The Day Jesus Died

CRUCIFIXION:
A Multidisciplinary Investigation of the Death of Jesus of Nazareth

Many fine books on the subject of crucifixion are available today, but no in-depth, multi-volume investigation of Roman crucifixion and Jesus' death has been available, until now. CRUCIFIXION: A Multi-disciplinary Examination of the Crucifixion of Jesus of Nazareth consists of seven volumes, each dedicated to an integral subject related to Jesus' crucifixion. *The Day Jesus Died* identifies the year, date, day, and hour of Jesus' death. And there's *From the Upper Room to Joseph's Tomb* which examines each location on Jesus' journey to Calvary. Other titles include: *Probing the Trials, Crucifixion, and Burial of Jesus of Nazareth*, *What Jesus' Crucifixion Accomplished for Us*, *Roman Crucifixion and the Death of Jesus*, *Watching Jesus Die*, and *Take Up the Cross*. With the CRUCIFIXION series, every aspect of Roman crucifixion and the cross is explored with specific reference to the crucifixion of Jesus. The scholar will appreciate each book's depth of research, often reflected in each chapter's extensive endnotes. The nonprofessional reader will enjoy the thoughtful and readable style of each book in the series. Every reader will quickly find value in each volume of this seven-book series.

The Day Jesus Died

Discovering the Year, Date, Day, and Time of Jesus' Crucifixion

WOODROW MICHAEL KROLL

Foreword by Darrell L. Bock

RESOURCE *Publications* · Eugene, Oregon

THE DAY JESUS DIED
Discovering the Year, Date, Day, and Time of Jesus' Crucifixion

Copyright © 2025 Woodrow Michael Kroll. All rights reserved. Except for brief quotations in critical publications or reviews, no part of this book may be reproduced in any manner without prior written permission from the publisher. Write: Permissions, Wipf and Stock Publishers, 199 W. 8th Ave., Suite 3, Eugene, OR 97401.

Resource Publications
An Imprint of Wipf and Stock Publishers
199 W. 8th Ave., Suite 3
Eugene, OR 97401

www.wipfandstock.com

PAPERBACK ISBN: 979-8-3852-3400-4
HARDCOVER ISBN: 979-8-3852-3401-1
EBOOK ISBN: 979-8-3852-3402-8
VERSION NUMBER 03/11/25

This book is dedicated to some of the scholars in my life who have encouraged me to "dig deeper"—scholars such as Paul E. Griffis (Practical Bible Training School), Marvin R. Wilson (Barrington College), Roger Nicole (Gordon-Conwell Theological Seminary), Bruce M. Metzger (Princeton Theological Seminary) and Harry Gamble Jr (University of Virginia).

Unearthing information about Jesus of Nazareth is not difficult because many writers of the earliest centuries refer to him. However, can these historians be trusted? Do we know they accurately portrayed the life, teaching, death, and resurrection of Jesus? Fortunately, we have three eyewitnesses and one first-century scholar who compiled a record of Jesus' life claiming, "Inasmuch as many have undertaken to compile a narrative of the things that have been accomplished among us, just as those who from the beginning were eyewitnesses and ministers of the word have delivered them to us, it seemed good to me also, having followed all things closely for some time past, to write an orderly account for you, most excellent Theophilus"

(LUKE 1:1–3).

If we are willing to trust the honesty and historicity of these four men, if we are willing to recognize the possibility that Matthew, Mark, Luke, and John knew what they were talking about, perhaps we can learn more about Jesus than we previously thought. We might even be able to use these eyewitness accounts of the first century to drill down to the year, the month, the date, the day, and yes, even the hour on that dark day when heaven's Sun failed and the Son of heaven succeeded.

The cross is God's exclamation point to his eternal plan for our salvation. Knowing the exact time of Jesus' death won't save us from our sin, but it may cause us to appreciate his sacrifice more, and if that's so, I have succeeded in my quest to dig deeper.

A mighty Fortress is our God
A Bulwark never failing
Our Helper He amid the flood
Of mortal ills prevailing

Did we in our own strength confide
Our striving would be losing
We're not the right Man on our side
The Man of God's own choosing

Dost ask who that may be?
Christ Jesus, it is He
Lord Sabaoth His Name
From age to age, the same
And He must win the battle

Let goods and kindred go
This mortal life also
The body they may kill
God's truth abideth still
His Kingdom is forever
—Martin Luther

Contents

Foreword by Darrell L. Bock	xi
Preface	xiii
Acknowledgments	xvii
Abbreviations	xix
List of Tables	xxiii
Introduction	xxv
Chapter 1 Calculating Time in Antiquity	1
Chapter 2 Calculating Time by Seasons and Sabbaths	31
Chapter 3 Was the Last Supper a Passover Seder?	58
Chapter 4 The Case for a Wednesday Crucifixion	86
Chapter 5 The Case for a Thursday Crucifixion	123
Chapter 6 The Case for a Friday Crucifixion	152
Chapter 7 Passion Week Timeline	187
Chapter 8 The Impact of Jesus' Birth Date on His Death Date	196
Chapter 9 Calculating the Year of Jesus' Crucifixion	229
Chapter 10 Candidates for the Year of Jesus' Crucifixion	258
Conclusion	278
What Does It Mean to Me? A final observation	284
Endnotes	287
Bibliography	301
Subject Index	309
Author/Person Index	325

Foreword

IT WAS THE MOST momentous week in the life of a figure whose global impact no one disputes. It is the most famous death in history. The events leading to the crucifixion of Jesus of Nazareth became a dispute over whether this Jewish Galilean teacher was someone of more cosmic significance or an imposter disturbing the peace of the fragile relationship between Jews and their faith. Even though these events took place in an obscure corner of the Roman empire, there was nothing insignificant about what was taking place.

The events of this volume zero in on all the cultural elements and historical discussion surrounding the "trials," crucifixion, and burial of Jesus. It takes a close look at a tightly compact series of events that led to Pilate's decision to permit the crucifixion of Jesus at the behest of the Jewish leadership who brought the legal complaint to the prefect that Jesus claimed to be a king Rome did not appoint. Just as the first-century Jewish historian Josephus said years later (*Ant.* 18.63), "When Pilate, at the suggestion of principal men among us, had condemned him to the cross," Dr Kroll takes us through the array of discussion that scholars have pondered leading up to this crucial historical event. The accounting starts with the dispute over whether we are dealing with a Passover meal and moves to the timing of the Jewish examination of Jesus where the leaders gathered their case to take to Pilate for the trial that did decide Jesus's earthly fate, namely, issues tied to the day and year of this crucial series of events.

The work here is careful and thorough. You can follow in detail the very issues scholars discuss. Some of these judgments are very close historical calls. Dr. Kroll is clear about that as well. The information here is first-rate and up-to-date. So I commend this volume to you and trust that by reading it you will have a better grasp of what led to the cross with all its momentous implications for humanity.

>   Darrell L. Bock
>   Senior Research Professor of New Testament Studies
>   Dallas Theological Seminary
>   Dallas, Texas

Preface

IT SEEMS AS IF the cross is everywhere today. Women wear it on a delicate chain around their neck. Many Catholics have a crucifix on the wall of their home. It can be found in cemeteries and churches, on tattoos and T-shirts, and so many other places. Some people are followers of Jesus Christ and love the cross. Others are not followers of Jesus but wear the cross anyway. The vast majority of people see it as little more than a wearable, an old symbol devoid of meaning in the twenty-first century.

This book is for skeptics of the cross because there are more than ample reasons not to be. It is for those who own a cross but have little understanding of its true meaning. And it's for Christ-followers who have picked up the cross and are carrying it daily in their lives. You will find yourself here somewhere.

Exploring the day and date of Jesus' crucifixion will feed the insatiable appetite of the scholar who regularly debates this issue. It will also inform the Christian who may not be a scholar but is amazed by the features of Jesus' crucifixion that demonstrate so clearly the sovereignty of God.

As you read this book or any of my works, you will quickly notice that I appeal often to the four Gospels for accurate historical information. I believe these writings are the earliest, most accurate, and best documents we have to inform us of the life and times of Jesus of Nazareth. I accept the Bible at face value, and while I incorporate the valuable insights and research of other scholars into my own, I also come to common sense conclusions that are often not evident in much of modern liberal scholarship. As the final authority, I appeal to those "men [who] spoke from God as they were carried along by the Holy Spirit" (2 Pet 1:21).

> "The death of the Incarnate Son of God on a Roman cross . . . marks the central point in the history of mankind."
> —F. W. Mattox

Some decades ago many scholars adopted the designations of B.C.E. and C.E. to indicate dates on the calendar. I completely understand why this change was made. The B.C.E. and C.E. designations are more inclusive because they do not specifically relate to Christianity. However, most of the Western world is steeped in the use of BC and AD; even many highly influential scholars have chosen to retain these designations.[1] However, I use BC and AD for a strikingly different reason.

Greek scholar Vincent Taylor noted:

> We are bound to consider how we think of time, whether past events are only isolated points in a series, or whether God invades history with abiding consequences. This issue seriously engages the attention of theologians today. It is best considered by reflecting upon (1) events as points in the time series, (2) events with permanent significance, and (3) events as divine invasions in time."[2]

I do not believe the advent of God's Son was part of a mere point-in-time series. I see the birth of the Messiah and Savior as an invasion of time by God himself. Thus, despite scholarly arguments to the contrary, I will use the designations BC and AD to reflect the incredible moment God changed the world forever by invading time, not simply indicating a timeshare for multiple religious communities.

Now some technical information. The Scripture references in this book are from the English Standard Version (ESV) of the Bible unless otherwise noted. The ESV is based on the Greek text in the 2014 editions of the Greek New Testament (5th corrected edition), published by the United Bible Societies (UBS), and *Novum Testamentum Graece* (28th edition, 2012), edited by Nestle and Aland. The Hebrew words in the text are from the Masoretic text of the Hebrew Bible, as found in *Biblia Hebraica Stuttgartensia* (2nd edition,1983). Words in Greek are taken from the 1993 editions of the Greek New Testament (4th corrected edition) and *Novum Testamentum Graece* (27th ed).

Since multiple words in the Greek language may be used for the same word in English, wherever I have highlighted a Greek word, and there is more than one Scripture associated with it, I have always used the Greek form of the first Scripture listed, as found in the 28th revised edition of the Nestle-Aland *Novum Testamentum Graece*.

According to the Oxford Dictionary, "time" is defined as "the indefinite continued progress of existence and events that occur in an apparently irreversible succession from the past, through the present, into the future." That sounds about right. Time is the measure of our existence from the distant past, beginning at the creation of the world [there is no time without matter] and stretching to the distant future when "time is swallowed up in eternity."

Time has been around for a very long time. Artifacts from the Paleolithic Period suggest that the moon was used to reckon time as early as 6,000 years ago.³ However, time is different for people at different locations. For example, when it is noon on Sunday where I live, it is already 2:00 am in Singapore and Shanghai, 3:00 am in Seoul, 5:00 am in Sydney, and 7:00 am in Suva (Fiji). But for each of these cities, it is Monday, while for me, it is still Sunday. Time changes every second worldwide, and that's important for your children living in Zurich to remember when they call you after their breakfast.

Time was measured differently depending on your location and the era in which you lived. Often how you measure time depends on your culture and the times. Time becomes of the utmost importance when attempting to fix the day and date of Jesus' crucifixion. Therefore, we must take the time to become familiar with time in antiquity.

> "When I consider the short duration of my life, swallowed up in the eternity before and after, the small space which I fill . . . I am terrified."—Blaise Pascal

As you read through these pages dedicated to exploring the day of the week Jesus was crucified, the year on the calendar of his execution, and the hour of his sacrifice, don't fail to keep the main thing as the main thing. Romans 5:6–8, "For while we were still weak, at the right time Christ died for the ungodly. For one will scarcely die for a righteous person—though perhaps for a good person one would dare even to die—but God shows his love for us in that while we were still sinners, Christ died for us."

If you miss this message, you miss the reason for this book, and so much more.

WOODROW MICHAEL KROLL
Ashland, Nebraska USA

ENDNOTES

1. Witherington, "Biblical Views," *BAR* 43.6 (2017): 26
2. Taylor, *The Cross*.
3. Carroll, *Eternity*, 54–55. See also Rudgley, *Lost Civilizations*, 86–105.

Acknowledgments

MY FIRST BOOK WAS published in 1977. I was thirty-three years old at the time and teaching Pauline Studies at a Christian university. That book had no acknowledgments page for I had no one to acknowledge. I wrote the manuscript, typed the manuscript, edited the manuscript, and did everything but publish the manuscript myself. Now, a hundred titles later, I have learned that I need help, and that help is available to me. This is especially important in this age of technology. Thus, I wish to express my deep appreciation to the following for their contribution to *The Day Jesus Died*.

As in my other works, I must acknowledge the sacrifice my wife Linda has made to this book. Not only has she aided me in checking the many Scripture references, but she has given up time with her husband to copious hours of research and writing. I am grateful for her patience and understanding.

Tina Work is my champion in getting this seven-book series on Roman crucifixion and the death of Jesus to the publisher. Tina is my chief tech officer, my photo enhancer, and the steady voice that has kept me following the necessary guidelines and procedures required by the publisher. I'm a big-picture person and the details sometimes escape me, but not Tina, for which I am very appreciative.

I wish to thank Darrell L. Boch for contributing the Foreword to this volume. He also invited me to be a guest on his podcast The Table on which we discussed the crucifixion and the historical evidence for it. His scholarship and friendship are much appreciated.

Books are written by authors but are published by publishers. Wipf & Stock Publishers has been kind enough, maybe brave enough, to undertake the publication of a seven-book series on crucifixion, focusing on the crucifixion of Jesus of Nazareth. Special thanks to Matt Wimer, Managing Editor,

Emily Callihan, Assistant Managing Editor, and George Callihan, Editorial Administrative Assistant for taking on this colossal project.

And, of course, I must acknowledge you, my reader. Books are written by authors and published by publishers, but without you, the reader, there is no satisfaction in writing or publishing a book. So, thank you for taking on the hard work of wading through history, archaeology, theology, and hundreds of Scriptures to drill down to the exact hour of Jesus' crucifixion. May the wonder of the Calvary event be enhanced by the discoveries you make in this book.

Abbreviations

BIBLE TRANSLATION

CEV	Contemporary English Version
CSB	Christian Standard Bible
ESV	English Standard Version
GNT	Good News Translation
HCSB	Holman Christian Standard Bible
JBP	J. B. Phillips
KJV	King James Version
TLB	The Living Bible
NAR	New Bible translation for Native American readers
NASB	New American Standard Bible
NCB	New Catholic Bible
NIV	New International Version
NKJV	New King James Version
NLT	New Living Bible
NRSV	New Revised Standard Version
RSV	Revised Standard Version

SCHOLASTIC ABBREVIATIONS

AASOR	Annual of American Schools of Oriental Research
AHJ	American Heart Journal
AJA	American Journal of Archaeology
Ant.	Flavius Josephus, Antiquities of the Jews
BA	Biblical Archaeologist
BAR	Biblical Archaeology Review
BKBC	The Bible Knowledge Background Commentary
BibSac	Bibliotheca Sacra
BW	Biblical World
CBQ	Catholic Biblical Quarterly
CE	Catholic Encyclopedia
CT	Christianity Today
DSS	The Dead Sea Scrolls
EBib	Études Bibliques
EBL	Encyclopedia of Biblical Literature
EQ	Evangelical Quarterly
ExpTim	Expository Times
HSNTA	Hennecke and Schneemelcher, New Testament Apocrypha
HTR	Harvard Theological Review
HUCA	Hebrew Union College Annual
IEJ	Israel Exploration Journal
ISBE	International Standard Bible Encyclopedia
JBL	Journal of Biblical Literature
JETS	Journal of the Evangelical Theological Society
JQR	Jewish Quarterly Review
JTS	Journal of Theological Studies
LXX	The Septuagint
NBD	New Bible Dictionary
NTS	New Testament Studies

NTG	Novum Testamentum Graece
OTP	The Old Testament Pseudepigrapha
PEQ	Palestine Exploration Quarterly
RevArch	Revue Archéologique
RB	Revue Biblique
RevQum	Revue de Qumran
SBLSP	Society of Biblical Literature Seminar Papers
SWJT	Southwestern Journal of Theology
TDNT	Theological Dictionary of the New Testament
VT	Vetus Testamentum
War	Flavius Josephus, Wars of the Jews
WJK	Westminster John Knox
ZNW	Zeitschrift für die Neutestamentliche Wissenschaft

List of Tables

The Months of the Jewish Calendar

Exclusive Versus Inclusive Calculation

Division of the Roman Night Watch

Jewish Priests and Roman Soldiers' Daily Schedules

Three Days and Nights Versus Third Day

Modern Translations

Roman Military Time

Translations of ὀψὲ (opsé)

Comparison of Passover Seder and the Lord's Supper

Wednesday Crucifixion

Saturday to Thursday

Friday to Thursday

The Sabbath in Leviticus

A Seventy-two Hour Wednesday Crucifixion

"The Sabbath" and the Weekly Sabbath

Jewish Time: Wednesday Crucifixion to Sunday Resurrection

Roman Time: Wednesday Crucifixion to Sunday Resurrection

Events Between Jesus' Death and Resurrection

Thursday's Three Days and Three Nights

Jewish Calculation: Thursday's Three Days and Three Nights by Jewish Calculation

Inclusive Calculation: Thursday's Three Days and Three Nights by Inclusive Calculation

Scenario One

Scenario Two

Scenario Three

Scenario Four

Scenario Five

"With" and "After" in the Gospels

Scenario Six

Thursday Through Sunday Night

"After," "In," and "Through"

Nisan 14—17

Scenario Seven

Friday—Sunday With Friday Crucifixion

Sequencing the Passover Weekend

Early Sunday Morning

Scholars Who Hold to a Friday Crucifixion

Between Jesus' Death and the Crucifixion Day Sunset

Traditional Passover Chronology

Humphrey's f Passion Week

Kroll's Crucifixion Timeline: Thursday Into Friday

Kroll's Crucifixion Timeline: Friday

Jesus' Early Life

Jesus Begins His Ministry

The Year of Jesus' Birth

Various Calendars

Luke 3:1,2 Human Date Indicators

Jesus' Birth, Ministry, and Crucifixion Dates

30 AD and 33 AD Crucifixion Timelines

Scholars Date Jesus' Crucifixion

Introduction

OF THE SEVEN BOOKS in this series on crucifixion, this is by far the most difficult to comprehend. Don't let that scare you off, but see this as a fair warning that we are going to drill deeper into a single subject in this book than any before it. Book One–*Roman Crucifixion and the Death of Jesus*–was more historical, archaeological, and sociological. It surveyed both the history of crucifixion and the historians who verified its use in the days of Jesus. Book Two–*Watching Jesus Die*–was more biographical, digging into the personal lives of every person who played a part in the last hours of Jesus' life. Book Three–*The Trials, Crucifixion, and Burial of Jesus of Nazareth*–helped us grasp the impact of every event on the day Jesus died. Now we come to Book Four–*The Day Jesus Died*–and to the deepest dive of all.

In this book, together we will farm every acre of our land. We will drill to the very depths of our mine. We will concentrate on the smallest time frame necessary, the fifty-seven hours into which are compacted the death, burial and resurrection of Jesus of Nazareth. From Thursday evening when Jesus and eleven of his twelve disciples arrived in the Garden of Gethsemane (perhaps 9:30 pm), to the moment on Sunday morning when the faithful women discovered the stone had been rolled away from Joseph's tomb (perhaps 6:30 am), is only fifty-seven hours.

If you got in your car in the beautiful city of Portland, Maine, and drove west through Boston, Chicago, Lincoln, and Boise, you would arrive in Portland, Oregon. You have driven from coast to coast across America, and it has only taken you forty-seven hours. To match the same time as Jesus' final hours, you would have to continue to drive south all the way to San Francisco. That's a fifty-seven-hour drive. During that same time, the International Space Station would have orbited the Earth thirty-eight times. To say the least, the most eventful period in the history of the world is crammed into a very short period. Our task is to unpack the events of that crammed period and learn as much as we can to come to biblical and factual conclusions about the year, date, day, and time of Jesus' crucifixion.

Put on your hip boots because we're going to wade in pretty deep.

Chapter 1

Calculating Time in Antiquity

In Judaism, all weekdays lead to the Sabbath. Jewish days do not have names; they have only numbers, and these numbers all anticipate the arrival of the seventh day, which the Jews do not number as seven but refer to as Shabbat, the Sabbath.

ON THE DESK IN my study, I have a sundial. While functional, it's largely ornamental, a wedding anniversary gift. Years ago I purchased a Galileo Thermometer at the Royal Observatory in Greenwich, England where Greenwich Mean Time (GMT) is established. I also have a solar-powered watch. I know it's solar-powered because when it stopped working, I attempted to purchase a battery and the sales clerk told me all I had to do was wear it in the sunlight. It had been in a dark closet for weeks.

Before we consider the options for the day Jesus died, we must understand the methods of calculating time in the first century AD. Many of the questions recorded in the narratives of the Gospels relate to time. Besides this, Jesus demonstrated a keen sense of time.

The writer of Ecclesiastes said, "For everything there is a season, and a time for every matter under heaven: a time to be born, and a time to die" (Eccl 3:1). No life has demonstrated this important principle clearer than that of Jesus of Nazareth.

The common Hebrew word for "time (Hebrew: עֵת; English: *'êth*) is found 258 times in the Old Testament. Fifty-three times the common New Testament word (Greek: χρόνος; English: *chrónos*) is used meaning "time." In one of its forms, the English word "time" occurs 683 times in the Bible, 179 of those in the New Testament.

Clearly, time is important. Thus, calculating time is also important, and must be done correctly and accurately if we are to understand the time references in the Bible correctly and accurately.

JESUS' INTEREST IN TIME

Jesus was keenly aware of the time. As Paul said, "When the fullness of time had come, God sent forth his Son, born of woman, born under the law" (Gal 4:4). When the birth of the Christ child became a threat to Herod the King, Matthew records, "Then Herod summoned the wise men secretly and ascertained from them what time the star had appeared" (Matt 2:7). God became a man at just the right time, the God-appointed time.

Later, when Jesus began his ministry among men and women, boys and girls, "At that time Herod the tetrarch heard about the fame of Jesus . . ." (Matt 14:1). When the religious crowds appeared too mentally dense to understand what Jesus was teaching them, he scolded the crowd, charging, "You hypocrites! You know how to interpret the appearance of earth and sky, but why do you not know how to interpret the present time?" (Luke 12:56). Sometimes he instructed his hearers not to reveal too much about him because, in his own words, "My time has not yet come" (John 7:6).

But in God's plan, Jesus did not come to Earth to be a teacher, a healer, a food distributor, or one who raised the dead. He came to be a Savior, and when it was right, "From that time Jesus began to show his disciples that he must go to Jerusalem and suffer many things from the elders and chief priests and scribes, and be killed, and on the third day be raised" (Matt 16:21).

To understand Jesus' concern for time, we must know how the first-century Jews reckoned time. How did they determine how long a day was? How did their calendar order their lives? These and similar questions need answers before we examine the day of Jesus' crucifixion.

No discussion about the crucifixion of Jesus Christ has produced more heat and less light than the debate over the day he died. Those who have diligently studied the day of the crucifixion have tended to come to one of three conclusions: (1) Jesus died on the traditional Friday; (2) he died on the less traditional Thursday; or (3) he died on the even less traditional Wednesday. Tradition is not a bad thing, but just because something is traditional does not mean it is correct. On the other hand, if people over the centuries have believed something to be accurate and it has become a tradition, there may be an excellent reason for that.

In researching this book, I have observed there is a great deal of interest in the topic of time, and everyone wants their opinion heard. Consequently, the Internet has become today's largest repository of unreliable information about Jesus' crucifixion. Since that is the case, this book is destined to spark both interest and controversy, friends and foes. That in itself is not a bad thing, as long as you, the reader, keep an open mind while reading the following chapters.

HOW FIRST-CENTURY JEWS CALCULATED YEARS AND MONTHS

Let's begin examining time in antiquity with the broadest category of time and narrow it down to any given day. That means starting with how the Jews determined what year it was, how their months were identified, what a week meant, and finally, what was unique about how the Jews reckoned a day.

In case you haven't noticed, Jewish people keep a calendar very distinctive from the rest of the world. Time is set by those momentous events in Jewish history remembered and celebrated on specific days in a yearly cycle of feasts and fasts. For this reason, the Jewish religious calendar has been nicknamed "the Catechism of the Jew."

Calculating Years

Since the Jewish calendar is pinned to cataclysmic events, what is the most earth-shattering event in history? Undoubtedly it is Creation itself. Only one event could serve as the beginning of history and that is the beginning of history itself. Therefore, Judaism counts the years of their calendar from the Creation of the universe. But how did the wise rabbis of the past determine precisely how old the Earth is? Even today, with all of our scientific advances, most scientists rely only on a theory. We know it as the "Big Bang" which is theorized to have taken place in the indeterminate past [13.8 billion years ago, give or take a billion] and was the genesis of all things.

With the "Big Bang" theory there is no precision in the matter at all. If you are off by a couple of hundred million years, you're close enough. If necessary, just adjust your figures, which happens frequently. But for Judaism, the only method for the rabbinic sages to date the age of the Earth was to count the years from the literal account of Creation as described in the book of Genesis.

> "Judaism preserves the exalted principles and the cataclysmic events of its history through a structured, well-defined, and specifically timed system of practices that it requires of its adherents."
> —Rabbi Maurice Lamm

As a result, every Hebrew year on their calendar reflects the number of years since God created the Earth in Genesis 1. So, for example, the year 2025 on the Gregorian calendar converts to 5785 on the Jewish calendar [except for September 23 to the end of the year which is 5786]. In the Jewish community, it is believed that 5,785 years have passed since God created Earth. According to the Torah's reckoning, it also means 5,785 years of God's sovereignty over the world.

This is very different from the methods used by other ancient peoples. Many societies began to count their calendar years anew with the reign of each new monarch. This made reckoning time very complicated and very confusing.

The original Roman calendar reckoned a year as being composed of ten fixed months, each of thirty or thirty-one days.[1] The calendar used by both the Roman Kingdom and later the Roman Republic included the reforms of Julius Caesar and became known as the Julian calendar, named after Julius Caesar. This calendar counted inclusively forward to the next of three principal days: the first of the month (the *kalends*); one day less than the middle of the month (the *ides*); and eight days—nine, counting inclusively—before this (the *nones*).

Judaism refused to divide history by the reign of a king or the death of a hero. It refused even the lives of Abraham or Moses as the starting point of its calendar. Nothing less than the beginning of all things would do. There were gaps in this commitment to a Creation calendar. For some centuries, the Jews began counting years from one event—the Exodus. After the destruction of the Temple in 70 AD, this cataclysmic event replaced the Exodus as the Jewish calendar's inaugural date. Ultimately, however, the Jewish calendar came back to using Creation as its starting point.

While this form of calendric reckoning served the Jewish community well, that community always existed as a minority. The Jews were always dominated by the calendars of their overlords. While it was still possible to date things according to their calendar, they had to adapt to living in an alien world. Of course, the Jews resisted, but ultimately they could not ignore the way the rest of the Roman world calculated years, months, and days. As a result, Jews lived their secular lives according to others' dating systems and their religious life according to their own. Orthodox Jews still do.

Calculating months

The Jewish calendar is lunar. The Jews count the months by the phases of the moon. That presents a problem because the Gregorian calendar adopted by most of Western civilization is a solar calendar. By approximately forty-eight minutes each day, the moon travels more slowly than the sun. At the beginning of the lunar month, the moon sets in the west just after sunset, but it is forty to forty-five minutes later each day. The moon continues to lag further and further behind the sun until, at the end of twelve months, the moon's year is eleven days shorter than the year of the sun. That means every three years, the moon loses a full month.

This spells trouble for the Jewish religious calendar. Passover must always be celebrated at the vernal equinox—springtime and harvest being its natural hallmarks. This coincided with and symbolized the resuscitation of nature with the redemption of the Jewish people.

The problem is, with the lunar calendar losing a month every three years, Passover kept moving further away from its beginning date. It began to move relentlessly out of the appropriate season of the year. This same phenomenon is observed by Muslims every year at the festival of Ramadan.

The sages of Judaism knew they had to do something to correct this "moon drift," so the teachers of the Talmud adjusted the calendar by adding seven leap months (called "Second Adar") in each nineteen-year cycle. This made Jewish holidays and festivals fall in the approximate season for which they were initially conceived.

In antiquity, the first day of the lunar month, called Rosh Chodesh, was proclaimed by the Sanhedrin in Jerusalem after the new moon was initially visually sighted and confirmed by two witnesses. That changed after the destruction of Jerusalem in 70 AD. From then on, Rosh Chodesh was calculated by the astronomical calendar to determine the days upon which holidays fell.

As you might guess, Jewish months do not line up perfectly with Gregorian calendar months, as Table 1 indicates. The Jewish calendar's first six months are Nissan, Iyar, Sivan, Tammuz, Av, and Elul. The final six months are Tishri, Cheshvan, Kislev, Tevet, Shevat, and Adar.

Table 1: The Months of The Jewish Calendar

Nissan	Nissan typically covers March into April. The most notable holiday during this time is Passover. This thirty-day month is the beginning of the Jewish year.
Iyar	Iyar runs 29 days from April into May. Lag B'Omer is the major holiday marking the *hillula* which celebrates the death of second-century mishnaic sage Rabbi Shimon bar Yochai.
Sivan	The third month consists of parts of May and June. Sivan's most important holiday is Shavuot which celebrates the giving of the Torah to the Jews on the sixth night of Sivan.
Tammuz	The 29-day Tammuz runs from mid-June into July with no major holidays.
Menachem Av	Often just called Av, this month of thirty days runs from July into August. Tisha B'Av (literally "the ninth of Av") is regarded as the saddest day in the Jewish calendar because it remembers the tragedies in Jewish history.
Elul	Elul lines up with mid to late August and it lasts into September. There is no major Hebrew holiday during this month. Elul is 29 days long
Tishrei	This seventh month lasts thirty days from September into October. During this time the High Holidays of Judaism occur—Rosh Hashanah, Jewish New Year, and ten days later Yom Kippur, the Day of Atonement.
Cheshvan	Cheshvan includes October into November. Depending on the year, Cheshvan can be 29 or 30 days.
Kislev	Kislev is the month of Hanukkah, the Jewish holiday celebrated for eight days and nights. It starts on the 25th of Kislev (late November until late December). This is the other month that is sometimes 29 days and sometimes 30 days.
Tevet	Tevet spans from December into January. Hanukkah is included in part of this month which ends during January. Tevet lasts for 29 days.
Shevat	Shevat covers January into February. The Tu B'Shvat more popularly called "Rosh Hashanah La'Ilanot," is literally "New Year of the Trees." In modern Israel, Tu B'Shvat is celebrated by planting trees as an ecological awareness day.
Adar	Adar, spanning February into March, wraps up the Jewish calendar. During Adar, Purim is celebrated to commemorate God's rescue of the Jews from the wicked Haman.

As you can see, each of these months is approximately equal to the number of days used in the Gregorian calendar, but their position in the year is somewhat different.

Jewish Leap Years

Rabbi Hillel II of the fourth century AD is credited with realizing that a lunar year is eleven days shorter than a solar year. Had this problem not been addressed, there would be no coordination between the historical event and the day it was celebrated. Hillel and other rabbis corrected the problem by adding a thirteenth month at the end of the year seven times in each nineteen-year cycle. This means that the 3rd, 6th, 8th, 11th, 14th, 17th, and 19th years have an extra month, which is called Adar Beit. It follows Adar and lasts 29 days.

The Jews have done remarkably well at maintaining their religious calendar while living daily in a world that uses a different one. I have never received a calendar from a Jewish friend in Israel that reflected the Gregorian system of dating, always the Jewish system.

Calculating weeks

Unlike the Gregorian calendar, the Jewish week does not run from Sunday to Saturday. The Jews count their weeks from Sabbath to Sabbath. This is the way Jesus' week would have been calculated. The Sabbath is much more than just a day. The Sabbath is the crown of their week. It is the zenith of Jewish weekdays. Theologically, the Sabbath is the Queen of Jewish expectations, a real foretaste of the world to come.

> "More than the Jews have kept the Sabbath, the Sabbath has kept the Jews."—Asher Ginsberg

In Judaism, all weekdays lead to the Sabbath. Jewish days do not have names; they only have numbers, and these numbers all anticipate the arrival of the seventh day, which the Jews do not number as seven but refer to as *Shabbat*, the Sabbath. Thus, the days of the week were called the first day, the second day, the third day, the fourth day, the fifth day, the sixth day, and the Sabbath. So in Hebrew, Monday would be "Yom Rishon" the first day, Tuesday would be "Yom Sheni" the second day, etc.

For observant Jews, both psychologically and physically, the days from Sunday to Friday are but steps leading to the *Shabbat*, the "palace in time." New clothes are worn first on *Shabbat*. Special foods are prepared for *Shabbat*. Distinguished guests are invited to join the family for *Shabbat*. All meaningful family discussions are delayed until *Shabbat*. It's easy to see just how vital *Shabbat* is to the Jewish community.

As a result of the build-up to *Shabbat*, Jews experience an abrupt freefall in their exhilaration and enthusiasm at the close of this special day. *Shabbat* departs, and life begins again at the bottom, working its way day by day toward the next *Shabbat*.

HOW FIRST-CENTURY JEWS CALCULATED DAYS

In history, before the invention of the modern clock, telling time at night was not an exact science. Indeed, during the day, you could look at the sun and determine approximately what hour of the day it was, but looking at the moon was much different. Some nights, the moon wasn't visible at all. Midnight was not a precisely distinguishable hour, nor could you tell when it was 3:00 am. Thus, the day had to begin with simple yet precise standards that everyone observed and adopted. This meant the Jewish day was calculated either from the beginning of the night or the beginning of the day. There was no third option.

Determining days

In all but secular matters, the Jews observe that the time the day begins with the arrival of night. They believe that when God created the world, he created night first and then day. "And there was evening and there was morning, the first day" (Gen 1:5). As a result, on the Jewish calendar, the date begins with the night beforehand. While a day in the secular calendar begins and ends at midnight, a Jewish day goes from nightfall to nightfall. The twilight period from sunset ("*shekiah*") until three stars are visible in the sky ("*tzeit hakochavim*") is a period known as "*bein hashmashot*." Nightfall is determined when the first medium-sized stars appear in the heavens. Technically, daybreak is defined as when the North Star becomes visible.

So firmly held is the belief that a day begins at nightfall, if the first of Tishrei fell on a Monday, and a child was born Monday night after dark, say 8:00 pm, the child's birthday is the second of Tishrei. Run that through your mind again.

Through the centuries, the Jewish people have also counted days differently from what others typically do in the West. Any portion of a day is counted as a full day. Any event that occurred at 3:00 pm, even though the sighting of the first three stars may only be hours away when a new day began, that event was counted as occurring on an entire day. So, in modern Israel, a three-day event, such as a rock concert in the Herodian theater at Caesarea Maritima, might start at noon on Monday and be done by noon on Wednesday. While this is only forty-eight hours, it is nevertheless considered a three-day concert, according to Jewish reckoning of time, not to mention ticket sales.

Here's what *The Jewish Encyclopedia* has to say.

> In Jewish communal life, part of a day is at times reckoned as one day; e.g., the day of the funeral, even when the latter takes place late in the afternoon, is counted as the first of the seven days of mourning; a short time in the morning of the seventh day is counted as the seventh day; circumcision takes place on the eighth day, even though on the first day only a few minutes remained after the birth of the child, these being counted as one day.[2]

It is a fact from secular historical records, as well as biblical documents, that the Jews considered portions of a day as a whole day. This was the conventional method of understanding time throughout much of the Middle East. Inclusive calculation meant counting both the first and the last unit of time as a complete unit. Source documents demonstrate this method was used generally by other ancient nations as well.

Roman dates were calculated inclusively. The difference between exclusive calculation and inclusive calculation is simple. In those languages, such as English, that use "exclusive" calculation, when counting eight days from Sunday, Monday will be day one, Tuesday the second day, and the following Monday will be day eight. When calculating "inclusively," Sunday (the start day) will be day one, and the next Sunday will be day eight. This becomes evident in some Romance languages. For example, a fortnight is a period of two weeks, fourteen days and nights. But the French phrase for "fortnight" is *quinzaine*, meaning fifteen days. In Spanish (*quincena*) and Portuguese (*quinzena*) the words are similar, both also related to fifteen.

Table 2: Exclusive Versus Inclusive Calculation

Exclusive	Sun	Mon	Tue	Wed	Thur	Fri	Sat	Sun	Mon
		Day 1	Day 2	Day 3	Day 4	Day 5	Day 6	Day 7	Day 8
Inclusive	Sun	Mon	Tue	Wed	Thur	Fri	Sat	Sun	Mon
	Day 1	Day 2	Day 3	Day 4	Day 5	Day 6	Day 7	Day 8	

Since in common usage the Romans calculated time inclusively, they called their market days *nundinae* (from *nonus*, ninth), every ninth day, when in reality, market day was held every eight days, as indicated on ancient calendars by the Roman letters, A through H (1 through 8).

The standing practice of inclusive calculation

An Egyptian inscription recording the death of a priestess on the fourth day of the twelfth month relates that her successor arrived on the 15th, "when twelve days had elapsed." Today, we would say that twelve days had elapsed after the fourth day and the date would be the 16th not the 15th. However, the Egyptians viewed counting time as did other societies in the Ancient Near East, using inclusive calculation. The Greeks followed this same all-encompassing method. The Olympiad was the four years between the Olympic Games, yet the Greeks called it a *pentaeteris* (five-year period).

The practice of inclusive calculation still occurs in some modern Asian cultures. There are even vestiges of this practice in the West. In some European languages, the phrase "eight days" means a week. The Beatles sang, "I ain't got nothin' but love, babe, eight days a week." You only get seven days a week if you do not use inclusive calculation as the ancients did.

In Roman Catholic tradition, the term "octave" for a festival refers to the day coming one week after the holy day, and yet the word "octave" derives from the Latin *octavus* meaning "eighth." In music, an octave is a series of eight contiguous notes.

The medical term "tertian fever" means a fever recurring every other day. A malarial fever with paroxysms typically recurs every forty-eight hours or every other day. And yet, the word *terian* in Latin means "third." This is because reckoning the day of the outbreak as the first, inclusively the recurrence is on the "third" day.

The point is that inclusive calculation permeates the world's underbelly even though most of us in the West have been unaware of it. Those who are not familiar with inclusive calculation, including most Western nations, do not appreciate this principle behind the calendar in much of the world.

A Hebrew boy was circumcised when "eight days old" (Gen 17:12), that is, "on the eighth day the flesh of his foreskin shall be circumcised" (Lev 12:3). Similarly, Luke speaks of circumcision "at the end of eight days" (Luke 1:59; 2:21). "At the end of eight days" does not mean eight full days from the date of birth, but eight inclusive days. The New American Standard Bible (NASB) uses the expression "when eight days had passed." The Holman Christian Standard Bible says, "When the eight days were completed."

The Jewish Encyclopaedia states. "A short time in the morning of the seventh day is counted as the seventh day; circumcision takes place on the eighth day, even though, of the first day only a few minutes after the birth of the child, these being counted as one day."[3]

Scores of contradictions would appear in both the Old and New Testaments if this principle were ignored. We must compare Scripture with

Scripture and use the idiom of the language in which the Bible was written, not the idioms with which we are comfortable today. This means the Jewish people consistently used inclusive calculation in numbering days, events, etc.

JEWISH CALCULATION OF DAYS IN THE OLD TESTAMENT

Nonetheless, any good student of the Bible wants to know if there are examples of inclusive calculation in the Bible. We are not disappointed. There are numerous scriptural examples of how inclusive calculation was used in the Scriptures. Of the nine examples below, six are from the Old Testament, three are from the New. One example would be enough, but here are nine.

In the days of Moses (c. 1450 BC)

When they take the time to look carefully, people are always amazed at how frequently the Bible includes time and place references in its narratives. You only do this if you are reporting the facts, not if you are making up stories. That's why lies are often devoid of details. When Moses and the Israelites entered the wilderness of Sinai, Exodus 19:1 reports, "On the third new moon after the people of Israel had gone out of the land of Egypt, on that day they came into the wilderness of Sinai."

Here is more evidence the Jews used a lunar calendar. The people had been traveling for three months before they entered the Sinai. God called Moses to the top of Mount Sinai to receive instructions. The Almighty said, "Go to the people and consecrate them today and tomorrow, and let them wash their garments and be ready for the third day. For on the third day the LORD will come down on Mount Sinai in the sight of all the people" (Exod 19:10–11).

Moses was to get the Hebrew people ready to encounter the presence of God. Day one: they would wash their garments to prepare to be in the presence of the Most Holy God. Day two: they would repeat washing their garments, to be absolutely certain they were ceremonially clean. Day three: the LORD would come down to the mountaintop in the presence of all the people. First day. Second day. Third day. But these days need not be full twenty-four-hour days because of the way the Jewish people counted days.

As they were accustomed to counting the number of days in a row, the first day may only be a portion of a day because the Jews used inclusive calculation. Day two would be a full twenty-four hours, but the third day could be just a portion of a day as well. We need to think as the Old Testament Jews did when counting the number of days.

First, second, and third would not always be seventy-two hours but could be only a portion of that. Because a new day began with the sighting of the first three stars at night, it was still considered a whole day if something happened just one hour before that. And if something occurred on the other end just an hour after the sighting of the North Star on the morning of the third day (see v. 16), three days could be as little time as only twenty-six hours. That would be extreme, of course, but it also demonstrates how tenacious the Jewish people were about counting partial days as full days.

In the days of King David (c. 1000 BC)

The biblical book of 1 Samuel records many of the exploits of David in subduing his enemies. After the Amalekites attacked Ziklag and carried off David and his men's families, David inquired of the LORD if he should pursue the marauders. God gave him the green light. As they were hunting down the Amalekites, they came across a lone Egyptian in the open country. David was not only wise, he was also kind. The man was hungry, so David fed him. "And when he had eaten, his spirit revived, for he had not eaten bread or drunk water for three days and three nights. And David said to him, 'To whom do you belong? And where are you from?' He said, 'I am a young man of Egypt, servant to an Amalekite, and my master left me behind because I fell sick three days ago'" (1 Sam 30:12–13).

Pay close attention to how David and his men reckoned the time this Egyptian had been abandoned. He had not eaten bread or drunk water for "three days and three nights." Yet when the sickly Egyptian relayed what happened to him, he said he fell sick "three days ago." The Egyptian was indicating one whole day and part of two others, as appears from verse 13, where he said three days ago he fell sick. In Hebrew it is, "this is the third day since I fell sick." David and his men noticed the Egyptian had not eaten for "three days and three nights" שָׁלוֹשׁ (shâlôwsh) יוֹם (yôwm) שָׁלוֹשׁ (shâlôwsh) לַיְל (layil) and the near-dead man repeated שָׁלוֹשׁ (shâlôwsh) יוֹם (yôwm) חָלָה (châlâh) "I fell sick three days ago." First day. Second day. Third day. In this sequence, there are only two nights, not three.

David's men discerned how long it had been since this Egyptian had anything to eat or drink, and his statement that he became sick and was abandoned by the Amalekite army three days earlier was understood to mean exactly the same thing. "Three days and three nights" can only be described as "three days" if the Jews were employing their standard method of inclusive calculation of time. Had the Egyptian man meant three full days and three full nights, he would have said four days, not three because any portion of a day was counted as a full day.

Obviously, David understood that "three days" did not mean three full twenty-four-hour periods, but three daylight periods and two nighttime periods, or three days and three nights in Jewish reckoning of time.

In the days of King Rehoboam (c. 930 BC)

After the death of Solomon, Rehoboam, Solomon's son and heir, went to Shechem to be crowned King. But the Jewish people came to him and expressed their concern about the heavy tax burden laid on them by his father. This funded the kingdom that has been called "the golden age of Israel." Rehoboam needed time to think, so he said to them, "Go away for three days, then come again to me" (1 Kgs 12:5). The people went away. But 1 Kings 12:12 says, "All the people came to Rehoboam the third day, as the king said, 'Come to me again the third day.'"

Rehoboam told the people to go away for three days, but in quoting him they said he told them to, "Come to me again the third day." There is no discrepancy between what Rehoboam said and what the people heard and repeated. The "third day" was "three days" when calculating how the Jewish people have always accounted for their days. Inclusive calculation has been the Jewish method of reckoning days since the beginning of the Hebrew nation.

In the days of King Jeroboam II (c. 793 BC)

"In the fifteenth year of Amaziah the son of Joash, king of Judah, Jeroboam the son of Joash, king of Israel, began to reign in Samaria, and he reigned forty-one years" (2 Kgs 14:23). "Amaziah, the son of Joash, king of Judah, lived fifteen years after the death of Jehoash, son of Jehoahaz, king of Israel" (2 Kgs 14:17).

Here are the facts as Scripture records them:

- Amaziah, King of Judah, had been reigning fifteen years when Jeroboam ll began his reign as King of Israel.
- Amaziah reigned as Judah's King fifteen years after Jeroboam ll began his reign as King of Israel.

Question: how long was the reign of Amaziah? For most people, this is a simple math problem. You add the fifteenth year of Amaziah to the fifteenth years he lived after the King of Israel's death, making Amaziah's reign thirty years. This seems very logical, except it wasn't the way time was calculated in the Middle East. And there is a problem. The Bible tells us how long Amaziah was the King of Judah. Verse 2 of 2 Kings 14 unmistakably says, "He was twenty-five years old when he began to reign, and he reigned twenty-nine years in Jerusalem."

If fifteen years plus fifteen years equals thirty years, why does the Bible say Amaziah reigned for only twenty-nine years? Likely the answer is the second fifteen years of his reign were not fifteen full years, but a partial year was counted as fifteen years. This is how Amaziah reigned for twenty-nine years. It's another example of inclusive calculation.

In the days of Shalmaneser, King of Assyria (c. 727 BC)

The book of 2 Kings, chapter 18, verses 9 and 10, record, "In the fourth year of King Hezekiah, which was the seventh year of Hoshea son of Elah, king of Israel, Shalmaneser king of Assyria came up against Samaria and besieged it, and at the end of three years he took it." The siege of Samaria lasted from the fourth to the sixth year of Hezekiah, King of Judah. This parallels the seventh to the ninth year of Hoshea, king of Israel.

Yet the city is said to have been taken "at the end of three years." Again, the math would be easy. We use simple subtraction and our calculation comes to two years. However, the Bible writer was calculating inclusively (years four, five, and six) when he noted that "at the end of three years" Shalmaneser king of Assyria would capture Samaria, the capital of the ten northern tribes. This is another example of inclusive calculation where any portion of years four or six would be counted as an entire year, just as year five was.

In the days of Queen Esther (c. 450 BC)

The story of Queen Esther reflects one of the proudest moments in Jewish history. King Ahasuerus, known in secular history as Xerxes, gave a feast in the Persian Empire in which all the men at the feast got drunk. The celebration lasted a week. On the seventh day, the drunken King ordered his consort, Queen Vashti, to appear before the ogling eyes of his drunken friends so he could show off her beauty.

But something happened no one could have foreseen. Vashti refused. Xerxes became furious and asked the men what he should do with his defiant wife. Concerned that a women's movement might erupt and threaten their male-dominated society, they suggested Vashti be banished from the King's presence and a new queen be selected. A beauty pageant was held, and a young Jewess named Hadassah was selected. She assumed the name, Queen Esther. But no one in Xerxes' court knew she was Jewish.

When the wicked anti-Semite Haman hatched a plan to eradicate the entire Jewish population, Esther's uncle appealed to the queen to save her people. Esther feared entering the King's presence without an official invitation, so she asked her fellow Jews to pray and fast. She begged, "Hold a fast on my behalf, and do not eat or drink for three days, night or day. I and my young women will also fast as you do. Then I will go to the King, though it is against the law, and if I perish, I perish" (Est 4:16). After fasting, Esther 5:1 records, "On the third day Esther put on her royal robes and stood in the inner court of the king's palace."

For our purposes, we must take note of how the Jews in Esther's time calculated days. She had requested that all the Jews fast, not eating or drinking "for three days, night or day," but Esther went to King Xerxes "on the third day" (Est 5:1). Therefore, it seems that fasting for part of the third day counted as fasting for the whole day. That is inclusive calculation.

If Esther intended the three days and three nights to be taken as a literal seventy-two-hour fast, she should have presented herself before the King on the fourth day. This would allow a full seventy-two hours to pass before approaching Xerxes. But just two verses later, the Bible says, "On the third day Esther put on her royal robes and stood in the inner court of the king's palace, in front of the king's quarters, while the king was sitting on his royal throne inside the throne room opposite the entrance to the palace" (Est 5:1).

Esther and her friends prayed for God's favor for three days, and on the third day, she appeared before the king. Unmistakably "three days and three nights" was equal to "the third day."

Suppose Esther asked her friends to pray on a Monday. Monday and that night would be the first day. Tuesday and that night would be the second day. Wednesday and that night would be the third day. If Esther had waited until three literal days and three literal nights passed, it would have been on day four that she appeared in King Xerxes' presence. Yet the biblical text distinctly indicates she stood before the King on the third day. There is no way around it. That's inclusive calculation.

A cardinal number is a number used in counting that indicates quantity. It answers the question, "How many?" An ordinal number is a number that shows something in a sequence with other numbers. So, "three" days is a cardinal number, and the "third" day is an ordinal number. You would say, "My relatives came to stay for three days (cardinal), and they left on the third (ordinal) day. While they may sound different, they are referring to the same number.

In Esther's case, "On the third day" was the same as "three days, night or day." That's how the Jews reckoned numbers. Any part of a day was considered a whole day.

Did you notice the spread of years covered in the examples just given? The days of Moses were somewhere in the vicinity of 1450 BC. The days of Esther were somewhere in the vicinity of 450 BC. Over one thousand years, history provides proof that the Jewish people of the Old Testament calculated days using inclusive calculation. Any part of a day was given the status of a full day.

It was approximately 1,000 BC when King David created Judah's nation, and after seven years, he reigned over both Judah and Israel. Israel's King Rehoboam (931—913 BC) ruled some 930 years before Jesus was born. King Ahasuerus (Xerxes) ruled from about 486 to 465 BC, almost 450 years before Jesus. Was this same inclusive method of counting days employed in the first century AD, during the days of Jesus? Let's investigate and let the evidence speak.

JEWISH CALCULATION OF DAYS IN THE NEW TESTAMENT

Nothing changed in those years of Babylonian exile or during the Intertestamental Period regarding how the Jewish people calculated time. They used inclusive calculation consistently during the years represented by both testaments. Both Old and New Testament people were living in the context of Judaism. The Romans were the Jews' overlords in the New Testament, just like the Amalekites were in David's day or the Persians in Esther's day.

Still, the Jews remained a people, a community separate and apart from their overlords. They did not assimilate into their overlord's society. In fact, they were commanded by God not to assimilate with the other nations (see Lev 20:23; Num 23:9; 36:6). So, we should expect Jewish literature to demonstrate the meaning of "three days and three nights" as equal to "the third day," and we are not disappointed.

The famous Jewish scholar, Rabbi Eleazar ben Azariah, who lived around 100 AD and was descended from the Old Testament priest Ezra, explained how Jewish people counted days. "A day and a night are an *Onah* [a portion of time], and the portion of an *Onah* is as the whole of it."[4] What the Rabbi was saying is that when the Jewish people numbered days, any portion of the twenty-four hours of a day and night was counted as a whole day and a night (an *Onah*).

But are there any New Testament-era examples of how the Jews calculated their days? Indeed there are.

An example from Jesus

Matthew records those lonely days when Jesus was in the wilderness being tempted by Satan. Matthew 4:1–2 notes, "Then Jesus was led up by the Spirit into the wilderness to be tempted by the devil. And after fasting forty days and forty nights, he was hungry." Matthew is quite clear: Jesus fasted forty days and forty nights.

Mark and Luke also record this event, but they express it somewhat differently. Mark 1:12–13, "The Spirit immediately drove him out into the wilderness. And he was in the wilderness forty days, being tempted by Satan." Luke 4:1–2 expresses, "And Jesus, full of the Holy Spirit, returned from the Jordan and was led by the Spirit in the wilderness for forty days, being tempted by the devil. And he ate nothing during those days."

While Matthew explicitly revealed Jesus fasted forty days and forty nights, Mark and Luke mentioned only forty days. Why? Because every Jew in Jesus' day knew that forty days and forty nights were calculated inclusively, any portion of the first day or the last day was counted as a day, and the overnight hours didn't change that. Mark and Luke feel no need to specify forty nights. They were naturally a part of the forty days.

The days before his final hours found Jesus in Jerusalem weeping over the heart-hardness and unrepentance of his fellow Jews. Some Pharisees who found truth in what Jesus taught tried to warn him of Herod Antipas' intention to kill the Nazarene. But Jesus responded to their pleas, "Go and tell that fox, 'Behold, I cast out demons and perform cures today and tomorrow, and the third day I finish my course'" (Luke 13:32). The word Jesus chose for "perfect" or "complete" (Greek: τελειοῦμαι English: *teleioumai*) is related to the word on the cross when he said, "It is finished" (Greek: τετέλεσται; English: *tetelestai*).

Jesus was not saying he would arrive in Jerusalem in three literal days. His point was he was given a mission from the Father, and he would stay the course until the mission was complete. He used an expression that indicated a brief period. Jesus said he would continue his ministry of healing the sick and casting out evil spirits "today." This is not a twenty-four-hour period, but an expression meaning the present. He would minister "tomorrow" as well, meaning the foreseeable future. But eventually "the third day I finish my course" meaning his crucifixion is coming when his task on Earth is complete.

We cannot help but see the metaphorical meaning of Jesus' words as they are applied to his death, burial, and resurrection. He must finish his mission "today" and "tomorrow." And on the "third day," he would complete his mission. According to Jewish inclusive calculation, that would mean any part of today, all of tomorrow, and any portion of the "third" day. Resurrection on the third day would be the culmination of his earthly mission. For this same idea of completion or finishing the mission, see John 19:30, Acts 20:24, and Hebrews 2:10; 5:8–9; 12:23. Jesus spoke using inclusive calculation, the method of reckoning days he had been taught as a child, as had all the Jews for millennia.

In the days of the Chief Priests and Pharisees

There is even a record of the chief priests and Pharisees demonstrating the Jewish method of inclusive calculation. The scene was after the crucifixion. Jesus had been placed in Joseph's tomb. But the religious leaders were concerned his disciples might pull a fast one and steal his dead body. Here's their story.

> The next day, that is, after the day of Preparation, the chief priests and the Pharisees gathered before Pilate and said, "Sir, we remember how that impostor said, while he was still alive, 'After three days I will rise.' Therefore order the tomb to be made secure until the third day, lest his disciples go and steal him away and tell the people, 'He has risen from the dead,' and the last fraud will be worse than the first" (Matt 27:62–64).

Notice once again the distinction between "after three days" and "until the third day." This is another example of cardinal versus ordinal numbering. "Three days" is the cardinal number; "third day" is the ordinal number. If you wanted to compute as the Jews did, you would count a portion of day one, a full day two, and a portion of day number three. That would be considered "three days and three nights," but, from our perspective, it would be three days and two nights. That's the way Jewish reckoning had always been.

An example from Cornelius, the Roman centurion

Of all the writers of the New Testament, Luke is the one who is most careful to give us time clues. He frequently uses phrases like "the next day" or "the following day." For example, in recording the historical details found in the book of Acts, Luke uses the time expression "the next day" seventeen times (Acts 4:3,5; 10:9, 23; 14:20; 20:7, 15; 21:1, 8, 26; 22:30; 23:32; 25:6, 17, 23; 27:3, 18) and "the following day" five times (Acts 7:26; 10:24; 16:11; 20:15; 21:18). Speaking of Christ's resurrection, Luke uses "the third day" equal to the total number of times the other Gospel writers combined use these words. In Greek, Matthew speaks of "the third day" concerning Jesus' rising from the dead four times; Mark uses the expression twice, Luke uses it six times (9:22; 13:32; 18:33; 24:7, 21, 46), and John not at all.

The most explicit biblical demonstration of inclusive calculation is the New Testament account of Cornelius and Peter (see Acts 10:30, where seventy-two hours were reckoned as "four days ago," not "three").

Cornelius was a leader in the Roman army. He was a centurion in the Italian Cohort.[5] One day, "About the ninth hour of the day," this Roman officer "saw clearly in a vision an angel of God." The angel called his name "Cornelius" (Acts 10:3). We are not told what day of the week it was, but this was day number one of Cornelius's experience.

Verse 9 introduces Peter into the story where he, too, has a vision. It was "The next day" when "Peter went up on the housetop about the sixth hour to pray." This was noon, and as F. F. Bruce, "The Dean of Evangelical Scholarship," pointed out, "Noon was not one of the appointed times for prayer, but pious Jews prayed three times a day (Ps 55:17)."[6] Bruce was for almost twenty years the Rylands Professor of Biblical Criticism and Exegesis at the University of Manchester. That phrase, "The next day," makes this day number two of Cornelius' experience.

In his vision, Cornelius was instructed to send men to Joppa to escort Peter to his residence. Day number three is indicated by verse 23. "The next day he [Peter] rose and went away with them, and some of the brothers from Joppa accompanied him." The distance between Joppa and Caesarea is approximately thirty-nine miles making it a two-day trip. As we would count days today, the episode involving Cornelius timed out to four days.

It is legitimate to ask why Luke would use inclusive calculation. Wasn't he a Gentile, untrained in the Jewish method of calculating dates? Indeed, he was. And wasn't the man he addressed the book of the Acts to also a Gentile? Again, yes, Theophilus was a Gentile.[7] And wasn't Cornelius, the man who shares the lead role with Peter in this account, a Roman centurion? Yes, that's true too. Cornelius himself said, "Four days ago, about this hour, I was praying in my house at the ninth hour." (Acts 10:30). Follow this logically.

Day #1—Verse 3: "About the ninth hour of *the day*." (3:00 pm)

Day #2—Verse 9: "The *next day*, as they were on their journey."

Day #3—Verse 23: "The *next day* he rose and went away with them."

Day #4—Verse: 24: "And on the *following day* they entered Caesarea."

Had Luke not used the Jewish method of inclusive calculation, Cornelius would have said, "Three days ago, about this hour, I was praying in my house at the ninth hour." It would have been approximately seventy-two hours± from the hour of Cornelius' vision to Peter's arrival at his house. Using the Jewish method of inclusive calculation, the ninth hour (3:00 pm) to sunset on the first day was understood to be the first full day (even though there may have only been four or five hours before nightfall). So, why would Luke use inclusive calculation when recording the "four days" of Cornelius's experience?

Remember that as a Roman centurion, Cornelius would have been somewhat familiar with the concept of inclusive calculation. Most Mediterranean societies conquered by the Romans used this method. Remember, too, that while Luke addressed Theophilus and the Jewish Christians of the Greek Peloponnese peninsula, there were also many Jewish believers living in Greece at the time.

Table 3: Division of the Roman Night Watch

Night watches adopted after the Roman occupation began in 63 BC	
Sundown to 9:00 pm	First Watch
9:00 pm to midnight	Second Watch
Midnight to 3:00 am	Third Watch
3:00 am to sunrise	Fourth Watch

Table 4 on the next page demonstrates how the day of a Roman soldier was both calculated and conducted differently from a Jewish priest's day.

Paul was quite inclusive when he addressed his first Corinthian letter to "the church of God that is in Corinth, to those sanctified in Christ Jesus, called to be saints together with all those who in every place call upon the name of our Lord Jesus Christ, both their Lord and ours" (1 Cor 1:2).

Calculating Time in Antiquity   21

Table 4: Jewish Priests' and Roman Soldiers' Daily Schedules

Jewish Time Calculation	Roman Time Calculation
6:00 pm to 9:00 pm	First Watch
9:00 pm to midnight	Second Watch
Midnight to 3:00 am	Third Watch
3:00 am to sunrise	Fourth Watch
The first hour	*From dawn to 8:00 am*
Priests prepare the altar (Lev 1:7; 6:1–13; Mishnah *Tamid* 1.2); first sacrificial lamb tied to the altar.	Morning workout doing weighted push-ups, squats, lunges, etc.*
The second hour	*From 8:00 am to 9:00 am*
Breakfast.	Morning drills and marching.
The third hour	*From 9:00 am to 10:00 am*
Incense is offered in the Sanctuary, the first lamb is sacrificed, and the Temple gates are opened (Mishnah *Tamid* 3.7; Edersheim, *The Temple*, 7, 108).	*Frumentatio* ("collection of grains"), Breakfast of cheese and cereals (mixed with salt and water to make bread) with tent companions.
The fourth hour	*From 10:00 am to 11:00 am.*
Reading the Law.	Building bridges, aqueducts, repairing walls, buildings, etc.
The fifth hour	*From 11:00 am to 12:00 pm (Noon)*
Discussion on various religious topics.	Continued engineering projects.
The sixth hour	*12:00 pm to 1:00 pm.*
The second lamb is tied to the altar at high noon. (Mishnah *Tamid* 4.1).	Continued work on engineering projects.
The seventh hour	*From 1:00 pm to 2:00 pm*
Service in the Temple.	Continued engineering projects.
The eighth hour	*From 2:00 pm to 3:00 pm.*
Rest at home with family.	Rest at the Antonia Fortress barracks.
The ninth hour	*From 3:00 pm to 4:00 pm.*
The second lamb sacrificed (*Ant.* 14.4.3); Philo *Special Laws* I, XXXV. 169).	Grunt work cleaning latrines, polishing armor, cleaning horse stalls, etc.
The tenth hour	*From 4:00 pm to 5:00 pm.*
Service in the Temple.	Afternoon drills and marching.
The eleventh hour	*From 5:00 pm to 6:00 pm.*
Burning incense and priestly benediction (Mishnah *Tamid.* 6:3—7:2; Num 6:24–26).	The second meal of cereals and sometimes meat (pork) plus posca to drink.
The twelfth hour	*From 6:00 pm to sundown*
Daily Temple service concluded.	Preparation for the next day.

The Apostle's second letter was addressed "to the church of God that is at Corinth, with all the saints who are in the whole of Achaia" (2 Cor 1:1). Achaia was situated in the northwestern corner of the Peloponnese peninsula. While Luke recorded the events in Acts primarily for a Gentile audience, he recorded those events mainly from a Jewish model.

I have carefully avoided applying the principle of inclusive calculation to the "three days and three nights" related to Jesus' death and resurrection. In the often-irrational debate on which day Jesus was crucified, we must remember that inclusive calculation did not magically appear in the Gospel narratives. This had been the established method of counting days since the earliest years of the Jews' existence. Twenty-first-century Westerners may not fully appreciate it, but that does not change the fact that the Jews practiced inclusive calculation in every corner of the world and throughout every century.

Only when speaking of night watches did the Gospel writers use Roman terminology. Jesus demonstrated his familiarity with the divisions of the night when he told the story of the master who went away and left his servants in charge. In a warning designed to incite his servants' watchfulness for his return, Jesus said, "Therefore stay awake—for you do not know when the master of the house will come, in the evening, or at midnight, or when the rooster crows, or in the morning" (Mark 13:35). The first watch is "evening"; the second watch is "midnight"; the rooster crows during the "third" watch; the fourth watch is "morning."

When reading the three Jewish and one Gentile evangelist's accounts, we must view each of these accounts through a Jewish lens of the first century, not our twenty-first-century Western lens.

INCLUSIVE CALCULATION AND THE JONAH STORY

Now we make a hard right turn. Should what we know about inclusive calculation be applied to the crucifixion story, or should it be set aside just this one time? If we say inclusive calculation was not used in Jesus' case, we are obligated to answer why. If we say that inclusive calculation was also used in the dying Savior's case, there is no need for a defense. Not using inclusive calculation with Jesus' crucifixion, burial, and resurrection would be a denial of centuries of standard practice. If the crucifixion weekend was recorded using inclusive calculation, it matches the rest of Scripture. If inclusive calculation is excluded, it does not.

That brings us to the one verse that is a stumbling block for so many when attempting to understand Jesus' crucifixion. The phrase "three days and three nights" is used just three times in the entire Bible. The first was in the lonely Egyptian story, whom David found had not eaten in "three days and three nights" (1 Sam 30:12). The second is in the story of the wrong-way prophet Jonah. Jonah 1:17 says, "And the Lord appointed a great fish to swallow up Jonah. And Jonah was in the belly of the fish three days and three nights." And the final time the phrase is used is in Jesus' prediction of his death, burial, and resurrection. "For just as Jonah was three days and three nights in the belly of the great fish, so will the Son of Man be three days and three nights in the heart of the earth" (Matt 12:40).

Those who insist Jesus meant he would be in the grave for three consecutive periods of twenty-four hours, a total of seventy-two hours, say, "There it is in black and white. Jesus said he would be in the grave for three days and three nights." But we have also seen this phrase in black and white in 1 Samuel 30:12 in which it did not mean a seventy-two-hour period.

Many theologians and historians today discount the veracity of the Jonah story. They say it is a myth and see this account as just another fish story. However, I see no reason to believe this had to be a myth, an allegory, or a fable. Does it stretch one's reason as well as one's faith? Of course, it does. But it is not beyond the realm of possibility. There is no reason there could not have been a man named Jonah and a gigantic fish that swallowed him and then vomited him out. I am not sure if the fish complained, "I must have gotten a bad piece of human," but I am quite confident his story could have happened.

Think in terms of possibilities and probabilities. Was Jonah three days and three nights in the belly of the great fish? It is a possibility. If you take the story at face value because there are other historical elements to the story, such as the existence of Nineveh, it could even be a probability. While a man treading water at sea being swallowed by a very large fish would be quite unusual, it could have happened. "With man this is impossible, but with God, all things are possible" (Matt 19:26).

The third and final time the "three days and three nights" phrase is used comes from the tongue of the Savior. "For just as Jonah was three days and three nights in the belly of the great fish, so will the Son of Man be three days and three nights in the heart of the earth." When Jesus used the phrase "three days and three nights," is it possible he meant three literal twenty-four-hour periods? It is possible. Is it probable that is what he meant? It is not probable. The phrase could mean seventy-two hours, but it would be an obvious outlier, and outliers are generally discarded when honestly judging anything.

THE PREPONDERANCE OF PROOF

Often the evidence we have before us is skewed by our subjectivity and biases. That's why we need some objective standards, some criteria by which to judge our understanding of the evidence. One such criterion is frequency. How often is one phrase used as opposed to another? How often is one site mentioned as opposed to another? That's weighted evidence because of frequency.

When determining the accuracy of a biblical manuscript, a science known as textual criticism, one criterion is frequency. If one translation is supported by a single manuscript and another translation is supported by ten manuscripts, the frequency of ten is chosen over the infrequency of one.

We can apply this principle to determine what Jesus meant by "three days" and "the third day." If "three days" were intended to indicate seventy-two hours, you would expect to find the phrase often in the Gospel narratives. If "third day" is evidence of inclusive calculation in the Passion narratives, you would expect to see it used more frequently.

In the language of the New Testament, the phrase "after three days" in Greek is μεττρεῖς ἡμέρα; English: *metá treîs hēméra*. The phrase "until the third day" in Greek is ἕως τρίτος ἡμέρα; English: *héōs trítos hēméra*. They are similar, but not the same.

If isolated from the context, the phrase μετά τρε ῖς ἡμέρα could confirm the literal interpretation of "three days and three nights" (Matt 12:40). By itself, with no other evidence to inform our understanding, the phrase would require that Jesus' resurrection take place after three whole days and nights from the time of his crucifixion or seventy-two hours. But there is significant evidence that would cause a careful reader of the Bible to question whether that is the true meaning.

Each of these terms is translated from the Greek words listed here:

Greek for "After Three Days" and "The Third Day"
Matthew 27:63—μετά τρεῖς ἡμέρα (after three days) *meta treis hemeras*
Mark 8:31—μετά τρεῖς ἡμέρα (after three days) *meta treis hemeras*
Mark 9:31—τρίτος ἡμέρα (the third day) *trite hemera*
Mark 10:34—τρίτος ἡμέρα (the third day) *trite hemera*

Although they are different Greek words, they are translated the same because of the Jewish calculation of time. All three references in Mark refer to the same sayings of Jesus and yet Mark uses a different word in sayings two and three.

It is a fundamental principle of interpretation that if a passage does not lend itself to a definite meaning or if the thought is interpreted differently in other places, the majority interpretation prevails. Consider the number of times "three days and three nights" is found in the Bible compared to the number of times "the third day" is found.

Table 5: Three Days and Nights Versus Third Day

Third-Day	Three Days and Three Nights
Matthew 16:21	
Matthew 17:23	
Matthew 20:19	
Matthew 27:63	
Luke 9:22	
Luke 13:32, 33	Matthew 12:40
Luke 18:33	
Luke 24:7	
Luke 24:21	
Luke 24:46	
Acts 10:40	
1 Corinthians 15:4	

Don't let the visual of Table 5 slide by you too quickly. "Three days and three nights" looks a little lonely on this table. If there is an embarrassing amount of white space on the right side of the table it's because the phrase "on the third day" is the common biblical phrase meaning three days.

Jesus' day of resurrection from the grave, "the third day," is used ten times in the Gospels (plus Acts 10:40 and 1 Cor 15:4) compared to only one time for "three days and three nights." That's heavy preponderance, and frequency would lend itself to understanding "the third day" as the appropriate interpretation.

The premier occasion where "after three days" is juxtaposed to "the third day" is Matthew 27:63 and 64. "Sir, we remember how that impostor said, while he was still alive, 'After three days I will rise.' Therefore order the tomb to be made secure until the third day, lest his disciples go and steal him away and tell the people, 'He has risen from the dead.'"

Most translations of the New Testament use these expressions interchangeably.

Table 6: Modern Translations

Modern Translations of Matthew 27:63 and Matthew 27:64				
KJV	Matt 27:63	"after three days"	Matt 27:64	"the third day"
ESV	Matt 27:63	"after three days"	Matt 27:64	"the third day"
NIV	Matt 27:63	"after three days"	Matt 27:64	"the third day"
NASB	Matt 27:63	"after three days"	Matt 27:64	"the third day"
CSB	Matt 27:63	"after three days"	Matt 27:64	"the third day"
TLB	Matt 27:63	"after three days"	Matt 27:64	"the third day"
NRSV	Matt 27:63	"after three days"	Matt 27:64	"the third day"
RSV	Matt 27:63	"after three days"	Matt 27:64	"the third day"
JBP	Matt 27:63	"after three days"	Matt 27:64	"the third day"
YLT	Matt 27:63	"after three days"	Matt 27:64	"the third day"

Since the preponderance of Scriptures indicates Jesus was raised on the third day, and not the fourth day, as a literal interpretation of Matthew 12:40 would require, we must consider the possibility that Jewish inclusive calculation is at work in determining Jesus' time in the grave. There is more than ample biblical precedent for this conclusion.

Two men on the Emmaus Road returning home on Resurrection Sunday were surprised Jesus did not know what had taken place that day in Jerusalem. Remember, there were three hours of pitch black skies, a strong earthquake, and Jesus rose from the dead. It would be difficult to be unaware of that. So, they spoke plainly:

> Concerning Jesus of Nazareth, a man who was a prophet mighty in deed and word before God and all the people, and how our chief priests and rulers delivered him up to be condemned to death and crucified him. But we had hoped that he was the one to redeem Israel. Yes, and besides all this, it is now the third day since these things happened (Luke 24:19-21).

Cleopas and his friend specifically said that the evening of the first day of the week—Sunday—was the third day since Jesus was crucified. The third day—one, two, three. All the evidence from the Bible, as well as from early Christian literature, agrees that Luke was using inclusive calculation.

The evidence is overwhelmingly in favor of inclusive calculation in the Gospel accounts of Jesus' crucifixion and resurrection. Yet, with strong evidence against them, some still cling to one verse in the face of ten others.

If Jesus were speaking these words today, counting back three days and three nights from a Sunday could indeed lead to a Wednesday or Thursday, depending on how one counted. But Jesus spoke these words in the first century. At that time, people did not number days as we do today. There are many biblical verses and a vast number of passages in early Christian literature that distinctly indicate Jesus died on a Friday. Have followers of Jesus and biblical scholars been wrong for centuries? It is possible, but is it probable?

How are we to interpret the "three days and three nights" of Matthew 12:40? Scholar Colin Humphreys concludes:

> Although this inclusive method of counting days and nights seems strange to us today, I do not think it would have seemed strange at all to Jewish people living in the second century AD, because this was the way they would have been brought up to count. In addition, Matthew would hardly have included the 'three days and three nights' words of Jesus in his Gospel if he felt they contradicted the Friday crucifixion and Sunday resurrection he clearly indicated later.[8]

The evidence for the "third day" equaling "three days and three nights" is weighty indeed. Using the inclusive calculation method of counting days is the only way to correctly settle the debate about the day Jesus was crucified.

THE INTERCHANGEABILITY OF PHRASES

One final observation about the phrases "three days and three nights" and "the third day." The evidence presented above establishes that these terms were used interchangeably in the New Testament. Often the evangelists would use one phrase or the other to describe the same event or time. For example, Mark 8:31 records, "And he [Jesus] began to teach them that the Son of Man must suffer many things and be rejected by the elders and the chief priests and the scribes and be killed, and *after three days* rise" (see also Matt 16:21 and Luke 9:22).

Later, in Galilee, Jesus said to his disciples, "The Son of Man is about to be delivered into the hands of men, and they will kill him, and he will be raised on *the third day*" (Matt 17:22-23). Mark records this same occasion by saying, "The Son of Man is going to be delivered into the hands of men, and they will kill him. And when he is killed, *after three days* he will rise" (Mark 9:31). The Gospels use these two phrases interchangeably because the phrases mean the same thing.

Another example of this interchangeability is found in Jesus' predictions of his death found in Mark 10:34, Matthew 20:19, and Luke 18:33.

Mark records Jesus' third prophecy of his death, "And they will mock him [the crucified Jesus] and spit on him, and flog him and kill him. And *after three days* he will rise."

For the third time, Matthew says, "And the Son of Man will be delivered over to the chief priests and scribes, and they will condemn him to death and deliver him over to the Gentiles to be mocked and flogged and crucified, and he will be raised on *the third day*" (Matt 20:18–19).

Luke documents for the third time, saying, "For he [Messiah Jesus] will be delivered over to the Gentiles and will be mocked and shamefully treated and spit upon. And after flogging him, they will kill him, and on *the third day* he will rise" (Luke 18:32–33).

If there was just one occasion where these two phrases were used interchangeably, that might be a coincidence. But we have just considered eight different references, by three different Gospel authors, using these phrases to mean the same thing. That's not a coincidence; that's evidence of frequency.

Forty days and forty nights

In the accounts of Jesus' temptation after his baptism, Luke notes that Jesus "was led by the Spirit in the wilderness for forty days" (Luke 4:1–2). This time it is Mark and Luke who agree using the identical phrase, "he was in the wilderness *forty days*, being tempted by Satan" (Mark 1:13), while Matthew uses the alternative phrase "after forty days and forty nights." "Then Jesus was led up by the Spirit into the wilderness to be tempted by the devil. And *after fasting forty days and forty nights*, he was hungry" (Matt 4:1–2). Mark and Luke indicate forty days; Matthew says forty days and forty nights. They are talking about the same time period.

There are several idiomatic expressions we use when talking about time. The people of the first century used them as well. Today, examples of idiomatic expressions like "third day" are frequently used with a clear understanding of their meaning.

For example, you are traveling, and you would like to get to your destination as soon as possible. But your eyes burn, your body aches, and you are getting sleepy. You're not going to make it all the way tonight. So, you stop about 8:00 pm and get a room at a motel. You want an early start in the morning, so you leave a wake-up call and get on the road at 6:00 am. You did not even use your room for twenty-four hours. In fact, you used it only 10 hours. When you received your bill, did you pay for 10 hours or an entire day?

If you spent any time overnight in that room, you paid for one full day. But you only used the room for less than half a day. It does not matter because a portion of a day is considered an entire day. That's inclusive calculation, and we experience it all the time. Jesus experienced it in Joseph's tomb. We understand the principle well, but some still have difficulty applying it to Jesus' hours in the grave. The Gospel authors did not.

THE IMPRECISION IN MEANING

In a brief but helpful column in the May/June 2016 *Biblical Archaeology Review,* Professor of New Testament Interpretation at Asbury Theological Seminary Ben Witherington III correctly comments, "We are a people obsessed with time—and with exactness when it comes to time—down to the nanosecond. In this regard, we are very different from the ancients, who did not go around wearing little sundials on their wrists and did not talk about seconds and minutes. They did not obsess about precision when it comes to time."

The phrases "three days and three nights" and "third day" are cases in point. To us in the twenty-first century, these phrases seem quite absolute. How much more specific can you get than "three days and three nights"? But our need for specificity in the twenty-first-century West was not at all felt by those living in the first-century Middle East.

In Matthew 12:40, when Jesus spoke of "three days and three nights," he was saying, "My experience in the grave and then being raised from it will be like the story of Jonah being in the great fish and then being expelled from it." The Savior was using Jonah and the fish as an analogy for death and resurrection. Jesus was not talking about time; he was talking about events. For him, using the story of Jonah was not about "three days and three nights" of time, but about Jesus' death and his resurrection on the third day. Jonah's "death" being swallowed by the great fish and then his "resurrection" by being spewed out, was a picture of Jesus' death, burial, and resurrection. The precision of time was not on the Savior's mind.

From the evidence presented in this chapter, including the Jonah reference by Jesus, the confirmation of inclusive calculation in the Bible is comprehensive, one might even say overwhelming. While others may deny or disregard this evidence, the Bible does not. To fail to apply inclusive calculation to the Passion narratives is to dishonestly treat the time references in those narratives since the precedent has been set in the rest of the Scriptures. Jesus did what he said he would do. He rose from the dead on the third day.

As Ben Witherington concludes, "I would suggest it's high time we showed these ancient authors the respect they deserve and read them with an awareness of the conventions they followed when writing ancient history or ancient biography and not impose our later genre conventions on them." I concur entirely. Using the understanding of those who wrote the Gospels, let's let them say exactly what they wanted to say. Let's faithfully interpret what they said using the criteria of their time.

Chapter 2

Calculating Time by Seasons and Sabbaths

The Jewish calendar is more like an ascending helix with recurring patterns or cycles that present the theme of God's goodness and salvation of his chosen people, Israel. So, rather than think in terms of months, religious Jews think in terms of seasons and the goodness of God for every season.

IN THE PREVIOUS CHAPTER, we examined how time was calculated in antiquity, with particular reference to the Jewish calculation of years, months, and days. But there is much more to calculating time in first-century Judaism. In this chapter, we want to explore how the Jews calculated time by seasons, Sabbaths, and sunsets.

In the centuries preceding the birth of Jesus, calendars and dates were established by various means. The Greek Olympiad was held every four years and for the Greeks, dating related to the Olympic Games. For the Romans, the calendar was determined by Rome's founding date, which the Roman historian Varro placed in the year 753 BC. In Syria, the calendar was set according to the victory of Seleucus I and the founding of the Seleucid dynasty.[9]

For Westerners, the calendar is linear. We move from day to day, week to week, year to year, and then on to the next year, *ad infinitum*. Not so with the Jewish people. Even those who use the Gregorian calendar in business, spiritually march to a different calendar.

The Jewish calendar is more like an ascending helix with recurring patterns or cycles that present the theme of God's goodness and salvation of his chosen people, Israel. So, rather than think in terms of months, religious Jews thought in terms of seasons and the goodness of God for every season. "For everything there is a season, and a time for every matter under heaven: a time to be born, and a time to die; a time to plant, and a time to pluck up what is planted" (Eccl 3:1).

I grew up on a chicken farm in western Pennsylvania in the United States. I understood the broiler chicken's life cycle, a bird raised for its meat, not for laying eggs. But it was not until 1990, when my family and I moved from New York State to America's heartland, that I gained a genuine appreciation for the seasons.

We now live in a small town in Nebraska (population 2,252). When I would occasionally go to Granny's, the only coffee shop in town, I would sit at my table and innocently listen to the farmers sitting at tables all around me. Their conversations always revolved around yield, rainfall, relative maturity, growing degree days, harvesting dates, etc. "If I don't get my TM YieldPro corn in by next Tuesday, I'll have to switch to Safeguard Pro." There were only two essential dates on their calendar: planting and harvesting. The rest of the year was waiting for God to give the increase.

THE IMPORTANCE OF THE SEASONS FOR JEWISH FEASTS

This is much the way it was for the Jewish farmers of Jesus' day. Israel was an agrarian society. They lived off the land, growing wheat, barley, etc., and tending to their vineyards. The Hebrew calendar was built precisely on agricultural dates like the barley harvest or the wheat harvest. Farmers have always known the paramount period in which to harvest and they planted accordingly, just like my flannel-shirted friends at the café.

The outpouring of God's Spirit on the church in Jerusalem came on the day of Pentecost. Just as the Jewish festival of the Firstfruits of the barley harvest occurred during Passover week, on Nisan 16, Pentecost was another Jewish first fruits festival. This time it was the wheat harvest (Lev 23:15). This Firstfruits festival was held precisely seven weeks after Nisan 16 (fifty days calculating inclusively as the Jew did, but forty-nine days [seven weeks of seven days] counting as we do today).

On the day of Pentecost, two leavened loaves, made from new wheat and yeast, were waved in the Temple by the priests. No Jew could harvest wheat, nor could any wheat product be eaten, until this offering to the LORD occurred first. It was the law. Just as the offering of a sheaf of barley on Nisan 16 marked the beginning of the barley harvest, so the offering of wheat loaves marked the beginning of the wheat harvest. Calculating inclusively, fifty days after Sunday, Nisan 16, leads to another Sunday. This is why the Christian Church traditionally celebrates the coming of the Holy Spirit on a Sunday, often called Whit Sunday.

> In general, the Jewish calendar in New Testament times (at least before 70 AD) followed the Sadducean reckoning, since it was by that reckoning that the Temple services were regulated. Thus the day of Pentecost was reckoned as the fiftieth day after the presentation of the first harvested sheaf of barley, i.e., the fiftieth day (inclusive) from the first Sunday after Passover (cf. Lev 23:15ff.); hence it always fell on a Sunday, as it does in the Christian calendar.[10]

We should keep this timeline in mind as we search to identify the day of Jesus' crucifixion. If we do not, we will be tempted to be guided by other, non-biblical, less accurate means that reach the wrong conclusions.

When it comes to calculating time by the Sabbath, all four Gospels agree that Jesus died the day before the Jewish Sabbath. Mark affirms Jesus' crucifixion occurred on "the day of Preparation, that is, the day before the Sabbath" (Mark 15:42). Which days are the "Preparation Day" and "the day before the Sabbath"?

Remember, from Judaism's earliest years, except for the Sabbath, all Jewish weekdays were numbered, not named. They were, and still are, called the first day, the second day, the third day, and so on unto the seventh, which differs because it is not called the seventh day but the Sabbath. The Jewish week's first day is the Christian Sunday; the seventh day, the Sabbath, is our Saturday. Friday was called "the eve of the Sabbath" or "the day of Preparation," both in the New Testament and by the Jewish historian Josephus. The Gospels agree that Jesus died the day before the Sabbath.

Mark alone details "morning" and "evening" events for three of those days: Sunday (11:1, 11), Monday (11:12, 19), and Thursday (14:12, 17). Also, Mark alone chronicles Friday's events in three-hour intervals (like Roman military time).

Table 1: Roman Military Time

6:00 am	"As soon as it was morning" (15:1)
9:00 am	"It was nine o'clock in the morning" (15:25)
12:00 Noon	"When it was noon" (15:33)
3:00 pm	"At three o'clock" (15:34)
6:00 pm	"When evening had come" (15:42)"[11]

As has been noted, the Jewish day began at sunset and lasted until sunset the next day. Therefore, the Jewish Sabbath runs from Friday evening to Saturday evening, and Preparation Day, the day before the Sabbath, is marked from Thursday evening to Friday evening. Although the Jews calculated the start of their day at sunset, they were accustomed to measuring the hours in the day from the daylight of sunrise.

Today we would view this as using both military time and standard time, using both a twenty-four-hour clock and a twelve-hour clock. At Passover time (March/April), sunrise in Jerusalem occurs at about 6:00 am. So midday is the sixth hour or noon. Matthew's Gospel informs us that Jesus died at "about the ninth hour" (Matt 27:46–50). That means Jesus died at about 3:00 pm.

There are, however, specific "indicators" that help us establish more precisely the day, date, and time of Jesus' crucifixion. Before examining the various days proposed as the crucifixion day, let's think about some of the factors—I call them "indicators"—that lead people to different conclusions.

THE SABBATH

References to keeping a holy Sabbath are found throughout the Old Testament, but primarily in the Pentateuch (cf. Exod 16:22–30; 20:8–11; 23:12; 31:12–16; 34:21; 35:2–3; Lev 23:3; 26:2; Num 15:32–36; 28:9–10; Deut 12–15). The Hebrew word Sabbath (שַׁבָּת shabbâth) means "to cease" or "to abstain." It refers to a work stoppage for holy communion with the Almighty. There is a similar word that means "seventh" (Hebrew: שְׁבִיעִי; English: *shebîyʿîy*), but this is not it. A Sabbath is observed every Friday evening from sunset through sunset on Saturday evening. In Israel, restaurants are sparsely attended on Friday night, but come Saturday evening, after *Shabbat*, you can't find a seat in the house.

Observing the Sabbath was a command of God. Exodus 20:8–11 reminded Israel that God rested from his creative activity on the seventh day (Gen 2:2). This grounds the Sabbath in the very act of creation. By Deuteronomy 5:12–15 the Jews were reminded of the years of slavery they endured in Egypt with no rest. On the Sabbath, all Jews (including family, hired servants, strangers, and even their domestic animals) were to stop every kind of labor. The penalty for ignoring the Sabbath restrictions was excommunication from any social interaction with others in Israel, or worse, the Sabbath-breaker could be put to death (Exod 31:12–16).

The purpose of the Sabbath

The Sabbath was observed for two reasons. First, it symbolized that the nation Israel had been set apart by the LORD God as his special people, his chosen people. "For you are a people holy to the Lord your God. The Lord your God has chosen you to be a people for his treasured possession, out of all the peoples who are on the face of the earth" (Deut 7:6; 14:2). Second, the Sabbath was both a celebration and an affirmation that the land belonged to God. Evidence of this is seen in the Sabbatical Year—one year out of every seven when the ground would lie fallow and not be cultivated, replenishing itself.

Unfortunately, over time Jewish religious leaders heaped burdensome rule after unnecessary rule on the Sabbath. The day of rest and communion with God became a day filled with heavy restrictions and almost impossible demands. The thrill of worship turned into the burden of observance. Jesus wanted to restore the Sabbath's true and original purpose (Matt 12:1–14; Mark 2:23—3:6; Luke 6:1–11). He preached, "The Sabbath was made for man, not man for the Sabbath" (Mark 2:27). Opposing these man-made restrictions on the Sabbath was the basis for much of the hatred directed toward Jesus from the chief priests, scribes, and Pharisees.

Sabbaths are not observed by the Jews only. Babylonians celebrated the 7th, 14th, 21st, and 28th as "holy days." In Eastern Christianity and some Sabbath-keeping traditions in the Western Church, notably among the Seventh-Day Adventists and the Mormons, the Sabbath is still observed. In Islam, the Qur'an acknowledges a six-part Creation Period (32:4, 50:38) and the biblical Sabbath as the seventh day (*yaum as-Sabt*: 2:65, 4:47, 154, 7:163, 16:124). However, Muslims replace Sabbath rest with *jumu'ah*, more popularly known as "Friday prayers." The *Uposatha* has been observed since Gautama Buddha's time (500 BC) and Theravada Buddhists are still keeping it today. It occurs every seven or eight days, following the four phases of the moon. Even the Cherokee Nation observes the first day of a new moon as a day of quiet reflection and oneness with the spirit world.

THE HIGH SABBATH

Besides the weekly Sabbaths, there were High Sabbaths related to the Hebrew Feasts (Festivals) described in Leviticus 23:4-44 and Numbers 28:16-18; 28:25. These special days, which were counted as Sabbaths, were appointed for Israel to keep and were separate from the regular weekly Sabbaths (Lev 23:3-8). One such feast was that of Trumpets. "And the LORD spoke to Moses, saying, 'Speak to the people of Israel, saying, "In the seventh month, on the first day of the month, you shall observe a day of solemn rest, a memorial proclaimed with a blast of trumpets, a holy convocation. You shall not do any ordinary work, and you shall present a food offering to the LORD"'" (Lev 23:23-25). Without using the word "Sabbath," all the earmarks of a Sabbath are there: a day of solemn rest, a memorial, a holy convocation (Exod 12:16; Lev 23:24; 23:35-36; Num 28:18), do no ordinary work (Exod 12:16; Lev 16:29; 23:25; 23:35-36; Num 28:18) and present an offering.

The same is true with the Feast of Atonement.

> And it shall be a statute to you forever that in the seventh month, on the tenth day of the month, you shall afflict yourselves and shall do no work, either the native or the stranger who sojourns among you. For on this day shall atonement be made for you to cleanse you. You shall be clean before the LORD from all your sins. It is a Sabbath of solemn rest to you, and you shall afflict yourselves; it is a statute forever (Lev 16:29-31).

In this case, God used both the word "Sabbath" and descriptions of a Sabbath.

The same phrases are used to describe the regular weekly Sabbath (Lev 23:3). It is not explicitly said in the Old Testament that the first day of the Feast of Unleavened Bread was a Sabbath, but these same two phrases were used to describe it (Exod 12:16; Lev 23:7; Num 28:18). In the New Testament, it was referred to as a Sabbath (Mark 16:1; John 19:31). It came on the same date every year, the fifteenth of the first month (Lev 23:6; Num 28:17). Thus, the High Sabbath was tied to a date, like Passover, not to a day of the week.

We understand this concept because we live with it today. One year Christmas comes on a Friday and another year it is on a Monday. The holiday is tied to a date, not to a day of the week.

John 19:31 informs us, "Since it was the day of Preparation, and so that the bodies would not remain on the cross on the Sabbath (for that Sabbath was a High Day), the Jews asked Pilate that their legs might be broken and that they might be taken away." The word translated "high" (Greek: μέγας; English: *mégas*) in the phrase "for that Sabbath was a High Day" is a common one. We have all become familiar with this word when we go shopping at the Mega Mart (*mégas*) or turn on the car radio to hear the latest "Mega Hit" (*mégas*) from the newest "Mega Star" (*mégas*). "High" in High Day is the word *mégas*.

But what was a "high Sabbath" or "High Day" in this Passion Week, and on what day did it occur? Leviticus 23:5–8 indicates:

> In the first month, on the fourteenth day of the month at twilight, is the LORD's Passover. And on the fifteenth day of the same month is the Feast of Unleavened Bread to the LORD; for seven days you shall eat unleavened bread. On the first day, you shall have a holy convocation; you shall not do any ordinary work. But you shall present a food offering to the LORD for seven days. On the seventh day is a holy convocation; you shall not do any ordinary work.

Leviticus clarifies that the "high Sabbath" was the first day of the Feast of Unleavened Bread. It was a day of "holy convocation" in which the Jews would do no routine work. Another holy convocation would be held seven days later at the end of the feast. Since the Passover was the fourteenth day of the month of Nisan, and the Feast of Unleavened Bread with its high Sabbath was the fifteenth day of the month, this particular Saturday was a special day indeed.

It was a High Day because it was the Sabbath. It was a High Day because it was the day on which all Jewish people presented themselves in the Temple according to God's command (Exod 23:17). And it was high because the sheaf of the first fruits was offered, according to Leviticus 23:10–11. This Sabbath Saturday was a "great" day because it was the first day of Unleavened Bread, occurring on an ordinary Sabbath. It was the most solemn season and the most solemn day of the Jewish ecclesiastical year. It does not get much better than that.

John calls the day after the crucifixion a special Sabbath or high Sabbath because in the year Jesus was crucified, the regular Saturday Sabbath (Friday evening through Saturday evening) coincided with the Passover Sabbath, on Nisan 15. Thus, the crucifixion occurred on Nisan 14, the day before the Passover meal. "John consistently says that the Last Supper (John 13:1,2), the trials of Jesus (John 18:28 and 19:14), and his crucifixion (John 19:31) were all before the Passover meal. The logical interpretation of John is that the crucifixion occurred on Nisan 14, and the Passover meal followed at the evening start of the next Jewish day, on Nisan 15."[12]

THE ANNUAL PASSOVER

In the Old Testament, references to the Passover, as well as the Feast of Unleavened Bread, are numerous (Exod 12:1—13:16; 23:15; 34:18-20,25; Lev 23:4-14; Num 28:16-25; Deut 16:1-8; Josh 4:19-23; 5:10-12; and 2 Chr 30:2,3,13,15). Passover (Pesach) was the first and primary of three great pilgrimage festivals for the Hebrew people, the other two being Shavuot (Weeks or Pentecost) and Sukkot (Tabernacles or Booths). These are called pilgrimage festivals because the Hebrew people would make a pilgrimage to the Temple in Jerusalem, as commanded by the Torah.

The original Passover occurred the night the angel of death passed through Egypt, slaying the firstborn as the last of the ten plagues on the Egyptians. The Jews smeared the blood of a lamb on the lintel and doorposts as a sign that the angel should "pass over" that home because God was protecting it. From the events of that fateful evening emerged the annual celebration of Passover. Unleavened bread was used in the celebration because it indicated the Jews had no time to allow their bread to rise before they hastily left on that Passover night.

The fixed date of Passover

For the Hebrew people, freshly released from 430 years of living under unbearable conditions, you would expect the celebration of the Passover to be frequently mentioned in the narrative of their wilderness journeys. It is not. There are only six specific examples of the Passover observance in the period from Moses (fifteenth century BC) to Judah's King Josiah (seventh century BC), besides the repeated Old Testament instruction concerning the time of celebration (Lev 23:5; Num 9:3; 28:16; Ezek 45:21). In each instance, the Passover lamb was slain on the Jewish "fourteenth" of the first month.

We have both early and late witnesses for the first Passover date in the time of the Second Temple. "They finished their building by decree of the God of Israel and by decree of Cyrus and Darius and Artaxerxes king of Persia; and this house was finished on the third day of the month of Adar, in the sixth year of the reign of Darius the king" (Ezra 6:14-15). Just a few weeks later, Passover was celebrated. Ezra 6:19 states, "On the fourteenth day of the first month, the returned exiles kept the Passover" (see also 1 Esdras 7:10).

In the late Second Temple Period, along with Jewish sources—Apocryphal literature, Aristobulus, Philo, and Josephus—the Bible mentions at least eight Passovers. The New Testament reports seven of these feasts, although no date is given. However, both the Passover and Paul's festival at Philippi are tied to a particular day of the week. According to the narrative in Acts 20, the twentieth day after Paul's Passover at Philippi coincided with Sunday.

The exact year of the Acts 20 narrative can be calculated through this synchronism, just as the precise year of the Passover. These synchronisms, together with the historical statements, fully establish the sacrificial date of the Passover as the 14th of Nisan during the time of the Roman occupation. From these sources, it can be demonstrated that Moses' fundamental laws governed the Jewish feasts until the Romans finally destroyed Jerusalem.

HOW PASSOVER WAS TO BE OBSERVED

God's instructions for celebrating Passover are quite clear in Exodus 12 and elsewhere. It was to be celebrated on the 14th day of the first month of the year, the month of Abib (Lev 23:5; Num 28:16–25), with the service beginning in the evening of that day. Wilhelm Bacher was a Hungarian Jewish scholar, rabbi, Orientalist, and linguist. He commented:

> In *Antiquities,* Josephus further explains his statement in *Wars* 6.9.3, namely, that it was the evening lamb sacrifice that was offered "about the ninth hour" *(Ant.* 14.4.3), or "at the ending of the day" *(Ant.*3.10.1) after which followed the slaying of the paschal lambs at sunset, when the lamps were lighted (Exod 30:8) and the incense was burned *(Ant.*3.8.3). This was the hour called *ben-ha-arbayim,* which did not include the whole afternoon, as in the later Halacha, but only the period from sunset to darkness.[13]

Even the apocryphal book of 1 Esdras mentions this date. "And the children of Israel that were of the captivity held the Passover the fourteenth day of the first month, after that the priests and the Levites were sanctified" (1 Esd 7:10).

In the medieval centuries (the fifth to the fifteenth century), Jewish manuscripts were still available for examination regarding the Passover date. Both the Arabian chronologer Albirani and the Jewish philosopher Maimonides had access to these sources. In 1634 AD, the French Jesuit and chronological scholar Aegidius Bucherius collected relevant chronological documents and published them in his *Doctrina Temporum*.[14] This historical evidence is invaluable in tracing the history of the Passover from antiquity to the present.

ANCIENT AUTHORS ON THE OBSERVANCE OF PASSOVER

Aristobulus of Paneas flourished in the second century BC. He was a Jewish Hellenistic philosopher who attempted a fusion of ideas in the Hebrew Scriptures with Greek thought. His entire work is said to have existed in a library on Patmos during the Middle Ages. Whether this is accurate or not, his description and explanation of Passover law and its relation to the full moon are of "definitive importance" to the ancient Jewish calendar.

Here is Aristobulus' statement about the Jewish Passover:

> Since there are two equinoxes, spring, and autumn, which are separated by equal distances, and since the Passover was appointed on the fourteenth day of the first month after the evening when the moon is caught in the region opposite to the sun, just as even the eyes can see, certainly the sun is found holding a part of the vernal equinox, and the moon, on the contrary, a part of the autumnal.[15]

Aristobulus's successor, Philo, who lived in the time of Christ, was an active author during the same period as when the book of Jubilees and the book of Enoch were written. He provides an even more complete analysis of the Jewish feasts and sacrifices than does Josephus. Regarding the slaying of the Passover lamb and the date of the Passover, Philo noted:

> On this day every dwelling house is invested with the outward semblance and dignity of a temple. The victim is then slaughtered and dressed for the festal meal, which befits the occasion. The guests assembled for the banquet have been cleansed by purificatory lustrations, and are there . . . to fulfill with prayers and hymns the custom handed down by their fathers. The day on which this national festivity occurs may very properly be noted. It is the fourteenth of the month.[16]

Although Josephus groups his references to the Passover around early Jewish history, he still insists there are accurate portrayals of Jewish practice in his own time. The importance here is not only do these portrayals explain the original Passover law, but they also corroborate Philo's testimony.

Josephus describes the Passover both in the language of the Egyptians and the Hebrews.

> But when God had signified, that with one plague he would compel the Egyptians to let Hebrews go, he commanded Moses to tell the people that they should have a sacrifice ready, and

> they should prepare themselves on the tenth day of the month Xanthicus, against the fourteenth . . . but when the fourteenth day was come, and all were ready to depart they offered the sacrifice, and purified their houses with the blood, using bunches of hyssop for that purpose . . . Whence it is that we do still offer this sacrifice in like manner to this day, and call this festival Pascha which signifies the feast of the Passover; because on that day, God passed us over, and sent the plague upon the Egyptians (*Ant.* 2.14.6).

In *Antiquities* 3.10.5, 6 Josephus refers to various observances of the Jews in their relationship with each other. This very instructive passage reads:

> In the month of Xanthicus, which is by us called Nisan, and is the beginning of our year, on the fourteenth day of the lunar month, when the sun is in Aries, (for in this month it was that we were delivered from bondage under the Egyptians,) the law ordained that we should every year slay that sacrifice which I before told you we slew when we came out of Egypt, and which was called the Passover . . . The feast of unleavened bread succeeds that of the Passover, and falls on the fifteenth day of the month, and continues seven days . . . But on the second day of unleavened bread, which is the sixteenth day of the month, they first partake of the fruits of the earth . . . [they] bring one-tenth deal to the altar, to God; and, casting one handful of it upon the fire, they leave the rest for the use of the priest. And after this, it is that they may publicly or privately reap their harvest. They also at this participation of the first fruits of the earth, sacrifice a lamb, as a burnt offering to God . . . When a week of weeks has passed over after this sacrifice, (which weeks contain forty and nine days,) on the fiftieth day, which is Pentecost, but is called by the Hebrews *Asartha*, which signifies Pentecost, they bring to God a loaf, made of wheat flour, of two tenth deals, with leaven; and for sacrifices, they bring two lambs.

I said this was a very instructive passage. Josephus has just corroborated what we already knew from the Old Testament. The sheaf of first fruits was to be offered to the Lord before they ate of the harvest of the land. The Jews began to eat the fruit of the land on the 16th day, following the Feast of Unleavened Bread. So the sequence of Passover events becomes more apparent:

- Nisan, 14th day—Slaying of the lamb for the beginning of Passover after sunset;
- Nisan, 15th day—Beginning of the seven-day Feast of Unleavened Bread;
- Nisan, 16th day—Wave offering presented to the LORD of the harvest's first fruits.

Fifty days following the wave offering, the Jewish people celebrate Pentecost, the Feast of Weeks. In the year Jesus was crucified, when followers of Jesus gathered in Jerusalem to celebrate the Feast of Weeks while observing the feast, the Holy Spirit fell on them powerfully and miraculously, and the Christian Church was born (Acts 2:1–4).

Surprisingly, Passover is not often mentioned in historical works outside of the Bible. Only once in the *Wars of the Jews* does Josephus mention it and its date ". . . being the fourteenth day of the month Xanthicus, [Nisan,] when it is believed the Jews were first freed from the Egyptians, Eleazar and his party opened the gates of this [inmost court of the] Temple, and admitted such of the people as were desirous to worship God into it" (*Wars* 5.3.1). However, he does mention Passover more often in his *Antiquities of the Jews*, equating it with the 14th of Nisan (*Ant*.11.4.8).

Even the great Maimonides, the medieval Sephardic Jewish philosopher, one of the most prolific and influential Torah scholars of the Middle Ages, confirms the date of the Passover in Moses' day as, "On the fourteenth day of the first month when the Passover offering was sacrificed."[17]

> "After a man has died for another, there can be no question raised about his love."—Charles Haddon Spurgeon

All these historical sources—Moses, Joshua, Ezekiel, the Apocrypha, Aristobulus, Philo, and Josephus—record the same date for the Jewish Passover observance. It was the 14th day of the first lunar month. This was the Passover date for slaying the lamb commanded by Moses, and it was the same Passover date in the Second Temple Period. This date has been consistent for 3,500 years. In the time of Christ, therefore, the national Passover must have been celebrated on the 14th day of the first month on the Jewish calendar. "It was about the sixth hour, says John, that is, midday, the hour when the preparations for the Passover began with the removal of all leavened bread. It was also the moment when preparations began for the ultimate Passover, with the sacrifice of the Lamb, Jesus."[18]

The crucifixion of Jesus of Nazareth can never be divorced from the slaughtering of the Passover lambs during Passion Week. If the death of Jesus on the cross does not align with the lambs' annual sacrifice in Jerusalem, the prophets, evangelists, apostles, and the writer of the book of Hebrews are all mistaken. Jesus came to fulfill the Passover Lamb prophecies, and the Gospels demonstrate he did just that.

The exactness of God's eternal calendar

The historian Josephus (*Wars* 6.9.3) indicates that in the first century AD, Passover lambs were slain between 3:00 pm and 5:00 pm on Nisan 14. Jesus died on the same day, Nisan 14, and the Gospels inform us he died at the ninth hour (Matt 27:45–50; Mark 15:33–37; Luke 23:44–46), that is, 3:00 pm. This would place his death precisely as the slaughter of the Passover lambs in the Temple began. Golgotha became the great Temple of God for those hours Jesus hung on the cross. There his sacrifice made atonement and paid the penalty for our sin. This is not just a convenient coincidence in timing; this is evidence of the eternal timetable of the Sovereign God.

The Jewish priests were very busy during those hours that Jesus hung on the cross. I imagine having three hours of pitch-black darkness put a crimp in their schedule. More than a few Jews made their way from all over the world to Jerusalem for Passover. Josephus informs us that the Syrian Governor Cestius Gallus requested the High Priest to take a census of Jerusalem to convince Nero of the importance of the city and the Jewish nation. How did the High Priest obtain an accurate count? He counted the number of lambs slain at Passover. That number was 256,500. Then he multiplied by 10, which was the average number of people served by each lamb slaughtered. This would yield a population in Jerusalem during Passover of approximately 2,565,000 or, as Josephus himself calculates it, 2,700,200 Jews (*Wars* 6.9.3). On an earlier occasion, Josephus computed the number of Jews present in Jerusalem at Passover to be not fewer than 3,000,000 (*Wars* 2.14.3). See, however, the comments on page 165.

It was in scurrying around to slaughter such a large number of lambs that most priests may have missed hearing Jesus say, "It is finished" as he handed his soul back to the Father. What a shame they missed the main event.

THE FEAST OF FIRSTFRUITS

Passover and the Feast of Unleavened Bread often get jammed together, and usually, it's the Feast of Unleavened Bread that gets lost in the shuffle.

Josephus almost equates the two (*Ant.*14:2.1; 17.9.3). Non-Jewish Americans don't have that problem because there are sufficient days or months between our major holidays (New Year, Easter, Memorial Day, Christmas, etc.). But the Feast of Unleavened Bread comes immediately on the heels of the annual Passover and, as a result, sometimes it gets overlooked.

The Feast of the Unleavened Bread began the night after the Passover. Here's how God described it to Moses.

> In the first month, on the fourteenth day of the month at twilight, is the LORD's Passover. And on the fifteenth day of the same month is the Feast of Unleavened Bread to the LORD; for seven days you shall eat unleavened bread. On the first day, you shall have a holy convocation; you shall not do any ordinary work. But you shall present a food offering to the LORD for seven days. On the seventh day is a holy convocation; you shall not do any ordinary work (Lev 23:5–8).

The critical points made by God in these verses are:

1. The fourteenth day of the first month of the Jewish year is always Passover.
2. The fifteenth day of the first month of the Jewish year begins the Feast of Unleavened Bread.
3. The Feast of Unleavened Bread would last for seven days.
4. The Jews were to eat bread made without yeast during the entire Feast of Unleavened Bread.
5. On the first day of the feast, the Jews were to observe a holy convocation, a Sabbath.
6. On the last day of the feast, the Jews also observed a holy convocation, a Sabbath.
7. The Jews were to present a food offering to the LORD each day of the feast.

During this seven-day festival, a morning and evening sacrifice was offered. Only unleavened bread was eaten, plus the meat of the sacrifices. Leaven is symbolic of sin, and the Passover was a memorial to the power of God's mighty arm to deliver the Hebrew people from Egyptian slavery. The Feast of the Unleavened Bread made God's deliverance and Israel's need for repentance current. It did more than memorialize; it had an immediate impact since it was also a time of repentance and putting away sin from their individuals' lives.

To illustrate the divine intentionality behind the timing of Jesus' crucifixion, we must consult the Apostle Paul. The apostle brilliantly used the striking symbolism of Jesus as the Passover lamb when he wrote, "Christ, our Passover lamb, has been sacrificed" (1 Cor 5:7). Later, in the same letter, Paul penned, "If in Christ we have hope in this life only, we are of all people most to be pitied. But in fact, Christ has been raised from the dead, the firstfruits of those who have fallen asleep. For as by a man came death, by a man has come also the resurrection of the dead" (1 Cor 15:19-21).

Paul was referring to Christ's resurrection, which he believed, in agreement with the very earliest Christian traditions, occurred on the third day after Jesus' crucifixion (1 Cor 15:4), that is, Sunday. But what does Paul mean by the word "firstfruits" in referring to Christ?

Those in his first-century AD audience would have understood this completely. The book of Leviticus describes what the Jewish people called a "firstfruits festival," which celebrated the beginning of the barley harvest. "Speak to the people of Israel and say to them, When you come into the land that I give you and reap its harvest, you shall bring the sheaf of the firstfruits of your harvest to the priest, and he shall wave the sheaf before the LORD, so that you may be accepted. On the day after the Sabbath the priest shall wave it" (Lev 23:10-11). What day is "the day after the Sabbath"? It's Nisan 16.

Here also is the testimony of the Jewish writers Philo and Josephus. Philo (c. 20 BC to 45 AD) wrote in *De specialibus legibus* (2.144-75) that the first sheaf of barley was presented in the Temple on the second day of the feast, which is Nisan 16. This makes the 16th of Nisan the only day possible for the wave offering at the beginning of the barley harvest—the Feast of Firstfruits.

It is not needed, but additional confirmation comes from the Mishnah, compiled about 100 AD. This record of the Oral Torah, transmitted in the aftermath of the destruction of the Second Temple in 70 AD, gives the following account of the festival of Firstfruits.

> On the eve after the first day of Passover, messengers from the court used to go to one of the barley fields near Jerusalem and in a festive ceremony would harvest a handful of barley which they then waved over the altar ... The ceremony on the 16th of Nisan permitted the people to eat from the fresh harvest of that year" (Mishnah *Menahot* 10.3 and 10.6).

The Apostle Paul cleverly used the symbolism of the festival of Firstfruits to refer to Jesus' resurrection. Paul was saying that just as waving the first sheaf of barley in the Temple enabled all of the barley harvests to be gathered, so too Christ's resurrection enabled all those who have died in faith to be resurrected and gathered into the bosom of God. The chronology underlying the symbolism Paul used is exact. By metaphor, Paul was acknowledging that Jesus' crucifixion was on Nisan 14, and his resurrection on Nisan 16. Otherwise, the basis for the symbolism is null and void.

Paul's implied chronology of the crucifixion events, recorded in one of the earliest New Testament documents (1 Corinthians—written about 55 AD), is identical to the chronology of John, which many scholars believe was the last Gospel written. Both are consistent with the Synoptic Gospels' chronology, perhaps written between 40 and 60 AD, provided the Last Supper is not understood as the Passover meal (see Chapter 3).

THE DAY OF PREPARATION

The Gospel of John is quite explicit. On the day Jesus was crucified just outside the gates of Jerusalem, John 19:14 says, "Now it was the day of Preparation of the Passover." And just a few verses later, John notes:

> Since it was the day of Preparation, and so that the bodies would not remain on the cross on the Sabbath (for that Sabbath was a High Day), the Jews asked Pilate that their legs might be broken and that they might be taken away. So the soldiers came and broke the legs of the first, and the other who had been crucified with him. But when they came to Jesus and saw that he was already dead, they did not break his legs (John 19:31–33).

Paraskeue, the Greek word translated as "Preparation Day," is "used to refer to the day or hours spent in preparation for the Jewish Sabbath or festivals."[19] It means the "eve of the Sabbath, the *Erev Shabbat* of the Jews, which has the special meaning of 'preparation' for the Sabbath, as Mark explains for the benefit of readers who are unfamiliar with this expression peculiar to Judaism."

These verses state categorically that the day of Jesus' crucifixion was the Preparation of the Passover. Since this is so explicit, we must be sure we correctly understand what is meant by "Preparation." Was "Preparation" (Greek: παρασκευὴ; English: *paraskeuē*) used only for the day before the Sabbath, or could it be used for the day before any feast day? Mark 15:42 indicates that it was used of Friday, and both Luke 23:54 and John 19:31 corroborate this. That it was generally understood to mean Friday is specified by its use in the *Didache* 8:1, in the *Martyrdom of Polycarp* 7:1, and by Josephus, *Antiquities* 16.6.2.

Charles C. Torrey and Solomon Zeitlin have contested this derivation of the term. Torrey, an American historian, archaeologist, and scholar, suggested that *paraskeuē* is the Greek word for the Jewish technical term denoting the Sabbath's eve, which was derived from the word for sunset. Zeitlin, from the Jewish university Dropsie College and an expert on the Dead Sea Scrolls, countered this. He maintained that the Hellenized Jews used *to sabbaton* to translate "eve of the Sabbath" and that *paraskeuē* could apply to any festival because it meant "act of preparation." In his later articles, Zeitlin asserted that Mark 15:42 does not prove *paraskeuē* means Friday but is an explanatory note for Jewish Christians who would not have understood its technical sense.

The preparation for the Passover or the Sabbath was an important day. It is mentioned six times in the New Testament, sometimes in advance of the crucifixion, sometimes as part of the crucifixion narrative itself, and sometimes after the crucifixion event was completed.

The John 19:14 reference is before Golgotha. "So when Pilate heard these words, he brought Jesus out and sat down on the judgment seat at a place called The Stone Pavement, and in Aramaic Gabbatha. Now it was the day of Preparation of the Passover. It was about the sixth hour. He said to the Jews, 'Behold your King!'"

The John 19:31 reference reads, "Since it was the day of Preparation, and so that the bodies would not remain on the cross on the Sabbath (for that Sabbath was a High Day), the Jews asked Pilate that their legs might be broken and that they might be taken away."

Luke 23:54 mentions that Preparation Day was observed just as Jesus was being removed from the cross and prepared for burial. "Now there was a man named Joseph, from the Jewish town of Arimathea.... This man went to Pilate and asked for the body of Jesus. Then he took it down and wrapped it in a linen shroud and laid him in a tomb cut in stone, where no one had ever yet been laid. It was the day of Preparation, and the Sabbath was beginning" (Luke 23:50, 52–54).

Mark 15:42–43 refers to the same event. "And when evening had come, since it was the day of Preparation, that is, the day before the Sabbath, Joseph of Arimathea, a respected member of the council, who was also himself looking for the kingdom of God, took courage and went to Pilate and asked for the body of Jesus."

John 19:41–42 says, "Now in the place where he was crucified there was a garden, and in the garden a new tomb in which no one had yet been laid. So because of the Jewish day of Preparation, since the tomb was close at hand, they laid Jesus there."

Matthew 27:62–64 relates to the day after Preparation as well. "The next day, that is, after the day of Preparation, the chief priests and the Pharisees gathered before Pilate and said, 'Sir, we remember how that impostor said, while he was still alive, "After three days I will rise." Therefore order the tomb to be made secure until the third day, lest his disciples go and steal him away and tell the people, "He has risen from the dead," and the last fraud will be worse than the first.'"

From these six references, we can draw six conclusions:

1. Even though the day of Preparation was a normal part of the Sabbath ritual, in the New Testament, it is exclusively mentioned in association with Jesus' crucifixion.
2. The day of Preparation was the day before the Sabbath.
3. The particular Sabbath in the Passion narrative was a High Day.
4. The day of Preparation faded into the beginning of the Sabbath.
5. The chief priests and Pharisees' request for a guard at the tomb was made on the Sabbath.
6. What is clear is that Jesus Christ died the day before the Sabbath, on the day of Preparation.

The reason the day of Preparation was important relates to the Sabbath restrictions as laid out in Exodus 16:23; 35:3 and elsewhere.

> On the sixth day they gathered twice as much bread, two omers each. And when all the leaders of the congregation came and told Moses, he said to them, "This is what the LORD has commanded: 'Tomorrow is a day of solemn rest, a holy Sabbath to the LORD; bake what you will bake and boil what you will boil, and all that is left over lay aside to be kept till the morning'" (Exod 16:22–23).

Moses continued to relate God's Sabbath regulations in Exodus 35:1–3:

> Moses assembled all the congregation of the people of Israel and said to them, "These are the things that the LORD has commanded you to do. Six days work shall be done, but on the seventh day you shall have a Sabbath of solemn rest, holy to the LORD. Whoever does any work on it shall be put to death. You shall kindle no fire in all your dwelling places on the Sabbath day."

Mark 15:42–43 affirms, "And when evening had come, since it was the day of Preparation, that is, the day before the Sabbath, Joseph of Arimathea, a respected member of the council, who was also himself looking for the kingdom of God, took courage and went to Pilate and asked for the body of Jesus."

Luke 23:53–54 also affirms, "Then he took it down and wrapped it in a linen shroud and laid him in a tomb cut in stone, where no one had ever yet been laid. It was the day of Preparation, and the Sabbath was beginning."

John 19:31 calls the day after the day of Preparation a "High Day." "Since it was the day of Preparation, and so that the bodies would not remain on the cross on the Sabbath (for that Sabbath was a High Day), the Jews asked Pilate that their legs might be broken and that they might be taken away." The day after the annual Passover is a God-designated holiday, the first day of the Feast of Unleavened Bread.

Interestingly, Matthew did not call the day after Jesus' crucifixion a Sabbath. Instead, he said, "The next day, that is, after the day of Preparation, the chief priests and the Pharisees gathered before Pilate" (Matt 27:62). Although a day of Preparation precedes each weekly Sabbath, a day of Preparation also precedes the Feast of Unleavened Bread. This Preparation Day is also the day of Passover preparation.

Preparation. Passover. Unleavened Bread. Firstfruits. The connection between them effortlessly slides between the hours from start to finish in the Passion narratives.

THE HOUR OF THE CRUCIFIXION

Initially, the Passover lamb was to be slain "in the evening at sunset." Deuteronomy 16:5–6 states, "You may not offer the Passover sacrifice within any of your towns that the LORD your God is giving you, but at the place that the LORD your God will choose, to make his name dwell in it, there you shall offer the Passover sacrifice, in the evening at sunset, at the time you came out of Egypt." The Karaites, who recognize only the *Tanakh* as their supreme authority excluding Jewish oral tradition, have always practiced an after-sunset paschal sacrifice. Even the few remaining Samaritans today still slay their lambs about sunset.[20]

Josephus also follows the practice that demands an evening sacrifice.

> In the month of Xanthicus, which is by us called *Nisan*, and is the beginning of our year, on the fourteenth day of the lunar month, when the sun is in Aries, (for in this month it was that we were delivered from bondage under the Egyptians,) the law ordained that we should every year slay that sacrifice which I before told you we slew when we came out of Egypt, and which was called the *Passover*; and so we do celebrate this Passover

in companies, leaving nothing of what we sacrifice till the day following (*Ant*.3.10.5).

Josephus ties both sacrifice and supper to one single date—the 14th. All these instances imply that the Passover lamb was slain about sunset.

In the Synoptics' account of Passion Week, the Last Supper takes place on the first night of Passover, defined in the Torah as occurring after daylight on Nisan 14. This places the crucifixion on Nisan 15th (Lev 23:5–6). The Gospel of John on the other hand positions the trial of Jesus before the Passover meal.[21] He places the sentencing of Jesus on the day of Preparation, before Passover. Thus, John's account places the crucifixion on Nisan 14 because the law dictated the lamb be sacrificed between 3:00 pm and 5:00 pm and eaten before midnight on that day.[22]

Reconciling the Synoptics and John

Reconciliation between the Synoptics and John is difficult, although many scholars have tried. In reviewing the more notable attempts, biblical scholar and Roman Catholic priest Raymond E. Brown, a member of the Sulpician Fathers, has concluded that they cannot be easily reconciled.[23] Steven L. Cox and Kendell H. Easley have argued that our modern precision of marking the time of day should not be read back into the Gospel accounts, written at a time when no standardization of timepieces or exact recording of hours and minutes was available.[24] Andreas Kostenberger, founding director of the Center for Biblical Studies, notes that in the first century, time was often estimated to the closest three-hour mark, and Mark intended to set the stage for the three hours of darkness during Jesus' crucifixion while John sought to stress the length of the proceedings, starting in the "early morning."[25]

If John was already living in Ephesus, a Roman city, when he wrote his Gospel, the sixth hour would be 6:00 am, for the Romans calculated their day commencing at midnight as we do today. This would coincide precisely with the other writers who used the Jewish reckoning of time. The trial was early in the morning, and the crucifixion began at approximately 9:00 am lasting until 3:00 pm. This explanation would coordinate the Synoptics with John as they used a different standard of time. J. V. Miller wrote an article entitled, "The Time of the Crucifixion" in which he attempted to harmonize the apparent conflicting accounts of Mark 15:25 and John 19:14 regarding the time of Jesus' crucifixion.[26]

The Roman versus Semitic calculation of time as an approach to reconcile the Synoptics with John has a long history of support. The internal confirmation comes directly from John's use of time within his Gospel. John makes four "time" notations, two of which uniquely refer to specific hours that are pinpointed to a quarter of a day (third, sixth, or ninth hour). In John 1:39, he says two of John the Baptist's disciples began their stay with Jesus at the tenth hour. According to Jewish time calculation, that would be 4:00 pm.

However, Brooke Foss (B. F.) Westcott, Bishop of Durham, scholar and theologian, noted of this passage:

> It is then scarcely conceivable that it was 4:00 pm (4 am is out of the question) before he reached the place "where he abode"; and even less conceivable that the short space of the day remaining should be called "that day," which appears full of incident. On the other hand, 10:00 am suits both conditions. It is an hour by which a wayfarer would seek to have ended his journey, and it would leave practically "a day" for intercourse [conversation].[27]

Another example of John's use of Roman calculation of time is in John 4:6, where Jesus' visit with the woman at the well was in the sixth hour. By Jewish reckoning, this would be noon. But 6:00 pm would be a more natural time for the events of this day, both the drawing of water by the woman and the disciples' purchase of food. We must remember in the first century, no one had access to a refrigerator, so food was purchased just before it was prepared to eat. Also, no one wandered out to draw water in the heat of the day.

A third example is John 4:52, which records the encounter of Jesus with the arrival at Cana in the seventh hour of a nobleman from Capernaum. This would be 1:00 pm by Jewish calculation, but 7:00 pm by the Roman method of time calculation. Westcott says, "It is more likely that the words of Jesus were spoken to the nobleman at Cana in the evening at seven o'clock when it was already too late for him to return home that night."[28]

That brings us to John 19:14, "Now it was the day of Preparation of the Passover. It was about the sixth hour." If John was using the Roman method of calculating the hours in a day, this would be about 6:00 am. To you and me, this may seem to be an extremely early hour for a trial to begin when we are accustomed to 9:00 or 10:00 am start times. But it was not at all unusual for Roman trials to begin this early. "A Roman court might be held directly after sunrise; and as Pilate had probably been informed that an important case was to be brought before him, there is nothing improbable in his being ready to open his court between 4:00 and 5:00 am."[29]

Another fact to reckon with is that John gave both the day ("the Preparation of the Passover") as well as the hour ("about the sixth hour") in identifying the time that Pilate released Jesus for crucifixion.[30] A Gospel narrative could not be more specific.

In his *Commentary on the Gospel of John*, the nineteenth-century President of Newton Theological Seminary in Newton, Massachusetts, Alvah Hovey, bravely proposed the following schedule for Jesus' trial.

- The *terminus a quo* would be about 3:30 am based on John's use of *proia* (John 18:28), which was customarily used for the fourth watch of the night from 3:00 am to 6:00 am.
- Hovey added one half-hour for the public charges against Jesus to be made.
- He added another half-hour for Jesus to be sent to Herod, reasoning that it could not have taken much time since Jesus refused to answer Herod's insincere inquiries.
- By 4:30 am Jesus would be back before Pilate again.
- The scourging and mocking Hovey figured would have covered from 5:00 am to 5:45 am.
- About 6:00 am would have come the *Ecce Homo* presentation of Jesus to the Jewish mob.
- By 6:30 am Pilate's pronouncement would have been given, and Jesus would have begun his *Via Dolorosa* journey to Golgotha.

This time frame would have well suited the Roman use of time. However, see Chapter 7, Table 4.

Of course, there are critics of those attempting to reconcile John and the Synoptics through the difference between Semitic and Roman time calculations. They say that in John 1:39 if the tenth hour was 4:00 pm, the disciples could have stayed with Jesus until the next morning. Regarding John 4, if Jesus and his disciples had begun their trip to Samaria early in the morning, noon (the sixth hour) would have been an appropriate time to seek rest and respite from the hot sun (although the evening hour would have also been accepted and perhaps more logical). Those who object to John's use of Roman time say the unusual hour for drawing water (if it were, in fact, uncommon, which is debated) may indicate more of the character and criticism of the Samaritan woman by the people of Sychar than the time of day.

Had the nobleman from Capernaum left for Cana about sunrise, he could have made the twenty-one-mile journey by 1:00 pm (at a twenty-minute mile pace) and simply not have completed the return journey until the next day. None of these objections, in my mind, rise to the level of verification enjoyed by John's use of Roman time and Matthew, Mark, and Luke's use of Jewish time.

JESUS' CRUCIFIXION AND THE END OF THE SABBATH

Matthew began his final chapter with this statement: "Now after the Sabbath, toward the dawn of the first day of the week, Mary Magdalene and the other Mary went to see the tomb" (Matt 28:1). Mark does similarly (Mark 16:1–2). Luke's final chapter begins not much differently. "But on the first day of the week, at early dawn, they went to the tomb, taking the spices they had prepared" (Luke 24:1). Nor does John's (John 20:1).

Each of the four evangelists records Jesus' resurrection from the dead. Matthew says the empty tomb was discovered by Mary Magdalene and the other Mary "after the Sabbath, toward the dawn of the first day of the week." That would be dawn on Sunday morning. Mark says the Marys with Salome went to the tomb "when the Sabbath was past." Luke adds that it was not only the first day of the week, but it was at dawn on Sunday. John rounds out the picture by saying it was Sunday, "the first day of the week," and when the women arrived at the tomb, it was still dark, before daybreak on Easter Sunday morning.

This all seems clear enough. The women came to the empty tomb early on Sunday, the morning after the Sabbath. But debate begins when you consider the words of Matthew 28:1 in the Greek language which say δὲ Ὀψὲ σαββάτων τῇ ἐπιφωσκούσῃ εἰς μίαν σαββάτων: "Now after the Sabbath, toward the dawn of the first day of the week . . ." This particular word for "after" (Greek: ὀψὲ; English: *opse*) is found twice more in the New Testament, both times in the Gospel of Mark.

After Jesus cleansed the Temple during Passion Week, Mark 11:19 states, "And when *evening* came they went out of the city." Again in Mark 13:35–36, using the budding of the fig tree as a metaphor for watching for signs of the Savior's return, Jesus warned his disciples, "Therefore stay awake—for you do not know when the master of the house will come, in the *evening*, or at midnight, or when the rooster crows, or in the morning—lest he come suddenly and find you asleep." In both cases, *opse* is correctly translated *evening*.

Modern translations of Matthew 28:1 are quite similar in pattern, dividing along two distinct lines: "the end of the Sabbath" and "when the Sabbath was over."

Table 2: Translations of ὀψὲ (opsé)

KJV:	"In the *end* of the Sabbath, as it began to dawn toward the first day of the week"
NASB:	"Now *after* the Sabbath, as it began to dawn toward the first day of the week"
RSV:	"Now *after* the Sabbath, toward the dawn of the first day of the week"
NIV:	"*After* the Sabbath, at dawn on the first day of the week"
JBP:	"When the Sabbath was *over*, just as the first day of the week was dawning "
CEV:	"The Sabbath was *over*, and it was almost daybreak on Sunday"
CEB:	"*After* the Sabbath, at dawn on the first day of the week"
CSB:	"*After* the Sabbath, as the first day of the week was dawning"

How are we to properly understand Matthew's time designation here? Was he speaking of the end of the Sabbath day at the appearance of the three first stars at night? Or did he have something else in mind? And what about that phrase indicating the Matthew 28:1 event occurred just before dawn? How does that square with the ending of the Sabbath?

Answers to these questions are important because they bear directly on the evidence for either a Wednesday crucifixion, a Thursday crucifixion, or a Friday crucifixion.

One writer, whose booklet on this subject has been around for many years, states: "The women came to the tomb 'late on the Sabbath.' The stone was rolled away 'late on the Sabbath.' The tomb was empty 'late on the Sabbath.' Since all these things happened 'late on the Sabbath,'" the author reasons, "Is it not the silliest kind of nonsense to say that the resurrection took place on Sunday morning?"[31] Actually no, it is not silly, and it's not nonsense. Here's why.

The words Matthew chose

To determine the meaning of these expressions we must look behind the modern translations of each evangelist's original words. "Now after the Sabbath, toward the dawn of the first day of the week..." (δέ ὀψὲ σάββατον ἐπιφώσκω εἰς μία σάββατον...) You do not have to read the Koiné Greek language to notice that the word σάββατον for "Sabbath" occurs twice in this phrase. That's because of the Jews' reverence for the Sabbath and how they treated all other days in deference to it. "After the Sabbath" or "first day of the week" meant one day after the Sabbath, the Jews reckoning their days in sequence from the Sabbath. Remember, we have already noticed that the Jews called the days of the week, the Sabbath's first day, the second day of the

Sabbath, etc. (Mishnah, *Ta'anit*, 4.3). In Matthew 28:1, σάββατον is found twice, once meaning the Sabbath Saturday and the second time meaning day one after the Sabbath Saturday, or the first day of the week (Sabbath + 1).

The second Greek word of note in Matthew 28:1 is ἐπιφώσκω. *Epiphosko* means to "grow light" or to "bring on the light." Hence, it is the word for "dawn," that moment when the light of the sun pierces the darkness of the night. The root word is *phosko,* meaning *"to shine."* From this word, we get our English word "phosphorescence," meaning an enduring luminescence.

This word is used in Scripture only one other time, also in the context of Jesus' crucifixion and resurrection. Luke 23:54 mentions that Joseph of Arimathea, Nicodemus, and the others had to hurriedly take Jesus' body from the cross and place it in Joseph's tomb. The reason? "It was the day of Preparation, and the Sabbath was beginning."

The word "beginning" is literally "dawning" in which ἐπιφώσκω is used in the metaphorical sense. This is the one text those who advocate for "three days and three nights" as seventy-two complete hours use to build their theory that Jesus rose at sunset on Saturday. However, when taken in the context of the other Gospel texts, the grammar establishes beyond doubt that the two Marys came to the tomb at dawn on Sunday morning.

Mark adds to our understanding of the discovery of Jesus' resurrection by saying the women came to the tomb, "very early on the first day of the week" (Mark 16:2). For "very early" Mark used an adverb (Greek: πρωΐ; English: *prōi*) of the word *"pro"* meaning "in front of" or "before." Very early means "in front of" the sun, "before" the darkness had completely dissipated and the sun arose. The women had set out in the darkness, but the sun was just rising when they arrived at the tomb. It was that moment between darkness and light.

The Gospel writers each used the natural breaks between day and night to describe the hour the women discovered Jesus was no longer in the tomb. They were not concerned with Jewish time or Roman time. They were concerned with the darkness of the twelve-hour night just ending and the twelve-hour light of the day after the Sabbath just beginning.

Twentieth-century French historian Bertrand Lançon remarks:

> [In the days of Jesus] hours were numbered in the same ways as in the times of the republic and early empire. An hour was the twelfth part of the day, so its value varied continually, and it equaled our sixty minutes only twice a year, at the equinoxes. At the winter solstice, an hour was shorter, about 45 minutes, but, at the summer solstice, it was longer, about 75 minutes . . . For Romans, as for us today, a day extended from midnight to midnight, or from the twelfth hour to the twelfth hour."[32]

Mark reaffirms the twelve-hour darkness giving way to twelve hours of light in Mark 16:9, "When he [Jesus] rose early on the first day of the week, he appeared first to Mary Magdalene." Again, the word Mark chose for "early" was *prōí* (before), meaning before sunrise.

"THE FIRST DAY OF THE WEEK"

"The first day of the week" soon became the common Christian designation for our day of worship. When Paul arrived at Troas, he met with the believers there, "On the first day of the week, when we were gathered together to break bread" (Acts 20:7). When Paul instructed the Corinthian believers about a collection for the famine-ravaged believers in Jerusalem, he said, "On the first day of every week, each of you is to put something aside and store it up, as he may prosper, so that there will be no collecting when I come" (1 Cor 16:2). The first day of the week was Resurrection Day and always will be.

Luke 24:1 informs us, "But on the first day of the week, at early dawn, they went to the tomb, taking the spices they had prepared." At "early dawn" is a word combination (Greek: βαθέως ὄρθρου; English: *batheōs orthrou*). The Greek means from the very rising of light, i.e., daybreak or dawn. It is the polar opposite of ὀψὲ (*opse*), meaning evening or the close of the day. This is the opening of a new day. Using this third Greek word meaning "dawn" or "early morning," Luke affirms beyond question that the women discovered Christ's resurrection occurred on Sunday morning, about sunrise.

The plain language of Scripture contradicts the arguments of those who advocate for any resurrection other than Sunday morning. The idea that Jesus rose Saturday evening after sundown contradicts Mark 16:9, which explicitly states Jesus rose at dawn on Sunday morning. It also invalidates the argument that Jesus did not rise on Sunday. According to Jewish time, Sunday had already begun at sunset on Saturday evening.

The Gospel accounts also rebuff the arguments of those who advocate a Saturday afternoon resurrection. The Bible evidence is clear that Jesus was buried just before sunset. Proposing an afternoon resurrection regardless of the crucifixion day contradicts Matthew 28:1; Mark 16:2, 9; Luke 24:1, 22; and John 20:1, all of which claim Jesus rose Sunday at dawn.

Any reading of the account of the early church in the book of Acts must take note that the New Testament church began to gather for worship on Sunday rather than to keep the Sabbath. That is not to say that these Jewish believers abandoned their Jewish heritage completely. They still celebrated the Jewish feasts and attended the Temple on Saturday. However, the resurrection of Jesus Christ from the dead ushered in a whole new era for them spiritually. From Pentecost onward, the Christians celebrated by gathering for their agape meals, communion, and worship on Sunday, the first day of the week.

So what have we learned from this chapter? To begin with, the Jewish feasts all had tremendous meaning to the Jews because they commemorated something God provided for their welfare. We learned that the Sabbath fell on Saturday but the High Sabbath could fall on any day of the week. The original Passover was punctuated with the killing of a lamb and the daubing of its blood over and on the sides of their doors. At just the time the lambs were being slaughtered in Jerusalem, the Lord Jesus was being slaughtered on Calvary's Cross. We noted the timing of the Feast of Unleavened Bread and the Feast of Firstfruits were effortlessly positioned after the Passover. We also learned how we can be sure of the exact hour Jesus was crucified.

But perhaps the most important lesson of this chapter is that Jesus' crucifixion brought to an end the need for sacrifices and the celebration of the Sabbath. For us, the purpose of the Sabbath was fulfilled in Christ Jesus. The "rest of the seventh" became the "rest of the Savior." Israel's favorite prophet clung to the promise, "For thus said the Lord God, the Holy One of Israel, 'In returning and rest you shall be saved; in quietness and in trust shall be your strength" (Isa 30:15). Isaiah's hope was fulfilled in Jesus who invited each of us to "Come to me, all who labor and are heavy laden, and I will give you rest" (Matt 11:28). "Thanks be unto God for his unspeakable gift" (2 Cor 9:15 KJV).

Chapter 3

Was the Last Supper a Passover Seder?

If you are not Jewish but are invited to join your Jewish neighbors for a Passover Seder, by all means, accept, and keep your eyes and ears, not to mention your taste buds, attentive and alert. When a Jewish family sits down to celebrate the Passover Seder, they facilitate the ritual aspects of the meal by using a book known as the Haggadah.

WE COME NOW TO one of the most critical questions in dating Jesus' crucifixion. Was the Last Supper the Savior celebrated with his disciples, where he broke bread with them, where he washed their feet, and where he identified his betrayer, was it a Passover Seder or just an informal gathering? This is one of the many issues on which biblical scholars are understandably divided.

Much of the problem in determining whether or not the Last Supper was a Seder or another type of meal is that the Synoptic Gospels present the meal differently than the Gospel of John. This difference is huge when dating Jesus' death.

Was it a Passover Seder or not? Nisan 15 could fall on any day of the week (just like our Christmas, December 25th), but when Nisan 15 fell on the regular weekly Sabbath, it was called a special Sabbath or a High Sabbath. High Sabbaths only occurred when the Passover Sabbath was the same day as the weekly Sabbath.[33]

This rare conjunction of the weekly Saturday Sabbath and annual Passover Sabbath still occurs today on the Jewish calendar. John called it a High Sabbath because in the year Jesus was crucified, the regular Saturday Sabbath (Friday evening through Saturday evening) coincided with the Passover Sabbath, on Nisan 15. Thus, according to the Gospel of John, the crucifixion occurred on Nisan 14, the day before the Passover.

Raymond E. Brown clarifies:

> The chronological relationship between the death of Jesus and the date of those two feasts (Passover and Unleavened Bread) is complicated by the fact that at face value, there is a contradiction between the Synoptics and John. The meal that Jesus ate on Thursday evening before he was arrested, according to the Synoptics, was the paschal (Passover) meal, whereas in John 18:28, on Friday morning when Jesus was being tried before Pilate, the Jewish authorities and people refused to "enter into the praetorium lest they be defiled and in order that they might eat the Passover (meal)"—a feast that according to John 19:14 was to begin the next day (i.e., Friday evening).[34]

Colin Humphreys, Professor of Materials Science at the Queen Mary University of London, comments.

> John consistently says that the Last Supper (John 13:1–2), the trials of Jesus (John 18:28 and 19:14), and the crucifixion (John 19:31) were all before the Passover meal. The natural interpretation of John is that the crucifixion occurred on Nisan 14, and the Passover meal followed at the evening start of the next Jewish day, on Nisan 15.[35]

On the other hand, according to Mark 14:12, "On the first day of Unleavened Bread, when they sacrificed the Passover lamb, his disciples said to him, 'Where will you have us go and prepare for you to eat the Passover?'" After instructions from Jesus, the disciples prepared the Passover meal (Mark 14:16), and that evening Jesus and his Twelve ate what we have come to call "the Last Supper" (Mark 14:17–18). Matthew and Luke provide a corroborating account. According to the Synoptics, both Jesus and his disciples refer to the Last Supper as "the Passover."

Here is the problem. For the authors of the Synoptic Gospels, the Last Supper really was a Passover meal, eaten in the evening at the start of Nisan 15, with the crucifixion occurring later that Jewish day (i.e., still on Nisan 15, since the Jewish day runs from sunset to sunset). Thus the Synoptics and John appear to disagree over whether the Last Supper was a Passover meal or just an intimate, meaningful dinner for Jesus and his disciples, as John presents it. Hence, we must examine all possibilities.

THE CASE FOR THE LAST SUPPER BEING A PASSOVER MEAL

Many people believe that Jesus' Last Supper was a Seder, the ritual meal held in celebration of the Jewish Passover. There are many good reasons for this assumption, as indicated by Mark 14:12. Since Jesus and his disciples were gathered in the Upper Room just before Passover, it is reasonable to assume they were celebrating the Passover Feast and that this meal was a Passover Seder.

The Hebrew people received God's instructions for observing the Passover on the night they exited from Egypt (Exod 12; cf. Lev 23:4–8; Num 9:3–14; Deut 16:1–8). On the tenth day of the first month (Nisan = March/April), a lamb was selected for each household (Exod 12:3). On Nisan 14, the lamb was slain "at twilight" (Exod 12:6; Lev 23:5; Num 9:3, 5), which, according to Josephus "they slay their sacrifices, from the ninth hour till the eleventh" (*Wars* 6.9.3). That would be from 3:00 pm to 5:00 pm. "That night" the Passover meal was eaten (Exod 12:8).

Exodus 12 requires the Israelites to repeat this practice annually, performing the sacrifice during the day and consuming it after the sun had set. Because the Jewish new day began at sunset, the sacrifice was made on the fourteenth of Nisan, but the Passover began and the meal was eaten on the fifteenth. Exodus 12 also declares a seven-day festival, which began when the sacrifice was consumed (Exod 12:15). That festival is the Feast of Unleavened Bread. The Passover was part of the weeklong Feast of Unleavened Bread and often that feast was simply referred to as Passover.

The original sacrifice described in Exodus 12 changed dramatically, however, once the Israelites settled into the Promised Land and the Temple of Solomon was built. Passover was designated as one of the Jewish Pilgrimage festivals where the Jewish people were expected to travel to Jerusalem to sacrifice a lamb at the Temple.

It seems the Jewish people drifted in their relationship with YHWH and once failed to keep the Passover for years. That's when good King Hezekiah reinstituted the observance of the Passover and the Feast of Unleavened Bread (2 Chron 30). Later King Josiah had to do the same, reviving the observance of the Passover while he was king.

> So all the service of the LORD was prepared that day, to keep the Passover and to offer burnt offerings on the altar of the LORD,

according to the command of King Josiah. And the people of Israel who were present kept the Passover at that time, and the Feast of Unleavened Bread for seven days. No Passover like it had been kept in Israel since the days of Samuel the prophet. None of the kings of Israel had kept such a Passover as was kept by Josiah, and the priests and the Levites, and all Judah and Israel who were present, and the inhabitants of Jerusalem in the eighteenth year of the reign of Josiah this Passover was kept (2 Chr 35:16–19).

Over time, the observance of the Passover became "institutionalized" with any number of practices, customs, traditions, and teachings leaching into the original celebration. According to rabbinic literature, so many practices in a specified order were attached to the meal that it became known as the Seder, from the Hebrew word for "order." Many of these customs continue today in the modern Seder meal, including the breaking of unleavened bread (*matzah*), red wine served, the Exodus story retold during the meal, and the significance of the unleavened bread, bitter herbs, and wine explained.

Parallels between Passover Seder and the Last Supper

There are evident parallels between the Passover Seder and the events of the Last Supper. In 1935, German Lutheran scholar and expert on Near East studies Joachim Jeremias published a book entitled *The Eucharistic Words of Jesus*.[36] In this book, Jeremias listed no less than fourteen distinct parallels between the Last Supper and the Passover Seder. Here are those parallels.

1. In obedience to the law (Deut 16:5–7), the meal was eaten in Jerusalem, the city of the Temple.
2. The Last Supper was held in a room made available to pilgrims for that purpose.
3. The meal was held during the night, after sundown.
4. Jesus celebrated the Last Supper with his "family" of disciples.
5. Jesus and the disciples reclined at a low table while they ate.
6. This meal was eaten in a state of ritual purity.
7. The Jews began each meal with the breaking of bread. But at the Last Supper and the Passover Seder, the breaking of bread was postponed until another dish had been served.
8. The wine was also consumed at the Last Supper, as it was for special occasion meals, like Passover.

9. Although red, white, and black wines were available in Palestine, the drink chosen for the Last Supper was red wine, just like the wine used in the Passover meal.
10. The meal came as a result of last-minute preparations.
11. After Jesus and his disciples finished the Last Supper meal, they gave alms to the poor.
12. Before leaving the table, Jesus and his disciples sang a hymn (Matt 26:30) as it was the custom of the Passover meal to sing Psalms 115 through 118 at the end of the meal.
13. Jesus and his disciples then remained in Jerusalem.
14. Jesus discussed the symbolic significance of the Last Supper. The one presiding over a Passover Seder also explains the meaning of each food.[37]

While this list is long, it is not particularly impressive. Many of the fourteen parallels would be true even if this were not the Last Supper. The disciples ate in Jerusalem, which they would have done anyway since that's where they were at the time. Jesus ate with his disciples, which he did daily throughout his ministry. They reclined at a low table, which was the custom in every home in those days. They drank red wine, perhaps a personal favorite. They gave alms to the poor, but that was the common practice of good people (Pss 41:1 and 112:9).

In Darrell L. Bock and Robert L. Webb's work, *Key Events in the Life of the Historical Jesus*, I. Howard Marshall contributes a chapter on "The Last Supper." In it, he surveys Jeremias's fourteen points of parallel between the Passover Seder and the Last Supper and dismisses or downplays most of them (especially points 1, 2, 3, 5, 8, 9, 10, 11, 12, and 13).[38] Upon deeper reflection, I am not so sure Jeremias' list strengthens the case for the Last Supper being a Passover Seder.

A more current presentation of the parallels between the Passover meal and the Last Supper is presented by Joel Marcus, Professor of New Testament and Christian Origins at Duke Divinity School.[39] Marcus argues that the correspondence between the Jewish Seder's various features and the Christian Last Supper indicates a connection between them that is stronger than mere coincidence.

For example, Marcus points out that the "*Ha lachma*" (Aramaic for "this is the bread"*)*, which is a brief passage that traditionally is recited at the beginning of the Seder meal, strongly parallels Jesus' words about the breaking of the bread and the suffering of his body. "And he took bread, and when he had given thanks, he broke it and gave it to them, saying, 'This is my body, which is given for you. Do this in remembrance of me'" (Luke 22:19).

God commanded ancient Israel, "Observe the month of Abib and keep the Passover to the LORD your God . . . You shall eat no leavened bread with it. Seven days you shall eat it with unleavened bread, the bread of affliction—for you came out of the land of Egypt in haste" (Deut 16:1–3). Grammatically, Jesus' statement about bread parallels the command to eat the bread of affliction, the unleavened bread of the Jews. This is the kind of parallel Marcus believes ties the Seder meal to the Lord's Table.

EVIDENCE THAT THE LAST SUPPER WAS A PASSOVER SEDER

Many scholars believe the Last Supper was indeed the Passover meal.[40] In summary form, they generally list the following arguments.

- The Synoptics explicitly identify the Last Supper as a Passover meal (Matt 26:17–19; Mark 14:12–16; Luke 22:8–15). This is a strong indicator.

The Last Supper meal took place, as required by Deuteronomy 16:7, within the gates of Jerusalem. It was Passover, and the city was super-crowded. Finding a room inside the city walls would not have been easy had it not been for God's sovereign direction. As he had on previous evenings, Jesus did not return to Bethany outside the enlarged limits of Jerusalem. The disciples and he spent the night after the Last Supper in the immediate Jerusalem area [Gethsemane]. According to the instructions for observing the Passover, after the meal, you were supposed to spend the Passover night in Jerusalem and not return to your home. "And you shall cook it and eat it at the place that the LORD your God will choose. And in the morning you shall turn and go to your tents" (Deut 16:7).[41]

- The Upper Room was made readily available in keeping with Passover customs.

The Last Supper was held after sunset, at night (Matt 26:20; Mark 14:17; see also John 13:30; 1 Cor 11:23).[42] This compares with the Old Testament requirement that the Passover lamb was to be killed "between the evenings," i.e., at nightfall, between day and night. The meal was then eaten after sunset that same evening. According to German Lutheran Near Eastern scholar Joachim Jeremias, the Passover meal was the only meal that began in the evening, after sunset.[43]

- Jesus limited himself to the Twelve rather than eating with his larger circle of followers.

This corresponds to the "family" orientation of the Passover celebration. It is difficult to imagine a "family" Passover meal (where the fathers of the household would kill a lamb for each household—Exodus 12:3) occurring with thirteen men instead of each man celebrating with his wife and children. If the disciples had families of their own, they would have been in Jerusalem for Passover as well. Still, this was a transitional night between law and grace, and we cannot say for certain exactly what happened.

- The meal was eaten in Levitical purity (John 13:10).
- The Last Supper ended with singing a hymn, which would correspond with singing the Passover *Hallel* (Matt 26:30; Mark 14:26).
- Jesus interpreted specific elements of the meal as part of the Passover ritual.

"These arguments are very forceful and seem to make good sense," claimed Harold H. Hoehner, American biblical scholar and late professor of New Testament studies at Dallas Theological Seminary.[44] Other scholars agree.

The Synoptics explicitly identify the Last Supper as a Passover meal (Matt 26:17–19; Mark 14:12–16; Luke 22:8–15). Luke tells us Jesus sent Peter and John into the city "to prepare the Passover for us, that we may eat it" (Luke 22:8). They were instructed how to find the house God had reserved for them and what to tell the owner of the house. "The Teacher says to you, Where is the guest room, where I may eat the Passover with my disciples?" (Luke 22:11). And in obedience, "they prepared the Passover" (Luke 22:13). The obvious question is, why would the Synoptics call this a Passover meal if it were held a whole day before the designated time?

THE SYMBOLISM OF JESUS' BODY AND BLOOD

Perhaps one of the most persuasive arguments for the Last Supper being a Passover Seder is the symbolic way Jesus spoke of his body and blood. Ordinarily, when we sit down for a meal, we are doing so because we are hungry. But we also do so to be sociable, to interact with those joining us at the table. We have a meal with others to enjoy the three "double Fs"—faithful friendship, festive fellowship, and fabulous food. At a family meal, there should be no "ICPs"—intrusive cell phones. At least Jesus didn't have to put up with that.

But there are two meals in which satisfying hunger is not the primary purpose for eating. One is a Jewish meal, the other is a Christian one. The purpose of the Passover Seder is instruction, reflection, and praise to God for his accomplishments on behalf of his people. The purpose of the Lord's Table in the Christian tradition is instruction, reflection, and praise to God for his accomplishments on behalf of his people. Two different celebrations. Two different faiths. One purpose.

If you are not Jewish but are invited to join your Jewish neighbors for a Passover Seder, by all means, accept, and keep your eyes and ears, not to mention your taste buds, attentive and alert. When a Jewish family sits down to celebrate the Passover Seder, they facilitate the ritual aspects of the meal by using a book known as the Haggadah. The Haggadah is a Jewish text that sets forth the order of the Passover Seder. It's a bit like a catechism book. It explains each element of the meal, what to read, when to eat, when to sing, what to sing, etc.

THE CASE AGAINST THE LAST SUPPER BEING A PASSOVER MEAL

While the Synoptics describe the Last Supper as a Passover meal, John does not. John's Gospel describes the Last Supper as occurring "before the Feast of the Passover" (John 13:1). He indicates that the Passover meal would follow the death of Jesus. John 19:14 describes Pilate on his portable judgment seat, the Gabbatha. "Now it was the day of Preparation of the Passover. It was about the sixth hour. He said to the Jews, 'Behold your King!' They cried out, 'Away with him, away with him, crucify him!'"

There are, to be sure, strong similarities between the Passover Seder and the Last Supper, but there are also evident differences. While nothing in John's narrative of Passover Week designates the Last Supper as a Passover meal, he presents the meal as taking place in the evening between Thursday and Friday. In chapter 18, verse 28, John details why these religious Jews would not enter Pilate's palace, i.e. "so that they would not be defiled, but could eat the Passover." In that last clause, John used the very same words (Greek: φάγωσιν τὸ πάσχα; English: *phagōsin to pascha*) the Synoptics used to describe what was done at the Last Supper (Matt 26:17; Mark 14:12; Luke 22:8, 15). This points to the fact that in John's mind at least, the Passover meal had not yet been celebrated.

Some scholars believe that the Last Supper's ritual context was not a Seder at all, but rather a typical Jewish meal.[45] These theologians provide evidence that the connection between the Passover Seder and the Lord's Supper is tenuous at best.

The order of events

John's order of events would seem to indicate the Lord's Supper was a day before the Passover. John 13:1 states, "Now before the Feast of the Passover, when Jesus knew that his hour had come to depart out of this world to the Father, having loved his own who were in the world, he loved them to the end." It is objected, however, that this does not refer to the Last Supper as occurring before the Passover, but rather that Jesus 'knew' before the Passover that his death was imminent.[46]

In the same chapter, John says, "Some thought that, because Judas had the moneybag, Jesus was telling him, 'Buy what we need for the feast,' or that he should give something to the poor" (John 13:29). But if this were Nisan 13, there would be no need to buy the necessities for the feast that night; they would have the whole next day (Nisan 14) to do that. The verse makes sense only if referring to the evening of Nisan 14, for you would not be able to buy on Nisan 15, a high feast day.[47]

Later, John remarks, "Then they led Jesus from the house of Caiaphas to the governor's headquarters. It was early morning. They themselves did not enter the governor's headquarters, so that they would not be defiled, but could eat the Passover" (John 18:28). But Jesus had already shared in the Last Supper the night before. This is substantiated by John 19:14 which states, "Now it was the day of Preparation of the Passover. It was about the sixth hour. He said to the Jews, 'Behold your King!'" This phrase identifies the Friday of Passover week.

John 19:36 speaks of the Old Testament's fulfillment (Exod 12:46; Num 9:12) when no bones of Jesus, the Passover Lamb, were broken. The analogy is best understood if Jesus was slain when the other Paschal lambs were slain (1 Cor 5:7); hence, the Last Supper had to be before Passover and the killing of the sacrificial lambs.

The unleavened bread

Then there is a question about unleavened bread. The Gospels do not specify that Jesus fed his disciples the unleavened bread Jews were required to eat at Passover. For example, Mark recorded this meal saying, "And as they were eating, he took bread, and after blessing, it broke it and gave it to them, and said, 'Take; this is my body'" (Mark 14:22).

However, the word Mark chose for "bread" (Greek: ἄρτον; English: *arton*) was not the word for unleavened bread (Greek: ἄζυμος; English: *azymos*) but the word for common bread. This does not preclude the possibility that Jesus used unleavened bread at the Last Supper; Jews commonly referred to unleavened bread (*matzah* in Hebrew) only as "bread" (Deut 16:3).[48] Still, while generic "bread" could encompass *matzah*, Jewish scriptural references to Passover always designate "unleavened bread." This makes Mark's choice of the generic term odd, especially here of all places.

This concern cannot be superficially brushed aside. It is a more serious objection than it is given credit. Each of the Synoptic Gospels describes this meal the same. Matthew 26:26, Mark 14:22, and Luke 22:19 all use the generic word ἄρτος for breaking bread at the meal Jesus ate with his disciples on the eve of his crucifixion.

Writing about 55–56 AD, the Apostle Paul also referred to the Last Supper. First Corinthians 11:23–24 says, "For I received from the Lord what I also delivered to you, that the Lord Jesus on the night when he was betrayed took bread, and when he had given thanks, he broke it, and said, 'This is my body, which is for you. Do this in remembrance of me.'" Here, too, Paul used the Greek for regular bread (ἄρτος) and not the word for unleavened bread (ἄζυμος). This weakens the case for the Last Supper being the Passover meal.

Other missing elements

Curiously absent from any of the Synoptic descriptions of the Last Supper (Matt 26–29, Mark 14:22–25, and Luke 22:14–30) are any of the four fundamental components of a Passover Seder in Jesus' day. Those four required elements were a lamb (the primary food), bitter herbs, unleavened bread or *matzah*, and four cups of wine. These were always the Seder meal's primary elements, and yet at least three out of four of them were absent at the Last Supper.

This suggests this meal was not a Passover meal at all. Professor of Divinity at the University of Durham C. K. Barrett argues that the Passover was so familiar there was no need to mention all the elements.[49] However, it would seem to be unthinkable that familiarity would prevent the mention of these most important components of the Seder. To me, Barrett's suggestion seems to be a stretch.

The Mishnah explains that drinking four cups at the Passover Seder was essential.

> And they must give him no fewer than four cups of wine, even from the charity plate. They pour the first cup [of wine] for [the leader of the Seder] . . . [who] then recites a blessing over the wine . . . They pour a second cup [of wine] for him. And here the son questions his father . . . After they poured for him the third cup, he blesses over his food. The fourth [cup of wine], he

completes over it the Hallel, and he recites over it the blessing of the song. Between these cups, if he wants to drink, he may drink, but between the third and the fourth, he may not drink.[50]

The tradition of using four cups at the meal, recalling Israel's deliverance from Egypt, is based on the four actions of God recorded in Exodus 6:6–7. Notice the four "I will" statements God makes upon which each cup is based.

> Say therefore to the people of Israel, 'I am the LORD, and *I will* bring you out [*Cup #1*] from under the burdens of the Egyptians, and *I will* deliver you [*Cup #2*] from slavery to them, and *I will* redeem you [*Cup #3*] with an outstretched arm and with great acts of judgment. I will take you to be my people, and *I will* be your God [*Cup #4*], and you shall know that I am the LORD your God, who has brought you out from under the burdens of the Egyptians.

However, at the Last Supper, only a single cup was used by Jesus instead of the usual individual Passover cups. Matthew 26:27 and Mark 14:23 say, "and he took a cup (Greek: ποτήριον; English: *potērion*) [singular]" while Luke 22:20 says, "And likewise the cup [singular] after they had eaten, saying, "This cup [singular] that is poured out for you is the new covenant in my blood." In Jesus' day, the use of a common cup [neuter singular noun] was normal. This does not seem to meet the four cups' criteria. The celebration of the Passover was a specific, ordered event, not something where a common cup would be appropriate.

The Family Passover Seder

The Passover Seder meal was always a family meal with close relatives around the table. The LORD's instructions to Moses were specific. "On the tenth day of this month, every man shall take a lamb according to their fathers' houses, a lamb for a household" (Exod 12:3). If possible, the disciples would celebrate each Passover with their family, not as a group of men. While we could argue that the Last Supper was different, it would be atypical for Jesus to breach the Passover meal's clear intent by celebrating with his disciples instead of sending them off to celebrate with their families. As practicing Jews, the wives, children, parents, and relatives of Peter, Andrew, James, John, etc. would also have been in Jerusalem for Passover.

Some scholars have claimed that the disciples were Jesus' "family." That would diminish the genuine meaning of the word "family." Besides, the word "family" occurs only three times in the New Testament (Luke 2:4; Acts

3:25; Eph 3:15) but in no instance does the word refer to the disciples. Interpreting the disciples as meeting the requirement for observing the Passover Seder with your family doesn't really deal with the problem of taking the Twelve away from their families at the Passover meal.

Some argue that several events occurring the day after the Lord's Supper were forbidden on a feast day, such as leaving Jerusalem to go to Gethsemane. Mishnah: *Shabbath* 6. 4 indicates that at Passover the permitted space for pilgrims extended beyond the city walls, including Gethsemane. They also say the Sanhedrin session, the condemnation of Christ on Passover night, Simon of Cyrene coming in from the fields where he likely was working, Joseph of Arimathea purchasing linen in which to wrap Jesus' body, and so on, all would have been prohibited on the Passover or a Sabbath day. However, all of these objections have been answered adequately by German Lutheran orientalist Gustaf Dalman and Lutheran minister and scholar of Judaism Paul Billerbeck.[51] They need not be repeated here.

In addition to the missing elements of the Passover Seder noted above, other considerations appear not to be a part of the Lord's Table. Jesus said to his Twelve, "I have earnestly desired to eat this Passover with you before I suffer. For I tell you I will not eat it until it is fulfilled in the kingdom of God" (Luke 22:15–16). We must not put words in Jesus' mouth here. He did not say he was eating the Passover meal at that time, just that he was anxious to eat it with them. This may be a small distinction, but it is an important one for preserving biblical accuracy.

But there is a much larger issue with putting words in the Savior's mouth than this. Jesus said to the disciples, "I have earnestly desired to eat this Passover with you before I suffer. For I tell you I will not eat it until it is fulfilled in the kingdom of God" (Luke 22:15–16). Perhaps you have noticed what may well be an exclusionary statement after Jesus told his Twelve of his earnest desire. Speaking of the Passover meal, God the Son said, "I will not eat it until it is fulfilled in the kingdom of God."

Luke's exact words (Greek: οὐ μὴ φάγω αὐτὸ ἕως ὅτου πληρωθῇ ἐν τῇ βασιλείᾳ τοῦ θεοῦ; English: *ou mē phagō auto heōs hotou plērōthē en tē basileia tou theou*) make no reference to Jesus celebrating the Passover with his disciples. Jesus was not saying, "I long to eat the Passover Seder with you and I will not do it again until the fulfillment of the Kingdom of God." Many understand Jesus' words this way, and perhaps you have as well. But Jesus didn't say that. In fact, he said he would not eat the Passover Seder until the Kingdom of God is fulfilled. Had he wanted to indicate this was the last time he would eat the Passover meal until God's Kingdom he would have said, "For I tell you I will not eat it *again* until it is fulfilled in the kingdom of God." There is no *again* in Jesus' statement because he was not eating the Passover Seder at the Last Supper. It was something else.

We must also consider that nowhere in the New Testament is the Last Supper meal ever called or even equated with the Passover Seder of Exodus 12. When Paul gave the Corinthian believers instructions about observing the Eucharist (1 Cor 11:23ff), he did not mention the Seder meal, but instead, referred to that evening as "the night when he was betrayed." Given that Passover was the premier festival in Judaism, you would think Paul would have referred to it as such if the Last Supper was a Passover Seder.

How the early church viewed the Eucharist

Some scholars do not equate the Last Supper with a Passover meal because of how the church viewed the Lord's Table commemoration in the centuries following Jesus' crucifixion. For example, Christians celebrated the Eucharist daily or weekly (Acts 2:46–47). This underscores that it may not have been viewed exclusively in a Passover context. If the early followers of Jesus had linked the Eucharist with the Passover, they would have celebrated it, like the Passover meal, only on an annual basis. They did not.

The standard practices of the early church are described in Acts 2:42–47.

> And they devoted themselves to the apostles' teaching and the fellowship, to the breaking of bread and the prayers ... And day by day, attending the Temple together and breaking bread in their homes, they received their food with glad and generous hearts, praising God and having favor with all the people. And the Lord added to their number day by day those who were being saved.

Beyond this, an ancient Christian Church manual called the *Didache* also suggests the Last Supper may have been an ordinary Jewish meal. The *Didache*, also known as *The Teaching of the Twelve Apostles*, is an anonymous early Christian manual of belief dated by most scholars to the first century AD. It is thought to be the oldest extant written catechism of the Christian religion. The Eucharistic prayers in chapters 9 and 10 of the *Didache* are remarkably close to the prayer Jews repeated after their meals (*Birkat ha-Mazon*).[52] Indeed, these prayers are recited after the Passover meal, but they are also recited after any regular meal where bread is eaten. This increases the likelihood that the Last Supper may not have been a special meal but an ordinary Jewish meal with some special meaning.

Perhaps the Last Supper was Jesus' final opportunity to sit with his disciples, wash their feet, enjoy a meal, and reveal his betrayer who, in just hours, would implement the most heinous betrayal in human history. This would be underscored by John's presentation of the Last Supper's timing and purpose.

DIVERSE INTERPRETATIONS OF THE LAST SUPPER

Those who conclude the Last Supper was not the Passover meal are left with the task of identifying exactly what the meal was. What was its purpose? Several alternative explanations deserve our attention.

First, there's the theory made prominent by George Herbert Box, a lecturer in the Faculty of Theology, University of Oxford.[53] Box identified it with the ceremony known as *Kiddush* or sanctification.[54] This was a ceremony that pronounced blessings at the commencement of each Sabbath and feast day. This view, however, cannot be supported because the sanctification of Passover did not occur at the beginning of the day, but at Passover meals. *Kiddush* was said over the first cup (Mishnah: *Peshim* x. 2).

Second, German Protestant theologian and church historian Hans Lietzmann from the University of Berlin suggested the Last Supper was a *haburah* meal, a meal eaten by a small company of like-minded friends.[55] Are we really to believe that, with the horrific crucifixion awaiting in just hours, Jesus and the disciples gathered as a group of friends to enjoy one another's company? This seems to give too little weight to the Last Supper.

There is no evidence that Jesus and his followers formed a *haburah* group. Besides, the circle of friends who had these *haburah* meals understood these were "exclusively duty meals such as those connected with betrothals, weddings, circumcisions, funerals in which participation as a paying guest was considered meritorious."[56] Indeed, this is not the picture of the Last Supper.

Another alternative is to understand John 13:1 not as a time reference to the Paschal meal, but generally to the love of Christ Jesus. Consequently, John 18:28 is taken to refer to Jesus' desire to eat the other meals during the Passover festival without hindrance. As a result, John 19:14 is not understood to mean the day of Preparation for the Passover (Nisan 14), but rather the day of Preparation for the Sabbath that falls within the weeklong celebration of the Feast of Unleavened Bread (see also John 19:31). These interpretations are held by several fine scholars among Evangelical ranks.[57]

Still, another variant interpretation is that Mark authored "an artistic and theological day rather than a historical and chronological day."[58] However, once the interpretation of a non-literal day is adopted, it's just a short hop to where the train runs off the tracks. For example, if the Passover was not a specific day with a specific meaning for that day, it could have been earlier in Passion Week allowing sufficient time for all the events of the Passion story to take place before a Friday crucifixion. This has led some to appeal to the solar Qumran calendar as the appropriate calendar for calculating the events of Passion Week.

Some have suggested Jesus engaged in an unofficial meal with his disciples, at an unofficial time for the Passover Seder, yet with something of a Paschal character to it. Some well-known Evangelical scholars have advocated this belief.[59] Oxford University's Markus Bockmuehl appeals to this as a possible interpretation of Luke 22:15–16, where the Jews wish to hold off on killing Jesus until after the Passover celebrations.[60] Their goal was to silence Jesus and his followers without causing a huge commotion. Still, after Jesus ascended to heaven, it was said of his disciples that they had "turned the world upside down" (Acts 17:6). Other interpretations abound, but we need not investigate them here.

However, I want to propose another possible interpretation. This is an original understanding, but I think it's worthy of consideration. If I were to attach a name to my understanding of the Last Supper, I would call it a transitional meal. To me, this previously unarticulated interpretation makes a great deal of sense and I eagerly anticipate the response of other scholars and non-scholars alike to my interpretation.

THE CASE FOR THE LAST SUPPER BEING A TRANSITIONAL MEAL

A transitional meal is exactly what the name implies. The divine intent of the Last Supper was to be the last supper under the old era and the first of the new. The old was represented by law; the new is represented by grace. The old required blind obedience to law and tradition; the new requires faith in the efficacy of the Savior's death. The Passover meal remembers the distant past; the Last Supper remembers the near past with a view to the future.

Here are some questions I raise about the Last Supper. Is it possible Jesus' intention in eating this meal, and more specifically the elements that comprised it, was designed for a different purpose than previously considered? Is it conceivable this one-off meal for Jesus and his disciples set the stage for ongoing meals to be observed by his future disciples? These are serious questions. The following considerations provide insight into them.

JESUS AS FULFILLMENT

There is no doubt that Jesus understood a primary component of his mission to Earth was to fulfill the demands of the Law. Before Passion Week the Master warned his disciples, "Do not think that I have come to abolish the Law or the Prophets; I have not come to abolish them but to fulfill them" (Matt 5:17). During Passion Week he reminded his Twelve, "But the word that is written in their Law must be fulfilled: 'They hated me without a cause'" (John 15:25). At the end of the Passion Week, he again reminded his disciples saying, "These are my words that I spoke to you while I was still with you, that everything written about me in the Law of Moses and the Prophets and the Psalms must be fulfilled" (Luke 24:44).

If the Last Supper is viewed through the lens of fulfillment, it takes on an innovative meaning. Could it be that the Last Supper was not a Passover Seder but the accomplishment of it? Was this meal a divinely-designed transition from the Passover Meal to the Eucharist? Consider Table 3.

Table 1: Comparison of Passover Seder and the Lord's Supper

Requirements Stated: OT Passover Meal [Exodus 12]	Requirements Fulfilled: NT Eucharist [1 Corinthians 11]
Observance for a new beginning (v. 2)	Observance for a new creation (2 Cor 5:17)
An eight-day observance (v. 18)	A single-event observance (v. 25, 33)
"The congregation of Israel" (v. 3)	The church: Jews and Gentiles (v. 18)
Celebrated once, annually (vv. 3, 14)	"As often as you eat and drink" (vv. 25–26)
Family observance (v. 3)	Believing community observance (vv. 27, 29, 33)
Celebrated in the home (vv. 3, 4, 7)	Celebrated in a gathering (v. 22)
Four cups of wine (Exod 6:6–7)	One cup of wine (ποτήριον) (vv. 23–24; Matt 26:27)
Unleavened bread (v. 15)	Likely common bread (Mark 14:22)
Three required elements: a lamb; bitter herbs, and unleavened bread (v. 8)	Three required elements missing from the Lord's Supper (vv. 23–26)
A "forever" observance (v. 24)	An "Until he comes" observance (v. 26)

What description of the Passover meal can we draw from Exodus 12? What features of the Passover celebration stand out to us? Here are some elements to think about.

ESSENTIAL FEATURES OF THE PASSOVER CELEBRATION

- The Passover was celebrated in faith that the God who delivered the Israelites from Egyptian bondage would escort them into the Promised Land (Heb 11:28)
- The Exodus was a new beginning for God's chosen people (Exod 12:2).
- Moses announced God's plan to the congregation (v. 3).
- Moses revealed, "Every man shall take a lamb" (v. 3).
- God requires, "Your lamb shall be without blemish" (v. 5).
- The lamb was to be "a male a year old" the right age for a sacrifice (v. 5).
- "The whole assembly of the congregation of Israel shall kill their lambs at twilight," the appointed time for the sacrifice (v. 6).
- "You shall eat it in haste (v. 11).
- "I will execute judgments: I am the Lord" (v 12).
- "The blood shall be a sign for you" (v. 13).
- "When I see the blood, I will pass over you" (v. 13).
- "This day shall be for you a memorial day" (v. 14).
- "As a statute forever, you shall keep it as a feast" (v. 14).
- "Kill the Passover lamb" (v. 21).
- "And when your children say to you, 'What do you mean by this service?' you shall say, 'It is the sacrifice of the Lord's Passover'" (v. 26).
- While the slaughter was being performed, the Levites in the Temple chanted Psalms 113–18, the same Hallel that Jesus and his disciples would have sung the night before he was crucified (Matt 26:30; Mark 14:26; *Pesachim* 5:1–7).

We can never over exaggerate the importance of the blood, nor can we ever over appreciate its power. The sacrifice of the lamb's blood was the finger pointing to that bloody cross and the sacrifice of God's Lamb, the one who takes away the sin of the world (John 1:29). Without the blood, there is no atonement for our sin. If the Last Supper was to remind us that God's Passover Lamb fulfilled the requirements of the Old Testament, what would that look like? What kind of fulfillment would we see?

Viewing the Last Supper through the lens of Jesus' fulfillment of God's promises enables us to see the Lord's Supper as the fulfillment of the Passover Seder. For any fulfillment two things are necessary: 1) you need an articulation of the fact to be fulfilled, and 2) you need a realization of that articulation. Consider that tandem in the following.

THE LORD'S SUPPER: FULFILLMENT OF THE PASSOVER SEDER

#1. Articulated:

"The Lord said to Moses and Aaron in the land of Egypt..." (Exod 12:1). The Passover was celebrated in the belief that the God who delivered the Israelites from Egyptian bondage would not abandon them in the wilderness but would escort them into the Promised Land (Heb 11:28).

#1. Realized:

"I give them eternal life, and they will never perish, and no one will snatch them out of my hand. My Father, who has given them to me, is greater than all, and no one is able to snatch them out of the Father's hand" (John 10:28, 29). Remembering the bread and wine of the Lord's Supper awakens in us Jesus' promise, "I will never leave you nor forsake you" (Heb 13:5; see John 6:37; Rev. 3:5).

#2. Articulated:

"This month shall be for you the beginning of months" (Exod 12:2).

#2. Realized:

The Lord's Supper demonstrates a new beginning for followers of Jesus and freedom from the mechanical display of the Mosaic and Levitical laws. "Therefore, if anyone is in Christ, he is a new creation. The old has passed away; behold, the new has come" (2 Cor 5:17). "Now we are released from the law, having died to that which held us captive, so that we serve in the new way of the Spirit and not in the old way of the written code" (Rom 7:6; see also Mark 16:6; Acts 2:36; 10:34–43; 1 Cor 1:22–24; 2:2, 8; 11:25; 2 Cor 3:4–6; Gal 6:14; Eph 1:3–14; Phil 1:11; Heb 2:11–12; 10:19—23; 13:15; 1 Pet 1:6–9; Rev 5:9; 14:3).

#3. Articulated:

Moses announced, "Tell all the congregation of Israel . . ." (Exod 12:3).

#3. Realized:

Jesus announced, "Go therefore and make disciples of all nations" (Matt 28:19; see also Matt 24:14; Mark 13:10; Luke 24: 46–48; Rom 16:25–27; Gal 3:8; Rev. 5:9; 7:9; 13:7; 14:6). The redeeming message of Christ and his cross was designed by God to be spoken to all of humankind, not just the "congregation of Israel."

#4. Articulated:

"Every man shall take a lamb . . ." (Exod 12:3).

#4. Realized:

"Men spoke from God as they were carried along by the Holy Spirit (2 Pet 1:21) and revealed that Jesus is the Lamb of God, the Messiah, and Savior (John 1:29, 36; Acts 8:32–35; 1 Cor 5:7; see also 1 Peter 1:18–19, Rev 5:6, 8, 12, 13; 7:9, 10, 14, 17; 12:11; 13:8; 14:1; 15:3; 19:9, 21:3; 22:1, 3). Salvation is an individual act of God, with every recipient taking the Lamb for themselves.

#5. Articulated:

God required, "Your lamb shall be without blemish" (Exod 12: 5).

#5. Realized:

Jesus, the Lamb of God, was entirely sinless, holy, and righteous (Mark 1:24; Luke 1:35; John 6:66–69; Acts 3:14; 4:27, 30; 7:52; Rom 3:21–26; 2 Cor

5:21; 1 Pet 2:21–24; 1 John 3:5). Jesus alone could be God's Passover Lamb because Jesus alone lived in perfect righteousness. There was no Plan B or second choice because no other person lived without sin.

#6. Articulated:

"Your lamb shall be without blemish, a male a year old" (Exod 12:5).

#6. Realized:

Just as the Passover lamb was the perfect age for the sacrifice, Jesus was in the prime of his life, the perfect age for our sacrifice (Isa 53:1–3; Luke 3:23; John 8:57).

#7. Articulated:

"The whole assembly of the congregation of Israel shall kill their lambs at twilight" (Exod 12:6).

#7. Realized:

Jesus died at the hour the Passover lambs were slaughtered and his body taken down from the cross at twilight in keeping with the law (Mark 15:42–45; Luke 23:54; John 19:31–34; Deut 21: 22, 23; Mishnah, *Pesachim* 5:1). While the Passover lambs were dying for the sins of Israel, Jesus, God's Passover Lamb, was dying for the sins of humanity.

#8. Articulated:

The Passover Seder was to be eaten in haste (Exod 12:11; Deut 16:3).

#8. Realized:

The evangelists do not indicate the Last Supper was eaten in haste, but Jesus told Judas, "What you are going to do, do quickly" (John 13:27) and revealed to his disciples, "Yet a little while I am with you" (John 13:33). When the women approached the empty tomb, the angel told them, "Come, see the place where he lay. Then go quickly and tell his disciples that he has risen from the dead" (Matt 28:6–7). There is an urgency to the Good News.

#9. Articulated:

"I will execute judgments: I am the Lord" (Exod 12:12).

#9. Realized:

While the Passover was a celebration of mercy for the people of God, it was also an unfolding story of God's wrath and judgment on his enemies (Matt 11:20–24; John 3:16–19; 5:22–30; 16:8, 11; Rom 2:3–5; 1 Cor 4:5; 2 Thess 1:5; Heb 9:27, 28; 10:28–31; 2 Pet 2:4, 9; 3:7; Jude 1:6, 9; 14; Rev 6:1, 16; 14:9–10). "Truly, truly, I say to you, whoever hears my word and believes him who sent me has eternal life. He does not come into judgment, but has passed from death to life" (John 5:24).

> "In faith there is enough light for those who want to believe. . . and enough shadows to blind those who don't."—Blaise Pascal

#10. Articulated:

"The blood shall be a sign for you" (Exod 12:3).

#10. Realized:

During his ministry, Jesus performed many signs proving who he was (John 2:23; 3:2; 6:14; 11:47; 20:30, 31), but the sign of the blood was the greatest of these. "You were ransomed from the futile ways inherited from your forefathers, not with perishable things such as silver or gold, but with the precious blood of Christ, like that of a lamb without blemish or spot" (1 Pet 1:18, 19; see also Matt 26:28; 27:26–28; Mark 14:24; Luke 22:20; John 19:34; Acts 20:28; Rom 3:21–25; 5:9; 1 Cor 1:22–24; 10:16; 11:25, 27; Eph 1:7; 2:13; Col 1:20; Heb 9:11–14, 18, 22; 10:19, 29; 12:24; 13:12, 20; 1 Pet 1:2; Rev 1:5; 5:9; 7:14; 12:11; 19:13).

#11. Articulated:

The Passover was celebrated because, when the angel of death saw the blood, he passed over that house (Exod 12:12–13).

#11. Realized:

When God sees us through the blood of Jesus, he passes over us and requires no judicial sentence of eternal death (Luke 22:20; Rom 3:21–26; Col 1:19–20; see also John 6:53, 54; Acts 20:28; Eph 1:7; 2:13; Heb 9:11–14, 24–28; 10:19, 20; 1 John 1:7; Rev 1:5; 5:9; 7:14; 19:13). "And as Moses lifted up the serpent in the wilderness, so must the Son of Man be lifted up, that whoever believes in him may have eternal life. For God so loved the world, that he gave his only Son, that whoever believes in him should not perish but have eternal life. For God did not send his Son into the world to condemn the world, but in order that the world might be saved through him. Whoever believes in him is not condemned, but whoever does not believe is condemned already, because he has not believed in the name of the only Son of God" (John 3:14–18).

#12. Articulated:

"This day shall be for you a memorial day" (Exod 12:14).

#12. Realized:

"And he took bread, and when he had given thanks, he broke it and gave it to them, saying, 'This is my body, which is given for you. Do this in remembrance of me'" (Luke 22:19; see 1 Cor 11:24–25). "For as often as you eat this bread and drink the cup, you proclaim the Lord's death until he comes" (1 Cor 11:26).

#13. Articulated:

"As a statute forever, you shall keep it as a feast" (Exod 12:14).

#13. Realized:

"As often as you eat this bread and drink the cup, you proclaim the Lord's death *until he comes*" (1 Cor 11:26). The Eucharist is to stimulate our memory of the crucifixion of Jesus until he reappears as King of kings and Lord of lords. That's when memory is swallowed up in reality. "He will wipe away every tear from their eyes, and death shall be no more, neither shall there be mourning, nor crying, nor pain anymore, for the former things have passed away" (Rev 21:4).

#14. Articulated:

"Kill the Passover lamb" (Exod 12: 21).

#14. Realized:

The fact that Jesus would be killed in Jerusalem is well attested both by the pronouncements of Jesus and by those who recorded his death (Matt 16:21; 17:22–23; 26:1–5; Mark 8:31; 9:31; 10:34; 14:1; Luke 9:22; 13:31; 18:33; John 5:18; 7:1; 7:25; 8:22, 37, 40; Acts 2:23; 3:15; 5:30; 1 Thess 2:14–16). That Jesus was killed in Jerusalem is corroborated by the writers of the Gospels (Matt 27:31; Mark 15:13, 14, 20; Luke 23:21; John 19:6, 13).

#15. Articulated:

"And when your children say to you, 'What do you mean by this service?' you shall say, 'It is the sacrifice of the Lord's Passover'" (Exod 12: 26).

#15. Realized:

While the Jews invited the responsibility for the blood of Jesus to be upon their heads and the heads of their children (Matt 27:25), the gospel story made a difference in the lives of God's children, young and old. Matthew 19:14, "Jesus said, 'Let the little children come to me and do not hinder them, for to such belongs the kingdom of heaven.'" "I have no greater joy than to hear that my children are walking in the truth" (3 John 1:4; see also Mark 10:29–30; Luke 1:16–17; 10:21; 18:15–16; Acts 2:39; 21:5–6; 1 Cor 7:14; Eph 6:1–4; Col 3:20–21; Titus 1:6; 2 John 2:13; 3 John 1:4).

#16. Articulated:

While the slaughter was being performed, the Levites in the Temple chanted Psalms 113–18, the same Hallel that Jesus and his disciples would have sung the night before he was crucified (*Pesachim* 5:1–7).

#16. Realized:

"And when they had sung a hymn, they went out to the Mount of Olives" (Matt 26:30; Mark 14:26). "He put a new song in my mouth, a song of praise to our God. Many will see and fear, and put their trust in the Lord" (Ps 40:3).

There's a parallel between the Lord's Supper and the Passover Seder that appears to demonstrate the former fulfilled the latter. Calvary changed everything. Jesus had been preparing his disciples for this day for many months (see Matt 16:21; 17:22–23; 26:1, 2; Mark 8:31; 9:31; 10:33, 34; Luke 9:22; 18:31–33; John 8:34–38). But nothing prepared them for the events of the next few hours like the bread and wine being likened to his body and blood, a body that would be brutally beaten and blood that would drain from his head, his hands, his feet, and his side. This was Jesus' final demonstration of his claim, "Do not think that I have come to abolish the Law or the Prophets; I have not come to abolish them but to fulfill them" (Matt 5:17).

Joseph Tabory, Professor Emeritus at Bar Ilan University in Israel, confirms the most significant difference between the Last Supper and the Passover Seder. He recognizes that while the Last Supper traditions focus on an interpretation of the wine (as well as the bread), the Passover traditions feature the wine without offering any explanation or interpretation for it, even while other symbols are explained in detail.[61] In the Christian tradition, however, the interpretation of these symbols is everything. How we interpret these elements determines how we understand the relationship between the Passover Seder and the Lord's Supper.

There is a finality to the Lord's Supper that is not found in any other act of the Lord Jesus before his crucifixion. It is a transition from law to grace, from old to new. It is a change from "doing" to please God to 'believing" to please him. It was Jesus' final lesson to his disciples. They had heard him speak of being a servant, but this time he washed their feet to demonstrate it. They had heard him teach moral and spiritual truth, but now he is promising they will see these qualities displayed under the most horrendous circumstances. They had watched him heal the sick, give sight to the blind, and even raise the dead, but now he was talking about his own death and resurrection, and his disciples were mentally numbed by it all.

Could it be that the Last Supper wasn't a typical Passover Seder or an everyday meal, but God's way of showing that, within a few hours when Christ died on Calvary's cross, everything would change? Within hours, every prophecy of Isaiah 53 would be completely fulfilled. Was the Last Supper both the last meal of the Old Covenant and the first meal of the New? Did it not observe the requirements of the past as it transitioned to the freedom of the future? Without concern for dotting every "i" or crossing every 't' of the Seder, perhaps the Last Supper is best understood as a transitional meal, morphing into a current reminder of Jesus' death on Calvary's Cross. I think it's worth considering.

WHERE IS THE LAMB?

In my opinion, the biggest question related to the Last Supper comes not with what is present in the meal but what is absent. At the Passover celebration, in addition to the four cups of wine, the horseradish for bitter herbs, and the *matzah*, the critical element—the essential food—was the roasted Lamb. This was the symbol of sacrifice. It was the lamb's blood that was sprinkled over the doors of the Israelites' homes that dark Egyptian night when the cries of death were heard throughout the land. The lamb was what made the Passover celebration a celebration. And yet, at Jesus' Last Supper, the lamb is conspicuous only by its absence. We find ourselves asking the same question Isaac did of Father Abraham on Mount Moriah, "Where is the lamb?" (Gen 22:7).

It can be argued that the lamb was missing from the Last Supper because Jesus wanted to impress upon his disciples that he is the Paschal lamb, he is the fulfillment of all the predictions and promises engraved in the Mosaic Law. What need did they have for the type when the antitype was right there in their midst? Frankly, I don't find this line of reasoning very satisfactory. If bread and wine were present in the Last Supper meal, why not the lamb? Again, I ask: where is the lamb?

I have many friends who live in Jerusalem—both Jews and Arabs. One of my Jewish friends I have known for more than fifty years. I have been entertained in his home. He sends me a Christmas card each year and I send him a Hanukkah card. I have looked to him for insight into the modern Jewish mind. He has been a true friend.

Once years ago, when we were sipping lemonade in his backyard, the subject of the Passover came up. He was explaining to me, a Gentile, how his family would celebrate the Jewish Passover. I was intrigued. He explained the use of horseradish to demonstrate the bitter years of slavery his people endured under the Egyptians. He showed me the four cups the family uses for their Passover Seder. After he explained everything he asked if I had any questions. I had but one. "Where is the lamb?" He responded, "What do you mean?" In tender love again I said, "I understand about the horseradish and the other elements of the celebration, but what do you do for a lamb? It seems that is the most important feature of the entire Passover. What do you use for a lamb?" I quietly asked.

There was an unusual blank stare on my friend's face. I had not seen it before. He appeared to be stumped by my question. After what seemed like a very long time, but probably was only twenty seconds, he strained at an answer. Stammering a bit, he finally was able to push out, "Well, we believe the State of Israel has fulfilled all the promises of the Messiah so we no longer need a lamb." I'm saddened every time I think about his answer. His fulfillment, his deliverer, his Messiah, his Savior is a government that since its inception in 1948 has had thirteen prime ministers (one of them in office three different times), from nine different political parties. Is this what you wish to believe is the fulfillment of the Old Testament promises?

> "The Christian community is a community of the cross, for it has been brought into being by the cross, and the focus of its worship is the Lamb once slain, now glorified."—John Stott

We may not all agree on the exact meaning and purpose of the Last Supper, but I think we can agree that the lamb was a pretty important element in the Passover meal, but no mention is made of it in the Last Supper.

Unity trumps discrepancy

We must keep in mind that while there is an inconsistency between the Synoptics and John in the matter of the Last Supper, this inconsistency occurs within the context of a widespread chronological agreement between them. The supposed inconsistency is by far the exception rather than the rule. Consider this.

- All four Gospels indicate the crucifixion occurred on the day of Preparation (Matt 27:62; Mark 15:42; Luke 23:54; John 19:31, 42).
- Three of the Gospels note that the next day was the Sabbath (Mark 15:42; Luke 23:54, 56; John 19:31).

- All four Gospels say the women visited the tomb on the first day of the week (Matt 28:1; Mark 16:1–2; Luke 24:1; John 20:1).

- Three of the Gospels report the Last Supper was eaten at night (Matt 26:20; Mark 14:17; John 13:30; *cf.* also 1 Cor 11:23).

- All four say that after the Last Supper, they journeyed to the Mount of Olives (Matt 26:30, 36; Mark 14:26, 32; Luke 22:39–40; John 18:1) where Jesus prayed and then was arrested.

- All four report that Jesus was ordered before the chief priests that night (Matt 26:57; Mark 14:53; Luke 22:54; John 18:12, 24).

- All four record that, as Jesus predicted, Peter would deny his Lord before the cock crowed twice (Matt 26:74; Mark 14:72; Luke. 22:60; John. 18:27).

- All four mention the priests seized Jesus and shuffled him off to Pilate at early dawn (Matt 27:1; Mark 15:1; Luke 23:1; John 18:28).

- Three mention Jesus' trial before Pilate was on the customary day Romans released a prisoner (Matt 27:15; Mark 15:6; John 18:39). Some have mistakenly taken Mishnah *Pesahim* 8:6 to refer to this prisoner release and to nullify the chronology of the Synoptics because it infers that the prisoner was released to eat the Passover that night. But Joachim Jeremias, quoting the Jerusalem Talmud, demonstrated that the Mishnah refers to a prisoner who is being held by Jewish authorities, not to the Roman Passover amnesty.[62]

While the differences between John and the Synoptics regarding the Last Supper are significant, in the bigger picture, there is remarkable unity among all four Gospel authors relating the story of Jesus' crucifixion. The Gospel writers say nothing to contradict the impression that the Last Supper was different from other Passover meals. The fact is, if not a Seder, this meal would not have broken any rule regarding Passover.

The debate about this issue has been long and sometimes contentious. Often it has slipped off the rails by dismissing the Gospel narratives as hopelessly confused. Nevertheless, scholars both liberal and conservative continue to seek insights into this question.

My opinion? This meal was not just Jesus' Last Supper, but the last supper of the Old Testament economy. The Old Testament records God's promises; the New Testament records his performance. What Jesus did on the cross was the fulfillment of a wealth of Old Testament prophecies. The fulfillment of these was celebrated with a transitional meal asserting, "The old has passed away; behold, the new has come" (2 Cor 5:17).

Good, astute, and honest scholars come down on all sides of this issue and will continue to do so. The real truth is that this question will not be settled until we sit with Jesus himself at the Marriage Supper of the Lamb (Rev 19:9). There we can ask him ourselves. Until then, the question remains unanswered and our best response is to be charitable to those with whom we disagree.

The quote below in Latin summarizes how followers of Jesus should approach issues like the Last Supper when they disagree with other followers of the Lamb. This was written by Marco Antonio de Deminis in his work *De Repubblica Ecclesiastic*, published in 1617.

> "Unitatem in necessariis, in non necessariis libertatem, in omnibus caritatem."—Marco Antonio de Dominis
> *"Unity in what is necessary, freedom in what is not necessary, in all things charity."*

The more answers we submit to reconcile John and the Synoptics, the more questions arise. The distinctions are important, to be sure, because this issue is one reason why there is an Eastern Orthodox Church and a Western Catholic Church. The Christian Orthodox Church continues to follow the Julian calendar when calculating Pascha's date (Easter). The rest of Christianity uses the Gregorian calendar. There is a thirteen-day difference between the two calendars, Julian being thirteen days behind the Gregorian.

We should ask ourselves if the Last Supper being a Seder or not is enough to foster two different and often competing branches of Christ's Church. Or is it something we don't have to agree on to have fellowship with other Christ-followers? What do you think?

Chapter 4

The Case for a Wednesday Crucifixion

A literal interpretation of "three days and three nights" is the cornerstone of the argument for a Wednesday crucifixion, and to a lesser extent, a Thursday crucifixion. But, if this argument fails, both theories are in jeopardy.

TWO TRUTHS ABOUT THE United States of America are undeniable. The first is that the Bible and the Christian religion had a profound impact on shaping early American culture. The second truth is this impact has been dying for the last half-century, and today is on life support.

When I was in high school, I remember being legally excused from class to attend special services from noon to 3:00 pm on Good Friday. Seven ministers from seven different churches and denominations would each take a turn expounding one of the "seven last words of Christ." The 3-hour service did not drag on as you might think. Try doing that today.

> "The exact date of the crucifixion is one of the great unanswered questions of our time."—John Sentamu

In the Christian Church of the West, the Friday before Easter was always celebrated as the day Christ died. It was called "Good Friday." At least it was good for sinners. Actually, "Good" Friday is probably a corruption of the German *Gottes Freitag* ("God's Friday"). However it came by that name, it was forever celebrated as the day of Christ's sacrifice at Calvary.

In recent years, some denominations, especially the Seventh-Day Adventists, have advanced the view that Christ was entombed on Wednesday afternoon and arose from the grave exactly seventy-two hours later on Saturday afternoon. "Among the churches that have accepted this view as one of their fundamental beliefs are The Church of God (Seventh Day), the Worldwide Church of God, the Church of God International, and The Assembly of Yahweh."[63]

Perhaps the most well-known proponent of the Wednesday view was W. Graham Scroggie. After pastorates in England, Scotland, New Zealand, Australia, Tasmania, the United States, and Canada, Scroggie became pastor of the famous Spurgeon Metropolitan Tabernacle in London. He presented his Wednesday crucifixion view in his book, *A Guide to the Gospels*.[64] Many years ago I used this as one of the textbooks in classes I taught on the Gospels. But Scroggie was not an Adventist. He was trained at Spurgeon's College in London as a Baptist pastor.

There are three principal reasons why Christians have concluded Jesus Christ was crucified on Wednesday.

First, they believe that a Wednesday crucifixion and Saturday burial better explain the Passion Week events. For example, while the traditional Friday crucifixion often involved a so-called "silent day" on Wednesday of Passion Week, a Wednesday crucifixion eliminates the need for such a day.[65]

Second, it treats Jonah's "three days and three nights" prophecy literally.

And third, those who hold to a Wednesday crucifixion feel it best explains the expression "end of the Sabbaths" as the time of Jesus' resurrection. We will examine each of these and other reasons in this chapter.

I sincerely appreciate the time and effort others have put into coming to their understanding of the Passion Week timeline. Any in-depth study of the Gospels' evidence is better than no study at all. Generally, those who have concluded that Wednesday is the correct day for the crucifixion of Jesus Christ have done so after many hours of study and research. I applaud that. The same is true for those who advocate a Thursday crucifixion and a Friday crucifixion.

But the predispositions we all bring to our investigation sometimes, at best color the truth, or at worst blind us to it. For those advocating Wednesday, the predilection is the necessity for seventy-two hours of grave time for Jesus. For those advocating Friday, the predilection is the church has traditionally held Friday as the correct day for nearly two millennia. And for those advocating Thursday, the predilection may be, if Wednesday and Friday are wrong, surely Thursday must be right. Thursday becomes the compromise candidate. Advocates for each day have their reasons and arguments, and those who do not advocate for that day have their doubts and questions.

THE ARGUMENT FOR WEDNESDAY FROM THE CALENDAR

If the argument for a Wednesday crucifixion of Jesus is correct, how would that look on a calendar? What happened, and when did it happen during Passion Week? Here's how it would look according to the Wednesday theory.

Sunday: Jesus rode the foal of a donkey from the top of the Mount of Olives into Jerusalem with cheering crowds proclaiming, "Hosanna to the Son of David! Blessed is he who comes in the name of the Lord! Hosanna in the highest!" (Matt 21:9; Mark 11:9–10; John 12:13).

Monday: Busy day for Jesus. He cursed the fig tree and cleansed the Temple. Parables were taught. Scribes and Pharisees were denounced. Jesus lamented over Jerusalem. The Greeks desired to see Jesus. He delivered the Olivet Discourse. Judas bargained to betray his Master.

Tuesday: Jesus Christ ate an evening Passover meal with his disciples. Here he initiated the symbols (bread and wine) of a New Covenant (Matt 26:26–28). After the meal, Jesus prayed to the Father reaffirming he was committed to the Father's will. Soon he was betrayed by Judas, arrested, and taken to the compound of the High Priest.

Wednesday: Jesus was crucified and died around 3:00 pm (Matt 27:46–50). This was the preparation day for the No italics on the word "annual"—not weekly—Sabbath, which began at sunset (Mark 15:42; Luke 23:54; John 19:31). Jesus' body was taken down from the cross and placed in Joseph of Arimathea's tomb just before sunset (Matt 27:57–60).

Thursday: This was the High-Day Sabbath, the first day of the biblical Feast of Unleavened Bread (John 19:31; Lev 23:4–7). Matthew refers to it as the day "after the day of Preparation" (Matt 27:62). Wednesday night and the daylight portion of Thursday were the first of three days and nights that Jesus' body was in the tomb, literally fulfilling Jonah's sign.

Friday: The High-Day annual Sabbath is now past. The women bought and prepared spices for anointing Jesus' body before resting on the weekly Sabbath day. This Sabbath began Friday at sunset (Mark 16:1; Luke 23:56). Thursday night and the daylight portion of Friday marked the second of three days and nights Jesus' body was in Joseph's tomb.

Saturday: The women rested on the weekly Sabbath day, according to the fourth Commandment of the Mosaic Law (Luke 23:56; Exod 20:8–11).

Jesus rose near sunset that evening, precisely three days and three nights after his body was placed in the tomb. The sign of Jonah was fulfilled.

Sunday: The women brought prepared spices to the tomb to complete the burial process. It was early Sunday morning and still dark (Luke 24:1; John 20:1). But Jesus was not in the tomb; he had already risen (Matt 28:1–6; Mark 16:2–6; Luke 24:2–3; John 20:1). He did not rise on Sunday morning but near sunset the day before—three days and three nights after being placed in Joseph's tomb.[66]

Table 1: Wednesday Crucifixion

Day of the Week	Events of the Day
Sunday	Jesus' Triumphal Entry into the City of Jerusalem
Monday	All events between the Triumphal Entry and the Last Supper
Tuesday	Jesus ate the Passover meal and was betrayed by Judas.
Wednesday	Jesus was crucified in the am and pronounced dead at 3:00 pm.
Thursday	On the 'High Sabbath' day Jesus' body was placed in Joseph's tomb.
Friday	The women prepared for the weekly Saturday Sabbath.
Saturday	Jesus rose from the grave near sunset on the 'third day'.
Sunday	The women brought spices to the tomb; Jesus was not there.

It appears the primary reason for advocating a Wednesday crucifixion is to satisfy a three full-day and three full-night entombment. Even though it was conclusively demonstrated in Chapter 1 that a literal seventy-two-hour requirement for Jesus in the grave would not be necessary, nevertheless, those who hold to a Wednesday or Thursday crucifixion cannot let go of this assumed seventy-two-hour necessity. Without the need for three full days and three full nights, the Wednesday crucifixion can provide little evidence for its validation.

Let's examine the Wednesday crucifixion theory based on the evidence at hand. There must be reasons why good people migrate to a mid-week crucifixion of Jesus. What are they?

THE ARGUMENT FOR WEDNESDAY FROM JONAH'S PROPHECY

The heart of the case for placing Jesus' crucifixion on Wednesday is the prophecy of Jonah, which was repeated by our Lord. The more days and months into his ministry, the more Jesus clashed with the pious chief priests, elders, and Pharisees. At times the confrontations were heated. In Matthew 12, Jesus called the Pharisees a "brood of vipers" (v. 34), which cannot have pleased them. In response, the Pharisees attempted to discredit Jesus. "Then some of the scribes and Pharisees answered him, saying, 'Teacher, we wish to see a sign from you'" (v. 38). No sign, no authority.

Culturally the Jews were given to requiring signs before they would believe or act. The pages of the Bible are strewn with God's signs to verify his promises. The rainbow was a sign to Noah (Gen 9:13) and his staff becoming a serpent was a sign to Moses (Exod 4:3). Gideon demanded of the LORD, "Show me a sign that it is you who speak with me" (Judg 6:17). He needed more than one. Paul said of his own people, "Jews demand signs" (1 Cor 1:22). Here we find the scribes and Pharisees demanding a sign from Jesus (Matt 12:38).

But hadn't Jesus already given plenty of signs of his messiahship and divine authority? After all, before Matthew 12 and this call for a sign, Jesus had cleansed a leper of his disease (Matt 8:3) and healed a Centurion's servant (Matt 8:13). After he healed Peter's mother-in-law in Capernaum, Matthew records, "That evening they brought to him many who were oppressed by demons, and he cast out the spirits with a word and healed all who were sick" (Matt 8:16). This was in Capernaum, the principal city of Galilee. Inevitably there were scribes and Pharisees around to witness these miracles.

Not enough? Okay, Jesus healed two men possessed by demons (Matt 8:32), he healed a person with paralysis (Matt 9:6), as well as two blind men and a mute (Matt 9:29–30, 33). On this last occasion, we know the Pharisees were present because they immediately accused Jesus of exorcism by demon possession. And these are just the signs found in Matthew.

These phony religious leaders had already witnessed more signs than necessary to know that Jesus was not just another would-be messianic figure. He was the real deal. So when they asked for yet another sign to prove his authority, Jesus was likely a tad disconcerted.

The next verses in Matthew 12 say, "But he answered them, 'An evil and adulterous generation seeks for a sign, but no sign will be given to it except the sign of the prophet Jonah. For just as Jonah was three days and three nights in the belly of the great fish, so will the Son of Man be three days and three nights in the heart of the earth'" (vv. 39–40).

The sign of Jonah was given as a rebuke to the faithless Pharisees and the scheming scribes. Still, Jesus advanced as fact that "Jonah was in the belly of the fish three days and three nights" (שְׁלוֹשָׁה יָמִים וּשְׁלוֹשָׁה לֵילוֹת, Jonah 1:17), and likened his time in the grave to the time Jonah spent in the belly of the great fish. For Jesus, the story of Jonah and the great fish was not a myth but something he could legitimately use to speak of his own death and resurrection. You don't link myth with fact; you link fact with fact.

A literal interpretation of "three days and three nights" is the cornerstone of the argument for a Wednesday crucifixion, and to a lesser extent, a Thursday crucifixion. But, if this argument fails, both theories are in jeopardy. We explored in great detail the use of "three days and three nights" in the first chapters and noted this expression was an idiom equivalent to our phrase the "day after tomorrow." Still, Wednesday crucifixion advocates cling to this single reference as proof of their theory, while dismissing the twelve other references that do not support their theory.

CARDINAL VERSUS ORDINAL NUMBERS

How are we to interact with this twelve-to-one ratio of references? The difference is simple. It is the difference between cardinal and ordinal numbers. It was noted in chapter one that a cardinal number is a number that says how many of something there are, such as one, two, three, etc. An ordinal number tells the position of something in a list, such as first, second, third, etc. Jesus' reference to Jonah indicates that he would rise after three days and nights (cardinal number), while all the other references in the New Testament indicate he would rise on the third day (ordinal number) from the grave.

Jesus typically spoke of his death and resurrection in ordinal numbers. "As they were gathering in Galilee, Jesus said to them, 'The Son of Man is about to be delivered into the hands of men, and they will kill him, and he will be raised on the third day'" (Matt 17:22–23). See Matthew 16:21; 20:19; Luke 9:22; 13:32–33; 18:33; and 24:46 as examples of Jesus saying he would rise on the third day.

The question remains: Did Jesus mean he would literally be in the grave for seventy-two hours, three full days, and three full nights, or was he counting inclusively, as was the custom of the Jews in his day? (See Chapter 1 for a discussion that inclusive calculation was the norm in the Ancient Near East countries and would have been for Jesus as well).

I believe Jesus rose from the dead on the third day—first, second, third—which would not require seventy-two hours. If inclusive calculation was the norm for Jesus and the Gospel writers, the major reason for holding to a Wednesday crucifixion vanishes.

To emphasize the three days and three nights that Jonah was in the stomach of the great fish is to miss the point of the prophetic sign. Again, in Matthew 12:40, Jesus said, "For just as Jonah was three days and three nights in the belly of the great fish, so will the Son of Man be three days and three nights in the heart of the earth." But when Luke records the same event, he completely ignores the three days and three nights saying, "This generation is an evil generation. It seeks for a sign, but no sign will be given to it except the sign of Jonah. For as Jonah became a sign to the people of Nineveh, so will the Son of Man be to this generation" (Luke 11:29–30).

If the seventy-two-hour duration is the essential factor in this passage, how could Luke fail to record it? Look again carefully. Luke's comparison between Jonah's experience in the belly of the great fish and Christ Jesus' experience in the belly of the earth is not in terms of the duration of interment but in terms of similar miraculous expulsions from death. "For as Jonah ... so will the Son of Man be ... something greater than Jonah is here." This is about his resurrection, not about days.

> The vast majority of biblical commentators agree in viewing Jonah's sign as being primarily the sign of Christ's resurrection. For example, Albert Barnes in his notes on the Bible comments: "Three days and three nights. It will be seen, in the account of the resurrection of Christ, that he was in the grave but two nights and a part of three days. See Matthew 28:6. This computation is, however, strictly in accordance with the Jewish mode of reckoning. If it had not been, the Jews would have understood it, and would have charged our Saviour as being a false prophet; for it was well known to them that he had spoken this prophecy, Matthew 27:63. Such a charge, however, was never made; and it is plain, therefore, that what was meant by the prediction was accomplished.[67]

"John 2:18–19 says, "So the Jews said to him, 'What sign do you show us for doing these things?' Jesus answered them, 'Destroy this temple, and in three days I will raise it up.'" Jesus was making his resurrection the unmistakable sign of his messiahship, not the three days. Since the text of John 2:18–19 parallels Matthew 12:40 (in both cases, a sign is requested and given), it is certainly legitimate to conclude that the sign of Jonah is given for the same reason in both places, namely, the sign of the resurrection, implicit in the Johannine text and explicit in the Matthean text.[68]

Recently I revisited the Catacombs of Saint Sebastiano, Saint Callixtus, and Saint Domitilla to photograph scenes and symbols that are important examples of Early Christian art in the second and third centuries AD. In many frescos that adorn these and other catacombs' walls, Christ's resurrection is symbolically represented as Jonah being ejected from the great fish. Jonah's scene (known as 'Jonah's cycle' because it consists of different scenes) is the most common symbolic depiction of Christ's resurrection and a favorite theme in Early Christian art. In the crypt of Lucina at the Catacombs of Callixtus, Jonah's story decorates the cubicula walls beginning in the second century and continuing well into the fourth century. The Jonah story is also dominant in the Via Latina catacomb, 315–60 AD.[69]

The catacombs are an artistic reminder that the early Christians identified Jonah's story as a sign of Jesus Christ's resurrection. It must be pointed out, however, that none of the Early Christian art depicts the time element of three days and three nights. It was immaterial to the early church. Their art was all about the resurrection story. This was true for Jesus as well whenever he spoke of the Jonah story.

Paul himself indirectly confirms this in introducing his most doctrinal letter—the Epistle to the Romans. The apostle writes:

> Paul, a servant of Christ Jesus, called to be an apostle, set apart for the gospel of God, which he promised beforehand through his prophets in the Holy Scriptures, concerning his Son, who was descended from David according to the flesh and was declared to be the Son of God in power according to the Spirit of holiness by his resurrection from the dead, Jesus Christ our Lord (Rom 1:1–4).

To Paul, what was important was not the time Jesus spent in the tomb, but the fact he rose from the dead and vacated the tomb. This fact is overlooked by those who hold to a Wednesday crucifixion. But they have other arguments we must consider.

THE ARGUMENT FOR WEDNESDAY FROM COUNTING BACKWARD

How do we know that Jesus' Triumphant Entry was on a Sunday? The fact is we don't, at least not from the Gospels. In none of the four Triumphal Entry accounts (Matt 21:9ff., Mark 11:9ff., Luke 19:28ff., and John 12:12ff.) will you find the word Sunday, the first day of the week, or any similar terminology? That doesn't mean it wasn't Sunday; it means we must come to that conclusion without the benefit of a direct reference in God's Word.

Those who hold to a Wednesday crucifixion love to count backward. The starting point is John 12:1, which says, "Six days before the Passover, Jesus therefore came to Bethany, where Lazarus was, whom Jesus had raised from the dead." With this cardinal number, we can determine a variety of things, the chief of which is the date of the Passover. Unfortunately, this is where the bias of Wednesday advocates comes into play.

To place Jesus' crucifixion on a Wednesday, proponents must assume the next day was Passover. So, with the assumption that Passover began at sunset on Thursday night and continued until sunset on Friday night, Wednesday crucifixion advocates count backward as expressed in Table 2.

Table 2: Counting Backward From Thursday to Saturday*

Day 1	Thursday (Passover began at sunset on Thursday night)
Day 2	Wednesday (Jesus was crucified at mid-day)
Day 3	Tuesday
Day 4	Monday
Day 5	Sunday
Day 6	Saturday (Jesus arrived at Bethany, in perfect agreement with John 12:1)
*"Six days before the Passover, Jesus therefore came to Bethany."	

Samuele Bacchiocchi, who was a Seventh-Day Adventist, commented:

> Some find this as the "final clinching proof" thinking it allegedly pinpoints the time of the resurrection as being Saturday afternoon. To the proponents of the Wednesday crucifixion, this text teaches that Christ arose before "the end of the Sabbath," because when the women arrived at the sepulcher "in the end of the Sabbath" they discovered that their Lord had already risen. Furthermore, they maintain that by counting backward from Saturday afternoon the prophetic three days and three nights of Christ's entombment, one arrives on Wednesday afternoon as the time of Christ's crucifixion.[70]

If Thursday beginning at sunset was Passover, the twenty-four hours before that (starting on Wednesday at sunset) is day one before Passover—Wednesday, not Thursday. Counting backward six days, as Table 3 indicates, means Jesus arrived in Bethany on Friday, not Saturday. The math is a problem for advocates of a Wednesday crucifixion.

Table 3: Counting Backward From Sunset Thursday to Sunset Friday

	Thursday (Thursday sunset to Friday sunset—Passover)
Day 1	Wednesday (Wednesday sunset to sunset Thursday—the day of Preparation)
Day 2	Tuesday (Tuesday sunset to sunset Wednesday)
Day 3	Monday (Monday sunset to sunset Tuesday)
Day 4	Sunday (Sunday sunset to sunset Monday)
Day 5	Saturday (Saturday sunset to sunset Sunday)
Day 6	Friday (Friday sunset to sunset Saturday)

Death before sunset

Reuben Archer Torrey was an American evangelist, pastor, educator, and prolific writer. Torrey was trained at Yale, as well as Leipzig and Erlangen in Germany. Still, he was decidedly conservative in his theology and a staunch defender of the authenticity and accuracy of the Bible. He also was a fierce advocate for a Wednesday crucifixion. He believed that a second Sabbath, a Passover Sabbath, occurred during the Passion Week, and much of what the Gospel writers had to say about the events of Jesus' crucifixion related to that Sabbath, not the weekly Saturday Sabbath.

Torrey wrote the following in a paper entitled "A Case for the Wednesday Crucifixion Theory."

> The Bible does not leave us to speculate which Sabbath is meant in this instance; for John tells us in so many words, in John 19:14, that the day on which Jesus was tried and crucified was, "the preparation of the Passover." In other words, it was not the day before the weekly Sabbath (that is, Friday), but it was the day before the Passover Sabbath, which came that year on Thursday—that is to say, the day on which Jesus Christ was crucified was Wednesday. John makes this as clear as day.

Well, clear for Torrey anyway. I admire Torrey. On the East Coast, he founded the Montrose Bible Conference (Montrose, PA) at which I have been the featured speaker many times. On the West Coast, he founded BIOLA University. He was a jet setter before there were jets. However, I believe he is incorrect in his assumptions about Passion Week. For example, he wrote:

> When we accept exactly what the Bible says, namely that Jesus was not crucified on the Passover day but on "the Preparation

of the Passover" (John 19:14), and that he was to be three days and three nights in the grave, then the fact that the "Preparation of the Passover" that year was on a Wednesday and his resurrection early on the first day of the week, allows exactly three days and three nights in the grave. To sum it all up, Jesus died just about sunset on Wednesday. Seventy-two hours later, exactly three days and three nights, at the beginning of the first day of the week, Saturday at sunset, he arose again from the grave.[71]

Torrey places Jesus dying before sunset on Wednesday. Exactly seventy-two hours later is Saturday afternoon, also before sunset. This means Jesus was not raised from the dead on the first day of the week but in the late afternoon of the Sabbath day of the week. Advocates of a Wednesday crucifixion cannot escape the fact that seventy-two literal hours before a sunset ends is also before a sunset ends. Thus, according to Torrey and the Wednesday crucifixion theory, Sunday is not the Lord's Day and is not connected to the resurrection. It is for this very reason that some Sabbath-keepers believe the Wednesday crucifixion theory. Torrey was not a Sabbath keeper, but he came to the same conclusions.

THE ARGUMENT FOR WEDNESDAY FROM DOUBLE SABBATHS

Those who advocate for a Wednesday crucifixion claim there were two Sabbaths during Passover Week. Often these people are convinced that the rest of the world hasn't discovered this. One United Church of God author wrote, "What few people realize is that the Sabbath spoken of here was not the *weekly* Sabbath day, which begins on Friday at sunset and lasts until Saturday sunset. The apostle John specifically tells us that the day on which Jesus was crucified immediately preceded a special Sabbath, not the regular weekly Sabbath."[72] Actually, what John said was the Sabbath that week was a "High Day." He said nothing about it not being the regular weekly Sabbath.

The fact is, the rest of the world is not ignorant of a second Sabbath celebration during certain weeks of the Jewish calendar. The rest of the world simply cannot validate applying this phenomenon to the middle of Passion Week, thus determining Wednesday as the day of Jesus' crucifixion.

Those promoting a Wednesday crucifixion understand Sabbath to be plural. This is a vital text for them because if Matthew says, "Now after the Sabbath*s* [plural], toward the dawn of the first day of the week," they believe that proves there were two Sabbaths that week with a day in between. The first Sabbath allegedly was "the annual High-Day Sabbath, the feast day of

The Case for a Wednesday Crucifixion 97

the days of Unleavened Bread," while the second was "the weekly Sabbath," Saturday.[73]

There are, however, two problems with this. First, this is not the exclusive interpretation of what Sabbaths (plural) can mean, as Wednesday crucifixion advocates imply. Second, not all Greek manuscripts contain the Greek word for Sabbath (Greek: σαββάτων; English: *sabbatōn*) in the plural form.

Matthew 28:1. "Now after the Sabbath(s), toward the dawn of the first day of the week, Mary Magdalene and the other Mary went to see the tomb." In the original language the word *Sabbath* (Greek: σαββάτων; English: *sabbatōn*)—the Greek equivalent of the Hebrew שַׁבָּת; English: *shabbâth*—is not in the plural number in most Greek manuscripts. The vast majority of English translations do not use the plural form of Sabbath. (The plural form of σαββάτων is never found in reputable translations like the ESV, CSB, KJV, NASB, NET, NIV, NLT, NRSV, RSV, TLB, the list goes on and on). This profoundly takes the wind out of the sails of Wednesday advocates.

While Wednesday's crucifixion supporters prefer to understand the word as plural and thus justify their interpretation of two Sabbaths during Passover Week, it could just as easily be singular and indicate only one Sabbath that week. Or, just as likely, if plural, it could mean something more spiritually symbolic, like the crucifixion of Jesus would be the end of a need for the Sabbaths when he became our rest (Matt 11:28). The plural word "Sabbaths" does not require a Wednesday or Thursday crucifixion.

Wednesday promoters believe after the Passover Sabbath (see Lev 16:29–31; 23:24–31, 39) passed, the women left their homes and purchased spices to apply to Jesus' body (Mark 16:1). They understand Luke 23:54–56 as proof, believing without two Sabbaths during Passion Week, the women could not purchase the spices "after the Sabbath" and still prepare those spices "before the Sabbath."

The Sabbath within the "Passover week" was used to determine the wave/sheaf/Firstfruits offerings on the day after the Sabbath.[74] "And truly he did not speak falsely in saying so; for the festival, which we call Pentecost, did then fall out to be the next day to the Sabbath" (*Ant.*13.8.4).

Scholar F. F. Bruce clarifies:

> The Passover meal was eaten after sunset, at the start of Nisan 15, so Leviticus indicates that this day was a day of rest which came to be called the Sabbath of the Passover. Nisan 15 could fall on any day of the week, but when it fell on the normal weekly Sabbath, it was called a special High Sabbath.[75]

Since such a conjunction of the weekly Sabbath and annual Passover still occurs in the Jewish calendar today, Colin Humphreys says, "Hence, according to John, the crucifixion was on Nisan 14, the day before the Passover meal."[76]

Humphreys continues:

> Clearly this special holy day of rest was the day on which the Passover meal was eaten, the first meal in the seven-day Feast of Unleavened Bread, which was eaten after sunset. This was the day on which families assembled for a sacred meal. Since Exodus 12:15–16 calls the first day of these seven days both the day on which leaven must be removed from houses and a sacred day of rest on which the Passover meal was eaten, a calendar with a sunrise-to-sunrise day must be being used in which both events occurred on Nisan 14.[77]

Hence, two Sabbaths did occur during Passover Week, but this fact alone does not prove a Wednesday crucifixion because, just as America's tax day April 15th can fall on any day of the week, the High Sabbath could fall on any day of the week as well. Both Bruce and Humphreys were hinting that the day of the "double Sabbath" was the day between Jesus' Friday crucifixion and Sunday resurrection.

THE ARGUMENT FOR WEDNESDAY FROM THE FEASTS OF ISRAEL

Holy convocations were also a part of the feasts of ancient Israel. A solemn assembly was held on the feast day at the end of Passover. "For six days you shall eat unleavened bread, and on the seventh day there shall be a solemn assembly to the LORD your God. You shall do no work on it" (Deut 6:8). These convocations were a part of the feast day at the end of the Feast of Tabernacles (*Sukkot*) (Lev 23:34–36).[78]

From my observation, it appears that every feast that called for a "holy convocation" received one. It was an integral part of that feast. But not every feast of Israel called for such a solemn assembly, nor was every feast called a "Sabbath."

The first time the word "Sabbath" is found in the Bible is in Exodus 16:22–26. These verses refer to the establishment of the weekly Saturday, the sixth-day Sabbath. In Hebrew, the Sabbath is mentioned fifteen times in Exodus, all relating to the weekly Sabbath. It is not until we get to the Levitical laws that the word "Sabbath" is used in a context that does not refer to the Saturday Sabbath. In Hebrew, the word "Sabbath" is found twenty-four times in Leviticus, sometimes referring to a special Sabbath, a High Day, associated with a feast of Israel.

Leviticus 23:2 introduces these as "appointed feasts of the Lord that you shall proclaim as holy convocations." Verses 37 and 38 wrap up by saying, "These are the appointed feasts of the LORD, which you shall proclaim as times of holy convocation . . . besides the LORD's Sabbaths." Still, as mentioned above and as indicated by Table 4, not all of these feasts called for a holy convocation, nor were all of them called a "Sabbath" (Hebrew שַׁבָּת; English: *shabbâth*). What are we to make of this?

Table 4: The Sabbath in Leviticus

Scripture	Meaning	Mentions Sabbath	Call for Holy Convocation
Leviticus 16:31	Day of Atonement	Yes	Yes
Leviticus 23:2	The Sabbath	Yes	Yes
Leviticus 23:4-5	The Passover	No*	No
Leviticus 23:6-8	Unleavened Bread	No*	No
Leviticus 23:11	The Feast of Firstfruits	Yes	No
Leviticus 23:15-26	The Feast of Weeks	Yes	Yes
Leviticus 23:24	The Feast of Trumpets	Yes	Yes
Leviticus 23:32	The Day of Atonement	Yes	Yes
Leviticus 23:33-36	The Feast of Booths	No*	Yes
Leviticus 19:3	The Weekly Sabbath	Yes	No
Leviticus 19:30	The Weekly Sabbath	Yes	No
Leviticus 23:3	The Weekly Sabbath	Yes	No
Leviticus 23:38	The Weekly Sabbath	Yes	No
Leviticus 24:8	The Weekly Sabbath	Yes	No
Leviticus 26:2	The Weekly Sabbath	Yes	No
Leviticus 25:2	Fallow Year Sabbath	Yes	No
Leviticus 25:4	Fallow Year Sabbath	Yes	No
Leviticus 25:6	Fallow Year Sabbath	Yes	No
Leviticus 26:43	Fallow Year Sabbath	Yes	No
Leviticus 25:8	Jubilee Year Sabbath	Yes	No
Leviticus 26:34-35	Jubilee Year Sabbath	Yes	No
*These verses may describe a day of no ordinary work, but no Sabbath.			

Curiously, the three annual feasts of Israel that do not mention the word "Sabbath" are the spring feast of Passover (Lev 23:4–5), the Feast of Unleavened Bread (Lev 23:6–8), which is tied to Passover, and the fall Feast of Booths (Lev 23:33–36). The failure to mention the Passover as a Sabbath seriously undermines the Wednesday (and Thursday) argument for the day of Jesus' crucifixion. If anything, you would think the Sabbath would be emphasized if it was an annual event that constituted a second Sabbath in the middle of Passion Week.

The sheaf of Firstfruits was to be offered to the LORD before the Jews ate the harvest of the land. Since they began to eat on the sixteenth day following the Feast of Unleavened Bread, they offered the Firstfruits on that day. The LORD commanded them to offer the first fruits of the harvest "on the day after the Sabbath" (Lev 23:11). It was on the day following the yearly Sabbath of Unleavened Bread that the wave sheaf was offered. Their new harvest began to be eaten that very day.

Now the sequence of Passover events appears in sharper focus:

1. *The fourteenth day*—Slaying of Passover lamb
2. *The fifteenth day*—Feast of Unleavened Bread
3. *The sixteenth day*—Firstfruits of harvest presented

To properly appreciate the Sabbaths that were associated with Israel's feasts, consider the timing and purpose of Israel's seven feasts, along with the weekly Sabbath.

The Weekly Sabbath [calls for a holy convocation]

Leviticus 23:3, "Six days shall work be done, but on the seventh day is a Sabbath (Hebrew: שַׁבָּת; English: *shabbâth*) of solemn rest, a holy convocation. You shall do no work. It is a Sabbath to the LORD in all your dwelling places."

The Passover [no call for a holy convocation]

Leviticus 23:4–6, "These are the appointed feasts of the LORD, the holy convocations, which you shall proclaim at the time appointed for them. In the first month, on the fourteenth day of the month at twilight, is the LORD's Passover." [No mention of a Sabbath]. The Passover, with the lamb slain, typifies the atoning work of the Lamb of God, i.e., his redemptive work on the cross. While Passover is a feast day, it is not called a Sabbath day.

The Feast of Unleavened Bread [calls for a holy convocation]

Leviticus 23:6-8, "And on the fifteenth day of the same month is the Feast of Unleavened Bread to the LORD; for seven days you shall eat unleavened bread. On the first day you shall have a holy convocation; you shall not do any ordinary work. But you shall present a food offering to the LORD for seven days. On the seventh day is a holy convocation; you shall not do any ordinary work." [No mention of a Sabbath]. The Feast of Unleavened Bread is closely connected with the Passover and should not be separated from it.

The Feast of Firstfruits [no call for a holy convocation]

Leviticus 23:9-11, "And the LORD spoke to Moses, saying, 'Speak to the people of Israel and say to them, When you come into the land that I give you and reap its harvest, you shall bring the sheaf of the firstfruits of your harvest to the priest, and he shall wave the sheaf before the LORD, so that you may be accepted. On the day after the Sabbath (Hebrew: שַׁבָּת; English: *shabbâth*) the priest shall wave it.'" While the Passover foreshadows the death of Christ, the waving of the sheaf of the Firstfruits signifies a new life, typifying the resurrection of our Lord Jesus Christ.

The Feast of Weeks [calls for a holy convocation]

Leviticus 23:15-16, 21 "You shall count seven full weeks from the day after the Sabbath (Hebrew: שַׁבָּת; English: *shabbâth*), from the day that you brought the sheaf of the wave offering. You shall count fifty days to the day after the seventh Sabbath (Hebrew: שַׁבָּת; English: *shabbâth*). Then you shall present a grain offering of new grain to the LORD . . . You shall hold a holy convocation. You shall not do any ordinary work." After seven Sabbaths had passed and fifty days counted, a new meal offering was offered and two wave loaves baked with leaven, typifying those who follow Jesus are one with him.

The Feast of Trumpets [calls for a holy convocation]

Leviticus 23:23-25, "And the LORD spoke to Moses, saying, 'Speak to the people of Israel, saying, In the seventh month, on the first day of the month, you shall observe a day of solemn rest, (Hebrew: שַׁבָּתוֹן; English: *shabbâthôwn*) a memorial proclaimed with blast of trumpets, a holy convocation. You shall not do any ordinary work, and you shall present a food offering to the LORD.'" The trumpets announced a forthcoming event, the regathering of God's people, and the return of the LORD for his people.

The Day of Atonement [calls for a holy convocation]

Leviticus 23:26–28, 32. "And the LORD spoke to Moses, saying, 'Now on the tenth day of this seventh month is the Day of Atonement. It shall be for you a time of holy convocation, and you shall afflict yourselves and present a food offering to the LORD. And you shall not do any work on that very day, for it is a Day of Atonement, to make atonement for you before the LORD your God . . . It shall be to you a Sabbath (Hebrew: שַׁבָּת; English: *shabbâth*) of solemn rest (Hebrew: שַׁבָּתוֹן; English: *shabbâthôwn*), and you shall afflict yourselves. On the ninth day of the month beginning at evening, from evening to evening shall you keep your Sabbath'" (Hebrew: שַׁבָּת; English: *shabbâth*).

The Apocalypse affirms that when the Great High Priest, our Savior, and Israel's King, comes the second time in power and glory, Israel will look on him whom they have pierced and will turn to him for their atonement.

The Feast of Booths [calls for a holy convocation]

Leviticus 23:33–36, "'Speak to the people of Israel, saying, "On the fifteenth day of this seventh month and for seven days is the Feast of Booths to the LORD. On the first day shall be a holy convocation; you shall not do any ordinary work. For seven days, you shall present food offerings to the LORD. On the eighth day, you shall hold a holy convocation and present a food offering to the LORD. It is a solemn assembly; you shall not do any ordinary work."'" [No mention of a Sabbath]. The Feast of Tabernacles [Booths] was a memorial to Israel's dwelling in tents in the wilderness. The festival foreshadows the Millennial Kingdom's coming glory, Israel's glorious inheritance when Gentiles are gathered with redeemed Israel in God's earthly kingdom.

Why is the mention, or lack thereof, of the day as a Sabbath necessary in the argument for a Wednesday crucifixion? Just where you would expect the Levitical Law to affirm that Passover was also a Sabbath celebration, that potential confirmation is missing. This does not mean the Passover of the Passion Week was not a Sabbath, only that it was not called a Sabbath by Leviticus 23, which describes the relationship between Israel's feasts and Israel's Sabbaths. If there was a second Sabbath during Passover Week, the Feasts chapter in the Old Testament appears not to support it, removing yet another block from the foundation of a Wednesday crucifixion.

THE ARGUMENT FOR WEDNESDAY FROM THE WOMEN AND THEIR SPICES

Okay, we've been through some pretty heavy stuff thinking about Sabbaths, High Sabbaths, feasts and festivals, Solemn Assemblies, and more. Maybe it's time we give our minds a break.

In the following pages, we will explore what is, in my opinion, the strongest argument for a Wednesday crucifixion. Advocates of Wednesday claim that after the first Sabbath (the one that occurred on the evening of the crucifixion—Mark 15:42; Luke 23:52-54), the women purchased spices. Take note that they made their purchase after the Sabbath (Mark 16:1). The Wednesday view claims this Sabbath was the Passover Sabbath (see Lev 16:29-31; 23:24-32,39). The second Sabbath that week would have been the weekly Saturday Sabbath.

Luke 23:54-56 reveals, "It was the day of Preparation, and the Sabbath was beginning. The women who had come with him from Galilee followed and saw the tomb and how his body was laid. Then they returned and prepared spices and ointments. On the Sabbath they rested according to the commandment."

Wednesday supporters say these verses prove the women who purchased spices after the first Sabbath returned and prepared the spices before they "rested on the [weekly] Sabbath." Their argument is these women could not possibly have purchased the spices "after" the Sabbath, yet prepared those spices "before" the Sabbath, unless, of course, there were two Sabbaths.

Wednesday advocates maintain two things. First, the only explanation that does not violate the biblical account of the women purchasing their spices on a day that was not a Sabbath is their view. Second, the Wednesday view holds to a literal understanding of Matthew 12:40 and a complete seventy-two-hour interment. Accordingly, the Sabbath was a High Day (Passover) and occurred on Thursday (Wednesday sunset to Thursday sunset). The women purchased spices after the Passover Sabbath was over on Friday (after sunset on Thursday evening). They rested beginning after sunset on Friday, the weekly Sabbath. Finally, to anoint Jesus' body, they brought the spices to the tomb early Sunday morning, twelve hours after the Sabbath ended when they discovered Jesus had risen from the dead.

You see the problem here. If the Passover Sabbath occurred on Thursday (i.e. Wednesday sunset to Thursday sunset), and the regular weekly Sabbath began at Friday's sunset and lasted through to Saturday's sunset, the women had plenty of time to purchase the spices during the daylight hours of Friday, before the weekly Passover began. This begs the question: Why did the women not buy the spices and go to the tomb to anoint Jesus' body during all of Friday's daylight hours before the Sabbath began? Why wait until Sunday morning?

Table 5: A Seventy-two Hour Wednesday Crucifixion

Wednesday: 3:00 pm–the execution of Jesus by crucifixion
Thursday:
First twenty-four hours: (day one)–the Passover High Sabbath
Wednesday, 6:00 pm–the beginning of night one through
Thursday, 12:00 am–6:00 pm [the rest of day one].
Friday:
Second twenty-four hours: (day two)
Thursday, 6:00 pm–the beginning of night two through
Friday, 12:00 am–6:00 pm [the rest of day two].
Saturday:
Third twenty-four hours: (day three)–the weekly Saturday Sabbath
Friday, 6:00 pm–the beginning of night three through
Saturday, 12:00 am–6:00 pm [the rest of day three].
Saturday, 6:00 pm–Jesus' resurrection

If Jesus died at 3:00 pm and was buried before sunset at 6:00 pm (exactly seventy-two hours), then the verses about early dawn (Matt 28:1; Luke 24:1), the rising sun (Mark 16:2), and while it was still dark (John 20:1) do not fit with a 6:00 pm Saturday resurrection. Since the whole case for Wednesday crucifixion is built on a literal seventy-two hours in the grave, what good is a theory based on a literal seventy-two-hour period that doesn't accommodate all the facts presented by all four of the Gospel authors? It's a serious problem for this interpretation.

THE ARGUMENT FOR WEDNESDAY FROM THE UNITED STATES NAVAL OBSERVATORY

Those who claim Jesus' crucifixion occurred on Wednesday, the fourth day of the week, often appeal to the findings of the U.S. Naval Observatory (USNO). However, their argument arises from an erroneous interpretation of a letter issued by the Observatory (USNO).⁷⁹ In January 1919, a table of full equinoctial moons from 24 to 38 AD was sent upon request to Church of God leader Elmer E. Franke. Following the Passover reckoning of this modern Jewish calendar, Wednesday advocates have decided the month of March is the month of the crucifixion full moon.

At that time, Captain W. S. Eichelberger was the director of the U.S. Naval Observatory. In his letter, later published by E. E. Franke in a pamphlet, Captain Eichelberger wrote:

> In reply to your letter of January 15, you are informed the astronomical full moon occurred Tuesday, March 27, AD 31, i h. PM, Jerusalem time, Julian calendar. This time may be accepted within two or three hours.
> [Signed] W. S. RICHELBERGER, Commander (Math.)
> Director Nautical Almanac.

The U.S. Naval Observatory Almanac Office does not establish historical dates; it accepts those dates for their chronological tables, confirmed by astronomy and history. What the USNO tables affirmed is that, according to Passion Week as recorded in the Gospels, from 8 Nisan to 14 Nisan, the Passion Week's events cannot be squeezed into any smaller number of days than is provided by a Friday crucifixion. This does not imply, however, that it should be stretched into more than the time allotted by a Friday crucifixion.

On March 28, 1924, Captain Eichelberger answered a similar inquiry from the editor of *American Sentinel* (Washington, D.C.). He was asking about the date of the Passover moon in 31 AD. Here is the Captain's reply to the *American Sentinel*:

> In reply to your letter dated March 27, 1924, you are informed as follows: The first astronomical full moon following the vernal equinox of 34 AD occurred, according to the Julian calendar, on Tuesday, March 27, at 2:00 h. PM, Jerusalem civil time. By direction of the superintendent, U. S. Naval Observatory, Very truly yours,
> W. S. EICIIELBERGER, Captain (Math.)
> U. S. Navy, Director Nautical Almanac.⁸⁰

It is here that some, certainly not all, advocates of a Wednesday crucifixion play fast and loose with the truth. You will notice in the two responses by Captain Eichelberger there is nothing to indicate that the date March 27 AD was tendered as a Passover moon, much less as the date of Jesus' crucifixion. Captain Eichelberger consistently called it the "first astronomical full moon following the vernal equinox." However, those who inquired about this full moon often referred to it as "the time of the Passover," "the year of Christ's crucifixion," and "the paschal full moon." Even though Captain Eichelberger mentioned none of these things, those who advocate for the Wednesday theory accept the Captain's letters as "proof positive of the day that Christ was crucified."

In a later correspondence (1929) concerning the same full-moon table, the director of the observatory further elucidated the meaning of the terms that he used in his previous correspondence. He wrote:

> The astronomical full moon next after the spring equinox of AD 31 (Julian calendar) occurred on Tuesday, March 27. The dates of the paschal full moons according to Jewish observance between AD 24 and AD 38 are uncertain. The rules employed in the present Jewish calendar are of later adoption . . . The Christian ecclesiastical calendar was not fixed until the Council of Nice[a], 325 AD. Some of the questions involved are discussed in the article on 'Bible' in the eleventh edition of the *Encyclopedia Britannica* (vol. 3, p. 890).
> [Signed] "W.S. Eichelberger, Captain (Math.)
> U. S. Navy, Director Nautical Almanac."[81]

Eager to establish a Wednesday crucifixion, those who use Captain Eichelberger's correspondence as proof have seriously erred in doing so. They read into his letter what they wanted to see. But what they wanted to see was not what the Captain wanted to say.

THE ARGUMENT FOR WEDNESDAY FROM HISTORICAL SOURCES

Presented as proof by some that Christ was crucified on Wednesday is an ancient document known as the *Didascalia Apostolorum*. This is a Christian treatise in the genre of church orders or rules of practice for the local churches. The *Didascalia* was patterned after the earlier *Didache*.[82] The author is unknown but likely was a bishop, maybe from northern Syria near Antioch.[83] Written in the third century, perhaps around the year 230 AD, the *Didascalia* purports to pass on apostolic instruction that the last Passover of Jesus and his disciples was on the Tuesday night of Passion Week.[84]

The document states:

> For when we had eaten the Passover on the third day of the week at even [Tuesday evening], we went forth to the Mount of Olives; and in the night they seized our Lord Jesus. And the next day,

which was the fourth of the week [Wednesday], he remained in ward in the house of Caiaphas the High Priest.

The earliest mention of the *Didascalia* is by Epiphanius, the fourth-century bishop of Salamis, Cyprus. Epiphanius wrote a huge work in three volumes cataloging eighty different heresies that plagued the church during his day. Unfortunately for the credibility of a Wednesday crucifixion, the *Didascalia Apostolorum* was found to be in use among the Audiani, a group of Syrian heretics.

Equally unfortunate is that the author of the *Didascalia* is notoriously inexact in his quotations and contradictory in his facts. For example, while he says the Passover was on the third day of the week (Tuesday evening through Wednesday evening), the author also says Jesus was crucified on a Friday. He exhibits no little confusion in the presentation of his facts. Epiphanius (367–403 AD) himself wrote, "Wednesday and Friday are days of fasting up to the ninth hour because, as Wednesday began the Lord was arrested and on Friday he was crucified."

By the fifth century, celebrations of Jesus' resurrection were consistently held on Sunday, the first day of the week. However, a fourth/fifth-century church historian named Socrates of Constantinople notes in a section of his history, "Differences of Usage in Regard to Easter," that some Christians celebrated the resurrection on the Sabbath rather than on Sunday. As he put it, "Others in the East kept that feast on the Sabbath indeed."

Socrates' *Historia Ecclesiastica*, a history of late ancient Christianity during the years 305 to 439 AD, is quite well-balanced. He is careful not to use hyperbole when referring to prominent figures in the church and the government. But Socrates is often thought to have been a follower of Novatianism because he gives great detail about this sect in his *Historia Ecclesiastica*. He is quite generous in his praise of them.[85] Socrates is also very kind in his treatment of the Arians and other heretical groups.[86]

Gregory of Tours (538–94 AD), the French bishop who wrote *Decem Libri Historiarum* (*Ten Books of Histories*), better known as the *Historia Francorum* (*History of the Franks*), noted that many believed Jesus rose on the seventh day of the week. Gregory clarified, however, stating, "In our belief, the resurrection of the Lord was on the first day, and not on the seventh as many deem." While others may have believed the resurrection occurred late on Saturday, Gregory wished his readers to know that he did not hold to this belief himself.

These historical records demonstrate that a slim minority of Christians during the first five centuries after Jesus' crucifixion understood the Passover to have begun on a Tuesday evening, with a corresponding Wednesday crucifixion and a late Saturday afternoon resurrection. However, it is only fair to note that many of these historical writers were also treated as heretics by the church.

THE MANY PROBLEMS WITH A WEDNESDAY CRUCIFIXION

While along the way I have noted some difficulties associated with a Wednesday crucifixion, there are many more than have been enumerated. Just as there are some points in favor of Jesus' crucifixion taking place on Wednesday, there are many more serious issues that deny that possibility. We now turn to some of the problems associated with a Wednesday crucifixion.

The issue of necessity

Most who hold to the Wednesday view also believe a double Sabbath occurred in Passion Week. The double Sabbath is a necessity for this position. One anonymous Internet author said, "The two sections of scripture that clearly and simply show there were indeed two Sabbaths during Passion Week are Mark 16:1 and Luke 23:56. Mark recorded the women buying the spices after the Sabbath, while Luke recorded them preparing the spices (must buy them first to prepare them) and then resting on the Sabbath." According to the Wednesday viewpoint, the only explanation that does not violate the biblical account of the women buying spices and then resting on the Sabbath is that Christ was crucified on Wednesday.

While the argument for the annual Passover Sabbath falling on Thursday is a necessary pillar of the Wednesday crucifixion theory, it is not as essential as you might think. If you do not separate Mark 16:1 from its context, the evangelist could very easily be talking about the weekly Saturday Sabbath. "When the Sabbath was past, Mary Magdalene, Mary the mother of James, and Salome bought spices, so that they might go and anoint him. And very early on the first day of the week, when the sun had risen, they went to the tomb" (Mark 16:1–2). Clearly, the context refers to Sunday morning when the women went early to Jesus' tomb and found it empty.

Luke 23:54–56 places the women in context as well. "It was the day of Preparation, and the Sabbath was beginning. The women who had come with him from Galilee followed and saw the tomb and how his body was laid. Then they returned and prepared spices and ointments. On the Sabbath, they rested according to the commandment." It was not until Sunday morning, the day after the Sabbath, that they could attempt to apply them to Jesus' body.

Nevertheless, without denying the possibility of two Sabbaths in Passion Week, there is no necessity for a double Sabbath when understood in the context of Mark and Luke.

The issue of timing

According to the mid-week theory, it was 4 or 5 days (depending on how you count them) between Jesus' crucifixion and the women anointing his body with spices.

I believe Ralph Woodrow justifiably asks, "If Jesus died and was buried on Wednesday, why would they wait until five days later—until the first day of the following week—before going to the tomb with their spices?"[87]

You don't have to be a New Testament scholar to see the problem here. If Jesus died on Wednesday, and the women did not go to the tomb to anoint his body until Sunday morning, why go at all? This four-day period would invalidate any effect the spices may have had on the Savior's body. Remember Martha's words when Jesus delayed coming to Bethany at the death of Lazarus? "Jesus said, 'Take away the stone.' Martha, the sister of the dead man, said to him, 'Lord, by this time there will be an odor, for he has been dead four days.'"

According to Dr. Arpad A. Vass, a Senior Staff Scientist at Oak Ridge National Laboratory and Adjunct Associate Professor at the University of Tennessee in Forensic Anthropology, human decomposition begins around four minutes after a person dies.[88] Rigor mortis sets in between two and four hours post-mortem. Within twenty-four to seventy-two hours, the internal organs decompose. In three to five days, the body starts to leak blood from the mouth and nose. If you have ever entered a room where there is a dead body you know immediately, for the stench is overwhelming. Martha was no doctor, but she was right about the decomposition of her brother's body.

It is a somewhat awkward problem that the faithful women had to wait until Sunday to anoint the Savior's body. With a 3:00 pm death on Wednesday, by Sunday dawn, eighty-six hours would have elapsed. By then decay and decomposition would have already overwhelmed the body. This obstacle alone dooms the Wednesday theory.

The issue of "a" Sabbath versus "the" Sabbath

Passover is never called "the Sabbath" in the Bible. Passover is always referred to simply as Passover. Thus, any time we encounter the definite article "the" before the word "Sabbath," we know the writer is referring to the weekly Sabbath, not to Passover or a High-Day Sabbath.

Table 6: "The Sabbath" and the Weekly Sabbath

Jesus' disciples husk corn on the Sabbath;	
He asserts himself as Lord of the Sabbath	Matt 12:1,2,4,8; Mark 2:23,24, 27,28; Luke 6:2,5
Jesus heals on the Sabbath:	
Man with the withered hand	Matt 12:10; Mark 3:2,4; Luke 6:7
Woman bent over	Luke 13:14–16
Man with dropsy	Luke 14:1–3
Crippled man at Bethesda	John 5:1,9,10,16,18
Man born blind	John 9:16
Circumcision versus healing	John 7:22,23
Doing necessary work on the Sabbath:	Matt 12:11,12; Luke 6:9
Jesus teaches on the Sabbath:	Mark 1:21; 6:2; Luke 4:16, 31; 13:10
Jesus' crucifixion and the Sabbath:	Matt 28:1; Mark 15:42; 16:1; Luke 23:54,56; John 19:31
Fleeing the Abomination of Desolation:	Matt 24:20 (NIV)
"A Sabbath"	Luke 6:1 (see verses 2, 5)*; 14:5; (see verse 3); John 9:14 (see verse 16)
"One Sabbath"	Mark 2:23 (see verses 24,27,28); Luke 14:1 (see verse 3)
"Another Sabbath"	Luke 6:6 (see verse 7)
*Even when "the" does not precede the word Sabbath, you will always find "the Sabbath" elsewhere in the context.	

In the Greek text, "the" Sabbath always and only applies to the Lord's Sabbath as commanded in Exodus chapters 16, 20, and many other places. So when John 19:31 says it was the preparation for "the Sabbath," grammatically he must be talking about the weekly Sabbath. The "preparation" for "the Sabbath" always refers to the day before "*the* Sabbath," meaning Friday. The only way "the Sabbath" can apply to the Passover Sabbath is if Passover falls on the same day as the weekly Sabbath. Even then it is still referring to the weekly Sabbath.

"Since it was the day of Preparation, and so that the bodies would not remain on the cross on the Sabbath (for that Sabbath was a High Day), the Jews asked Pilate that their legs might be broken and that they might be taken away." On God's calendar, this happened during Passion Week. Passover Sabbath and the Lord's seventh-day Sabbath fell on the same monumental day. This is why it is called the "High Sabbath" and why so many historic theologians and commentators of note, such as Albert Barnes, Adam Clarke, John Gill, John Wesley, etc. claim that at the end of the Passion Week, a double Sabbath did occur, a "High" Sabbath, i.e., Passover Sabbath and the weekly Sabbath occurring on the same day.

This important truth—that "the" Sabbath always refers to the weekly Sabbath—must be kept in mind if we are to accurately interpret the Passion narratives.

The issue of the tenth to the fourteenth

The command of God to Moses was crystal clear in Exodus 12:1–6. The Passover lamb was to be a male, one-year-old, and in perfect condition. Israel was not to offer a diseased or disabled lamb, but only the best of the flock. That lamb was selected on the 10th day of Nisan and inspected by the priests. They would look at its ears, feet, coloration, eyes, and all sorts of things looking for blemishes. If the lamb met the priest's expectations, it was penned separately from the other lambs and examined daily to make certain no developing disqualifications would arise. Then, on the 14th day of the month, the lamb was killed as a sacrifice to God in remembrance of his sparing the Israelites' lives on that deadly night of the tenth plague in Egypt.

But this presents another problem with the Wednesday crucifixion. If you place Nisan 14 on Wednesday and count back six days—the number of days they were permitted to work before the weekly Sabbath—it places Jesus' journey to Bethany on Thursday, Nisan 8. This is not the problem. The problem is counting backward also places the 10th of Nisan on a Saturday. Why is this a problem? The 10th would be the day the Jews presented the Lamb to the priest in the Temple, and the 10th of Nisan was a Saturday—the weekly Sabbath. It was the day of rest. No travel. No work. No lamb.

If the Jews slaughtered the lamb and presented it on a Sabbath, they would have violated numerous Sabbath laws. For the followers of Jesus, his Triumphal Entry into Jerusalem on that day would have meant they also broke many Sabbath laws, i.e., the people cutting and waving palm branches, forcing a donkey to carry a burden, plus the many and varied goings-on at the Temple on this day. It is much more likely that Jesus stayed at Lazarus' house until after the Sabbath. This would put his Triumphal Entry on Sunday. Problem solved, right? Not so fast.

The problem now is that the date is not Nisan 10 but Nisan 11. God clearly instructed the Jews to select and present the lambs on Nisan 10 and inspect them until Nisan 14. If you count backward from Wednesday the 14th, Tuesday the 13th, Monday the 12th, and Sunday the 11th, you have the problem of the wrong date. If you count four whole days backward from Wednesday the 14th Tuesday the 13th; Monday the 12th; Sunday the 11th; and Saturday the 10th you encounter the problem of the right date but the wrong day—a weekly Sabbath. A Wednesday crucifixion simply cannot make either of those dates occur on the appropriate day.

The issue of the Firstfruits

With a Wednesday crucifixion and literal seventy-two hours in the grave, the resurrection would occur on a Saturday Sabbath, which should precisely match the day of Firstfruits, but does not. With a Wednesday crucifixion, Firstfruits falls on Friday. This requires the resurrection also to be on Friday. However, this is trouble for the advocates of a Wednesday crucifixion because it is a day short of the seventy-two-hour span to which they have committed themselves.

Advocates obviously cannot put Firstfruits on Friday. Proponents of a Wednesday crucifixion are forced into a Saturday resurrection because of their strict adherence to the three days and three nights being seventy-two hours. This means that if Saturday was the day Jesus rose from the dead, it should also be the day of Firstfruits. But this violates Leviticus. 23:10–11, "When you come into the land that I give you and reap its harvest, you shall bring the sheaf of the firstfruits of your harvest to the priest, and he shall wave the sheaf before the LORD, so that you may be accepted. On the day after the Sabbath, the priest shall wave it." This would be Nisan 15, the Sabbath, the first day of Unleavened Bread. So, Firstfruits cannot have been on Saturday; it would not fall after a Sabbath.

But the difficulty for the Wednesday crucifixion theory grows even thornier. According to this theory, Firstfruits cannot have fallen on Sunday. That would fix the feast after a Sabbath, but it encounters an even more significant problem. A Sunday Firstfruits would extend past the seventy-two hours to which Wednesday proponents are tethered. A Sunday resurrection would make it the fourth day after Jesus' crucifixion. To accommodate a Wednesday crucifixion and Sunday Firstfruits, you must inject two days into the Passover Week. This would not only deny Nisan 16th as the day of the resurrection and the day of Firstfruits, but it would also destroy Jesus as the antitype to the waving the sheath in the hope of a harvest to come. These are dual deadly threats to the validity of a Wednesday crucifixion of Jesus of Nazareth.

The issue of a Saturday resurrection

Wednesday crucifixion proponents maintain that Jesus rose from the dead at sunset on Saturday, just as Sunday was beginning with the first three stars' appearance in the darkening sky. This gets their required seventy-two hours in, and just sneaks the resurrection inside the door of Sunday (Saturday 6:00 pm to Sunday 6:00 pm). But the Wednesday narrative completely ignores the many references to dawn on Sunday morning. Some advocates understand the "dawn" to mean the beginning of the day [as in "the dawn of the day"], which would occur shortly after sunset in Jewish calculation. But this is not a literal interpretation. If Wednesday proponents hold tightly to a strict, literal interpretation of a seventy-two-hour, three-day interment, why abandon the literal interpretation when it comes to the dawn of a new day? This inconsistency damages the Wednesday hypothesis.

As noted back in Chapter 2, one Wednesday crucifixion promoter states, "The women came to the tomb 'late on the Sabbath.' The stone was rolled away 'late on the Sabbath.' The tomb was empty 'late on the Sabbath.' Since all these things happened 'late on the Sabbath,' he reasons, 'Is it not the silliest kind of nonsense to say that the resurrection took place on Sunday morning?'"[89]

But this is not silly at all, especially when you recognize this author's words are a clear case of beginning with an error and enhancing it with more errors. It appears this author made his own translation of the Bible, for the phrase "late on the Sabbath" occurs in no legitimate translation of the Greek language, which is the epicenter of his argument. It is not found in the KJV, NASB, CSB, RSV, NIV, ESV, CEV, JBP, NKJV, and dozens of legitimate translations. If the author's bogus translation of "late on the Sabbath" is incorrect, the argument must be incorrect as well.

If it was "late on the Sabbath" when the women went to the tomb and found it empty, why do all the other Gospel writers place their visit "early in the morning"? And instead of being "late on the Sabbath," why do legitimate translations all say it was on "the first day of the week" which is not the Sabbath at all?

If it was "late on the Sabbath" when the women discovered the empty tomb, why do the other accounts link it with the dawn? Why does Matthew 28:1 even say it was "toward the dawn of the first day of the week?" By definition, dawn is when the sun is coming up, not when it is going down!

If it was "late on the Sabbath" when the women found the tomb empty, why would they be taking spices to anoint the dead body the next morning, knowing it was not there? (Luke 24:1).

If it was "late on the Sabbath" when the women discovered the stone was rolled away, why would they be asking the next morning, "Who will roll away the stone for us from the entrance of the tomb?" (Mark 16:3).

If it was "late on the Sabbath" that Mary Magdalene visited the tomb, found it empty, and saw the resurrected Christ, why would she be weeping the next morning at the tomb and asking the man she assumed was the gardener where the body was? (John 20:1, 11, 15). She would already have known.

If it was "late on the Sabbath," when the angel told the two Marys to "go quickly and tell his disciples that he is risen" (Matt 28:7), why would Peter and John calmly wait until morning before going to see the empty tomb for themselves? The fact is, John 20:4 says, "Both of them were running together, but the other disciple outran Peter and reached the tomb first." Peter and John ran to the tomb as soon as they heard it was empty!

The plain reading of Scripture will not permit the forced interpretation of "late on the Sabbath." Matthew 28:1 is clear: "Now after the Sabbath, toward the dawn of the first day of the week, Mary Magdalene and the other Mary went to see the tomb." I find it odd that, according to the Wednesday crucifixion view, they would go to "see" the tomb just after sunset when seeing would be more difficult.

But Mark is even more specific than Matthew, and his words place the final nail in the coffin for a Wednesday crucifixion. Mark says, "When the Sabbath was past, Mary Magdalene, Mary the mother of James, and Salome bought spices so that they might go and anoint him. And very early on the first day of the week, when the sun had risen, they went to the tomb" (Mark 16:1–2) The women's journey to the tomb was just after dawn, not just after dark.

"Very early on the first day of the week" could be interpreted by Wednesday proponents as "early just after the day began at sunset," but there is no way to get around Mark's addition, "When the sun had risen." The sun does not rise minutes after it sets. Most assuredly Mark is talking about Sunday morning at daylight, not Sunday as the Jewish day began the evening before. At some point, common sense has to prevail.

Luke affirms the timing of the women coming to the tomb. "But on the first day of the week, at early dawn, they went to the tomb, taking the spices they had prepared" (Luke 24:1). John does the same when he writes, "Now on the first day of the week Mary Magdalene came to the tomb early, while it was still dark, and saw that the stone had been taken away from the tomb" (John 20:1). Those Wednesday advocates who believe Jesus' resurrection came after 6:00 pm on Saturday find validation in John's "while it was still dark." However, if Jesus rose from the grave shortly after the sun went down on Saturday, shouldn't John have said, "while it was *just* dark" instead of "while it was *still* dark"? Think about it.

A late Saturday resurrection simply does not fit the facts. Since a Wednesday crucifixion requires a late Saturday resurrection, Wednesday likewise does not fit the facts for Jesus' crucifixion.

The issue of too many days

A Wednesday crucifixion has another devastating problem. There are too many days between Jesus' crucifixion and his resurrection. Wednesday advocates are fond of saying, "You can't get three days and three nights into a Friday crucifixion and a Sunday resurrection." In fact, you can, as we will see in a later chapter. What you cannot do is limit to only three days and three nights in a Wednesday crucifixion to a Sunday resurrection. If Jesus literally rose "three days" from his crucifixion and burial on Wednesday, resurrection would be on the fourth day, not the third.

I don't want to nit-pick here, but if Joseph and Nicodemus hustled to get Jesus' body in the grave before sunset on the day he was crucified, exactly seventy-two hours later would also be before sunset. So if Jesus' body was placed in Joseph's tomb before 6:00 pm on Wednesday, the first twenty-four hours would be before 6:00 pm on Thursday, the second twenty-four hours before 6:00 pm on Friday, and the third twenty-four hours would be before 6:00 pm on Saturday. This not only negates a Sunday dawn resurrection, but it also negates a Saturday post-6:00 pm beginning of a Sunday resurrection.

Jesus said, "Destroy this temple, and in three days I will raise it up" (John 2:19). If Jesus' crucifixion took place from 9:00 am to 3:00 pm on Wednesday, and Thursday did not begin until after sunset that day, Wednesday would have to be counted as the first day as the ancients counted days.

According to the Jewish method of calculating days, the count would look like Table 7

Table 7: Jewish Time: Wednesday Crucifixion to Sunday Resurrection

Tuesday sunset to Wednesday sunset (1st day) (Crucifixion 9:00 am–3:00 pm Wednesday)	One day: Wednesday
Wednesday sunset to Thursday sunset (2nd day)	One day: Thursday
Thursday sunset to Friday sunset (3rd day)	One day: Friday
Friday sunset to Saturday sunset (4th day)	One day: Saturday
Saturday sunset to Sunday sunset (5th day)	One Portion of Sunday
Total: 5 days	

According to the Roman method of calculating days, the count would look like Table 8.

Table 8: Roman Time: Wednesday Crucifixion to Sunday Resurrection

According to Roman Time Calculation	
Wednesday sunrise to Wednesday sunset (1st day) (Crucifixion 9:00 am–3:00 pm Wednesday)	One day: Wednesday
Thursday sunrise to Thursday sunset (2nd day)	One day: Thursday
Friday sunrise to Friday sunset (3rd day)	One day: Friday
Saturday sunrise to Saturday sunset (4th day)	One day: Saturday
Sunday resurrection after Saturday sunset	
Total: 4 days	

Those who advocate for a Wednesday crucifixion are attempting to be honest with the Scriptures. But their calculations are consistently mired in the swamp of mathematics. In attempting to get things right, they begin their defense of a Wednesday crucifixion with a wrong conclusion.

It is evident that the most critical piece of information to Wednesday advocates is Matthew 12:40, "For just as Jonah was three days and three nights in the belly of the great fish, so will the Son of Man be three days and three nights in the heart of the earth." They simply cannot get past the idea that the twelve verses that say Jesus would rise on "the third day" carry less weight than this single verse. It appears as if Wednesday supporters have placed Matthew 12:40 as frontlets between their eyes (Exod 13:16; Deut 6:8; 11:18). They can see nothing else, and this is their downfall.

But worse, it appears to me that those who believe in a Wednesday crucifixion, having swallowed the three-day/three-night pill, began searching for supposed corroborating evidence to support their position. They needed the second Sabbath in Passion Week, so they divined one. No Gospel of the New Testament ever mentions this second Sabbath in the middle of Passion Week. None. There is no Jewish literature to corroborate a mid-week Sabbath. There is no evidence anywhere that a Passover occurred in the middle of Passion Week.

I have followed carefully all the charts, graphs, counting days backward, all the attempts to support a Wednesday crucifixion, each one more confusing and less convincing than the one before. I have found no historical proof for any of them. They remind me of Paul's admonition to Timothy to remain in Ephesus to help those who "promote speculations rather than the stewardship from God that is by faith" (1 Tim 1:4).

The issue of the Roman Guards at the tomb

The chief priests and the Pharisees were concerned that someone would steal Jesus' body from Joseph's tomb. They thought the most likely candidates were his disciples. If the disciples secretly removed Jesus' body from the tomb and hid it elsewhere, they could claim Jesus had risen from the dead just as he predicted.

Matthew records the Jewish leaders' request to Pilate to prevent this.

> The next day, that is, after the day of Preparation, the chief priests and the Pharisees gathered before Pilate and said, "Sir, we remember how that impostor said, while he was still alive, 'After three days I will rise.' Therefore order the tomb to be made secure until the third day, lest his disciples go and steal him away and tell the people, 'He has risen from the dead,' and the last fraud will be worse than the first." Pilate said to them, "You have a guard of soldiers. Go, make it as secure as you can." So they went and made the tomb secure by sealing the stone and setting a guard" (Matt 27:62–66).

Notice that the chief priests and Pharisees wanted the tomb guarded only until the third day because that is when the resurrection would occur, not on the fourth day! The timing is critical here. The watch at the tomb began on the day "after the day of Preparation," and continued until "the third day." If Wednesday were the day of the crucifixion, that evening after sunset would begin the "The next day, that is, after the day of Preparation." That would be Thursday, and that evening after sunset through Friday at sunset would be the second day. Friday at sunset to Saturday at sunset would then be "the third day." This reckoning would only provide security through Saturday, not Sunday.

Regardless of how you slice it, a Wednesday crucifixion does not fit the events' timing, as reported in the Gospels.

The issue of the walk to Emmaus

The day of Jesus' crucifixion was filled with activity, but the day of his resurrection was no less a flurry of activity. Jesus rose from the dead. An angel stationed himself at the empty tomb. The guards fled the scene in fear. The women came early to the tomb only to discover it empty. Peter and John were summoned. They, too, found the tomb empty. Jesus appeared to Mary Magdalene. Later in the day, Christ mysteriously entered the room where his followers were gathered.

But the activity of Resurrection Sunday was still not over. Luke 24:13 records, "That very day two of them were going to a village named Emmaus, about seven miles from Jerusalem." What follows is the account of Jesus encountering Cleopas and his friend on the road to Emmaus. We dare not miss the time reference Luke provides for us: "That very day." It was still Sunday, the day of Jesus' resurrection. It was a very long and eventful day for everyone involved.

Although God prohibited the two from recognizing Jesus, they did respond to his question about what was going on in Jerusalem. What was everyone talking about? Stunned that he would not know about the crucifixion just days before and Jesus' resurrection that very morning, they asked the Son of God, "Are you the only visitor to Jerusalem who does not know the things that have happened there in these days?" (Luke 24:18).

At this point, the two disciples, wearing their disappointment on their sleeves, poured out their hearts to Jesus. Jesus could hear the pathos in their voices when they bemoaned, "We had hoped that he was the one to redeem Israel. Yes, and besides all this, it is now the third day since these things happened" (Luke 24:21).

They were stunned, as were others of Jesus' followers when he died on the cross. This was no way for the Messiah to die. They were certain Jesus was the one they had awaited, and now their hopes were dashed. Equally as difficult to swallow was the fact that "it is now the third day since these things happened."

"The third day." Cleopas used an ordinal number—third. Sunday was the third day since Jesus was crucified. Friday the first day, the day on which the Savior died. Saturday the second day, when the Jewish religious leaders begged Pilate to provide security at Jesus' tomb. And now here we are on Sunday evening of the third day. When Cleopas spoke of Sunday being the third day since the crucifixion, he virtually eliminated the possibility that Jesus' death took place on Wednesday, or Thursday for that matter. Sunday will never be "the third day" from either Wednesday or Thursday, as the days were calculated in Jesus' time.

The issue of chapter division

Finally, if we accept the obvious, that the women came to the tomb at sunrise, how are we to understand the statement of Matthew 28:1, "Now after the Sabbath, toward the dawn of the first day of the week, Mary Magdalene and the other Mary went to see the tomb"? How should we especially comprehend the words, "Now after the Sabbath"? We will better understand those words if we remember that the New Testament text originally did not have chapter and verse divisions. The chapter divisions commonly used today were developed by the Archbishop of Canterbury Stephen Langton around 1227 AD. The Wycliffe English Bible of 1382 was the first Bible to use these chapter divisions. The chapter and verse numbers were not inspired by God, as was the text itself. There are not very many, but occasionally a division between verses or chapters seems a bit off. Matthew 28:1 is one such example.

Those who advocate for a Wednesday crucifixion need "Now after the Sabbath" to link to "toward the dawn" to claim that Jesus rose from the dead shortly after sunset on Saturday. Their interpretation is that "dawn" does not mean sunrise but the beginning hours of the Jewish day at sunset. But what if the chapter break was in an unfortunate place and changed the intent of Matthew?

Without changing a word of Scripture, just adjusting the placement of the words in what may be a more appropriate chapter and verse division, the phrase "Now after the Sabbath" becomes perfectly understood. "So they went and made the tomb secure by sealing the stone and setting a guard after the Sabbath. Toward the dawn of the first day of the week, Mary Magdalene and the other Mary went to see the tomb."

You see how the placement of words in context is important. The literal phrase "late on the Sabbath" belongs to the thoughts expressed in verse 66 of chapter 27, not in verse 1 of chapter 28. (The word "Now" in English does not appear in the Greek text: ὀψὲ σάββατον ἐπιφώσκω εἰς μία σάββατον). Change nothing in Scripture; change only the human chapter division, and any ambiguity completely disappears. A proper chapter division seriously weakens the Wednesday crucifixion argument.

Remember. The weekly Sabbath began at sunset on Friday evening and ended at sunset on Saturday evening. The chief priests and the Pharisees likely frittered all day on Saturday because they were concerned that someone would steal Jesus' body from Joseph's tomb. They wanted a guard set at the tomb, but they couldn't leave their houses to go to Pilate until after the Sabbath ended. "So they went and made the tomb secure by sealing the stone and setting a guard after the Sabbath" fits the timetable perfectly. Then, "Toward the dawn of the first day of the week, Mary Magdalene and the other Mary went to see the tomb." This also fits the timetable perfectly. No changes here, just common sense.

WHAT IF PASSOVER WAS ON THE SATURDAY OF PASSION WEEK?

The following passage is from the Babylonian Talmud. It's the text of a *Baraith* that stipulates that it was "On Passover Eve they hung the corpse of Jesus the Nazarene."[90] Baraith is the generic name for the teachings of the Mishnaic Period (10–220 AD) which were not included in the Mishnah. Note the author did not say "on the eve of the Sabbath" but "on Passover Eve." That is critical.

Passion Week is the most important week on the Jewish calendar. And yet, none of the four Gospel narratives ever mentions a second Passover Sabbath during that special week. We should ask why.

John 19:31 calls the Sabbath a "High" day. Nowhere does John imply that this was a second Sabbath day in the mid-week of Jesus' Passion. Nowhere. "Since it was the day of Preparation, and so that the bodies would not remain on the cross on the Sabbath (for that Sabbath was a High Day), the Jews asked Pilate that their legs might be broken and that they might be taken away." It was the day on which the paschal feast properly commenced. It was called a "High Day" because that year the Feast of the Passover began on the weekly Sabbath.

This 'High Day' Sabbath was a special day for several reasons. It was indeed the Sabbath day, which was the day sanctified by the LORD God to the LORD God. Besides, this was a special day because it was the first day of the Feast of Unleavened Bread (Exod 23:17). It was from this feast the Jews calculated the weeks to Pentecost. They had to get the "High Day" correct, or Pentecost would be celebrated on the wrong day.

Furthermore, this was a 'High Day,' a great day, an extraordinary day, because it was also the day for presenting and offering the sheaf of new corn (Lev 23:10–11). The Talmudists of the second and third centuries refer to this 'High Day' Sabbath as "the great day of the Sabbath" (Hebrew: נקרא שבת הגדול; 'the great Sabbath') on account of the miracle or sign of the Passover (*Piske Tosephot Sabbat*, art. 314). *Piske Tosephot Sabbat* is a collection of halakhic decisions gathered into thirty-six treatises. Tosafot (Hebrew: תּוֹסָפוֹת; literally "additions") are collections of comments written in the margins of the Talmud but extracted, arranged according to the order of the Talmudic tractates, and printed.

Also, Jewish Liturgy shows this was called a "great Sabbath" because the Jews exercised extreme caution so that day would not be polluted (*Seder Tephillot*, fol. 183. 2, etc. Ed. Basil). The Jews typically called the weekly Sabbath a "High Day" when it coincided with Passover, as it did during Jesus' Passion Week.

So this particular Sabbath was a day of tremendous solemnity and importance. This was not an extra Sabbath day in the Passion Week. The expression "high" or "great" describes the gravity of the Passover Sabbath day, which overlaps the normal day for the Sabbath of the Jews. It was special because it was like a theological, cosmological aligning of several Jewish super-significant days.

In light of the biblical text and the Talmudist's confirmation, we must conclude that the phrase "three days and three nights" (Matt 12:40) is simply an idiomatic expression and not meant to be a literal seventy-two-hour period. Neither the days of Jonah nor the days of Jesus in Joseph's tomb necessitate three complete twenty-four-hour periods.

The primary research interest of W. Graeme Waddington (D.Phil. in Astrophysics, Oxford University) is Solar Physics. But when Sir Colin Humphreys asked if he would be interested in calculating the date of Jesus' crucifixion by charting the new moons' sightings, Waddington jumped at the chance. He traced all the new moons back as far as the height of the Roman Empire. Humphreys said of his colleague's work, "Waddington checked the predictions of his calculations against 1,282 recorded observations of new moons, and they gave the correct answer every time." That's impressive![91]

Based on the crescent moon's earliest possible sightings (Nisan 1st), Waddington's calculation of that Nisan 14 in 30 AD falls on Friday, April 7th; in 33 AD it is Friday, April 3rd. The truth is that in both years 30 and 33 AD, the "first" day of unleavened bread" fell on the weekly Sabbath day, thus making a two Sabbath theory unnecessary.

If someone chooses to hold to a Wednesday crucifixion, they must do so in the face of a mountain of evidence to the contrary. A Wednesday crucifixion conflicts with almost the unanimous Christian tradition that has been maintained for twenty centuries. To believe Christ was crucified on

Wednesday is to understand what contemporary and past theologians and scholars, both liberal and conservative, have deemed untenable.

I am sympathetic with my fellow Christians who wish to place Jesus' death on the Wednesday of Passover Week. They are merely seeking to make sense of the facts they believe to be true. But I must disagree with what they believe to be facts and with the conclusions they draw from those supposed facts. From my investigation of their position, I find the case for a Wednesday crucifixion unconvincing. As a result, I can only conclude Jesus' death did not occur on Wednesday. We must continue our search for truth.

Chapter 5

The Case for a Thursday Crucifixion

If you hold to the Thursday theory of Jesus' burial, you get what the Friday theory cannot give you—three nights. But it forces you to count the days and nights in the Roman method of the first century.

THE CASE FOR A Wednesday crucifixion during Jesus' Passion Week is, in my view, untenable. It appears to be a constructed view to preserve "three days and three nights" as a literal seventy-two-hour period. If we rightly understand this idiomatic phrase as did Jesus, Pilate, Peter, and Paul, the underpinning of a Wednesday crucifixion evaporates.

Not so with the Thursday crucifixion theory. This view's evidence is much more robust, and the conclusions more reasonable than those for a Wednesday crucifixion. This is an attractive view for some Christians because it appears to answer many of the questions the Wednesday view could not. Yet, it advances some of the same arguments and faces many of the same issues as did the Wednesday crucifixion.

The Thursday view was advocated by the Greek scholar Brooke Foss Westcott. B. F. Westcott was a towering nineteenth-century British biblical scholar and theologian, he served as Bishop of Durham, England from 1890 until he died in 1901. Although it has not enjoyed widespread acceptance, its adherents are confident they have discovered a worthy resolution between the Wednesday and the Friday views of Jesus' crucifixion. The Bible does not explicitly state on which day of the week Jesus was crucified. The most widely held view is Friday. The Thursday view employs something of a synthesis of both the Friday and Wednesday arguments. Let's investigate them together.

THE ARGUMENT OF THREE DAYS AND THREE NIGHTS

The bedrock of the Thursday view is the same as the Wednesday view, namely the words of Jesus, "For just as Jonah was three days and three nights in the belly of the great fish, so will the Son of Man be three days and three nights in the heart of the earth" (Matt 12:40).

The Thursday view argues that there are simply too many events that occur between Christ's burial and Sunday morning for a Friday crucifixion. Some count as many as twenty; I count fourteen in Table 1. Advocates of this view claim the problem is compounded by the fact that the only full day between Friday and Sunday was Saturday, which, of course, was the Jewish Sabbath. Adding an extra day (the Thursday view) or two extra days (the Wednesday view) removes that issue, but do they solve the problem?

If you look carefully at the events in Table 1, you will note that some are just historical notes that do not require much elapsed time, e.g., Mark 15:43, "Pilate marveled that Jesus was already dead." Also, Luke 23:56 indicates that after they witnessed Joseph, Nicodemus, and servants roll the stone over the tomb entrance, the women "returned and prepared spices and ointments. On the Sabbath, they rested according to the commandment." The women were aware the Sabbath was fast approaching, and they did not want to profane the sacred day. Still, Luke reports they had time to return home and get the ointments and spices ready before the beginning of the Sabbath, a fact often overlooked in calculating the day of Jesus' crucifixion.

Thursday crucifixion supporters follow the same line of thinking as Wednesday supporters. In researching countless sources on this subject, I can't tell you how many times I've seen the phrase, "There is absolutely no way to get three days and three nights between Friday to Sunday." However, as we demonstrated in Chapter 1, not only is there a way, but it was also the ordinary, typical, everyday way of speaking about three days and three nights. Failure to accept what is historically proven to be normative is the largest stumbling block to understanding the hours between Jesus' death and his resurrection. Table 2 demonstrates how those who propose a Thursday crucifixion count the days from Friday to Sunday.

Table 1: Events Between Jesus' Death and Resurrection

Event	Scripture
Joseph asks Pilate for Jesus' body.	Matt 27:58; Mark 15:43; Luke 23:52;
Pilate marveled that Jesus was already dead.	Mark 15:43
The centurion confirms Jesus is dead.	Mark 15:44
Pilate releases Jesus' body.	Mark 15:45; John 19:38
Nicodemus brings 75 pounds of myrrh and aloes.	John 19:39
Joseph wraps Jesus' body in clean linen cloth.	Matt 27:59; John 19:40
Joseph lays Jesus' body in his new tomb.	Matt 27:60; Mark 15:46
A stone is rolled over the entrance.	Matt 27:60; Mark 15:46
The faithful women witness Jesus' burial.	Matt 27:61; Mark 15:47; Luke 23:55
Women returned home, prepared spices.	Luke 23:56
They all rested on the Sabbath day.	Luke 23:56
Jews remember Jesus' three-day prediction.	Matt 27:62–64
They ask Pilate to secure the tomb for three days.	Matt 27:64
Pilate charges the Temple Police not Roman soldiers to guard the tomb.	Matt 27:65

Table 2: Thursday's Three Days and Three Nights

Thursday's Three Days and Three Nights	
Night 1	Thursday sunset—Friday sunrise
Day 1	Friday sunrise—Friday sunset
Night 2	Friday sunset—Saturday sunrise
Day 2	Saturday sunrise—Saturday sunset
Night 3	Saturday sunset—Sunday sunrise
Day 3	Sunday sunrise—Resurrection

This calculation of days and nights assumes Jesus died and was buried before sunset on Thursday and rose from the dead after sunrise on Sunday. However, the Bible does not say this. The Scriptures only say that Mary Magdalene and the other women arrived at the tomb about daybreak on the Lord's Day. The fact is, we do not know the hour Jesus rose from the dead. The Gospels do not tell us. It could have been any time from one minute after the stone was rolled over the entrance of Joseph's tomb to one minute before Mary Magdalene and the other women arrived at the tomb on Sunday morning.

If you hold to the Thursday theory of Jesus' burial, you get what the Friday theory cannot give you—three nights. But it forces you to count the days and nights in the Roman method of the first century. If you count days and nights in the Jewish way, the periods will look like Table 3.

Table 3: Jewish Calculation: Thursday's Three Days and Three Nights

Night and Day 1	Thursday sunset—Friday sunset
Night and Day 2	Friday sunset—Saturday sunset
Night and Day 3	Saturday sunset—Sunday sunset

Already you can see a problem. Determining the days and nights as the Jews did by beginning the day at sunset and continuing to the next sunset, does not help the Thursday theory because we know Jesus rose before sunrise on Sunday, not Saturday sunset.

If you applied inclusive calculation to these days and nights, it would look like Table 4:

Table 4: Inclusive Calculation: Thursday's Three Days and Three Nights

Day 1	Daylight hours of Thursday (3:00—6:00 pm)
Night and Day 2	Thursday sunset—Friday sunset (24 hours)
Night and Day 3	Friday sunset—Saturday sunset (24 hours)
Night and Day 4	Saturday sunset—Sunday sunrise (12 hours)

Using the normal inclusive calculation, the Thursday crucifixion would be three nights but four days. This is why Thursday advocates reject inclusive calculation.

Why do people cling to three days and three nights?

Why do proponents of a Wednesday or Thursday crucifixion cling so fiercely to this one verse, Matthew 12:40? In the face of ten verses (twelve counting Acts 10:40 and 1 Cor 15:4) that claim Jesus rose "on the third day," why hold so tightly to this one? After years of research, I have come to just two conclusions. First, the "three days and three nights" is really all these two views have. It's the launching pad for their calculations. It's the sum and substance of their arguments. Everything else offered in favor of either view is either support or mere supposition. All other arguments are suppositions or they are a rearrangement of feasts and dates specifically to support Matthew 12:40. Advocates must cling to "three days and three nights," for without it, there is no case for anything but a Friday crucifixion.

But there must be a more spiritual reason than that, and I think there is. Advocates of the Wednesday or Thursday theories know these words came from the lips of Jesus himself. How can you deny the words of Jesus? No one should, and no one is. The problem is not with Jesus' words but with our understanding of his words. Yes, they are Jesus' words, and if they were the only words Jesus spoke concerning his death, burial, and resurrection, perhaps it would be case closed. But they are not. Any honest investigation must include consideration of Matthew 16:21; 17:22–23; 20:17–19; Luke 9:21–22; 13:32–33; 18:31–33; 24:5–7. Failure to do so is failure to be honest with 2 Timothy 3:16, 17.

Even the words in Luke 24:5–7 from one of God's angels corroborate Jesus' claim he would rise again on the third day. Beyond this, there are Peter's words in Acts 10:39–40, Paul's words in 1 Corinthians 15:3–4, Cleopas' words in Luke 24:21, and even Jesus' fiercest enemies' words in Matthew 27:62–64.

Suppose the "three days and three nights" argument is shown to be irrelevant to the question of Jesus' resurrection. In that case, advocates of a Thursday crucifixion are left with the two significantly lesser arguments we now investigate.

THE ARGUMENT OF SIX DAYS BEFORE PASSOVER

John 12:1 reports, "Six days before the Passover, Jesus therefore came to Bethany, where Lazarus was, whom Jesus had raised from the dead." This Passover would be Jesus' last, and he knew it. Jesus dined at the house of Lazarus, Martha, and Mary, his dear friends and followers. They lived in the village of Bethany on the Mount of Olives range just two miles (fifteen furlongs) from Jerusalem. Advocates of the Thursday crucifixion point out that if Jesus' crucifixion took place on Friday, which they believe also had to be Passover, Jesus' journey would have taken place on the Sabbath.

The Passover Calendar is much like the Christian Advent Calendar. With an Advent Calendar, you count down the days until Jesus' incarnation, his advent on Earth. With the Passover Calendar, you count down each day until Passover arrives. Like Christmas, Passover is not a fixed date on the calendar. According to the Thursday view, here's how the Passover Calendar would have looked that Passion Week.

From the perspective of a Thursday crucifixion, the meal Jesus ate at the house of Lazarus was on the night of Nisan 8, the night they arrived at Bethany. This night was the beginning of the weekly Sabbath. But after the end of the weekly Sabbath at sundown on Nisan 9, "they made him a supper and Martha served" (John 12:2).

The Sabbath travel ban

Traveling from Bethany to Jerusalem on the Sabbath would have been prohibited by the Mosaic Law (Exod 16:29). Nevertheless, there is some evidence the Israelites could travel a very short distance on the Sabbath. This would allow them to journey from their homes to the Tabernacle or later to the Temple, even if they lived outside Jerusalem's walls. This permission became known as a "Sabbath day's journey."

The Jews have always been masters at finding (or creating) loopholes in the Law, which would permit them more freedom while claiming they had fulfilled the Law of Moses. They have recalculated the distance of a Sabbath day's journey several times. In ancient days the priests determined a Jew could travel a fixed 2,000 cubits (approximately 3,000 feet) on the Sabbath from within the city boundaries.[92] They arbitrarily based this number on Joshua 3:4, which gave the distance the Jews had to stay away from the ark of the covenant. "Yet there shall be a distance between you and it, about 2,000 cubits in length. Do not come near it."

Over the centuries, the rabbis found ingenious ways to expand the Sabbath day's journey, giving travelers more flexibility. Eventually, they interpreted the word "place" in Exodus 16:29 "Remain each of you in his place; let no one go out of his place on the seventh day," to mean city so that it would be acceptable to travel 2,000 cubits outside the city limits on the Sabbath day. Later the Pharisees doubled the distance you could lawfully travel. They decided if you had your food stored at a location other than your home, that "place" figuratively became your home. You were permitted to travel there up to 2,000 cubits and then another 2,000 cubits back to your real home, which made the whole journey 4,000 cubits, about 6,000 feet or 1.13636 miles.

Table 5: Scenario One

						(Annual Passover)	
Nisan 8	Nisan 9	Nisan 10	Nisan 11	Nisan 12	Nisan 13	Nisan 14	Nisan 15
Friday	Saturday	Sunday	Monday	Tuesday	Wednesday	Thursday	Friday

Counting Backward Six Days to Jesus' Arrival at Bethany from Thursday, the Annual Passover, Being the First Day

6 pm >– 14 th –< 6 pm DAY 1

6 pm >–13th–< 6 pm DAY 2

6 pm >–12th–< 6 pm DAY 3

6 pm >–11th–< 6 pm DAY 4

6 pm >–10th–< 6 pm DAY 5

6 pm >–9th–< 6 pm DAY 6 Arrival day at Bethany the 9th (Saturday).

The Lamb selection was on the 10th (Sunday). The Triumphal Entry was on the 10th. The Crucifixion was on the 14th (Thursday). This configuration requires Jesus' journey to Jerusalem to be on the weekly Sabbath.

After Jesus ascended into heaven from the midst of his disciples, Acts 1:12 says, "Then they returned to Jerusalem from the mount called Olivet, which is near Jerusalem, a Sabbath day's journey away." So in the Roman first century, Jews understood that the distance they could legally travel on the Sabbath was from the city wall of Jerusalem to the top of the Mount of Olives. This means when Jesus and his disciples slept overnight in the Garden of Gethsemane on the side of the Mount of Olives, they were well within the law of Sabbath travel. It also means that the house of Lazarus and his sisters in Bethany was beyond the limitations of a Sabbath day's journey. Traveling from Jericho to Bethany or Bethany to Jerusalem on the Sabbath was legally out of the question for a devout Jew.

Remembering how the Jews calculated a day

It is critical to remember that in the Roman era during the late Second Temple Period, the Jews calculated a day as beginning the night before around twilight. Thus, the weekly Sabbath began Friday night as the day got dark and continued through the Saturday daylight hours until dark.[93] I know this has been mentioned several times already, but understanding this dimension of time is so important, if we miss it, we will be hopelessly off in our calculations of Jesus' death, burial, and resurrection.

In Deuteronomy 16:6 YHWH commanded, "You shall offer the Passover sacrifice, in the evening at sunset, at the time you came out of Egypt." Leviticus further defined the hour of the Passover sacrifice. "In the first month, on the fourteenth day of the month at twilight, is the Lord's Passover" (Lev 23:5–8). The word "twilight" (Hebrew: עֶרֶב; English: 'ereb) means "between the two evenings." It designates the time between the going down of the Sun and the appearance of the first three stars of the night.

"Six days before the Passover"

So what did John mean when he said, "Six days before the Passover, Jesus therefore came to Bethany"? If we count the day of the Passover itself to be the first of the six days, as indicated by Table 5, Scenario 1, our Lord came to Bethany on the Sabbath, the 9th of Nisan, when he ate with Lazarus and his sisters. The next day, Nisan 10, Jesus made his public entry into Jerusalem (John 12:12). This is the view of those who advocate for a Thursday crucifixion.

But when John said, "six days before the Passover," what if he meant the sixth day before the Passover, meaning there would be six whole days between Jesus' arrival at Bethany and the Passover? If this is what John intended, Jesus' arrival must be the day before the Jewish Sabbath. This would be more likely than Jesus traveling on the Sabbath.

If the 14th of Nisan were the day on which the Passover sacrifice was killed "between the two evenings," the 13th would be counted as the first day before the Passover, and the day before the sixth day separating Passover and Jesus' arrival at Bethany would be the 7th of Nisan. However, if the weekly Sabbath coincided with the Passover Sabbath, the day before the previous Sabbath would have been the 9th. Jesus would have arrived in Bethany at "the end of the Sabbath" which would have been about 7:03 pm Saturday. The feast would be on the following day.

Following these days and dates is difficult. Perhaps Table 6 will help.

But this also creates a problem. It means Jesus and those traveling with him journeyed up from Jericho on a Friday/Saturday, which would have been the time of the weekly Sabbath when no one could travel. It seems every time you solve one issue, you create another.

Counting the annual Passover as the first of the six days does not help. In the first scenario with a Friday annual Passover, everything favors a Thursday crucifixion, except this configuration places the Triumphal Entry on Monday instead of Sunday. "The next day the large crowd that had come to the feast heard that Jesus was coming to Jerusalem" (John 12:12).

The fourth scenario is equally problematic. Counting backward from a Saturday annual Passover places the lamb selection on the 10th of the month and the lamb slain on the 14th, Good Friday. This scenario has Jesus arriving at Bethany on Monday and the Triumphal Entry the next day, Tuesday, as in Table 8.

Sir Colin J. Humphreys has proposed an intriguing solution to the days of Passion Week. He added a midweek day for Jesus to complete the many activities that faced him. This removes the traditional Wednesday "day of silence" in which it was thought Jesus spent this midweek day resting at the house of Lazarus.[94]

Table 6: Scenario Two

Counting Backward from Saturday with Six Days Between the Annual Passover and Jesus' Arrival at Bethany								
								(Annual Passover)
Nisan 7	Nisan 8	Nisan 9	Nisan 10	Nisan 11	Nisan 12	Nisan 13	Nisan 14	Nisan 15
Friday	Saturday	Sunday	Monday	Tuesday	Wednesday	Thursday	Friday	Saturday
								6 pm >–15 th–< 6 pm DAY 1
							6 pm >–14 th–< 6 pm DAY 2	
						6 pm >–13 th–< 6 pm DAY 3		
					6 pm >–12 th–< 6 pm DAY 4			
				6 pm –11th–< 6 pm DAY 5				
			6 pm >–10th–< 6 pm DAY 6					
		6 pm >–9th–< 6 pm DAY 7						

6 pm >–8th–< 6 pm DAY 7 Arrival day with 6 days between Passover and Bethany. The lamb was selected on the 10th (Monday). The lamb was slain on the 14th (Good Friday). The Triumphal Entry was on Sunday the 9th placing Jesus' journey from Jericho to Jerusalem on the weekly Sabbath.

Table 7: Scenario Three

Counting Backward Six Days to Jesus' Arrival at Bethany from Friday, the Annual Passover, as the First Day
					(Annual Passover)	
Nisan 9	Nisan 10	Nisan 11	Nisan 12	Nisan 13	Nisan 14	Nisan 15
Saturday	Sunday	Monday	Tuesday	Wednesday	Thursday	Friday
						6 pm >– 15 th –< 6 pm DAY 1
					6 pm >– 14 th –< 6 pm DAY 2	
				6 pm >–13 th –< 6 pm DAY 3		
			6 pm >– 12 th –< 6 pm DAY 4			
		6 pm >–11th –< 6 pm DAY 5				
6 pm >–10th –< 6 pm DAY 6 Arrival day at Bethany on the 10th (Sunday). Lambselection on the 10th (Sunday). The Triumphal Entry was on the 11th (Monday); "the next day." The Crucifixion was on the 14th (Thursday).

Table 8: Scenario Four

Counting Backward Six Days to Jesus' Arrival at Bethany from the Annual Passover, as the First Day

					(Annual Passover)	
Nisan 9	Nisan 10	Nisan 11	Nisan 12	Nisan 13	Nisan 14	Nisan 15
Sunday	Monday	Tuesday	Wednesday	Thursday	Friday	Saturday
						6 pm >– 15 th –< 6 pm *DAY 1*
					6 pm >– 14 th –< 6 pm *DAY 2*	
				6 pm >– 13 th –< 6 pm *DAY 3*		
			6 pm >– 12 th –< 6 pm *DAY 4*			
		6 pm >– 11 th –< 6 pm *DAY 5*				
6 pm –10th –< 6 pm *DAY 6* Arrival day at Bethany on the 10th (Monday). The lamb selection was on the 10th (Monday). The Triumphal Entry was the 11th (Tuesday). The lamb was slain on the 14th (Good Friday).						

Table 9: Scenario Five

Counting Backward According to Humphreys with Six Days Between Saturday and Jesus' Arrival at Bethany

Nisan 7	Nisan 8	Nisan 9	Nisan 10	Nisan 11	Nisan 12	Nisan 13	Nisan 14 (Annual Passover)	Nisan 15
Friday	Saturday	Sunday	Monday	Tuesday	Wednesday	Thursday	Friday	Saturday

6 pm >–8 th –< 6 pm DAY 7. Jesus arrives at Bethany on the 8th (Saturday). Triumphal Entry is on the 9th (Sunday). The lamb was selected on the 10th (Monday) and was slain on the 14th (Good Friday). The day before the six days is Saturday which would place Jesus' journey from Jericho to Jerusalem on the weekly Sabbath.

6 pm >–9 th < 6 pm DAY 7

6 pm >–10th –< 6 pm DAY 6 Jesus curses the fig tree

6 pm >–11th –< 6 pm DAY 5 Other events of Passion Week

6 pm >–12 th –< 6 pm DAY 4 Events of Passion Week

6 pm >–13 th –< 6 pm DAY 3 The Last Supper

6 pm >–14 th –< 6 pm DAY 2 Early arrest of Jesus

6 pm >–15 th –< 6 pm DAY 1 Trial

What if the crucifixion took place on Thursday? This would certainly add the additional night needed to fulfill Jesus' "three days and three nights" prophecy. Still, it raises further problems, including counting partial days for either the crucifixion or the resurrection, but not for both. This use of inclusive calculation cannot be employed here but denied in the case of "three days and three nights" as advocates of a Thursday crucifixion tend to do. Such an inconsistency does not bode well for the Thursday view.

THE ARGUMENT OF THE WOMEN AT THE TOMB

In the Gospels, Mark declares, "And very early on the first day of the week, when the sun had risen, they went to the tomb" (Mark 16:2). Matthew says, "Now after the Sabbath, toward the dawn of the first day of the week, Mary Magdalene and the other Mary went to see the tomb" (Matt 28:1). Luke 24:1 concurs, as does John 20:1.

Three things upon which all four Gospel writers agree. First, it was the first day of the week when the women came to the tomb of Jesus. Second, it was very early in the morning, around dawn, on that day. Third, Jesus was not in the tomb; he had already risen from the dead by Sunday dawn.

When Matthew wrote that the women arrived "after the Sabbath" or as some translations have it, "in the end of the Sabbath," those who propose Jesus was crucified on Thursday understand this to mean the end of two Sabbaths—the High Holy Sabbath and the weekly Sabbath. As explored in Chapter 4, the argument is that the word Sabbath in Hebrew is plural (Greek: σαββάτων; English: *sabbatōn*). The word does indeed appear in the plural form, but only the context can determine its number, singular or plural. For Thursday advocates, it must be plural, but that cannot be proven. Interpretation of the text influences whether Sabbath is singular or plural. The double Sabbath during Passover Week supports the plural; the single Saturday Sabbath supports the singular, as does the possibility that the High Sabbath and the weekly Sabbath fell on the same day.

This begs the question of why the women waited until Sunday morning to return to the tomb. As noted in the last chapter, promoters of a Wednesday crucifixion reason that the Feast of Unleavened Bread would have begun at sundown, Thursday Nisan 15. The High Sabbath would have ended at sunset the following day, which would be the beginning of the nighttime hours of Friday (Nisan 16). When the Sun rose following those overnight hours, the women could have gone to the tomb on Friday during the daytime hours to anoint the Lord's body but did not. The weekly Sabbath would not have started until the next sundown, Saturday, Nisan 17. So why didn't the women go to the tomb during the daylight hours of Friday Nisan 16?

While Wednesday promoters struggle to answer this question, Thursday supporters have a ready answer. While Nicodemus brought a massive amount of myrrh and aloes to prepare the body of Jesus for burial, the women brought only ointments and spices to anoint the body (compare John 19:39–40 with Mark 16:1). With a Thursday crucifixion, the women could not go to the tomb on Friday because it was the High Day Sabbath of the Feast of Unleavened Bread. And they could not go on Saturday because it was the regular weekly Sabbath. The earliest day they could go to the tomb and anoint the body of Jesus was Sunday.

With the two-Sabbath view, if Christ was crucified on Thursday, the High Holy Sabbath (the Passover Sabbath) would have begun Thursday at sundown and ended at Friday sundown. This would place the end of the High-Day Sabbath up against the beginning of the weekly Saturday Sabbath. No room for shopping.

THE ARGUMENT OF "AFTER THREE DAYS"

A final argument for a Thursday crucifixion is one that not many Thursday advocates ever use. This is surprising because I believe it is their most persuasive argument. The question arises, did Jesus rise from the dead "in three days" or "after three days." The Gospels' authors use both phrases.

Here are the eight verses in question.

- John 2:18–21, "So the Jews said to him, 'What sign do you show us for doing these things?' Jesus answered them, 'Destroy this temple, and in (ἐν; English: *en*) three days I will raise it up.' The Jews then said, 'It has taken forty-six years to build this temple, and will you raise it up in (Greek: ἐν) three days?' But he was speaking about the temple of his body."

- Mark 8:31, "And he began to teach them that the Son of Man must suffer many things and be rejected by the elders and the chief priests and the scribes and be killed, and after (Greek: μετὰ; English: *meta*) three days rise again."

- Mark 14:57–58, "And some stood up and bore false witness against him, saying, 'We heard him say, "I will destroy this temple that is made with hands and in (Greek: διὰ English: *dia*) three days I will build another, not made with hands."'" In the original language, verse 58 says "within three days" using *dia*, meaning through, within, or among.

- Matthew 27:39–40, "And those who passed by derided him, wagging their heads and saying, 'You who would destroy the temple and rebuild it in (Greek: ἐν; English: *en*) three days,' save yourself! If you are the Son of God, come down from the cross."
- Matthew 27:63, "The next day, that is, after the day of Preparation, the chief priests and the Pharisees gathered before Pilate and said, 'Sir, we remember how that impostor said, while he was still alive, "After (Greek: μετὰ; English: *meta*) three days I will rise."'"
- Matthew 29:59–61, "Now the chief priests and the whole council were seeking false testimony against Jesus that they might put him to death, but they found none, though many false witnesses came forward. At last two came forward and said, 'This man said, "I am able to destroy the temple of God, and to rebuild it in (Greek: μετὰ; English: *meta*) three days."'"

There are even verses in the Gospels where the word *meta* is translated both as "after" and "with." John 3:22 says, "After (μετὰ) this Jesus and his disciples went into the Judean countryside, and he remained there with (μετὰ) them and was baptizing" (see also in Greek: Matt 25:19; Luke 22:20–21; Luke 22:58–59; and John 20:26). Unmistakably, the first usage is a time reference, while the second refers to an accompanying presence.

What do we learn about the use of this word by comparing Scripture with Scripture? Used frequently in the Gospels, the preposition *metá* occurs in Greek 247 times in the four Gospels (Matthew: seventy-one times; Mark: fifty-four times; Luke: sixty-four times; John: fifty-eight times). It is equally evident it can mean either "with" or "after." The only way to determine which translation is appropriate is the context of the passage itself.

If you examine the verses in Table 10 carefully, you will see that "with" is used when speaking about someone's accompanying presence with others, and "after" is used as a time reference. For John, *metá* was a favorite transitional time word. He used it as the first word at the beginning of chapters 5, 6, and 7.

This inevitably led to the conclusion that in Passion Week's verses referring to time, *metá* must always be understood as meaning "after." If Jesus rose from the dead after three days, with a Thursday crucifixion, day one would be Thursday into Friday, day two would be Friday into Saturday, and day three would be Saturday into Sunday—"after three days."

Proponents of a Thursday crucifixion believe this requires three days to be fulfilled. If Jesus rose "after" three days, a Friday does not provide those three days. But this is just another wrinkle on insisting that "three days and three nights" must be literal twenty-four-hour days. Inclusive calculation also permits "after" three days to be applied. Thus the impact of Jesus' resurrection taking place "after" three days is certainly diminished.

Table 10: "With" and "After" in the Gospels

Scripture	Word	Citation
Matt 1:23	with	"God *with* us."
Matt 12:30	with	"Whoever is not *with* me is against me . . ."
Matt 17:1	with	" Jesus took *with* him Peter and James, and John . . ."
Matt 24:29	after	"Immediately *after* the tribulation of those days . . ."
Matt 26:23	with	"He who has dipped in the dish *with* me will betray me . . ."
Matt 27:34	with	"They offered him wine to drink, mixed *with* gall, . . ."
Matt 27:62	after	"The next day, that is, *after* the day of Preparation, . . ."
Matt 28:19,20	with	"I am *with* you always, to the end of the age."
Mark 1:14	after	"Now *after* John was arrested, Jesus came into Galilee . . ."
Mark 2:16	with	"Why does he eat *with* tax collectors and sinners? . . ."
Mark 8:38	with	"He comes in the glory of his Father *with* the holy angels."
Mark 14:14	with	"I may eat the Passover *with* my disciples?"
Mark 14:28	after	" But *after* I am raised up, I will go before you to Galilee."
Mark 15:31	with	"The chief priests *with* the scribes mocked him."
Marl 16:12	after	"*After* these things, he appeared in another form to two of them."
Luke 1:28	with	"Greetings, O favored one, the Lord is *with* you!"
Luke 2:46	after	"*After* three days they found him in the temple."
Luke 8:13	with	"When they hear the word, receive it *with* joy."
Luke 10:1	after	"*After* this, the Lord appointed seventy-two . . ."
Luke 12:13	with	"Teacher, tell my brother to divide the inheritance *with* me."
Luke 15:29–31	with	" 'Son, you are always *with* me . . .' "
Luke 23:43	with	"Today you will be *with* me in paradise."
John 3:2	with	"No one can do these signs . . . unless God is *with* him."
John 8:29	with	"And he who sent me is *with* me."
John 12:8	with	"For the poor you always have *with* you."
John 13:27	after	"Then *after* he had taken the morsel, Satan entered into him."
John 14:16	with	"He will give you another Helper, to be *with* you forever"
John 19:18	with	"There they crucified him, and *with* him two others."
John 19:28	after	"*After* this, Jesus . . . said, 'I thirst.'"
John 19:38	after	" *After* these things Joseph of Arimathea . . ."

Table 11: Scenario Six

Three Days and Three Nights—Thursday to Sunday			
	(Passover High Sabbath)	(Weekly Sabbath)	
Nisan 14	Nisan 15	Nisan 16	Nisan 17
Thursday	Friday	Saturday	Sunday
Day 1: Daylight to Sunset.			
	Day 2: Sunset >- Night 1 -> Sunset: "High Day" Sabbath		
		Day 3: Sunset >- Night 2 -> Sunset: *Weekly Sabbath*	
			Day 4: Sunset >-Night 3-<Sunrise: Resurrection

Thursday proponents also claim that at the very moment Jesus hung his head and died, the veil of the Temple was ripped in two. Since this event rendered useless the old Holy of Holies, it is the perfect antitype of pulling down the old religious system and the physical need for a priest to approach God to forgive our sins. We now may come boldly to his throne of grace with a contrite heart and receive the pardon we so desperately need (Heb 4:16; Ps 51:17).

Those who champion a Thursday crucifixion understand that when Jesus majestically rode into Jerusalem on the foal of a donkey, he was fulfilling a prophecy of Zechariah 9:9. But these claims are not unique to those who believe Jesus was crucified on Thursday. They also apply to those who hold to a Wednesday or a Friday crucifixion.

The Thursday view has much to commend it. However, it is not without problems, some of which are explored here.

THE ARGUMENT FROM THE CALENDAR

By Jewish reckoning, adherents to the Thursday crucifixion view assign as Day 1 the yet-daylight portion of Thursday, Nisan 14 called "evening" when Jesus was entombed (Matt 27:57; Mark 15:42). Nisan 15 began at sunset Thursday and was the beginning of three nights. Nisan 15 was also the first day of the Feast of Unleavened Bread when the Passover meal was eaten. No work was allowed on the first and seventh days of this feast. Hence Nisan 15 was a special Sabbath known as a "High Day" (John 19:31).

Friday began Day 2 with sunset on Thursday night and continued to sunset on Friday evening. Nisan 16 began the regular weekly Sabbath at Friday sunset. This would mean there were two Sabbaths back-to-back, Nisan 15 and 16 in the Thursday theory. Night 2 started Friday evening and lasted until Saturday dawn.

Day 3 was Saturday (the weekly Sabbath) during the daylight hours. The first day of the Jewish week began Nisan 17 at Saturday sunset and was Night 3. Jesus was raised from the dead sometime during this third night but before sunrise on Sunday morning.

Here's how that would look on a Jewish calendar.

PROBLEMS WITH A THURSDAY CRUCIFIXION

If you hold to the Thursday theory of Jesus' burial, you get what the Friday theory cannot give you—three nights. But it forces you to count the days and nights by the Roman method of the first century. Each calculation of the day Jesus Christ died has some positive points and some negative points. Just when you think you have solved all the issues, someone points out another one. Therefore we must examine the issues that cause misgiving about the Thursday crucifixion just as we did with the Wednesday view.

The matter of too many days in seventy-two hours

One of the most suspect details of a Thursday crucifixion is you cannot hold to a Thursday crucifixion and seventy-two hours in the grave at the same time. Thursday adherents do; in fact, this is one of the most persuasive arguments in their minds. But let's do the math.

From Table 12 illustrating the Thursday scenario, take note that Thursday adherents count the "evening" (Mark 15:42–43) on Thursday as day one in his three days and three-night ordeal. That would be the remaining hours of sunlight after Jesus' crucifixion on Thursday. But this is faulty for two reasons.

First, it uses inclusive calculation, which all non-Friday crucifixion adherents claim they reject. Still, when it is needed to make their case, it is used without question. But second, if Jesus was placed in the tomb before 7:03 pm on that Preparation Day, and was in the grave a full seventy-two hours, he cannot have risen just after sunset on Saturday evening, during the first hours of Sunday. Again, it's a matter of simple math. Let's use 7:03 as the supposed time of his burial as it is the astronomical moment of twilight in each potential Passover Week.

Table 12: Thursday Through Sunday Night

Thursday Through Sunday Night Using Inclusive Calculation	
Day and Time of Day	Comments
Thursday, Day 1: between 3:00 and 7:03 pm	Joseph seeks Pilate's permission to bury Jesus; Jesus is buried before sunset.
Friday, Night 1 & Day 2: At 7:03 pm	Jesus has now spent a full 24 hours in the tomb.
Saturday, Night 2 & Day 3: At 7:03 pm	Jesus has now spent 48 hours in the tomb.
Sunday, Night 3 & Day 4: At 7:03 pm	Jesus has now spent 72 hours in the tomb but is 11 hours late for his resurrection.

The Thursday view of Jesus' crucifixion does accommodate seventy-two complete hours, which the Friday view does not, but again, there is a problem with the math. If Jesus remained in the tomb for seventy-two hours beginning sometime before sunset on Thursday, he could not have arisen from the grave any earlier than late Sunday evening, before sunset. If he arose before or after that, it would not be a literal seventy-two hours.

The Friday view is disparaged because "there's no way you can get seventy-two hours between Friday and Sunday." But is not that also true of the Thursday view?

Count with me. Thursday sunset to Friday sunset equals twenty-four hours. Friday sunset to Saturday sunset equals twenty-four hours. Saturday sunset to 6:00 am Sunday morning is eleven hours. The number of hours between 7:03 pm Thursday and 6:00 am Sunday equals fifty-nine not seventy-two. And if you wait for the full seventy-two hours, Jesus would not have risen until after sunset on Sunday night. No one believes that to be true. This is a significant mathematical setback for the Thursday crucifixion view.

The Issue of the back-to-back Sabbaths

Those who advocate for a Wednesday crucifixion maintain there were two Sabbaths in the Passion Week. Wednesday promoters believe that the first Sabbath that week, which they understand as a Passover Sabbath (see Lev 16:29–31; 23:24–31, 39), fell on a Thursday. Those who promote a Thursday crucifixion also understand there were two Sabbaths that week. They believe the first one, the High-Day Sabbath, was on Friday, followed by the regular weekly Sabbath on Saturday.

Both Wednesday and Thursday advocates base this on their interpretation that the word Sabbath is plural in number in the crucifixion narratives. We have already sufficiently explored that only the context can determine if this is a singular or plural noun.

Matthew sets some time markers that help us know the timing of the crucifixion. Read Matthew 27:17—28:7. Here are the time markers in this passage with no interruptions of other verses.

> When it was evening, there came a rich man from Arimathea, named Joseph, who also was a disciple of Jesus. He went to Pilate and asked for the body of Jesus . . . The next day, that is, after the day of Preparation, the chief priests and the Pharisees gathered before Pilate and said . . . Therefore order the tomb to be made secure until the third day . . . Now after the Sabbath, toward the dawn of the first day of the week, Mary Magdalene and the other Mary went to see the tomb.

Do you see any need for another Sabbath in the straightforward narrative? Does Matthew give us any reason to think that the Preparation Day (Friday) was also a High Day? Joseph asked Pilate for permission to bury Jesus' body at the end of the day on which Christ was crucified. Matthew indicates it was "the next day, that is, after the day of Preparation" that the chief priests were so concerned Jesus' disciples would steal his body they asked Pilate to place Roman guards at the tomb.

The very next words in the text are, "Now after the Sabbath, toward the dawn of the first day of the week." Does not this give us enough information to make a reasonable determination that Jesus' crucifixion took place on Friday! The guards were added to the tomb on Saturday. The women came to the tomb on the third day, which was Sunday, the first day of the week. If there wasn't that street hump of Matthew 12:40 to get over, if you didn't need to get seventy-two hours into the mix, everything would fit perfectly as presented in the Gospels.

Could there have been back-to-back Sabbaths? Yes, there could have been. The first day of the Feast of Unleavened Bread was treated as a Sabbath, as was the last day of this feast (John 19:31)

Now, follow carefully. The day of Preparation was always the day before the Sabbath. The Sabbath of the Passion Week was a High Day meaning a special Sabbath because of Passover. The Jews asked Pilate to break the legs of the crucifixion victims on the day of Preparation, so they would not remain on the cross and violate the Sabbath, particularly since that Sabbath was a High Day.

Is there anything in the texts of the Gospels to indicate they were not talking about the weekly Saturday Sabbath? I find nothing. Is it possible that the regular Saturday Sabbath was also the High Day Sabbath of the Passover? It is absolutely possible.

Scripture makes no direct mention of two consecutive Sabbath days in any of the Gospel narratives. It makes no explicit mention of two Sabbaths at all. So why do advocates of a Wednesday or a Thursday crucifixion endorse a double Sabbath, separate from the High Day falling on the weekly Sabbath? It's done out of necessity. And what is that necessity? It's their intrinsic need to fit three full days and three full nights, a literal seventy-two hours, into the Passion Week between Jesus' crucifixion and his resurrection. That is the keystone of the two Sabbath arguments. Take away that stone, and the building begins to crumble.

THE ISSUE OF THE "DAY OF PREPARATION"

John (John 19:31-33) and the other Gospel authors make it clear that the day of Preparation was the day just before the weekly Sabbath. Since it is mentioned six times in the Gospels, it is evident that the "Preparation" (Greek: παρασκευή; English: *paraskeuē*) for the Sabbath was an important day. John 19:14 cements the claim that Jesus was crucified on the Preparation for the Sabbath. "Now it was the day of Preparation of the Passover. It was about the sixth hour. He [Pilate] said to the Jews, 'Behold your King!'"

Luke 23:54 mentions the preparation day was just as Jesus was being removed from the cross and prepared for burial. Mark 15:42 refers to the same event. Even though the Preparation was a normal part of the Sabbath ritual, take note that it is mentioned in the New Testament only in connection with the crucifixion of Jesus (Matt 27:62, Mark 15:42, Luke 23:54, John 19:14, 19:31, and 19:42). The day of Preparation faded into the beginning of the Sabbath. What is clear, however, is that Jesus Christ died the day before the Sabbath, on the day of Preparation.

Why the Preparation was important

This day of Preparation was crucial to the Jewish people because of the Sabbath restriction in Exodus 16:22-23 and elsewhere. Later, Moses "assembled all the congregation of the people of Israel" and repeated the commandment of the LORD that everything for the weekly Sabbath was to be prepared the day before (Exod 35:1-3). No preparations, no cooking, no housekeeping, nothing could be done on the day wholly dedicated to the LORD.

But here is an important note regarding the Preparation day. In the Bible, only the sixth day of the week is defined as the Preparation day (Exod 16:5), and it is preparation for the seventh-day Sabbath. Nowhere in God's Word is the day of Preparation associated with the day preceding a yearly festival Sabbath. In the Holy Scriptures, the term "Preparation day" or "day of Preparation" always means the day we call Friday. Always!

As before noted, from Judaism's earliest years, all the days of the Jewish week were numbered not named, except for the Sabbath. They were, and still are, called the first day, the second day, and so on unto the seventh, which is not the seventh day, but the Sabbath. On our Friday, the sixth day was called 'the eve of the Sabbath' or "the day of preparation" both in the New Testament and by extra-biblical sources.

Another important note is this. In Leviticus 23, there is an essential but often overlooked distinction between the seventh-day Sabbath and the first day of Unleavened Bread. Regarding the weekly Sabbath, absolutely no work of any kind was permitted on the seventh-day Sabbath (Lev 23:3).

But the nuance is different in Leviticus 23:7 when speaking about the Passover. God commanded, "On the first day you shall have a holy convocation; you shall not do any ordinary work." The words "ordinary work" mean "servile work" (Hebrew: עֲבֹדָה; English: *'ăbôdâh*). In the NIV and RSV, they are "laborious work." They mean work outside the house, work on the job, laboring, farming, etc. This is the kind of work you do for an employer, the kind of work that earns you wages.

The difference is subtle, but it is there. On the weekly Sabbath, everything in a Jewish household shut down. No work was done around the house or out of the house. On the Sabbaths associated with the Jewish feasts, it appears that only labor as employment was prohibited.

How the day of Preparation impacts the day of Jesus' crucifixion

Since all work was banned, burial could not happen on a seventh-day Sabbath. If this is what was meant by the Gospel writers, the "no work" rule on the weekly Sabbath was why the Jews wanted the crucified men to be taken down from their crosses before sunset. Although the High Day Sabbath coincided with the weekly Sabbath at the end of Passion Week, it was the weekly Sabbath that caused Joseph to seek Pilate's permission to bury Jesus' body before sunset.

The twelfth-century Sephardic Jewish philosopher Maimonides was the most prolific and influential Torah scholar of the Middle Ages. In the *Hilchot Yom Tob* (Law of the Holidays), he gave this account of the matter. "On a common day they 'prepare' for the Sabbath, and on a common day they prepare for a feast day; but they do not prepare on a feast day for the Sabbath, nor is the Sabbath, מכינה, 'a preparation' for a feast day" (*Hilchot Yom Tob*, 1.19).

Preparation of meals, housekeeping, and other chores determined to be "work" by Jewish law were difficult enough for one day before a Sabbath, let alone two days, back-to-back, as the Thursday view demands. In fact, the Jewish priesthood would deliberately delay the new moon's declaration (*Kiddush Hachodesh*) by one day to prevent the inconvenience of back-to-back Sabbaths. This practice continues today and argues strongly against a Thursday crucifixion.

The understanding of timing

I mentioned that in my opinion, this is the strongest argument for a Thursday crucifixion. But it is only strong in comparison with the other arguments. It is not so strong as a standalone argument.

First, some of the verses in which *metá* (see Table 13 below) appears that are usually translated "after" are not time-specific. In Mark 14:28, for example, Jesus said, "But after I am raised up, I will go before you to Galilee." Jesus was saying, "I am going to be crucified. I will be laid in a grave. And when I have been raised from the dead, I will go to Galilee. Meet me there." There is a lack of specificity.

The same is true in many Greek texts (see Matt 1:12; 26:32, 73; Mark 1:14; 13:24; 14:70; 16:12, 19; Luke 1:24; 5:27; 10:1; 12:4-5; Luke 15:3; 17:8; 18:4; 22:20, 58; John 2:12; 5:1, 4, 14; 6:1; 7:1; 11:7, 11; 13:7, 27; 19:28, 38; 21:1). In fact, the only Greek texts in which more specificity is found are Matt 17:1; 24:29; 25:19; 26:2; 27:53, 62, 63; Mark 8:32; 9:2; Luke 2:46; 9:28; John 4:43; 20:26.

Second, many times *metá* is found when the Gospel author is specific, but there is still no critical time reference. For example, "And after six days Jesus took with him Peter and James, and John, his brother, and led them up a high mountain by themselves" (Matt 17:8; Mark 9:2; Luke 9:28). This was a very significant event, both in the life of Jesus and especially in the lives of his three top disciples. But what is the significance of the six days? Apparently none. It is just a detail the author included. The fact that it was six days later is no more impactful on the transfiguration than had it been three days later.

Table 13: "After," "In," and "Through"

Word in Greek	Word in English	Scriptures
μετά	After	Matt 27:63; Mark 8:31; 9:31; 10:34
διά	n, through	Matt 26:61; Mark 14:5
ἐν	In	Matt 27:40; Mark 15:29; John 2:19-20

Third, when the chief priests and Pharisees went to Pilate and recounted what Jesus said 'After three days I will rise," they immediately requested, "Therefore order the tomb to be made secure until the third day." (Matt 27:64). Their understanding of Jesus' "after three days" appears to be until "the third day."

The issue of the Firstfruits

The proposed chronology with a Thursday crucifixion suffers from several problems, not the least of which is that Firstfruits must occur on Sunday. However, it does not if Jesus was crucified on Thursday, 14 Nisan.

Remember, Jesus was tried in the early morning on the day he was crucified, he was placed on the cross around 9:00 am. There was darkness from noon to 3:00 pm He committed his spirit to the Heavenly Father around 3:00 pm In the Thursday view, all this was accomplished on 14 Nisan. But if Jesus rose from the dead on the third day and Thursday Nisan 14 was the first day of his Passion, the third day would be Nisan 16, but it would not be a Sunday. It would be Saturday—another problem with a Thursday calendar.

Table 14: Nisan 14—17

Nisan 14—17			
Thursday	Friday	Saturday	Sunday
14 Nisan	15 Nisan	16 Nisan	17 Nisan

Thursday Crucifixion and Sunday Firstfruits

Firstfruits was a Jewish feast held in the early spring at the very beginning of the barley harvest. It was always observed on Nisan 16. Bringing the first of your harvest as an offering to God was a way of tangibly thanking him for the land, for seasonal rainfall, and for his gracious provision of a good grain harvest.

In Ancient Israel, firstfruits, or the "wave offering" (Hebrew: רֵאשִׁית; English: *rê'shîyth*) as it was often called, was that portion of the harvest selected first and set apart from the rest of the harvest. It was the symbolic act where the priests physically waved the first portion of the harvest in the air, indicating that this was an offering to the Lord. The festival is derived from the word (Hebrew רוּם; English *rûwm*) meaning "to lift." In Jewish literature, the festival of Firstfruits is discussed in the *Bikkurim* tractate of the Talmud as a sacrificial gift brought to the altar (*Bikkurim* 3:12). The obligation to bring the first fruits of your harvest to the Temple began with the festival of Shavuot and continued until the festival of Sukkot (*Bikkurim* 1:6). God established Firstfruits as recorded in Leviticus 23:9–14.

Some irrefutable facts can be extracted from these verses.

- God provided the harvest for his people, Israel.
- Israel was to bring a bundle of that harvest to the priest in the Tabernacle or Temple.
- Israel was forbidden to eat anything from the annual harvest until this offering was first made to God.
- The priest would lift that bundle high and wave it as a token of thanks to the LORD.
- God would only accept Israel if the wave offering was first presented to him.
- The priest was to wave the offering to God on the day after the Sabbath.
- On the same day, Israel was to offer a yearling male lamb without blemish as a burnt offering.
- A grain offering was to be made of twenty percent of an ephah of finely ground flour mixed with oil.
- A drink offering was also to be made of a hin of wine (a liquid measure equal to about eight quarts).
- Firstfruits (the wave offering) was to be a statute forever.

For our purposes, from Leviticus 23, we must glean at least two facts: first, the wave offering was always the day after the Sabbath, and second, Firstfruits was to be observed forever, throughout all generations.

For the Christian, Firstfruits has an even greater meaning. The Apostle Paul used the Jewish Firstfruits as a symbol of Jesus' resurrection from the dead. Firstfruits was God's promise that, while Jesus was the first of a kind in his resurrection, he would not be the last. Just as more of the harvest would follow the wave offering, more followers of the Lord Jesus would rise from the dead, just as he did. For Christians, the Firstfruits offering found its fulfillment in Jesus Christ. "But in fact Christ has been raised from the dead, the Firstfruits of those who have fallen asleep" (1 Cor 15:20).

Jesus' resurrection paved the way for our resurrection. Significantly, if Jesus had been crucified at Passover, his resurrection on the third day would have fallen on Nisan 16—the Feast of Firstfruits. While the Passover Lamb atoned for our sins, the Firstfruits anchored the promise of our eternity. The Passion weekend was extremely relevant for those with faith in Christ!

The proposed chronology with a Thursday crucifixion fails to make Firstfruits on Sunday, which does not square with the Jewish calendar in which Firstfruits is always Sunday. This appears to be a significant problem for this position.

Table 15: Scenario Seven

Counting Backward Six Days to Jesus' Arrival at Bethany from Thursday, the Annual Passover, Being the First Day						
					(Annual Passover)	
Nisan 8	Nisan 9	Nisan 10	Nisan 11	Nisan 12	Nisan 13	Nisan 14	Nisan 15
Friday	Saturday	Sunday	Monday	Tuesday	Wednesday	Thursday	Friday
						6 pm >–14th–< 6 pm DAY 1
					6 pm >–13th–< 6 pm DAY 2	
				6 pm >–12th–< 6 pm DAY 3		
			6 pm >–11th–< 6 pm DAY 4			
		6 pm >–10th–< 6 pm DAY 5				
6 pm >–9th–< 6 pm DAY 6 Arrival day at Bethany the 9th (Saturday). Lamb selection was on the 10th (Sunday). Crucifixion was on the 14th (Thursday). The Triumphal Entry was on the 10th (Sunday). This requires Jesus' journey from Jericho to Jerusalem to be on the weekly Sabbath.							

The issue of travel on the Sabbath

Those who advocate for a Thursday crucifixion of Jesus of Nazareth encounter another difficulty with the 10th of Nisan. If Nisan 14 was the annual Passover and also the day Jesus was crucified, and if Nisan 14 was on a Thursday, Nisan 10 had to be on a Sunday. It would have begun at the sighting of the first three stars on Saturday night and continued through the night, all the next day until sunset on Sunday night. Again, in the Jewish calendar, while the day began after sunset the evening before, all the daylight hours were during the second half of that day, which from our modern perspective would have been the next day.

The problem here is Jesus and his company would have arrived at the house of Lazarus, Martha, and Mary in Bethany on the 9th of Nisan. The next morning (Nisan 10) was the Triumphal Entry into Jerusalem. With this scenario, however, Jesus and his company would have had to travel from Jericho up to Jerusalem on Nisan 9, which began when the first three stars appeared at sunset on Nisan 8 and continued through the night and all the next day (Nisan 9). But Nisan 9, according to the Thursday crucifixion view, was a Saturday. That meant Jesus and those who traveled with him made the journey from Jericho to Jerusalem on the weekly Sabbath day. This would have put them far outside a Sabbath Day's journey (see above).

To be fair, travel on the Sabbath seems to be a problem for scenarios one, two, and five. In scenario one, Jesus and those accompanying him would have journeyed from Jericho to Bethany on Saturday, Nisan 9, thus breaking the Sabbath ban on travel. This would also be true of scenario five. In scenario two, there are two days unaccounted for between Jesus' arrival at Bethany and his Triumphal Entry on Sunday morning. If Jesus arrived on Nisan 7, what did he do all day on Friday, Nisan 8? In none of the Gospels is this extra day mentioned or even hinted at.

In comparison to the other arguments in favor of a Thursday crucifixion, this one may seem the most persuasive, but when examined more closely, its strength dissipates.

While those who hold to a Thursday crucifixion do so passionately, some of their reasoning is faulty, and most of their arguments can easily be answered. I find the Thursday position a great deal more appealing than the Wednesday theory, but not so appealing that it unseats the traditional Friday crucifixion, which we must now investigate.

Chapter 6

The Case for a Friday Crucifixion

In the Gospels, Jesus referred to his crucifixion and resurrection in cardinal numbers only one time—Matthew 12:40. However, he referred to these events in ordinal numbers ten times: Matthew 16:21; 17:23; 20:19; Luke 9:22; 13:32–33; 18:33; 24:7, 21, 46. At the very least, that should tell us something.

THAT THE CRUCIFIXION OF Jesus of Nazareth occurred on the traditional Good Friday is held by the vast majority of Christians, certainly by the vast majority of scholars. I have made no effort to hide that I believe it is the most defensible of the three views of the day Jesus died. Those who propose a Wednesday or Thursday crucifixion are passionate about defending their position. They should be. If they have searched the Scriptures and have concluded that Jesus could not have been crucified on Friday because "there is no way you can get three days and three nights between Friday and Sunday," at least they have searched the Scriptures. This is more than many who hold to a Friday crucifixion have done.

I am not a traditionalist in one sense of the word. Just because my parents and grandparents celebrated Good Friday doesn't mean I have to. Just because the traditions of the church have concluded that Jesus was crucified on Friday doesn't mean I must come to that same conclusion. But if the facts indicate Friday was the day of Jesus' crucifixion, I am compelled to follow them, just as any honest person would.

In this chapter, I will not appeal to tradition. I will appeal to the Gospel narratives and confirmed history. That being said, we must honestly ask, "What do we find in the Bible that would lead a person to conclude that Jesus was crucified on a Friday? What are the arguments advocated by those who hold to a Friday crucifixion?" Let's explore together.

THE ARGUMENT OF LITERARY SOURCES

We who live in the twenty-first century are not the first to wonder about the day of Jesus' death. Saints and sinners have discussed this issue for millennia. Throughout those generations, the position that Jesus was crucified on Friday and raised on Sunday morning has become the acknowledged opinion, accepted by all but a few. The literary sources in support of this view are many and varied. This list represents a selection from multiple periods of early church history.

Christian Authors

It is important to know what Christ-followers in history have understood about the day Jesus died. They often represent Christian tradition and give us insight into what those who have gone before us held as truth. So, before we investigate secular authors, here is what two key players in the history of the church believed about the day of Jesus' crucifixion.

Ignatius of Antioch

Ignatius of Antioch, the third bishop of the Christian church in Antioch, is recognized as an Ante-Nicene Father.[95] He lived from approximately 30/35 AD through 107/108 AD, which makes him a near-contemporary of the Gospels authors.

In his *Epistle to the Trallians*, written around 60 AD, Ignatius addressed Jesus' reference to Jonah in the great fish's belly. He explained how Christians of his time (first century AD) understood the meaning of "three days and three nights."

> On the day of the preparation, then, at the third hour, he received the sentence from Pilate, the Father permitting that to happen; at the sixth hour he was crucified; at the ninth hour

he gave up the ghost, and before sunset, he was buried. During the Sabbath, he continued under the earth in the tomb in which Joseph of Arimathea had laid him. At the dawning of the Lord's day, he arose from the dead, according to what was spoken by Himself, "As Jonah was three days and three nights in the whale's belly, so shall the Son of man also be three days and three nights in the heart of the earth." The day of the preparation, then, comprises the passion; the Sabbath embraces the burial; the Lord's Day contains the resurrection" (*The Epistle of Ignatius to the Trallians*, chapter 9).

This near-contemporary of Matthew, Mark, Luke, and John confirms the understanding of the Church during the earliest days of its existence. Ignatius recorded that Jesus was crucified on Friday [the day of preparation], his body lay in the tomb on the Saturday Sabbath, and he rose on the third day [the Lord's Day], using inclusive calculation, which was the norm for the first century. But Ignatius is not alone.

Justin Martyr

Born around 100 AD into a pagan family in Samaria, Justin became an early Christian apologist.[96] He is called Justin Martyr because he was martyred for the faith, along with some of his students. In his *First Apology*, Justin explained the prevailing view of Jesus' crucifixion on the day before Saturday. He wrote:

> But Sunday is the day on which we all hold our common assembly, because it is the first day on which God, having wrought a change in the darkness and matter, made the world; and Jesus Christ our Saviour on the same day rose from the dead. For he was crucified on the day before that of Saturn (Saturday); and on the day after that of Saturn, which is the day of the Sun, having appeared to his apostles and disciples, he taught them these things, which we have submitted to you also for your consideration.[97]

Using the terms popular in his academic circles, Justin recorded that Jesus was crucified the day before Saturday, meaning Friday, and that he rose from the dead on the day of the Sun, Sunday. We now have a witness from the first century and one from the second century, leaders in the early church, explaining how they viewed Jesus' hours in the grave.

However Christian authors were not the only early historians to understand the concept of "the third day." Other historians did as well because it was the normal way of viewing calendar days. There are secular authors who, while not addressing the day of Jesus' crucifixion, nevertheless establish his crucifixion and the day celebrated as the day of his resurrection. Let's see what some of them have to say.

Secular Authors

Understanding what the Church Fathers believed about the day Jesus died focuses internally on the church, but appreciating what those outside the church understood is equally important. Often their writings confirm those of the Church Fathers and even the Gospels themselves.

Pliny the Younger

Pliny was born about 61 AD, in Como, the most beautiful region of the Italian Alps. Pliny was of the equestrian rank, a member of the aristocratic order of *equites* (knights), the class just beneath the senatorial order. Pontius Pilate was of this same rank. Pliny's military and political career began at the age of eighteen. In his late twenties, he was elected to be a public official known as a Quaestor in ancient Rome.[98] As an observer throughout the Roman Empire, Pliny became a historian by writing about the things he experienced.

While he was the Roman governor of Bithynia, Pliny wrote of the Christians:

> They were in the habit of meeting on a certain fixed day before it was light, when they sang in alternate verses a hymn to Christ, as to a god, and bound themselves by a solemn oath not to [do] any wicked deeds, never to commit any fraud, theft, or adultery, never to falsify their word, nor deny a trust when they should be called upon to deliver it up; after which it was their custom to separate, and then reassemble to partake of good food—but food of an ordinary and innocent kind.

Pliny explicitly stated these early Christians observed the Ten Commandments. Most early Christians were of slave stock or from other lower classes, and the vast majority had heathen masters or employers. Thus, they were forced to work on their day of rest, which was, unfortunately, an official working day throughout the empire until Constantine's "Sabbath" Edict in 321 AD. The specific "fixed-day" [Latin: *certum diem*] on which the Christians met was Sunday.[99]

While Pliny does not address the day of Jesus' crucifixion directly, he does mark the day of Jesus' resurrection as Sunday, ruling out any crucifixion theory that places Jesus' resurrection on Saturday.

Lucian of Samosata

Lucian of Samosata (125–200 AD) was an Assyrian rhetorician and satirist who wrote in the Greek language. He had a quick mind and a sharp tongue, writing witty and often deriding satires. In his parody called *The Passing of Peregrinus*, he verifies the non-Christian perception of Christianity. In recording the death of Peregrinus, Lucian writes:

> It was now that he came across the priests and scribes of the Christians, in Palestine, and picked up their queer creed. I can tell you, he pretty soon convinced them of his superiority; prophet, elder, ruler of the Synagogue—he was everything at once; expounded their books, commented on them, wrote books himself. They took him for a God, accepted his laws, and declared him their president. The Christians, you know, worship a man to this day—the distinguished personage who introduced their novel rites, and was crucified on that account.

Lucian corroborates the accounts of the Gospels and others who record that Jesus was crucified, even if he does not reveal the exact day.

In addition to secular authors, some Jewish authors mention Jesus' crucifixion and the day they understood his death to have occurred.

Jewish Authors

Like the secular authors, you would not expect Jewish authors to go out of their way to affirm what the Gospels recorded about Jesus or the day he was crucified. This makes the contribution of Jewish writers all the more interesting.

Flavius Josephus

The Jewish military leader turned prolific historian for the Roman Empire, Josephus mentions Jesus and his crucifixion several times in his writings. In *Antiquities of the Jews*, he wrote of the relation of the day of Preparation to the Sabbath day following.

> Caesar Augustus, High Priest and tribune of the people, ordains thus: Since the nation of the Jews hath been found grateful to the Roman people ... it seemed good to me ... that the Jews have liberty to make use of their own customs, according to the law of their forefathers ... that they be not obliged to go before any judge on the Sabbath day, nor on the day of the preparation to it, after the ninth hour (*Ant*.16.6.2).

Josephus has eliminated any lawful trial on the Sabbath or the day of Preparation after the ninth hour. Jesus' trial, of course, was not held on a Sabbath day, and the Sanhedrin avoided this prohibition by holding Jesus' trial before the ninth hour on the day of Preparation. In Jewish minds, everything about Jesus' trial was on the up and up.

The Talmud, Mishnah, and Tosefta

The Babylonian Talmud (*Sanhedrin* 43a) specifically places Jesus' crucifixion on the eve of Passover, the eve of the Sabbath.

> On the eve of the Passover, Yeshu [the Nasarean] was hanged. For forty days before the execution took place, a herald went forth and cried, "He is going forth to be stoned because he has practiced sorcery and enticed Israel to apostasy. Anyone who can say anything in his favor, let him come forward and plead on his behalf." But since nothing was brought forward in his favor, he was hanged on the eve of the Passover.

Perhaps the most important tidbit that comes from this Talmud entry is that Jesus was hanged (crucified) "on the eve of the Passover." Jesus was nailed to the cross on the day before the annual Passover celebration. This is significant since the Babylonian Talmud confirms that whenever the Passover occurred in the year of Jesus' death, the Savior was crucified specifically on the day before it. A Florentine manuscript adds, "and the eve of Sabbath."

Another Jewish source relating to execution and the Passover is a Baraita of the Jerusalem Talmud. This Baraita describes a man named Ben Stada's practice of writing (tattooing) on his flesh. It is found in *Shabbat* 11:15; 12:4; 13d. The first passage reports a dispute concerning these markings. In support of Ben Stada, Rabbi Eliezer said, "Isn't it true that Ben Stada (other readings say Sitra, Sotra, or Stara) learned in this way?" To this, the Sages replied, "And because of one idiot, we should hold all of the normal people liable"?

Here is where the *sugya* ends in the later printed editions. A *sugyot* (plural: *sugya*) is a passage from the Gemara discussing a specific Mishnah topic. But the earliest published text continues by saying . . .

> [Was he] the son of Stara (or: Stada)? Wasn't he rather the son of Pandira! Rav Ḥisda said, "Stara was [his mother's] husband; Pandira was [his mother's] lover." [But his mother's] husband was Papos the son of Judah! Rather, his mother was Stara (or Stada), and his father was Pandira. [But] his mother was Mary the hairdresser (*magdala*)! Rather [she was called Stada] because of what they say in Pumbedita: She cheated (*sata da*) on her husband.

The name "Ben Pandira" was understood in the Babylonian Talmud as a euphemism for Jesus (cf. *Tosefta Ḥullin* 2:24; the Babylonian Talmud Av. Za. 16b-17a). Hullin (Hebrew חֻלִּין meaning "profane") is a tractate found in the Mishnah, Tosefta, and Babylonian Talmud. This entire Talmudic passage is seen as an anti-Christian polemic, ridiculing the doctrine of Jesus's virgin birth.[100] Some scholars see the reference to the execution of Ben Stada on the eve of Passover, as well as the eve of the Sabbath, as a reference to Jesus' crucifixion.[101]

If, indeed, this passage is speaking of Jesus, which appears to be quite possible, it confirms that Jesus was crucified on the eve of the Sabbath which was also the eve of the Passover. Adherents to a Friday crucifixion should be pleased with that, although many don't even know about the Babylonian Talmud or this passage in it.

> "I am a Jew, but I am enthralled by the luminous figure of the Nazarene. No one can read the Gospels without feeling the actual presence of Jesus. His personality pulsates in every word."
> —Albert Einstein

Jesus was not always treated kindly in the Talmud. He was accused of being a sorcerer, a black magic practitioner, and leading the Jews into idolatry (*Sanhedrin* 43a). He was also accused of being sexually immoral (*Sanhedrin* 107b; *Sotah* 47a) and performing his miracles by witchcraft (*Shabbos* 104b).

Perhaps most distasteful of all, in the Babylonian Talmud (*Gittan* 57a), the Gemara relates a story about Onkelos bar Kalonikos, the son of Titus' sister, who wanted to convert to Judaism. To make the right decision, he raised three individuals from the dead to seek their advice. First was Titus himself; then Balaam; and finally, Jesus of Nazareth. In each case, Onkelos asked what the punishment would be in the next world for "that man," meaning Titus, Balaam, or Jesus. The Savior's answer: "He is punished with boiling excrement." This does not sound much like the Good Shepherd of the Gospels.

Nevertheless, it is established by others who did not write one of the four Gospels that Jesus' crucifixion was on the day of Preparation, on the eve of the Sabbath, and the eve of Passover. These accounts corroborate the evangelists' accounts that Jesus was crucified on Friday.

THE ARGUMENT OF THE DAY OF PREPARATION

One of the issues of debate on the day of Jesus' crucifixion is the timing of Mary and the women who bought and prepared spices to anoint Christ's body. Both Luke and Mark inform us of the sequence and timing of these events.

Luke 23:54–56, "It was the day of Preparation, and the Sabbath was beginning. The women who had come with him from Galilee followed and saw the tomb and how his body was laid. Then they returned and prepared spices and ointments. On the Sabbath they rested according to the commandment."

Mark 16:1–2, "When the Sabbath was past, Mary Magdalene, Mary the mother of James, and Salome bought spices, so that they might go and anoint him. And very early on the first day of the week, when the sun had risen, they went to the tomb."

The word "preparation" is used six times in the four Gospels, each time having the ordinary meaning of the day we call "Friday." In requesting a guard be placed at the tomb of Jesus, Matthew 27:62 says, "The next day, that is, after the day of Preparation (Greek: παρασκευή; English: *paraskeuné*), the chief priests and the Pharisees gathered before Pilate." Mark 15:42–43 and Luke 23:54 record the same, as does John 19:14, 31, and 42, all referring to the day of Preparation. The Gospels all firmly establish that Jesus was crucified on the normal "day of Preparation," that is, the day before the weekly Sabbath, i.e. Friday.

Friday as the ordinary meaning for the day of Preparation

It is important to note that when Mark said, "It was the day of Preparation (Greek παρασκευὴ), and that the Sabbath (Greek: προσάββατον; English: *prosabbaton*) was beginning," he used two Greek words to describe the day of Preparation. These two words have identical meanings and they represent just one day—the day before the Sabbath. The word *prosabbaton* (*pro*–before and *sabbaton*–Sabbath) is also a technical term indicating the day of the Preparation for the Sabbath, that is, Friday evening.

Later its use seems to have been extended to denote the sixth day (Friday) of each week. This is how the first-century *Didache* (8) and the second-century *Martyrdom of Polycarp* (7) use the word *prosabbaton*. Hellenistic Jews used the term *prosabbaton* (Sabbath-eve) explicitly and exclusively for "the day before the Sabbath" (*Judith* 8:6; 2 *Maccabees* 8:26).

In the twenty-first century, we often have difficulty understanding why the word *paraskeué* is so definitively associated with Friday, because in our context "the day before the Sabbath" could mean just about anything. But that was not the case in Jesus' day. In the Second Temple Period, the word *paraskeué* was commonly accepted as a synonym for Friday and only Friday. It is the Greek equivalent of the Aramaic word "*arubtaeve*," both of which were widely known among the people of the Roman Empire to mean Friday.

Tertullian was born about 155 AD and died about 240 AD. That means he was a second/third-century Church Father, and by his time, *paraskeué* had the fixed meaning of Friday, so much so Tertullian said it had been the name for Friday since creation.[102]

The famous eighteenth-century English Baptist scholar and voluminous author John Gill spoke of the day of Preparation as "Friday; on which day, it is clear, Christ suffered, died, and was buried."[103] It is useless to argue against the historical understanding that Friday was the day of Preparation because it is a fact of history. Jesus was crucified on the day of Preparation.

THE ARGUMENT OF THE "HIGH DAY" SABBATH

The Gospel of John asserts that the day following Jesus Christ's crucifixion was a high Sabbath (John 19:31). John makes no mention of a second Sabbath in Passion Week. He speaks only of the day following the "day of Preparation." That day was Nisan 15, the first day of the Feast of Unleavened Bread and the "holy convocation" or Passover Sabbath.

The next day, after the day of Preparation and after the first day of the Feast of Unleavened Bread, which in the year Jesus died was also the weekly Sabbath, was called the day of Firstfruits (*Yom HaBikkurim*), more commonly known in Judaism as *Reishit Katzir*. This was the day that initiated the forty-nine-day countdown to the harvest festival of Shavuot (Pentecost).

So, the sequence of inter-connected days becomes clear.

Table 1: Friday–Sunday With Friday Crucifixion

Friday	Saturday	Sunday [Easter]	Sunday + 50 days
Nisan 14	Nisan 15	Nisan 16	Sivan 6
Day of Preparation	Weekly Sabbath	Day of Firstfruits	Shavuot
Crucifixion	Passover	Resurrection	Pentecost
	High Day Sabbath		Feast of Weeks
	First Day of Unleavened Bread		

Those who hold to a Friday crucifixion understand this particular Sabbath to be a day of tremendous solemnity and importance. This was not an extra Sabbath day in Passion Week. The expressions "high" or "great" describe the gravity of the Sabbath day which was also Passover, the most beloved and revered day on the Jewish calendar.

THE ARGUMENT OF THE THIRD DAY

Not to be missed in discussing a Friday crucifixion is the power of the phrase "the third day." Those who believe that Jesus was crucified on Friday understand the third day to mean 1st, 2nd, 3rd day, not a literal seventy-two hours—1, 2, 3. There is power and meaning in "the third day" that does not relate to the crucifixion story. God did many marvelous things on "the third day." Here are some examples.

The movement of God on the third day

Some would argue that the frequent references to the "third day" are simply examples of Hebrew poetry. In some cases, that may be true. But for most cases, there is no reason to believe the author intended anything other than the usual meaning—day three, the third day.

- Genesis 1:13, "And there was evening and there was morning, the third day." The middle day of God's creation saw our planet spring to life with trees, grass, seeds, and vegetation of all kinds.
- Genesis 22:4, "On the third day Abraham lifted up his eyes and saw the place from afar." This was the day God performed one of the most transparent pictures of Jesus' crucifixion in the Old Testament—the intention of Abraham to sacrifice his only son Isaac.

- Exodus 19:10–11, "The Lord said to Moses, 'Go to the people and consecrate them today and tomorrow, and let them wash their garments and be ready for the third day. For on the third day the Lord will come down on Mount Sinai in the sight of all the people.'"
- Esther 5:1, "On the third day Esther put on her royal robes and stood in the inner court of the king's palace, in front of the king's quarters, while the king was sitting on his royal throne inside the throne room opposite the entrance to the palace." Queen Esther saved the Jewish people from extinction as she stood before King Xerxes on the third day.
- Hosea 6:1–2, "Come, let us return to the LORD; for he has torn us, that he may heal us; he has struck us down, and he will bind us up. After two days he will revive us; on the third day he will raise us up, that we may live before him." Hosea was appealing to Israel and Judah to repent of their sins and allow God to bring them new life. This sounds remarkably like what Jesus did when he was crucified and rose on the third day to give us new life (see also Gen 42:17–18; 2 Kgs 20:5–6; Ezra 6:14–15).

While there are many similarities, none of these references are prophecies of Jesus' death or resurrection. However, they demonstrate the powerful movement of God on the third day, meaning that Jesus' crucifixion is not without precedent. God moved on other days as well, but Christ did not rise on other days; he rose from the dead on the third day.

> "The mockers taunted Jesus to come down from the cross and save himself. But he would do something more miraculous than that. Jesus would come up from the grave."—Woodrow Michael Kroll

There appears to be a "third-day" theme running through the pages of the Old Testament. The context of each of these verses is historical, not poetic, and there appears no reason to assume a literal third day is not intended. God often chose to work mightily on the third day.

THE ARGUMENT OF SLAYING THE PASSOVER LAMB

The Old Testament command was for the Passover lamb to be slain on the afternoon of the 14th of Nisan and eaten after sunset, which became the 15th

of Nisan in Jewish reckoning. This is firmly established both in the biblical text and in Jewish history (see Exod 12:1–6,18; Lev 23:5; Num 9:3,5; 28:16; Josh 5:10; 2 Chr 35:1; Ezra 6:19; Ezek 45:21). Yet, according to Exodus 12:18, unleavened bread was also to be eaten beginning on the 14th of Nisan, known as the Lord's Passover, which is the day before the Festival of Unleavened Bread (Exod 12:18–19).

Those who advocate a Friday crucifixion understand Jesus to have eaten a meal consisting of bread and wine only, no roast lamb, on Thursday evening with his disciples. He then went with those disciples (minus Judas) to the Garden of Gethsemane to pray. Jesus was arrested, given a preliminary hearing by Annas, questioned by Caiaphas, thrown into prison in the High Priest's house, tried early the next morning at the Chamber of Hewn Stone, sent to Pilate, and was nailed to the cross by 9:00 am. Later that same day, at 3:00 pm in the same city, the Passover lambs were slain for each household among the Jews.

Estimates of the population of Jerusalem in Jesus' day are all over the map. The Roman historian Tacitus projected the city's population at the time of the Jewish wars to be 600,000. The Jewish historian Josephus estimated it at 2,700,200 Jews (*Wars* 6.9.3). As mentioned in Chapter Two, Hillel Geva, the Director of the Israel Exploration Society, claimed there were only 20,000 living in Jerusalem in AD 70.[104] Perhaps the most reliable estimate comes from Magen Broshi writing in the *Biblical Archaeology Review*. He approximates the population of Jerusalem at 80,000 during the first century AD.[105]

But that only includes the permanent inhabitants of Jerusalem. What about the swell of Jews that arrived from all over the known world for Passover? They, too, would need a lamb for a family.

It is valuable to quote Josephus here.

> These High Priests, upon the coming of that feast which is called the Passover, when they slay their sacrifices, from the ninth hour till the eleventh, but so that a company not less than ten belong to every sacrifice, [for it is not lawful for them to feast singly by themselves,] and many of us are twenty in a company, found the number of sacrifices was two hundred and fifty-six thousand five hundred; which, upon the allowance of no more than ten that feast together, amounts to two million seven hundred thousand and two hundred persons that were pure and holy (*Wars of the Jews* 6.9.3).

Most of these numbers appear to be too high. Slaying 256,500 lambs would be a logistical nightmare, and would seriously deplete the shepherds' flocks.

Suppose during the years of the Savior's ministry we use Magen Broshi's estimation that Jerusalem's population was about 80,000, and one lamb was needed for each average household consisting of a mother, father, grandmother, grandfather, four children, and six other relatives. In that case, each family was fourteen people (Josephus says between ten and twenty for each household). A family of fourteen seems to be a just estimate. That means, just for residents of Jerusalem, 5,714 lambs needed to be slaughtered in Jerusalem each year at Passover, a much more manageable number. But the number of lambs slain is not the critical consideration here; the time of their slaughter is.

The slaying of the Passover lambs began at 3:00 pm on Friday. The Jewish historian Josephus confirms that the Passover lambs were slain from the ninth hour to the eleventh hour, meaning from 3:00 pm to 5:00 pm.[106] Therefore, the two saving events—the time for the killing of the Passover lamb and the death of Jesus the Lamb of God—coincided precisely that Friday afternoon, Nisan 14th at 3:00 pm. This correlates with the timing of the original Passover in Egypt, Nisan 14th (Num 33:3-4). In Egypt, Passover was the 14th; the Hebrew pilgrim journey with unleavened bread began on the 15th of Nisan.

The striking symbolism of Jesus as the Passover Lamb was used effectively by the Apostle Paul. To the Corinthian believers, he wrote:

> Do you not know that a little leaven leavens the whole lump? Cleanse out the old leaven that you may be a new lump, as you really are unleavened. For Christ, our Passover lamb, has been sacrificed. Let us therefore celebrate the festival, not with the old leaven, the leaven of malice and evil, but with the unleavened bread of sincerity and truth" (1 Cor 5:6-8).

Paul used the double symbolic reference of leaven and the Passover to show that just as leaven had no place in a Jewish home during Passover, there was no place for the leaven of malice and evil in the house [life] of the one saved by the blood of the Lamb. "If anyone is in Christ, he is a new creation. The old has passed away; behold, the new has come" (2 Cor 5:17). The act by which our old life has been swept away and replaced by new life in the Spirit was the death of the Passover Lamb at the exact hour the Passover lambs were being slain that Friday in Jerusalem.

The Argument of the Feast of Unleavened Bread

There are times when the Bible speaks of the Feast of Unleavened Bread and the Passover to describe the combination of Nisan 14 (The Lord's Passover) with Nisan 15–22, (the subsequent week-long Feast of Unleavened Bread). The Feast and Passover are not interchangeable, but they are connected. Therefore, the first day of the Feast of Unleavened Bread would sometimes be Nisan 14, with Passover as a Pre-Unleavened Bread day (see Matt 26:17; Mark 14:12; Luke 22:1, 7–8).

Referring to Passover as a part of the Feast of Unleavened Bread was entirely understood by the Jews of the first century. However, it is often confusing to Gentiles of the twenty-first century. While these verses appear to be saying the Passover lamb was slain on the first day of Unleavened Bread (15 Nisan), they actually refer to 14 Nisan, Passover day.

The Passover observance, as outlined in Exodus 12:5–6, is specific. "Your lamb shall be without blemish, a male a year old. You may take it from the sheep or from the goats, and you shall keep it until the fourteenth day of this month, when the whole assembly of the congregation of Israel shall kill their lambs at twilight." Constructed of (Hebrew בֵּין; English: *bêyn* = between) and (Hebrew עֶרֶב; English: *'ereb* = eventide or dusk), "twilight" literally means "between the evenings."

After the daylight hours of Passover, when the sun had set, the Jews would eat the meat from the Passover. First, they offered it to God; then, and only then, they ate it for their own physical needs.[107] The sequencing of events in Exodus 12 for that first Passover in Egypt is significant.

- Kill the lamb on the 14th day at twilight.
- Spread the blood on the doorposts and lintel of your house.
- Roast the lamb, do not eat it raw or boiled.
- Eat the roasted lamb after the blood has been applied to the door.
- Burn any leftover lamb; do not save it for the next day.
- No leaven in your bread.
- Keep your clothes on, belt fastened, sandals on your feet, and staff in your hand as you quickly eat.

The Jews could only follow these specific instructions if the night of the Passover unwrapped into the next day, the seven-day Feast of Unleavened Bread. The calendar of events fits perfectly with a Friday crucifixion, not so much with Thursday, and not at all with Wednesday.

The Argument of the Feast of Firstfruits

According to the Bible, the three-day Passover weekend progression of events is as follows:

Table 2: Sequencing The Passover Weekend

	Passover →	Unleavened Bread →	Firstfruits
Or how about this:	Nisan 14 →	Nisan 15 →	Nisan 16
Said differently:	Crucifixion →	Sabbath →	Resurrection
Said differently still:	Friday →	Saturday →	Sunday

The wave (omer), which was a sheaf of barley offered in conjunction with the Feast of Unleavened Bread, directly followed the Passover. Barley is a self-pollinating member of the grass family. Found in abundance on grasslands throughout the Fertile Crescent of Western Asia and the northernmost parts of the Middle East, domesticating and growing barley has been going on for thousands of years.[108]

The first fruits of the second harvest, the loaves of bread, are offered at Shavuot. Both were wave offerings.[109] The Feast of Shavuot celebrated the wheat harvest in Israel. In ancient times, the grain harvest lasted seven weeks. It began with the harvesting of the barley during Passover and ended with the wheat harvest at Shavuot, which concluded the harvest festival.

In the first century AD, every Jew and almost everyone else knew what the days of Passover, Unleavened Bread, and Firstfruits meant. So when Paul said, "For Christ, our Passover lamb, has been sacrificed" (1 Cor 5:7), even the Gentiles in Corinth would make the connection. They also would have no difficulty understanding the sequence of days when Paul read to them from Leviticus 23, "On the day after the Sabbath the priest shall wave it," meaning the wave offering of the Firstfruits. What could the day after the Sabbath mean? Certainly not a Sabbath somewhere in the middle of the Passion Week. The day after the Sabbath was Sunday. Everyone knew that. It was the first day of the week, Resurrection Day.

Jewish writers of that era knew that Sunday was the day after the Sabbath. Philo and Josephus are decisive. Philo (c. 20 BC to AD 45) wrote in his *De specialibus legibus* (2.144–75) that the first sheaf of barley was presented in the Temple on the second day of the feast, that is, Nisan 16. Josephus agrees and records a critical sequence of events related to Passover, Unleavened Bread, Firstfruits, and Pentecost (*Ant*.3.10.5).

The word in the New Testament for "firstfruits" is not found frequently. It occurs only eight times—six times by Paul, once by James, and once by John in the Revelation. Paul used the word (Greek: ἀπαρχὴν; English: *aparchēn*, derived from ἀπό meaning *from* or *with* and ἄρχομαι meaning *to commence*) in three different ways.

First, he used the word spiritually in Romans 8:23, "We ourselves, who have the firstfruits of the Spirit" (also in Rom 11:16 and again in 1 Cor 15:20).

Second, Paul used *aparchēn* in 1 Corinthians 15:23 when speaking of our physical, bodily resurrection. "But each in his own order: Christ the firstfruits, then at his coming those who belong to Christ."

Third, he used it in Romans 16:5, "Greet also the church in their house. Greet my beloved Epaenetus, who was the first convert [the word is *aparchēn*, firstfruits] to Christ in Asia." Epaenetus was the first person to turn from sin and to Christ as Savior in Western Greece. Epaenetus appears to be of the family of Stephanas who placed their faith in Jesus as a family (see 1 Cor 16:15). Paul used *aparchēn* as a reference to the first to become believers in Achaia, with others who would follow.

Given these examples, coupled with the use of firstfruits in the Old Testament, it's evident that the Feast of Firstfruits embodies the concept of a beginning. Jesus' death on Friday afternoon was the end of life lived under the Law. His resurrection on Sunday morning was the beginning of our new life of grace found only in Christ. He is the Firstfruits, but our day of resurrection will come as well. That's the promise of Sunday.

THE ARGUMENT OF JOSHUA AND THE SIXTEENTH OF THE MONTH

Jesus' crucifixion was on the day of Preparation, Friday Nisan 14, the Feast of Unleavened Bread began officially on Saturday Nisan 15, and Firstfruits was celebrated on Sunday, Nisan 16. But how do we know Firstfruits was on the 16th?

For those who hold to a Wednesday crucifixion, Nisan 16 is on a Friday; for those who advocate a Thursday crucifixion, it falls on a Saturday. None of these theories can be right if the day of Firstfruits is not right.

We first read about Firstfruits in Exodus 23, more in Exodus 34, but we really get going in Leviticus 23. Nonetheless, a Scripture often overlooked about Passover and Firstfruits is Joshua 5:10–12.

> While the people of Israel were encamped at Gilgal, they kept the Passover on the fourteenth day of the month in the evening on the plains of Jericho. And the day after the Passover, on that

very day, they ate of the produce of the land, unleavened cakes and parched grain. And the manna ceased the day after they ate of the produce of the land. And there was no longer manna for the people of Israel, but they ate of the fruit of the land of Canaan that year.

The Israelites first kept the Passover on Nisan 14 after they entered the Promised Land. That very day the manna which had fed them during their forty-year journey stopped. It was no longer needed because they had entered a land of plenty, a land that oozed with milk and honey. But how do we know they celebrated Firstfruits in their new homeland? Because keeping the Passover was not the only Leviticus 23 directive of God.

Leviticus 23:10–12 was also God's command to Moses:

> Speak to the people of Israel and say to them, "When you come into the land that I give you and reap its harvest, you shall bring the sheaf of the firstfruits of your harvest to the priest, and he shall wave the sheaf before the Lord, so that you may be accepted. On the day after the Sabbath the priest shall wave it. And on the day when you wave the sheaf, you shall offer a male lamb a year old without blemish as a burnt offering to the Lord.

They were to bring the first of their harvest to the priests and wave the sheaves on the day after the Sabbath. But what Sabbath? Did God mean the weekly Sabbath or the yearly Passover Sabbath? Look more closely at that Leviticus passage.

God told them that after entering the Promised Land, they must offer him the first fruits of the first harvest before eating anything themselves from that harvest. Joshua 3:14–16 describes what happened:

> So when the people set out from their tents to pass over the Jordan with the priests bearing the ark of the covenant before the people, and as soon as those bearing the ark had come as far as the Jordan, and the feet of the priests bearing the ark were dipped in the brink of the water (now the Jordan overflows all its banks throughout the time of harvest), the waters coming down from above stood and rose up in a heap very far away, at Adam, the city that is beside Zarethan, and those flowing down toward the Sea of the Arabah, the Salt Sea, were completely cut off. And the people passed over opposite Jericho.

That clause, "the Jordan overflows all its banks throughout the time of harvest," is key to our understanding. When the priests bearing the ark of the covenant began to cross the River Jordan, God miraculously rolled back the waters so the people crossed the springtime-flooded Jordan on dry ground.

The distance from Israel's crossing at Jericho to Adam, the city near Zarethan, is approximately sixty-five miles. That's more than enough space for two to three million Israelites to cross the Jordan in a timely way. Walking five feet apart, 68,640 people could cross side-by-side, row after row. The people came out of the Jordan on the tenth day of the first month, and they encamped at Gilgal on the eastern edge of Jericho. Gilgal is perhaps a mile and a half northwest of Jericho (Josh 4:18–19).

Again, take note of the date—the tenth day of the first month. This would be Nisan 10, the very day the Passover lamb was selected for the four-day inspection period. While they had just set foot in a foreign and hostile land, in obedience to the LORD's command, these weary travelers took time to select the best lamb of their flocks, and four days later on Nisan 14, they slew that lamb in celebration of the Passover. This was their first Passover in the Promised Land.

Joshua 5:10–11 describes the day after their first Passover. "While the people of Israel were encamped at Gilgal, they kept the Passover on the fourteenth day of the month in the evening on the plains of Jericho. And the day after the Passover, on that very day, they ate of the produce of the land, unleavened cakes and parched grain."

The Israelites observed the Feast of Unleavened Bread on the Nisan 15 after the Nisan 14 slaying of the lambs for Passover. They consumed the last of their old grain because it was the time of year to harvest a new crop (v. 12).

The book of Joshua confirms that these Jewish settlers observed the Passover on the 14th and the Feast of Unleavened Bread began on the 15th. Nevertheless, how do we know they also celebrated Firstfruits on the 16th? Because they had to, it was the command of God, and it is unthinkable that the Israelites would take the time to observe the Passover and the Feast of Unleavened Bread without adding the third celebration in the trilogy—Firstfruits (Lev 23:10–11).

It is quite evident that this is not talking about the weekly Saturday Sabbath. It is unmistakably referring to those annual, interrelated, and connected feasts—Passover, Unleavened Bread, and Firstfruits. There can be no question about the timeframe: Nisan 14, slaying the Passover lamb; Nisan 15, the Feast of Unleavened Bread begins; Nisan 16, Firstfruits of the harvest waved before the LORD.

This is confirmed by Josephus' *Antiquities of the Jews* 3.10, as well as in the Mishnah's description of the Festival of Firstfruits. "On the eve after the first day of Passover, messengers from the court used to go to one of the barley fields near Jerusalem and in a festive ceremony would harvest a handful of barley which they then waved over the altar . . . The ceremony on the 16th of Nisan permitted the people to eat from the fresh harvest of that year" (Mishnah *Menahot* 10.3 and 10.6).

The Joshua account presents a thorny problem for both advocates of the Wednesday and Thursday crucifixion days. Neither fit the New Testament pattern and now we discover they do not fit the Old Testament pattern either.

THE ARGUMENT OF THE FIRST DAY

We have already explored the argument for the third day in affirming the Friday crucifixion. The Gospel writers used the ordinal number "third" in each case to place the resurrection on Sunday morning. Now we explore the argument of the other ordinal number delineating the Passover weekend—the "first day."

If we can free ourselves of the captivity of Matthew 12:40, and the idea that Jesus must have been seventy-two hours in the grave, we can look unhinderedly for corroboration of that third day in the Gospel narratives. Here are the verses where all four of the Gospel writers note that Jesus rose from the dead on the first day of the week.

Matthew 28:1, "Now after the Sabbath, toward the dawn of the first day of the week, Mary Magdalene and the other Mary went to see the tomb."

Mark 16:2, "And very early on the first day of the week, when the sun had risen, they went to the tomb." And verse 9, "Now when he rose early on the first day of the week, he appeared first to Mary Magdalene, from whom he had cast out seven demons."

Luke 24:1, "But on the first day of the week, at early dawn, they went to the tomb, taking the spices they had prepared."

John 20:1, "Now on the first day of the week, Mary Magdalene came to the tomb early, while it was still dark, and saw that the stone had been taken away from the tomb."

If we work backward from the first day of the week, that is, the third day after Jesus' crucifixion, the days of Passover weekend look like this:

- Sunday (Firstfruits)—the third day, Resurrection Day.
- Saturday (Sabbath)—the second day; Jesus' body is in the tomb.
- Friday (Preparation day)—the first day; Jesus was crucified, 9:00 am to 3:00 pm.

Keep this calendar of days in mind as we explore additional proof for a Friday crucifixion.

Table 3: Gospel Designations for Early Sunday Morning

Expression	Scripture
"After the Sabbath"	Matt 28:1
"Toward the dawn"	Matt 28:1
"At early dawn"	Luke 24:1
"Very early"	Mark 16:2
"Early"	Mark 16:9; John 20:1
"When the sun had risen"	Mark 16:2
"While it was still dark"	John 20:1
"The first day of the week"	Matt 28:1; Mark 16:2, 9; Luke 24:1; John 20:1

Proof from Jesus' encounter with Cleopas

It was Sunday, a momentous day for these faithful followers of Jesus. The women's report that Jesus rose from the dead was confirmed. The news began spreading across Jerusalem like a prairie fire. But when Jesus encountered Cleopas and his friend on the way to Emmaus late in the day on Sunday, notice when Cleopas began his account of the things that had happened in Jerusalem. He did not begin with Jesus' resurrection even though it had just occurred that day, but with his crucifixion that was three days earlier. Read Luke 24:19-21. Cleopas put the resurrection day in context with the crucifixion day. "It is now the third day since these things happened."

The text connects the "first day" Sunday, Resurrection Day, with the "third day" that Cleopas spoke about. "But Peter rose and ran to the tomb; stooping and looking in, he saw the linen cloths by themselves; and he went home marveling at what had happened. That very day two of them were going to a village named Emmaus, about seven miles from Jerusalem . . ." (Luke 24:12-13).

Luke could not have made it any plainer. Even the clause construction in Luke's original Greek will not permit any other meaning. Luke, who was a stickler for details, confirms that the first day of the week, Resurrection Day, is also the third day since Jesus was crucified.

There is no possibility that the four evangelists' reference to the first day of the week was to the dark hours after sunset when the first day began. This would be a very odd time for Mary Magdalene and the other faithful women to stumble through the darkness to the tomb.

Nevertheless, even if we make those concessions to Matthew 28, Luke 24, and John 20, we must account for Mark 16:2. "And very early on the first day of the week, when the sun had risen, (Greek: τοῦ ἡλίου ἀνατείλαντος) they went to the tomb." We cannot merely ignore this reference that the sun had already risen when the maid from Magdala and the other women arrived at the open tomb of Jesus.

THE ARGUMENT OF TYPE AND ANTITYPE

In teaching both the masses and his own disciples, Jesus often employed types and antitypes. A type is a person, place, or thing used to demonstrate the resemblance between it and something future, called the antitype. In the New Testament, the prominent word for a type is τύπος, meaning a pattern or mold. When artisans would create clay or wax figures, they would press the clay into a mold shaped precisely as they wanted their figure to appear. The mold was the type; the figure was the antitype.[110]

For example, Romans 5:14 connects the first Adam (the type) and the last Adam (Christ, the antitype). "Yet death reigned from Adam to Moses, even over those whose sinning was not like the transgression of Adam, who was a type (Greek: τύπος), of the one who was to come."

Jesus often taught the crowds publicly and his disciples privately by using types and antitypes. In John 6, while Jesus was teaching the crowds at Capernaum, they asked him some piercing questions:

> What sign do you do, that we may see and believe you? What work do you perform? Our fathers ate the manna in the wilderness; as it is written, "He gave them bread from heaven to eat." Jesus then said to them, "Truly, truly, I say to you, it was not Moses who gave you the bread from heaven, but my Father gives you the true bread from heaven. For the bread of God is he who comes down from heaven and gives life to the world." They said to him, "Sir, give us this bread always." Jesus said to them, "I am the bread of life; whoever comes to me shall not hunger, and whoever believes in me shall never thirst" (John 6:30–35).

The manna was the type; Jesus was the antitype.

The slaying of the Passover lamb was an Old Testament type or sign pointing to the reality of God's true Passover Lamb, the Lord Jesus. The Sabbath of rest was an Old Testament type pointing to the reality of God's true rest in Christ Jesus (Matt 11:28). So, too, Firstfruits is an Old Testament type of the celebration of new life, as the first of the grain was offered to God. The antitype to that was the resurrection from the dead that Jesus Christ celebrated on the third day, the first day of the week. Firstfruits was not a Sabbath; it occurred on Sunday, just as Jesus' resurrection did. Keeping the Sabbath does not save us; the Savior saves us.

Those who hold to the Wednesday or Thursday crucifixion would agree that Firstfruits was a type of Jesus' resurrection. However, neither places Nisan 16 on Sunday, where the Bible puts it. A Friday crucifixion keeps that calendar intact.

The only day that can reconcile with Scripture at every point is the Friday crucifixion of Jesus and his Sunday resurrection. Only this view matches the Old Testament feast days (the type) and corresponds completely with their New Testament fulfillment (the antitype). There is not a single discrepancy!

THE ARGUMENT OF SCHOLARSHIP

Genuine scholarship must be respected. After all, if a woman or a man has given a whole life to studying crucifixion, specifically the crucifixion of Jesus of Nazareth, they usually can speak with some authority on his crucifixion. If they have studied both the Greek and Hebrew languages and can get behind our modern translations to the original meaning of the writer, they deserve to be heard. Even if they propose a hypothesis that turns out to be proven false, they still have put multiple hours into developing that hypothesis and often publish it. For that, their hypothesis should at least be considered.

Scholarship and a Friday

Scholars do not always agree. In fact, for every ten scholars who advocate one theological scenario, there will be ten who support a different one. That is almost universally true. The one exception where this is not true is the discussion about the day of Jesus' crucifixion. The scholarly opinion that Jesus died on Friday of Passion Week is overwhelming. The vast majority of scholars who have exercised any kind of depth in their study have concluded Jesus was crucified on Friday and rose from the dead on Sunday morning. Here are some of those scholars who have concluded Jesus was crucified on Friday.

Specifically, notice the diversity in their religious affiliations and theological persuasions.

Table 4: Scholars Who Hold to a Friday Crucifixion

Darrel L. Bock, Senior Research Professor at Dallas Theological Seminary, is an elder emeritus at Trinity Fellowship Church in Dallas, TX.
S. G. F. Brandon was an Anglican parish priest.
Raymond E. Brown was an American Catholic priest and member of the Sulpician Fathers.
F. F. Bruce was a member of the nonconformist evangelical group known as the "Open Brethren."
Justice Haim Cohn was once a Hazzan (Cantor) in the ultra-orthodox Jerusalem neighborhood of *Mea Shearim* but experienced a gradual crisis of faith
Bart D. Ehrman was raised as a fundamentalist Christian but eventually abandoned his faith and became an agnostic, leaning toward atheism.
Craig A. Evans is the John Bisagno Distinguished Professor of Christian Origins at Houston Baptist University.
Jack Finnegan was an ordained minister in the Disciples of Christ denomination.
Joel B. Green is an ordained elder of the United Methodist Church.
John F. MacArthur is senior pastor of the non-denominational Grace Community Church, Sun Valley, CA.
Martin Hengel was once a Lutheran parish minister.
Paul L. Maier is not only a New Testament scholar but a lifelong Lutheran. His father, Walter Maier was the founder and longtime radio speaker on *The Lutheran Hour*.
Ernest L. Martin was a minister in the Worldwide Church of God for nearly 20 years.
John P. Meier is an American biblical scholar and Roman Catholic priest.
J. A. T. Robinson was an English New Testament scholar, author, and the Anglican Bishop of Woolrich, England.
A. N. Sherwin-White was a member of the village church in tiny Fyfield, England.
R. C. Sproul was a Reformed theologian, member of the Presbyterian Church in America.
N. T. Wright is a senior research fellow at Oxford, was the Anglican Bishop of Durham.
Solomon Zeitlin not only obtained a doctorate in theology from the *École Rabbinique* in Paris, but received his rabbinical ordination there as well.

As you can see, the list is diverse indeed. While these scholars may not agree on many points of theology, they all agree on one thing. That Jesus was crucified on a Friday. In a world where it is difficult to get scholars to agree on anything, this is quite amazing.

Every honest enquirer must ask, "Why have so many scholars over the centuries and today concluded that Jesus was crucified on Friday and first appeared alive on Sunday"? You should be stunned at the theological and denominational diversity among these scholars. Just because something is of the majority opinion does not mean it is correct. But while challenges to the Friday view have been made for many years and continue today, the consensus opinion remains.

These words from John P. Meier are typical of the learned opinion that Jesus was crucified on a Friday.

> The natural inference is that the women would have proceeded to anoint the body immediately after preparing the spices if the Sabbath had not intervened. The reader almost automatically concludes that the events surrounding the burial—and, indeed, all the occurrences narrated since Luke 22:66 ("and when day came")—are to be placed on Friday. Counting backward, we see that the women came to the tomb on Sunday, rested on Saturday, and saw Jesus executed and buried on Friday.[111]

Most biblical and historical scholars hold that the Savior was crucified on Friday. Those who hold to a Wednesday or Thursday crucifixion may not care, but they should.

THE ARGUMENT OF COMMON SENSE

As just inferred by Meier, with the most natural reading of the New Testament you would conclude that Jesus died on Calvary's Cross on Friday and rose from Joseph's tomb by dawn on Sunday. This is also the near-universal consensus of the Church Fathers and scholars throughout church history. There must be a reason.

First-time readers of the Gospel narratives never come away with any doubt that Jesus was crucified on Friday and arose on Sunday. It fits the facts. It is common sense. So, if a Friday crucifixion makes sense, why do some well-meaning Christians adhere to a Wednesday or Thursday crucifixion?

I believe they are seeking the truth as we all are, but they stub their toe on the curb of Matthew 12:40, and now, living with that stubbed toe, they must hobble on an alternative route to the truth. Unfortunately, that wounded toe frequently leads them to choose a path that directs them away from the established Gospel timeline.

While the evidence for a Friday crucifixion is compelling, that does not mean those who advocate for another day have no reason to question the Friday view. Here are some of the complications identified with a Friday crucifixion.

PROBLEMS WITH A FRIDAY CRUCIFIXION

Those who do not believe Jesus was crucified on Friday, regardless of what day they believe he was, must have some reasons for rejecting Friday. You do not hold a divergent view of something when all the experts believe it without some assumed cause. So, what are the reasons people may doubt the Friday crucifixion? These concerns are not given in any kind of order, certainly not in the order of their consequence.

The issue of the women and their spices

Both Luke and Mark inform us about the sequence and timing of events related to the women and their spices on the day of Preparation. Luke 23:54–56 says, "It was the day of Preparation, and the Sabbath was beginning. The women who had come with him from Galilee followed and saw the tomb and how his body was laid. Then they returned and prepared spices and ointments. On the Sabbath they rested according to the commandment." Mark 16:1–2 notes, "When the Sabbath was past, Mary Magdalene, Mary the mother of James, and Salome bought spices, so that they might go and anoint him. And very early on the first day of the week, when the sun had risen, they went to the tomb."

Some have pointed to these women as reasons for objecting to the traditional Friday crucifixion.

The reason for the spices

Spices come from pungent plant substances and were both highly prized and very expensive in antiquity. They were carried to Palestine from India, Arabia, Persia, Mesopotamia, and Egypt. King Solomon traded for spices with Hiram, king of Tyre (1 Kgs 10:15). The land of Sheba, which is present-day Yemen, had considerable spice commerce. The queen of Sheba made a long journey of 1,630 miles to see the extent of Solomon's wisdom and riches. She came "bearing spices and very much gold and precious stones" (2 Chr 9:1). Verse 9 of this chapter says, "There were no spices such as those that the queen of Sheba gave to King Solomon." That's quite an endorsement of the variety and quality of the spices from the land of Sheba.[112]

Spices were of great importance in the everyday lives of the Jews of Israel. As then, still today, incense, perfumes, and ointments were used for personal hygiene in regions of the world where bathing is not frequent. Myrrh and aloes were used in anointing the dead before burial.

Unlike the Egyptians, Jews did not practice embalming. Instead, they committed the dead person's body to the ground, "dust to dust" (Gen 3:19). The main reason for anointing the dead with spices was to diminish the odor of the decomposing body. When Jesus asked for the stone to be rolled away from the mouth of Lazarus' tomb, Martha objected: "Lord, by this time there will be an odor, for he has been dead four days" (John 11:39). The women's spices brought to the tomb on Sunday morning were intended to honor Christ's body and eliminate just such an odor.

No women brought spices to the tomb except on Sunday morning.

Matthew informs us that Joseph of Arimathea wrapped Jesus' body in a clean linen shroud. Mark tells us he placed a stone over the face of the tomb. Luke adds that this was the day of Preparation and the Sabbath was fast approaching. John explains that Nicodemus brought seventy-five pounds of myrrh and aloes to anoint Jesus' body.

In the four Gospel accounts of the women coming to the tomb of Jesus at the same time as Joseph of Arimathea and Nicodemus, none records the women having spices with them (Matt 27:59–61; Mark 15:46–47; Luke 23:52–56; John 19:39–40).

So, let's get one thing straight. While the women followed Joseph and Jesus' body to the tomb, the women did not anoint Jesus' body at his burial. Every act of devotion by these women was to be done early on Sunday morning, the first day of the week. This is important because it means the argument of too little time for the women to prepare spices has too little evidence.

Besides, this Sabbath also being a "High Day," the women would have visited the spice markets earlier in the week to purchase some extra spices for household use in advance of the special Sabbath The spices they needed on Sunday morning may already have been in their kitchen pantry or on their spice rack. It was Nicodemus who brought the excessive amount of spices that Good Friday, not the women. What's more, both the Passover Sabbath and the weekly Sabbath ended at Sundown on Saturday evening. At that point, shops in Jerusalem would reopen with a flurry of business and stay open into the night. The women could have purchased more spices during the hours after the Sabbath had passed. The whole issue of timing for the women buying spices is a moot point. It is irrelevant. They had more than ample opportunity to buy spices for Sunday morning.

The issue of a Saturday night resurrection

Dated to approximately 180 AD, the so-called *Gospel of Peter* has fired the theory that Jesus rose from the dead, not early on Sunday morning, but just after the Jewish day began, which was Saturday night after sunset. Many who hold to a Thursday crucifixion, and all who hold to a Wednesday crucifixion, appeal to the apocryphal *Gospel of Peter* for proof that it was during those first hours of Sunday, shortly after sunset Saturday night, that Jesus arose.

Here is Raymond E. Brown's translation of that portion of the *Gospel of Peter*.

> But in the night in which the Lord's day dawned, when the soldiers were safeguarding it two by two in every watch . . . But that stone which had been thrust against the door, having rolled by itself, went a distance off the side; and the sepulcher opened, and both the young men entered . . . Now at the dawn of the Lord's Day Mary Magdalene, a female disciple of the Lord . . . with her women friends, came to the tomb where he had been placed (*Gospel of Peter* 9:35–37; 12:50–51).

After these words, a narrative of the resurrection follows.

For some, this apocryphal passage links the Lord's resurrection with those women coming to the tomb during the night watch when the Roman soldiers were sleeping. You have to wonder why they would come at night instead of in the morning when it was light and they could see much better. But adherents to a Wednesday crucifixion cling to the idea that the phrases "In the night in which the Lord's day dawned" and "Now at the dawn of the Lord's Day." They believe these phrases show Jesus rose from the dead late on the third day after he was crucified, but before the fourth day had begun.

The problem with this view is not a Friday crucifixion but that adherents to a non-Friday crucifixion appeal to this *Gospel of Peter* passage to squeeze in a day that is simply not there. They need that one additional day to get seventy-two hours in before Jesus rises from the grave. The Wednesday crucifixion theory violates one of two facts we know from the Gospels. Either Jesus rose precisely seventy-two hours after he was buried about 6:00 pm on Wednesday, which makes his resurrection on Saturday at 6:00 pm, or he rose seventy-two hours after sunset on Saturday, which would be the beginning of Sunday, which adds up to more than seventy-two hours. Either option makes the Wednesday theory insupportable.

Those who hold to a Thursday crucifixion come a little closer to the truth of the Gospel accounts, but are still wide of the mark. As pointed out in the last chapter, if Jesus died at 3:00 pm on Thursday and was buried by a 6:00 pm sunset (7:03 pm to be precise), and if he rose just after sunset on Saturday night (at the start of Sunday), he was not in the grave a full seventy-two hours but only a little over fifty hours. Thursday adherents must count the "evening" (Mark 15:42–43) on Thursday, that is, the remaining hours of sunlight after Jesus' crucifixion, as day one in his three-day and three-night ordeal. That may squeeze "three days and three nights" into the timeline, but it still fails to add up to seventy-two hours, a literal reading of the text.

Ironically, Thursday adherents must use inclusive calculation to keep Jesus' resurrection from falling sometime between 3:00 pm and 7:03 pm on Sunday. This is the same inclusive calculation that both Wednesday and Thursday crucifixions soundly reject when it comes to Matthew 12:40.

Traditionally, Jesus is thought to have died on the Friday of Passion Week. Harold W. Hoehner spoke for the scholastic world when he wrote, "Some conclude Jesus could not have died on Friday; Jesus may have died on Wednesday or Thursday, thus allowing for three days and three nights. However, when one recognizes that the Jews reckoned a part of a day as a whole day, Jesus' death on Friday does not present a real problem."[113]

Hoehner is correct. Jesus' death on Friday does not present a real problem, but his death either on Wednesday or Thursday presents some insurmountable problems.

The issue of breaking the Sabbath travel ban

Another perceived problem with the Friday crucifixion is that if Christ were crucified on a Friday, both he and all his disciples would have broken the Sabbath by traveling to Lazarus' house on the weekly Sabbath. "Six days before the Passover, Jesus therefore came to Bethany, where Lazarus was, whom Jesus had raised from the dead" (John 12:1).

However, this assumption itself presents several problems. First is the math. As noted in the previous chapter, if Jesus was crucified on Friday (the day of Preparation) and the next day was both the weekly Sabbath and the Passover Sabbath, six days before that Passover Sabbath would be Sunday, not Saturday. Counting backward six days from the Passover:

Day 1 = Friday

Day 2 = Thursday

Day 3 = Wednesday

Day 4 = Tuesday

Day 5 = Monday

Day 6 = Sunday

The second difficulty is, that if Jesus and his disciples broke the Sabbath day's journey rule, that would only be true if Friday was the "High Day," not Saturday. Those who adhere to a Thursday crucifixion believe Friday to be the annual Passover Sabbath, and thus six days prior would be the Sabbath of the week before. But that is built on a faulty assumption that Friday was the Passover Sabbath and is a problem only for a Thursday crucifixion, not a Friday one. If Saturday, the day of the weekly Sabbath, was also the day of the annual Passover Sabbath, this perceived problem evaporates.

There is a third consideration answering why Jesus and his disciples did not break God's Sabbath rule. Traveling to Bethany on the Sabbath may have been a violation of Jewish tradition, but it was not a violation of God's law. The closest to a travel restriction for Jewish families is God's statement in Exodus 16:29. "The Lord has given you the Sabbath; therefore on the sixth day he gives you bread for two days. Remain each of you in his place; let no one go out of his place on the seventh day." But this does not precisely address the situation of the traveler. Jesus drew a sharp distinction between the Law of God and the traditions of men (see Mark 7:1–9).

Again, John 12:1 details, "Six days before the Passover, Jesus therefore came to Bethany, where Lazarus was, whom Jesus had raised from the dead." From the close of John 11, we know that "the Passover of the Jews was at hand, and many went up from the country to Jerusalem before the Passover to purify themselves" (verse 55). But "at hand" (Greek: ἐγγὺς; English: *engys*) means "akin" or "near" and is non-specific. Was the Sabbath hours away, days away? The text does not tell us.[114]

What's more, where is the town of Ephraim in the desert wilderness? Was Jesus residing there until the weekly Sabbath before Passion Week? This village appears to be the Ephrain or Ephron (2 Chr 13:19; Josh 15:9) in the hill country five miles west of Jericho, just eight miles north of Jerusalem. Bethel and Ephraim are linked in the writings of Josephus, who chronicled the victories of General Vespasian (*Wars* 4.9.9; see also 1 Macc 5:46; 2 Macc 12:27).

A Friday crucifixion presents fewer obstacles than either the Wednesday or Thursday theories. It also offers more definitive proof. In fact, the only serious challenge to a Friday crucifixion is the incorrect interpretation of Matthew 12:40.

The Case for a Friday Crucifixion   181

This leads us back to the historical belief that Jesus was crucified on Friday, died around 3:00 pm, was buried before sunset that same day, and rested in the grave Friday/Saturday night, all day Saturday, and Saturday/Sunday until the moment he rose from the dead. His resurrection was affirmed by Mary Magdalene and the other women who arrived at the empty tomb just before dawn on Sunday morning. This has been the historical, biblical, and consistent position of the Christian faith for nearly 2,000 years.

The issue of too little time

One of the major reasons why advocates of either a Wednesday or a Thursday crucifixion reject the traditional Friday crucifixion is the issue of time. As one Internet scribe put it:

> The crucifixion of Jesus had actually to take place on Thursday! Hebrew days begin at sunset . . .If Jesus had been crucified on Hebrew Friday, there would have been too many time-consuming things for Joseph to do before sunset when the Sabbath would have begun][115]

In the entry entitled "Crucifixion" in the *Jewish Encyclopedia*, Reform Jewish scholars Kaufmann Kohler and Emil G. Hirsch make this same argument saying, "On that day [the day Christ died], in view of the approach of the Sabbath (or holiday), executions lasting until late in the afternoon were almost impossible." They cite the Talmud, *Sanhedrin* 35 b, as evidence.

But is this really a strong argument? Remember what we know from the Gospels themselves.

- Jesus was crucified outside the gate of the walls of Jerusalem (Matt 27:32; John 19:17).
- The distance from the Church of the Holy Sepulcher, the supposed site of ancient Golgotha, to the location of Herod's Palace where Pilate resided when in Jerusalem is merely 3/10 of a mile (just 528 yards).
- Specific studies have found pedestrian walking speeds ranging from 2.8 miles per hour (mph) (4.51 kilometers per hour—kph) to 2.95 mph (4.75 kph) for older individuals. Younger people walk faster. As a member of the Sanhedrin, Joseph of Arimathea and Nicodemus both fit in the "older individuals" category.

So, after Jesus died, which the Bible says occurred around 3:00 pm (Matt 27:45), and after the Roman soldier pierced Jesus' side to ensure that he was dead, how long would it take Joseph to walk to Pilate's palace and ask for the body of Jesus for burial?

- Let's say he was even slower than the average older adult, and Joseph could only walk 2.5 mph. At that rate, he could walk between Golgotha and Pilate's residence in just over seven minutes.

- We have no idea how long it took for him to get an audience with Pilate, but it could not have been too long on this day. Jesus was much on Pilate's mind. At the most, it had only been eight hours since Pilate released the Savior to the howling mob to be crucified. But let's suppose it took thirty minutes to obtain the interview. It may have been three minutes, but we will err on the side of caution.

- Pilate asked the centurion to confirm Jesus was dead, which he did. Every implication is the centurion was already at Pilate's palace because Mark 15:44 says that Pilate was "summoning the centurion." That verb (Greek: προσκαλεσάμενος; English: *proskalesamenos*) is composed of two smaller words, *prós* (πρός), which is a preposition of direction meaning *toward*, and the verb *kaléō* (Greek: καλέω) meaning *to call*. "Call toward" suggests Pilate turned in the direction of the centurion and called him to come closer.

- With gratitude, Joseph hurriedly returned to Golgotha. With the help of others, Joseph removed Jesus' body from the cross and placed it on the preparation slab in his tomb's antechamber. Theoretically, these activities took another thirty minutes, although realistically it was probably much less.

- We know the tomb was nearby because John 19:41 records, "Now in the place where he was crucified there was a garden, and in the garden a new tomb in which no one had yet been laid."

- Mark 15:46 tells us that Joseph had the linen shroud with him when he returned to Golgotha. "And Joseph bought a linen shroud, and taking him down, wrapped him in the linen shroud and laid him in a tomb that had been cut out of the rock."

- Nicodemus rejoined Joseph at the tomb, perhaps having procured the burial spices while Joseph was at Pilate's palace requesting Jesus' body (John 19:39).

- The faithful women followed Joseph to the tomb to identify its location, but then returned to their homes to prepare for the Sabbath (Luke 23:55–56).

- Joseph and Nicodemus hurriedly prepared Jesus' body as best they could, and also returned to their homes for the Sabbath.

So, the clock is ticking. Sunset in April in the city of Jerusalem at this time of year is 7:03 pm. To the best of our ability, let us add up the hours and minutes between 3:00 pm and sunset to see if all the activity recorded in the Bible fits or not.

Table 5: Activity Between Jesus' Death and the Crucifixion Day Sunset

Time	Activity As Recorded in The Gospels
3:00 pm	Jesus breathed his last; God's veil of darkness lifted.
3:25 pm	Jesus' side was pierced; Joseph left Golgotha for Pilate's Palace.
3:45 pm	Joseph arrived at Pilate's palace, a 528-yard walk of less than 10 minutes.
4:00 pm	Joseph received an audience with Pilate.
4:15 pm	The centurion confirmed Jesus was dead.
4:30 pm	Joseph arrived back at Golgotha with a linen shroud.
5:00 pm	Jesus was removed from the cross by Nicodemus, Joseph, and his servants.
5:20 pm	Joseph and the others arrived at his nearby tomb.
5:30 pm	The faithful women left for their homes to prepare for the Sabbath.
5:50 pm	Perhaps the women purchased spices on the way, but now are home.
6:00 pm	Joseph and Nicodemus finished a hurried preparation of Jesus' body.
6:30 pm	Joseph and Nicodemus were back in their homes for the Sabbath.
7:03 pm	Sunset in April in the Holy City, Jerusalem

I have attempted to be super generous in allotting the time for each activity. Please remember. As the psalmist said, Jerusalem is a "city that is compact together" (Ps 122:3). The distance between Golgotha and Pilate's palace was about 528 yards or a little more than five football fields in length. It was only a seven or eight-minute walk. Joseph and Nicodemus could have removed Jesus' body from the cross, carried it to Joseph's nearby tomb, thoroughly washed it, rubbed it with spices, and wrapped it in a shroud, then returned to their homes for the Sabbath—with thirty-three minutes to spare. The women also were safely back in their homes with an hour and thirteen minutes to spare.

The argument about not having enough time is a figment of the imagination that does not stand up to the clock. It's not valid and should be discarded as you would an urban legend.

CONCLUSION

Much has been said in the preceding chapters about the traditional Friday being the day upon which Jesus was crucified. I have not just assumed a Good Friday crucifixion; I have carefully done a deep dive into the pros and cons of the other days, and as Daniel 5:27 says, they "have been weighed in the balances and found wanting." Here are my conclusions regarding what day Jesus was crucified. Others may draw their own conclusions.

First, Friday is not a newcomer to the discussion of the day of Jesus' death. Observing Good Friday dates from antiquity. Wednesday and Thursday are the newcomers.

No evidence exists to indicate the Christian population over the centuries ever placed Jesus' death on any other day. While periodically, someone in history would raise the issue and opt for another day, it was not until the twentieth century that the Wednesday or Thursday theories of Jesus' crucifixion took root. It may not be coincidental that these theories found favor at a time that corresponds with the rise of the Internet. Of course, age is not the equivalent of authenticity. After all, before the ancient Greek Pythagoras, who asserted the Earth is round, and Aristotle who may have been the first to prove it, people thought the Earth was flat. However, it was the prevailing theory that fell flat.

Still, ancient literature supplies no evidence that Jesus' crucifixion ever referred to any day but Friday. If the church knew Jesus was crucified on a day other than Friday, they certainly did not show it. How could Christians hold onto a Friday crucifixion so long if Wednesday or Thursday presents better options? It appears that since the vast majority of Christians throughout the centuries believed Jesus was crucified on Good Friday and rose from the dead on Resurrection Sunday, we should not be in a rush to abandon that traditional belief.

Second, all four Gospel accounts claim Jesus was crucified on the day of Preparation for the Sabbath, not the day before the day of Preparation or the day before that.

Matthew 27:62, Mark 15:42, Luke 23:54, and John 19:14, 31, 42 find agreement on this issue. The day of Preparation for the weekly Sabbath fell on Friday, and if Saturday was the annual Passover Sabbath as well, the day before still fell on Friday. Early on, the day of Preparation was commonly referred to as "Friday." How can other theories hold that Jesus was crucified on the day of Preparation? Easy. They move the goalpost. The meaning or implication of the word Sabbath is changed to fit their theory.

Third, the death, burial, and resurrection of the Lord Jesus Christ is the gospel's central theme, just as it is the New Testament's central theme.

Paul claimed, "For I decided to know nothing among you except Jesus Christ and him crucified" (1 Cor 2:2). "Jesus Christ and him crucified." It was always the substance of the Gospel. And Jesus' resurrection is linked with his crucifixion with equal importance because Jesus promised, "Because I live, you also will live" (John 14:19).

The key expression associated with Jesus' crucifixion is, "Father, forgive them" (Luke 23:34). The key expression associated with his resurrection is, "on the third day." In the Gospels, this expression is found ten times (Matt 16:21; 17:23; 20:19; 27:64; Mark 9:31; 10:34; Luke 9:22; 13:32; 18:33; 24:7). The fact that Jesus rose from the dead on the third day is affirmed in the Gospels (Luke 24:46), in the book of Acts (Acts 10:40), and in the epistles (1 Cor 15:4). This particular expression is a deciding factor in determining that Jesus was crucified on Good Friday and raised from the dead on Easter Sunday morning.

Finally, the texts of the Gospels, the weight of time, the Church Fathers, past and present scholarship, and common sense all come down on the side of a Friday crucifixion.

The Internet debate, the ongoing posts, and the endless threads of discussion from those who are certain they have the only correct answer, are not always healthy. Many display a little slice of knowledge but fail to consider the broader range of factors necessary to make an informed decision about this question.

If you live in an island nation, you may feel a kinship with those who lived in the days of the New Testament. Your environment may cause you not always to be aware of the time. But if your life is the hectic pace of an urban dweller, you know what it means to be looking at your smartphone or atomic watch at least every other minute.

Time is important. Accuracy is important. However, none of us should lose sleep over the year or the day of the week on which Jesus was crucified. Wednesday and Thursday advocates can still have good fellowship with those who support a Friday crucifixion. That fellowship is based on the Crucified One, not the day of his crucifixion. The most critical issue here is the fact, not the day.

> Wounded for me, wounded for me,
> There on the cross he was wounded for me;
> Gone my transgressions, and now I am free,
> All because Jesus was wounded for me.
>
> Dying for me, dying for me,
> There on the cross he was dying for me;
> Now in his death my redemption I see,
> All because Jesus was dying for me.

Risen for me, risen for me,
Up from the grave he has risen for me;
Now evermore from death's sting I am free,
All because Jesus has risen for me.
—William Gilbert Ovens

Chapter 7

Passion Week Timeline

Creating an accurate hour-by-hour, minute-by-minute timeline of the Passion Week would only be attempted by a fool. But as Alexander Pope said in his 1711 poem, An Essay on Criticism, "Fools rush in where angels fear to tread." That line seems eminently appropriate here.

IDENTIFYING THE CORRECT YEAR and day of Jesus' crucifixion has not proven to be as easy as one might think. Scholars have given a lifetime to deciphering these issues and are still at odds with the results. You should not expect to find the answer to this issue in a Bible study, discussion group, or blog post.

In this chapter are presented various timelines devised by scholars indicating the variety of opinions about Jesus' last few days on this side of the grave.

At the very outset, anyone who proposes a timeline for the last week of Christ's life must truthfully admit he or she may be wrong. There is so much we do not know, so many things we cannot prove, affecting any timeline. So, I admit it. The room for error is the largest room in the house. My conclusions in this chapter could be off the mark. Nonetheless, I hope to present a reasoned case for the order and timing of Passion Week events. First, we must examine both the traditional timeline and some alternative timelines for Passion Week.

TRADITIONAL AND ALTERNATIVE CHRONOLOGIES FOR PASSION WEEK

The long-held traditional chronology of the last week of our Lord's life places the Triumphal Entry on Sunday, the crucifixion on the following Friday, and the resurrection on Sunday. It is also characterized by what came to be known as the "Silent Wednesday." The traditional Passion Week is Table 1.

Table 1: Traditional Passover Chronology

Saturday	Jesus and his disciples had supper at Bethany.
Sunday	Jesus' Triumphal Entry into Jerusalem. He spent the day in the Temple.
Monday	Jesus cursed the fig tree and then cleansed the Temple.
Tuesday	Jesus' authority was challenged by Jerusalem's religious leaders.
	Jesus declared the Messiah to be the son of David.
	Jesus wept over Jerusalem's stubborn unbelief.
	Jesus delivered the "Olivet Discourse."
	Judas made plans to betray Jesus.
Wednesday	The "Silent Day" when no activity is recorded of Jesus or his disciples.
Thursday	The day of Preparation for the Passover.
	Jesus delivered the "Upper Room Discourse."
	Jesus ate the Last Supper and instituted the Lord's Supper.
	Jesus agonized in prayer, but yielded to the Father's will.
	Jesus arrested, taken to Annas for interrogation.
Friday	Jesus sent to Caiaphas for a make-shift trial with a quorum of the Sanhedrin.
	Peter denied Jesus three times before the rooster crowed twice.
	Early in the morning, Jesus tried at the Chamber of the Hewn Stone.
	Jesus was transferred to Pilate to pronounce the sentence of death.
	Roman soldiers severely beat Jesus before releasing him to a Jewish mob.
	Jesus walks the Via Dolorosa to Golgotha, where he is crucified.
	Joseph of Arimathea removed Jesus' body from the cross and buried it.
Saturday	Jesus' body remained in the tomb of Joseph of Arimathea.
Sunday	Jesus rose from the dead.
	At dawn, the women discovered the tomb was empty.
	Jesus entered the room where the disciples were gathered.
	Jesus encountered Cleopas and his friend on the road to Emmaus.

More and more scholars are challenging this long-held chronology and configuring the week's timeline differently. One of the more ingenious Passover Week timelines comes from Sir Colin J. Humphreys. Sir Colin is a British physicist and Director of Research at the University of Cambridge. Table 2 is his reconstruction of Passion Week.

ASTRONOMICAL CALENDAR OF PASSION WEEK

The astronomical calendar numbers each year based on the AD year numbering system. However, it strictly follows the standard decimal integer (whole numbers). The astronomical calendar has a year 0. The years before 0 are designated with negative numbers, e.g., –5 BC. The years after year 0 are designated with positive numerals, e.g., +33 AD. The addition of the year 0 only affects the years before it, but not afterward.[116]

Table 2: Humphrey's Passion Week

From the Last Supper to the Crucifixion		
Event	*Gospels*	*Day and Time*
The Last Supper	All	Wednesday, ends 12:00—2:00 am
The Walk to Gethsemane	All	Early Thursday am
Jesus Prays in Gethsemane	The Synoptics	Early Thursday am
Jesus is Arrested	All	Early Thursday am
Jesus is interrogated by Annas	John	Thursday, about 3:00—4:30 am
Peter's First Denial; Cock Crows	All	Thursday, about 3:00 am
Peter's Third Denial; Cock Crows	All	Thursday, about 4:30 am
Jesus is Taken to Caiaphas	All	Thursday, about 5:00 am
Jesus' Trial by the Sanhedrin	The Synoptics	Thursday after sunrise; 5:46 am
Trial by Pontius Pilate	All	Friday morning
Trial by King Herod	Luke	Friday morning
Resumed Trial by Pilate	All	Friday morning
Jesus is Brutally Flogged	Matt/Mark/John	Friday morning
Roman Soldiers Mock Jesus	Matt/Mark/John	Friday morning
Simon Carries Jesus' Cross	The Synoptics	Friday morning
Jesus is Crucified at Golgotha	All	Friday about 9:00 am
Jesus Dies on the Cross	All	Friday about 3:00 pm

Astronomers use the Julian calendar for those years before 1582 AD, including the year 0. However, they used the Gregorian calendar for years after 1582 AD.[117] The standard designations of BC (BCE) or AD (CE) are not used. Instead, year 1 BC is numbered 0, so year 2 is simply labeled—1.

Although the astronomical calendar's numerical values only differ from the historical timeline before year 1, the difference is critical when calculating astronomical events like solar or lunar eclipses. Here, then, is Table 2 representing a calendar of the Passion Week based on the astronomical calendar.

As you can see, Humphreys' Passion Week timeline places the Last Supper on Wednesday night instead of Thursday night. He continues to put Jesus in front of Pilate and subsequently on the cross on Friday morning but elongates the trials of Annas and Caiaphas so they occupy the timespan between early Thursday morning and early Friday morning. Traditionally these trials would be allotted only a few hours; Humphreys extends them to approximately twenty-four hours.

This begs the question of how we arrive at the correct Passion Week timeline. What are the sources of verifiable information from which we can draw?

Here is one scholar's account of what happened that Friday.

> About six o'clock in the morning, Pilate passed sentence upon Jesus, executing the order that he should be crucified. Almost three hours passed before the crucifixion took place . . . At Calvary, they drove the nails into his hands and feet, and the cross was mounted with Jesus upon it by nine o'clock. For three hours, Christ hanged upon the cross, while the burning eastern sun intensified the agony of the crucifixion. At noon the light of the sun was extinguished, and a cloak of darkness was cast over the earth for a period of three hours. About three o'clock in the afternoon, the darkness was dispelled as suddenly as it had appeared, and the light of the sun shone down upon the earth once more. Nine hours had passed, therefore, since Jesus had been led forth from Pilate's judgment hall, nine hours of suffering, nine hours of pain, nine hours without a crust of bread.[118]

As stressed earlier, creating an accurate hour-by-hour, minute-by-minute timeline of Passion Week is nearly impossible. I have assigned some of the times below based on the distance traveled, the reasonable time necessary for an event, and informed speculation about other periods. Sometimes that informed speculation is little more than a conjecture. But at least the timeline I propose is plausible and fits within all the timeline clues provided by the Gospels. What are those timeline clues?

TIMELINE CLUES FROM THE GOSPELS

We do not have many time clues from the Gospels to create an accurate crucifixion day timeline, but we do have some. Here they are:

5:00 am—Matthew 27:1 tells us that "When morning (Greek: Πρωΐας; English: *Prōia*) came, all the chief priests and the elders of the people took counsel against Jesus to put him to death." Mark confirms Matthew's words (Mark 15:1), and John agrees (John 18:28). The word πρωΐα means the dawn or early morning. It indicates an event that takes place at first light. Sunrise in Jerusalem this time of year occurs at 6:24 am.

5:45 am—Matthew 27:2 indicates, "And they bound him and led him away and delivered him over to Pilate the governor." Mark confirms this. "And they bound Jesus and led him away and delivered him over to Pilate" (Mark 15:1). John 18:28 says, "Then they led Jesus from the house of Caiaphas to the governor's headquarters. It was early morning." Again, *prōia* is used indicating it was very early in the morning.

9:00 am—Mark 15:22, 25, "And they brought him to the place called Golgotha (which means Place of a Skull) . . . And it was the third hour when they crucified him." The third hour in Roman time corresponds with our 9:00 am.

According to John, it was midday when Jesus' sentence was passed (John 19:24). How are we to reconcile these contradictory statements? Each evangelist is following his own plan. John's sixth hour (midday) has something of a liturgical meaning; it is the moment when the Passover begins. Jesus, therefore, was sentenced at the beginning of the Jewish Passover. Mark uses the simpler three-hour reckoning periods, as the Romans did. The meeting of the Sanhedrin took place at dawn, that is, the first hour (Mark 15:1); at the third hour, Jesus' crucifixion; at the sixth, the darkness; at the ninth, the Savior breathed his last. His division of time is schematic.[119]

> "The hour had come! The Lamb slain from the foundation of the world was now to be slain before the eyes of the world."
> —Jessie Penn-Lewis

Noon—Matthew 27:45, "Now from the sixth hour there was darkness over all the land until the ninth hour." Mark 15:33 and Luke 23:44-45 concur. "It was about the sixth hour, says John, that is, midday, the hour when the preparations for the Passover began with the removal of all leavened bread [from the house]. It was also the moment when preparations began for the ultimate Passover, with the slaughter of the Lamb, Jesus."[120]

3:00 pm—Mark 15:34 reports, "And at the ninth hour Jesus cried with a loud voice, 'Eloi, Eloi, lema sabachthani?' which means, 'My God, my God, why have you forsaken me?'" Matthew 27:46 confirms this. Upon making this cry, the three-hour interlude of darkness was lifted from the earth.

4:10 pm—Matthew recorded, "When it was evening (Greek: Ὀψίας; English: *Opsias*), there came a rich man from Arimathea, named Joseph, who also was a disciple of Jesus" (Matt 27:57). The word translated "evening" means late afternoon (early evening) as opposed to the hours after nightfall (later evening). Mark 15:42-43, "And when evening had come, since it was the day of Preparation, that is, the day before the Sabbath, Joseph of Arimathea, a respected member of the Council, who was also himself looking for the kingdom of God, took courage and went to Pilate and asked for the body of Jesus" (see also Mark 1:32; 14:17; John 20:19). The word *ópsios* implies a time approaching the "golden hour" before sunset.

6:30 pm—It is now the evening of Jesus' crucifixion. "The Greek word translated 'Preparation' means the eve of the Sabbath, the *Erev Shabbat* of the Jews, which has the special meaning of 'preparation for the Sabbath,' as Mark explains for the benefit of readers who are unfamiliar with this expression peculiar to Judaism."[121]

7:03 pm—At this time of year, this is the exact time the sun sets in Jerusalem. Everyone settles in for the night [to the house, not the bed].

6:00 am—It's now the morning of the third day. Jesus' body has been captive to Joseph's tomb for thirty-six hours. Luke 24:1-3 confidently records, "But on the first day of the week, at early dawn, they went to the tomb, taking the spices they had prepared. And they found the stone rolled away from the tomb, but when they went in they did not find the body of the Lord Jesus." Later in that chapter, Luke says of these women, "They were at the tomb early in the morning" (Luke 24:22).

The beloved physician wanted to stress that the women came extremely early to the tomb because he used two words, not one, to indicate the time of day. Luke used one word (Greek: ὄρθρος; English: *órthros*) meaning "at the rising of the light" immediately before (Greek: βαθύς: English: *bathýs*) the word meaning "very early."[122]

Armed with these time clues, I hesitantly offer this hour-by-hour account of the final days of Jesus' Passion Week.

A POSSIBLE HOUR-BY-HOUR, MINUTE-BY-MINUTE TIMELINE

As mentioned, creating an accurate hour-by-hour, minute-by-minute timeline of the Passion Week would only be attempted by a fool. But as Alexander Pope said in his 1711 poem, *An Essay on Criticism*, "Fools rush in where angels fear to tread." That line seems eminently appropriate here. Here is my best estimate of the order and timing of the events from Thursday to Sunday of Jesus' Passion Week.

Table 3: Kroll's Crucifixion Timeline: Thursday Into Friday

Possible Crucifixion Timeline: Gethsemane to Golgotha		
Thursday		
9:30 pm	Jesus Wrestles With God's Will	Matt 26:37–46; Mark 14:33–42
10:30 pm	Judas Arrives to Betray Jesus	Matt 26:47–50; Mark 14:43–50;
11:00 pm	Annas' Interrogation Begins	John 18:12–13, 19–24
11:40 pm	Quick Sanhedrin Quorum Trial	Matt 26:59–68; Mark 14:55–65;
Midnight	Jesus in Caiaphas' palace prison	Luke 22:66
Friday		
5:00 am	Sanhedrin Meet, Confirm Verdict	Matt 27:1–2; Mark 15:1
5:45 am	Jesus Sent to Pilate for Trial	Matt 27:11–14; John 18:28–37 15:2–5
6:45 am	Jesus Sent to King Herod	Luke 23:6–12
7:45 am	Jesus Returned to Pilate	Luke 23:11
8:00 am	Jesus Sentenced to Crucifixion	Matt 27:26; Mark 15:15;
8:10 am	Jesus Abused by Roman Soldiers	Matt 27:27–31; Mark 15:16–20
8:30 am	Jesus Led Away to Golgotha	Luke 23:26–31; John 19:16–17

The events in Table 4, while reasonable and likely, are a bit more precise because of the Gospels' record of 9:00 am (Mark 15:25) and 3:00 pm (Matt 27:45, 46; Mark 14:33, 34). What is best to be gained from the possible timetable of Golgotha to the Grave (Table 4) is the demonstration that there was sufficient time for Joseph of Arimathea and Nicodemus to prepare Jesus' body for burial and both of them to return home before sunset and the first three stars of the evening appeared. They could have accomplished all the Gospels say they did and not have violated any Sabbath prohibitions. They were safely at home when the Sabbath began.

The inadequacies you may detect in this attempt to create a crucifixion timeline are likely well-founded. The most authoritative sequence of events during Passion Week came directly from the lips of Jesus Himself.

> And as Jesus was going up to Jerusalem, he took the twelve disciples aside, and on the way he said to them, "See, we are going up to Jerusalem. And the Son of Man will be delivered over to the chief priests and scribes, and they will condemn him to death and deliver him over to the Gentiles to be mocked and flogged and crucified, and he will be raised on the third day" (Matt 20:17–19).

Table 4: Kroll's Crucifixion Timeline Friday

Possible Crucifixion Timeline: Golgotha to the Grave		
Friday		
9:00 am	Jesus nailed to the cross	John 19:17–18
10:00 am	Jesus said, "Father, forgive. . ."	Luke 23:34
11:00 am	Jesus spoke to the criminals	Luke 23:39–43
11:30 am	Jesus spoke to Mary and John	John 19:26–27
12:00 pm	Darkness covered the land	Matt 27:45; Mark 15:33; Luke 23:44
3:00 pm	Jesus moaned, "My God, my God, why?"	Matt 27:46; Mark 15:34
3:01 pm	Jesus said "I thirst"	John 19:28
3:02 pm	Jesus declared, "It is finished"	John 19:30
3:02 pm	Earthquake, veil torn, graves opened	Matt 27:51; Mark 15:38
3:03 pm	Jesus said, "Into your hands"	Luke 23:46
3:25 pm	Roman Soldier pierced Jesus' side	John 19:34–37
4:00 pm	Joseph asked for burial permission	Matt 27:57–58; John 19:38
4:15 pm	Pilate granted permission	Matt 27:57–58; John 19:38
4:45 pm	Jesus' body was removed from the cross	Mark 15:46; Luke 23:53; John 19:38
5:15 pm	Jesus' body was washed, spiced	John 19:40
6:00 pm	Jesus' body was placed in the tomb	Luke 23:53; John 19:40
6:30 pm	Joseph and Nicodemus were back in their homes before 7:03 pm sundown	Lev 23:5, between the two evenings

Regardless of how we arrange or rearrange the events and days of Passion Week, this does not change the bottom line.

He suffered under Pontius Pilate,
was crucified, died, and was buried;
He descended to hell.
The third day he rose again from the dead.
He ascended to heaven
and is seated at the right hand of God the Father almighty.
—*The Apostles' Creed*

Chapter 8

The Impact of Jesus' Birth Date on His Death Date

We must begin with the assumption that Luke was a competent historian, careful of his facts, and not prone to unverified statements, and his writings generally support such a reputation.

> O little town of Bethlehem
> How still we see thee lie,
> Above thy deep and dreamless sleep
> The silent stars go by.
> Yet in thy dark streets shineth
> The everlasting light,
> The hopes and fears of all the years
> Are met in thee tonight.
> —Phillips Brooks

I HOPE YOU DWELT long enough thinking about Phillips Brooks's Christmas carol to recognize one of the most meaningful contrasts ever put to paper. In that little town of Bethlehem, on that fateful night when the Savior who is Christ the Lord was born, Brooks noted, "The hopes and fears of all the years, are met in thee tonight."

It's the balance of history. On one side are our hopes, hopes for a better life, hopes for shelter and safety, hopes for a brighter future. On the other side are our fears, fears life won't get better, fears that shelter and safety are tenuous, and fears that the future grows dimmer each day. Hopes on one side, fears on the other. And where will they be brought together so our fears can be diminished even destroyed by our hopes? In the babe in the Bethlehem manger.

It was quite a night. Relatives of residents packed the little town of Bethlehem. They had come for the census ordered by Augustus Caesar. Streets were booming with the din of donkeys, nervous sheep, street vendors, and people greeting each other. Joseph and his pregnant wife Mary arrived from Nazareth to discover his relatives had no more room for their out-of-town guests. Stars ignited the sky with an aura of majesty. There were angels among those stars, ready to descend to Earth. There were shepherds in the star-lit fields, drowsily protecting their flocks. It was the perfect scene for a modern Christmas card.

But this book is about Jesus' crucifixion, not his birth. It's about the end of his life, not the beginning. What does Jesus' birth in Bethlehem have to do with his death in Jerusalem? As you will see, being able to determine the year Jesus was born, along with some clear biblical clues, helps us identify the date of Jesus' death.

> "Forgiveness is the reason for the crucifixion, and the crucifixion is the reason for the Incarnation."—Peter Kreeft

A "nativity-based" approach to estimating the year of Jesus' death relies on an analysis of the nativity narratives in the Gospels of Luke and Matthew, along with other corresponding historical data.[123] Neither Luke nor Matthew mentions the day, date, or even time of year Jesus was born, although Luke 2:2 does refer to the fact there was a census taken near that time by the Roman aristocrat Quirinius. Also, both Luke and Matthew associate Jesus' incarnation with the days of Herod the Great.

We should not construe the paucity of historical dating as proof that Jesus never existed. There is no scarcity when establishing the historical Jesus. Credible historians and theologians agree with American New Testament scholar and theologian Marcus Borg. "Some judgments are so probable as to be certain; for example, Jesus really existed."[124] Baptist theologian and apologist Bernard Ramm added, "There is almost universal agreement that Jesus lived."[125] The issue of Jesus' existence is not in question. It is the relationship of his birth to his death that is the focus of this chapter.

THE QUESTION OF QUIRINIUS' CENSUS

Since the census taken by Quirinius is one of the few biblical clues we have for the year of Jesus' birth, it is necessary to explore what we know about Quirinius and his census. Here's how first-century Roman historian and politician Tacitus described Quirinius.

> An indefatigable soldier, he had by his zealous services won the consulship under the Divine Augustus [in 12 BC], and subsequently the honors of a triumph for having stormed some fortresses of the Homonadeises in Cilicia. He was also appointed adviser to Caius Caesar [from 2 to 4 AD] in the government of Armenia and had likewise paid court to Tiberius, who was then at Rhodes (*Annals* 3:48).

The most controversial aspect of dating Jesus' birth is the census commanded by Caesar Augustus and carried out by Quirinius.

For centuries the Roman aristocrat Publius Sulpicius Quirinius (c. 51 BC–21 AD), governor of Syria, and his census have been the subject of much debate in the academic community. The British academic and ancient historian A. N. Sherwin-White commented, "There is one name that has caused more controversy than any other of the Roman phenomena in the New Testament, that of Quirinius, the governor of Syria."[126] Luke's Gospel used the census of Quirinius to establish the timeframe for the birth of Jesus Christ (Luke 2:1–5). But Luke also placed the census within the reign of Herod the Great, who died years earlier.[127]

Most liberal scholars believe Luke was simply in error when he placed the birth of Jesus during the census of Quirinius, which took place in 6 AD. Some say, "Luke has thoroughly confused the facts"[128] Others say, "There is, in fact, no alternative but to recognize that the evangelist based his statement on uncertain historical information."[129] And more recently some have expressed their doubts, saying that, "Attempts to reconcile [Luke's text] with the facts of ancient history are hopelessly contrived."[130] And yet there must be good reasons why more conservative scholars adhere tenaciously to the authenticity and accuracy of Luke's record.

Why the Quirinius census?

Quirinius became the Roman governor of Syria when the Roman armies seized control of the area in 6 AD. The census associated with his name was taken of Judea's inhabitants. Josephus says in his *Antiquities*, Book 18.1.1, "Cyrenius came himself into Judea, which was now added to the province of

Syria, to take an account of their substance." Most of what we know about Quirinius we learn from Tacitus, the Roman historian. His *Annals* (3.48) describe the rise and fall of Publius Sulpicius Quirinius.

The edict of Augustus Caesar, recorded in Luke 2:1–2, is also recorded by the second/third-century Roman historian Cassius Dio. Rome had been systematically moving across the world, conquering empire after empire. By 5 AD, expenditures to keep the Roman legions moving forward exceeded Rome's income. Rome had moved so quickly conquering the world that there was a chance the empire would be flat broke. Cassius Dio records that "Augustus lacked funds for all these troops."[131]

To meet this challenge, in 6 AD Caesar established a military treasury. "Augustus made a contribution himself toward the fund and promised to do so annually, and he also accepted voluntary contributions from kings and certain communities; but he took nothing from private citizens.... this proved very slight in comparison with the amount being spent."[132]

Cassius Dio conclusively described the action taken to overcome this mounting deficit. "[Augustus] established the tax of five percent, on the inheritances and bequests which should be left by people at their death to any except very near relatives or very poor persons, representing that he had found this tax set down in Caesar's memoranda ... In this way, then, he increased the revenues."[133]

> "The knotty question of Quirinius is the major historical problem of the New Testament."—Jerry Vardaman

So, in 6 AD, Caesar Augustus issued an empire-wide decree that, for a second time, there would be a five percent inheritance tax on estates; this was above the regular taxation. Such taxation required a census to register transferable assets, such as land, or record genealogies to establish "very near relatives."

The journey to Bethlehem

Luke's account of Joseph and Mary traveling to Bethlehem as required by the census is familiar to almost everyone (Luke 2:1–7). Critics of the Lucan account maintain there was no need for Joseph, not to mention Mary, to make that arduous journey from Nazareth to Bethlehem. Joseph could have registered in Nazareth, where he lived. They deny the need for Jews to return to their tribal headquarters to be "numbered" as required by a census under Herod.[134] Nonetheless, it is a fact that a census usually occurred in one's hometown.[135] F. F. Bruce mentions an Egyptian papyrus dating from 104 AD reporting that people living under Roman rule must always return to their home city for the taxation census.[136] There were no online registrations in those days.

Justin Martyr's second-century writings defended Christians against persecution. Once, Justin remarked, "Now there is a village in the land of the Jews, thirty-five stadia[137] from Jerusalem, in which Christ was born, as you can ascertain also from the registries of the taxing under Quirinius your first procurator in Judea" (*First Apology*, 34).

Despite liberal protests, the historical record is clear that inheritance taxation would also require a census to be conducted where tribal records were kept, regardless of who performed the census. Joseph was a descendant of David, of the tribe of Judah. David's ancestral home was Bethlehem, and only in Bethlehem were the land records and genealogies kept required for such a census.

Historians corroborate the Gospel narratives that taxing the local Jewish population during the years Jesus was born, lived, and died was a fact. But there have been other apprehensions.

ARGUMENTS AGAINST THE ACCURACY OF LUKE'S ACCOUNT

We must begin with the assumption that Luke was a competent historian, careful of his facts, and not prone to unverified statements, and his writings generally support such a reputation. These assumptions were scientifically verified by Sir William Ramsay.[138] However, one of the main apprehensions scholars have is an apparent contradiction between the date of the census of Quirinius and the reign of Herod the Great. For some scholars, this has led to the opinion that Luke was an inaccurate historian and should not be trusted.

Luke 1:5 tells us, "In the days of Herod, king of Judea" Zechariah and Elizabeth were told they would have a son, John the Baptist. This places Jesus' birth during the same time frame, just six months later (Luke 1:24–27). Matthew concurs (Matt 2:1–7). However, Luke also places the birth of Jesus during the Syrian governorship of Quirinius (Luke 2:1–2). Quirinius was governor of Syria from 6 to 9 AD, an apparent discrepancy that has triggered much debate.

The objections to Luke's account and the challenge to his historical accuracy were solidified by the nineteenth-century German Protestant theologian Emil Schürer's work, *A History of the Jewish People in the Time of Jesus Christ*. Schürer's book was published near the end of the nineteenth century, at the very height of the literary criticism movement.[139]

Emil Schürer posited five reasons why Luke could not be historically accurate:

- (1) Nothing in history is known of a general census in the time of Augustus;

- (2) In a Roman census, Joseph would not have had to travel to Bethlehem but would have registered in the principal town of his residence, and Mary would not have had to register at all;

- (3) No Roman census would have been made in Palestine during Herod's reign;

- (4) Josephus records nothing of a Roman census in Palestine in the time of Herod—instead, the census of 6–7 AD was something new among the Jews; and

- (5) A census held under Quirinius could not have occurred during Herod's reign, for Quirinius was not governor until after Herod's death.[140]

As weighty as these objections may seem, all can be answered with ease. In his equally weighty work, *Chronological Aspects of the Life of Christ*, Harold W. Hoehner convincingly counters each of Schürer's objections.[141]

Opinions on whether or not Luke was in error tend to fall along theological lines. While conservative theologians maintain reasonable explanations for the apparent discrepancies, more liberal theologians say Luke was blatantly mistaken. For example, Candler School of Theology professor Luke Johnson's assertion that, "On the basis of exhaustive research, Luke's dates seem to be out of kilter: Quirinius and the census under him do not match the other dates."[142]

John P. Meier says, "Luke makes chronological errors at times." Still, Meier attempts to verify his statement by citing only Luke 2:2 and Acts 5:36 as examples of supposed errors, the two references to the census in Luke and Acts.[143] That is hardly proof. Even though Raymond Brown tends to create a monumental, often conservative-leaning work when he writes, in his massive two-volume *magnum opus* entitled *The Birth of the Messiah*, he builds his entire case on the assumption that Luke 2:2 is not at all historically accurate.[144]

Historian David J. Hayles sums up the argument against Luke's accuracy in the Quirinius matter. He says, "It is urged that a general census of the Empire is a fabrication, that the local one under Herod an impossibility, that the enrollment requiring a return to one's own city quite improbable, and that any association of Quirinius with a census this early is completely anachronistic."[145]

But while Luke's accuracy has its critics, so too it has its defenders, and they must be permitted to have their say.

ARGUMENTS FOR THE ACCURACY OF LUKE'S ACCOUNT

Attempts to counterpunch the blows of liberal scholars on Luke's accuracy have exhibited varying degrees of plausibility. Here are a few theories that, in my opinion, have proven to be inadequate.

Author and publisher George Ogg proposed that Quirinius did not rule Syria in 6–7 AD but instead 8 to 14 years earlier. Ogg claimed that those sources giving a 6–7 AD are simply wrong; this would include Josephus.[146]

Others have suggested that the name Quirinius in Luke 2:2 instead should have been Saturninus, a first-century Roman *quaestor* and tribune. As proof, a few scholars have pointed to a statement made by Tertullian about the birth of Christ. The eminent Church Father said, "There is historical proof that at this very time [a census] had been taken in Judea by Sentius Saturninus, which might have satisfied their inquiry respecting the family and descent of Christ."[147] Those who hold to this theory think that an early scribe mistakenly changed Saturninus's name to Quirinius.

These views have not garnered much support, likely because they do not satisfy the need for critical evidence or even plausibility.[148]

Many arguments are more credible supporting Luke as accurate in placing Quirinius' census during the reign of Herod the Great. Below are only the most reasonable explanations.

#1 Explanation: A census by Quirinius earlier than 6 AD

Some scholars say an earlier census was taken by Quirinius, which would eliminate the problem of the difference in Luke's dating. According to Josephus, when Quirinius liquidated Archelaus's estate, by the thirty-seventh year after Caesar's defeat of Antony at Actium [6 AD], all property registrations were complete (*Ant*.18.1.1). The first registration under Herod the Great was done to count the number of citizens in the Roman Empire, but must not be confused with the 6 AD census which was taken only in Judea by Quirinius. The two censuses did not have the same geographical scope, nor did they have the same purpose.[149]

Ben Witherington III, Professor of New Testament Interpretation at Asbury Theological Seminary, helps clarify the issue.

> This census was an obvious historical landmark that many would be familiar with. Luke uses it to provide Theophilus with a general frame of reference. Luke is saying, in essence, "You remember the cause célèbre that happened when Quirinius took a census as governor of Syria. Well, there was a less famous census before that one, the very first census of its kind, which precipitated a journey by Jesus's family to Bethlehem." Chronological precision was not required even in very good Hellenistic historiography, and so Luke is content to let Theophilus know that the census he has in mind transpired before AD 6.[150]

Baptist archaeologist Jerry Vardaman says when Agrippa died in March 12 BC, "It is my opinion that Quirinius took his place in the region of Syria (at least between 12 and 10 BC). He was serving as consul in Rome when Agrippa died—consul being the normal post held before appointment as governor of Syria." Vardaman based his belief that Agrippa's sons, Gaius and Lucius (the grandsons of Augustus), were too young to rule in his place. Thus, until Gaius and Lucius were mature enough to rule, Quirinius stepped in to rule in their stead.[151]

One last thing. Sir William Ramsay, knighted by King Edward VII, was the first Professor of Classical Art and Architecture at Oxford. Ramsay discovered several inscriptions that indicated Quirinius was governor of Syria on two occasions, the first time several years before this 6 AD date.[152] Thus, some propose there was a census by Quirinius before the 6 AD census, which would clear up the confusion in dating.

#2 Explanation: One elongated census, not two

Other scholars have proposed that a census could take years to complete and thus Quirinius' two censuses were just one. Research professor Darrell L. Bock notes, "It is here often noted that censuses were giant undertakings, surely taking several years to complete (e.g., a 40-year-long census in Gaul)."[153] A variant of this view was proposed by twentieth-century German Protestant theologian Ethelbert Stauffer. He advocated that in 7 BC, Luke's "*apographa . . .* began" and in "AD 7 the work of the census was completed with the *apotimesis.*"[154] Apographa, from the Greek meaning "copied," are copies or transcripts of texts copied from the original autographs of the original authors.

But Bock points out, "Luke's use of *apographēs* (απογραφης) in his description of the AD 6 census points away from this [one elongated census] (Acts 5:37), as does Josephus's use of both terms in his description of this census (*Ant.*18.2–4; cf. also *Wars* 7.8.1)."[155]

While it is reasonable, the idea of one elongated census covering the years of an earlier and later census by Quirinius does not seem to fit all the facts.

#3 Explanation: The pattern of multiple censuses

Census taking was not unusual during the time of Christ. Cassius Dio writes, "For the Britons seemed likely to make terms with him, and the affairs of the Gauls were still unsettled, as the civil wars had begun immediately after their subjugation. He took a census of the inhabitants and regulated their life and government."[156]

Dio mentions that when Agrippa died, Augustus would not even look at Agrippa's corpse because, according to some explanations, it was the year of a census (12/11 BC).[157] Cassius Dio also referred to a census that Augustus conducted himself in 11 BC (*Roman History*, 54.35.1ff). Livy mentions that Drusus, the father of the future Roman Emperor Claudius, conducted a census in Gaul in 12 BC.[158] This census is alluded to by Tacitus (*Annals* 11.23.1–11.25.1). It is also thoroughly documented in the famous Tablet of Lyon inscription.[159]

There is ample historical proof that taking a census was not uncommon. Indications are that the Romans took an empire-wide census every fourteen years, with regional or specific-purposes censuses more frequent. Other such evidence indicates these procedures were widespread.[160] An earlier census by Quirinius would fit the pattern of frequent censuses taken in the days of Rome.

#4. Two governorships of Quirinius; Two epigraphic witnesses

Besides Luke, there are two other historical witnesses to the two governorships of Quirinius. The *Titulus Venetus,* an ancient Latin inscription, indicates that a census took place in Syria and Judea about 6 AD. It suggests this was typical of the censuses taken throughout the entire Roman Empire from Augustus's time (27 BC-14 AD) until at least the third century AD.

The second historical witness is *Titulus Tibertinus* who says a person fitting the description of Quirinius served twice as governor of Syria. Since the inscription does not bear Quirinius's name, we cannot say for sure that he is the person described. Since the inscription was broken, scholars have speculated that it referred to several governors, such as Varus, Saturninus, Piso, and Quirinius. But only Quirinius matches the entire description, and he does so exactly.

[PUBLIUS' SON, P. SULPICIUS QUIRINIUS; CONSUL; PRAETOR; PROCONSUL]
[OF THE PROVINCE OF CRETE & CYRENE HE HELD, AS LEGATE]
[PROPRAETOR OF THE DIVINE AUGUSTUS OF GALATIA HE WAGED WAR ON GESSTI]
[WITH THE PEOPLE OF THE HOMONADES WHO HAD KILLED AMYNTAS THE]
[K]ING, WHICH* HAVING BEEN BROUGHT INTO THE POW[ER OF IMPERATOR CAESAR]
AUGUSTUS AND THE ROMAN PEOPLE, THE SENAT[E DECREED TO THE IMMORTAL GODS]
TWO THANKSGIVINGS FOR SUCCESS[FUL ACHIEVEMENTS]
LIKEWISE BY TRIUMPHAL ORNAMENTS [ANOTHER TIME AWARDED];
AS PROCONSUL OF THE PROVINCE OF ASIA HE HE[LD; AS LEGATE PROPRAETOR]
OF THE DIVINE AUGUSTUS ONCE MORE SYRIA AND PH[OENICIA HE HELD];

Titulus Tibertinus, Quirinius' Epitaph (by Gerard Gertoux)

Inscription of Tibur, CIL XIV 3613

As a side note, according to epigraphic science, the Latin word *iterum* "again" means the renewal of the same term of office in the same place. For example, *duumvir iterum* in Pompeii[161] designated Publius Paquius Scaeva as the proconsul of Cyprus "again." When it means the second term of office at a different location and not a renewal at the same place, inscriptions would include the letters "*II.*" For example, the name Q. Varius Geminus, who was legate twice, appears in the form: *leg. divi Aug. II.*

#5. A normal Roman census

Jerry Vardaman breaks down how a census was conducted in the Roman Empire. From an examination of over two hundred Roman Period census returns, recovered by archaeological investigations, it is possible to reconstruct the normal course of a census.

- About May or June, an edict was posted by the provincial governors informing the populace that the time of the periodic Roman census was near.
- The people then had one year to file their returns.
- Normally, people would wait until the last weeks to file (like our modern income tax), but there are indications that some filed at once.
- As applied to the census of Quirinius in 12 BC, the citizens of Bethlehem could have filed their census returns any time between May/June 12 BC and May/June 11 BC.[162]

An earlier census would be dated between 10 BC and 4 BC within the cycle of censuses for taxation. F. F. Bruce prefers the date for the empire-wide census as 10–19 BC, with the Judea-only census occurring a few years later.[163] Thus, the earlier census could have been the normal, empire-wide census of the people under Rome's foot, overseen by Quirinius.

#6 Explanation: Quirinius served in positions other than governor.

Others have made the plausible suggestion that Luke 2:2 does not say Quirinius was "governor" of Syria when the census was taken. It says only that he was in a position of authority within the Roman Empire. Adherents of this view say Quirinius had a place of responsibility, which included taking a census but was not "governor" at the time. They contend the word Luke used (Greek: ἡγεμονεύοντος; English: *hēgemoneuontos*) could mean a prefect, procurator, ruler, auxiliary, or even a guide. If this is the case with Quirinius, it would mean Luke's dating may be entirely correct, but his Greek was not specific.

The historian Josephus recorded the effects of Quirinius' decree in 6 AD on Rome's non-citizens, in this case, the Jews of Judea. He wrote:

> Now Cyrenius [Quirinius], a Roman senator, and one who had gone through other magistracies, and had passed through them till he had been consul, and one who, on other accounts, was of great dignity, came at this time into Syria, with a few others,

being sent by Caesar to be a judge of that nation, and to take an account [census] of their substance (*Ant*.18.1.1).

Josephus' words affirm that Quirinius held several governmental positions in his public service career before becoming a Roman governor. This makes *#6 Explanation* more attractive.

#7 Explanation: Quirinius concluded a census begun by Varus.

Some scholars suggest the office Quirinius held at the time of Jesus' birth was a special census commission (*legatus ad census accipiendos*), or a procuratorship,[164] a generalissimo of the East,[165] a *maius imperium*,[166] or the governor of Asia.[167] The possibilities are many.

It is generally acknowledged that if Quirinius had previously served as governor of Syria, that service could not have taken place during the time Luke describes (i.e., during the year of Jesus' birth).[168] It is believed that this is indicated by Josephus, who clearly states that P. Quinctilius Varus[169] was governor of Syria after Herod's death.[170] However, some scholars suggest that a census begun by Varus at the direction of Caesar Augustus was not completed until years later, and thus became associated with his successor, which is presumed to be Quirinius.[171]

#8 Explanation: A linguistic possibility

Linguistic solutions to Luke 2:2 involving textual evidence are proposed in at least three ways.

First, although it is usually a superlative, you could understand the word (Greek: πρώτη; English: *prōtē*) in Luke 2:2 as a comparative and render the verse, "This census was before [the census] which Quirinius, governor of Syria made."[172] F. F. Bruce suggested the Greek in Luke 2:2 could appropriately be translated, "This was the first registration when Quirinius was governor of Syria." Nevertheless, it could justifiably be translated, "This enrollment (census) was before that made when Quirinius was governor of Syria."[173]

The Greek word *prōtos* means "foremost in order of importance, before, first (of all), or former." This would indicate Luke was dating the taxation census before Quirinius became governor of Syria. If, as is legitimate, Luke 2:2 was translated, "This was the census before the one taken while Quirinius was governor of Syria," there would be no problem with the dating, and Luke's critics would have one of their major arguments against him evaporate before their eyes.

A second and equally valid understanding of *prōtos* is in the adverbial form. Understood this way, the sentence would simply read, "This census took place before Quirinius was governor of Syria."[174] The census mentioned in Luke 2:2 was not the census of 6 AD by Quirinius, but an earlier census only hinted at in Luke's Gospel.

Harold Hoehner suggested a third alternative translation. "This census was before that [census] when Quirinius was governor of Syria."[175] This would imply Quirinius was governor of Syria long enough for two official censuses, and Luke 2:2 was referring to the first census by Quirinius, not the 6 AD census. All three of these renderings are wholly valid and do no damage to the intent of the word *prōtos*.[176]

Nigel Turner, a Reader in Theology at the University of Rhodesia (now the University of Zimbabwe), commented on the use of Greek words pertinent to the Luke 2:2 text.

> Luke should not be convicted before we have considered that small point of grammar. Greek at this period was as relaxed as any modern language in observing the correct distinction between comparative and superlative with regard to "former" and "first." There was in Hellenistic Greek, as there is in English today, a preference for "first" when in fact "former" or "prior" is more grammatical. Strictly, "first" means number one among at least three, while "former" is the word which compares only two. St. Luke was professional, but many use "first'" where the meticulous prefer "former."[177]

Turner notes that Marie-Joseph Lagrange, a Dominican priest and founder of the École Biblique in Jerusalem, offered a solution that completely vindicates St. Luke's accuracy. "'First census' must be taken in its Hellenistic connotation as the first of two, and then we must expand the clause a little. This census was before the census which Quirinius, governor of Syria, made."[178]

With any of these renderings, the difficulty of Luke's reference to Quirinius is assuaged. Harold Hoehner maintained that Luke's reference translated this way would accommodate either Quirinius' well-known governorship and census in 6 AD or his hypothesized governorship and census in 3–2 BC.[179]

#9 Explanation: A census years before Quirinius became governor

Angus John Brockhurst (A.J.B.) Higgins, Senior Lecturer in New Testament Language and Literature at the University of Leeds, argued the word πρῶτον in John 15:18, when used as an adverb, carries the same meaning as the (Greek: πρῶτον; English: *prōton*) preposition πρός meaning "before."[180] "If the world hates you, know that it has hated me *before* it hated you." Given this to be accurate, πρῶτον would adjust the participial phrase and appropriately be translated, "This census took place before Quirinius was governor of Syria." According to Higgins' argument, instead of placing the census during Quirinius's governorship, Luke intended to say the census took place in the years before Quirinius became the Syrian governor in 6–7 AD.

I find Higgins' explanation reasonable. If correct, Luke was not distinguishing an earlier census from the one during the governorship of Quirinius. He was indicating that the census at the time of Jesus' birth was conducted in the years before Quirinius became governor of Syria.

Nonetheless, liberal scholars refuse to accept the reasoning of conservative scholars. Jesuit priest Joseph A. Fitzmyer, former professor emeritus at The Catholic University of America, said succinctly: "Publius Suplicius Quirinius' career is fairly well known and defies all attempts either to attribute to him two censuses in Judaea or to date the start of his legateship of Syria to any other period than A.D. 6–7."[181] The evidence against Fitzmyer's assumption, however, is strong and should be considered.

I have belabored this discussion of the Quirinius census because it is crucial in dating the Christ child's birth, and Jesus' birth is critical in dating his death.

Luke had much better access to historical sources than his modern critics. Dennis M. Templeman noted, "These writers were much closer in time to the event of Herod's death and had historical records and testimony which are lost to us today."[182] The good doctor claimed to have "followed [investigated] all things closely for some time" (Luke 1:3) Additionally, he claimed to have written under the inspiration of God's Holy Spirit. It seems ludicrous for today's scholars to judge Luke's accuracy by today's methodology.

THE MAGI AND THE STAR

We know little of these Magi and even the things we think we know we don't. Beyond this, the Gospel of Matthew is our only reliable source of information about them.[183] Matthew is the only canonical Gospel to mention their visit to Bethlehem. Still, there are many things people believe about the Magi that are not found in Matthew.[184]

Let's clear up some misconceptions that almost everyone has. We have been taught things about Jesus' birth and have believed them for most of our lives, things that have no factual basis. We must explore what the Gospel accounts of Jesus' birth do not tell us before being confident about what they do. Here is a sampling of things that Matthew does not say.

Matthew does not identify the wise men's country of origin.

Matthew only says they were "wise men from the east" (Greek: ἀπὸ ἀνατολῶν; English: *apo anatolōn*) (Matt 2:1). The word *anatolē* simply translated as "east" literally means the "dawn" or "rising," i.e., the rising of morning light. By implication, it is believed these men came from the East, where the sun rises. So, were the Magi Japanese from "the land of the rising sun"? Not likely. For those living in the Levant, the lands upon which the sun rose were not China, India, or Japan. They were the lands we know today as Jordan, Syria, Iraq, and Iran. That's where people living in ancient Israel saw the sunrise, not 5,000 miles further east. [The distance between Jerusalem and Shanghai is 4,927 miles or 7,929.24 kilometers]. Even the worldly Romans, let alone Palestinian peasants, knew little of the Far East.

These "wise men" were "Magi," a Greek term that could be understood as "sages" or "astrologers," as implied by the 500 AD Armenian Infancy Gospel.[185]

> "In the three Magi let all people worship the author of the universe: and let God be known not in Judea alone, but in all the world."
> —Leo the Great

In 490 AD, the Byzantine emperor Zeno claimed to have discovered these Magi's remains in Persia, and he brought them to Constantinople. Today they are found in a large gilded triple sarcophagus placed above the Cologne Cathedral's high altar. There they are known as the "Three Kings of Cologne." The place of Zeno's apparent discovery may be a hint that the Magi were from Persia, modern Iran today.

Others believe their names suggest they came from Babylon, one of the most important centers of astronomical and astrological knowledge in its day. From the early second millennium BC, Babylonian astronomy was associated with astrology and divination. The royal courts interpreted celestial events as warnings sent from the gods to the reigning king. They knew well the prophecy of a coming Jewish Messiah. In their minds, this unique star's appearance triggered the need to journey to Jerusalem to investigate.

In the eighth century AD, the Anglo-Saxon theologian Venerable Bede wrote of a tradition that understood the three Magi were signifying the three parts of the world—Africa, Asia, and Europe—and they may have been descendants of the sons of Noah who fathered the three dominant races of Earth (Gen 10).[186] The truth is, we do not know for sure what country they called home and this last suggestion seems a little far-fetched.

Matthew does not tell us they were kings.

Their identification as kings came later when Christian authors associated Isaiah 60:3, Psalm 68:29, and 72:11 with the messianic prophecy, "May all kings fall down before him."[187] The earliest extant image of the Magi is dated to the mid-third century AD. It appears on a fresco above an arch in the Catacomb of Priscilla, one of Rome's oldest Christian cemeteries.[188] As is the case in almost all early depictions of the Magi, there are three of them, wearing a similar type of dress (although their clothing's color varies in the catacomb painting) and they are all of the same race. Matthew's Magi were not commonly portrayed as kings until the thirteenth century.

In almost all early depictions of the Magi, each one carries a gift of some kind. Unfortunately, in the Catacomb of Priscilla fresco, the gifts are faded and difficult to make out. Nonetheless, one of the wise men usually carries a wreath, one a bowl, and one a jug or box-shaped article. Sometimes their camels also grace the pictures, as in a fourth-century sarcophagus relief in the Vatican Museum.

"Adoration of the Magi," Fourth-century sarcophagus in the Vatican Museum

The dress, the regal aura of the Magi, the expensive gifts they brought, and a popular Christmas carol have all led to the assumption, but not the fact, that the Magi were kings.

Matthew does not mention the number of Magi.

John Henry Hopkins Jr. wrote, "We three kings" in 1857. These lyrics have become indelibly pressed into our minds. Too bad not everything Hopkins wrote was accurate.

> "We three kings of Orient are,
> Bearing gifts we traverse afar.
> Field and fountain,
> Moor and mountain,
> Following yonder star."
> —John Henry Hopkins, Jr.

In Western Christianity, we have traditionally assumed the Magi numbered three based mainly on the fact they brought three gifts.[189] In Eastern Christianity, principally in Syriac churches, the Magi are often numbered at twelve.[190] A wall painting in the Roman catacomb of Domitilla shows four Magi, and the Catacomb of Peter and Marcellinus depicts only two. Again, the number is traditional, not biblical. Do not stop singing one of your favorite Christmas carols, but sing it with the knowledge that the author was an American clergyman, not a Middle Eastern historian.[191]

> "The now-standard number, three, did not appear until the third century when the Church Father Origen derived it from the three gifts: gold, frankincense, and myrrh."—Mary Joan Winn Leith

In the apocryphal infancy gospel *Protoevangelium of James*, one of the earliest extra-biblical accounts of the Magi's journey, these men remain unnamed, unnumbered, and unnecessary to the birth narrative. The *Protoevangelium of James* was written to enhance the role of Jesus' mother, Mary, in the Christian tradition. Likely composed in mid-second-century Syria, it provides no new information about the Magi. It does, however, describe the place where Jesus was born as a cave, rather than a wooden or stone stable.

Matthew does not reveal the names of the Magi.

Tradition provides names for these men; the New Testament does not. However, traditions and legends do not agree on their names.[192] The most popular traditional names are Melchior (who was assumed to be a Persian scholar), Caspar (whose name is spelled in various ways—Gaspar, Jaspar, Jaspas, Gathaspa, etc.), and Balthazar (who was assumed to be a Babylonian scholar).

However, *The Encyclopaedia Britannica* offers a different origin for these "kings." "According to Western Church tradition, Balthasar is often represented as a king of Arabia, Melchior as a king of Persia, and Gaspar as a king of India."[193] The *Armenian Infancy Gospel* gives their names as Melkon, King of Persia, Gaspar, King of India, and Baldassar, King of Arabia. These are the closest eastern counterparts to Melchior, Gaspar, and Balthasar of the Medieval Latin Church.[194]

The truth is, we do not know any of the Magi's names. These names have come into church tradition through years of speculation and the desire to refer to the Magi by personal names. But there is still more we do not know about the Magi.

Matthew does not identify the nature of the star

Perhaps the most enigmatic part of the Magi's journey is the star that mysteriously informs them where to locate the Jewish Messiah. Endless books have been written, blogs posted, and DVDs produced claiming to identify the so-called "Star of Bethlehem." Explanations for the star range from pious tradition to a comet, or to Johannes Kepler's suggestion that it was the alignment of planets Regulus, Jupiter, and Venus. Some have even suggested it was a supernova. Perhaps Babylonian astronomy gives us the best clues to this age-old mystery.[195]

Professor Emeritus of Assyriology at the University of Helsinki, Simo Papola notes that, "Attempts to identify the star with historical celestial phenomena have been inconclusive at best, leading many to dismiss the Gospel account as a beautiful but imaginative myth."[196] However, some scholars' dismissive attitude may be hiding important clues to a better understanding of Jesus' life.

It is not within the scope of this book to pursue further the various theories attempting to identify this star. Suffice it to say that whatever it was, it helps us date the birth of the Christ child and, consequently, the crucifixion date.

Matthew does not tell us the Magi followed the star to Jerusalem.

This shocks most Christians. Sometimes what your Sunday school, Catholic school, or Hebrew school teacher taught you was more tradition than fact.[197] The story of the Magi following the star suffers from this kind of inaccurate tradition.[198] Most of us were taught that a star appeared in the East which the Magi followed from there to Jerusalem and eventually to Bethlehem. Countless films, documentaries, and blogs have been produced depicting three kingly old men riding through the desert sands on camels, making their way to Jerusalem, with a guiding star overhead. Early depictions of this scene often have the Magi pointing upward toward the star. But the Bible does not say this happened.

Matthew 2:2 records the Magi came to King Herod and asked, "Where is he who has been born king of the Jews? For we saw his star when it rose and have come to worship him." The verb Matthew chose is in the past perfect tense in Greek. "We *saw* his star when it rose." The verb implies a completed action, something that happened once at a point in the past. This diminishes the need to identify the nature of the guiding star. It was not shining during the Magi's entire trip to Jerusalem. The star did not lead the Magi to Jerusalem, as most have believed.

From that one-time appearance in their country, the Magi understood the need to journey to Jerusalem and find the young Messiah. The Christian Standard Bible translates Matthew 2:9 as, "After hearing the king, they went on their way. And there it was—the star they had seen at its rising." This rendering correctly indicates that the Magi saw the star when it first arose in their homelands and now they were happy to see it again over Jerusalem.

> "A star that rose in the East, appeared over Jerusalem, turned south to Bethlehem, and then came to rest over a house would have constituted a celestial phenomenon unparalleled in astronomical history: yet it received no notice in the records of the times."
> —Raymond E. Brown

After visiting with Herod the king, the Magi left his Jerusalem palace and again saw the same star. Matthew 2:10 says, "When they saw the star, they rejoiced exceedingly with great joy." This suggests the Magi had not seen the star along their journey, just in the beginning, before they left the East. Much to their delight, the star reappeared and led them to Bethlehem, to the house where the young Messiah was living with his parents, Joseph and Mary. It was from Jerusalem to Bethlehem and the place where the infant Jesus was staying that the star led them, there and only there.

Upon seeing the child, they did the only appropriate thing when in the presence of the Messiah, the Savior of the world, God the Son. "They fell down and worshiped him" (Matt 2:11). Flat on their faces, these wealthy, distinguished, respected Magi worshipped the true King of the Jews and the King of Kings.

Matthew does not directly say how old Jesus was when the Magi visited.

That the young Jesus was an infant and not a babe in arms when the Magi located him in Bethlehem can be deduced from three facts.

(1) When Luke spoke of the "baby" Jesus, he used the word (Greek: βρέφος; English: *brephos*) for a newly born child (Luke 2:12). Matthew, however, spoke of Jesus as an infant (Greek: παιδίον; English: *paidíon*) in Matthew 2:8, 9, 11, 13, 14, 20, 21. In 2:16, Matthew refered to the children who were slaughtered using the word for a child that is at least one year old, not a newborn (Greek παῖς; English: *paîs)*. However, Harold Hoehner argued that this distinction between "baby" and "boy" is not entirely evident. He noted the word *paidíon* is used of infants in Luke 1:59, 66, 76; 2:17, 27, as well as John 16:21 and Hebrews 11:23. The word *paîs* is used six out of twenty-four times in the New Testament for a baby child. Thus, Hoehner hypothesized the visit of the Magi could well have been a short time after Jesus was born.

(2) Matthew 2:11 indicates the Magi went "into the house" to lay their gifts before Jesus. Matthew chose the word "house" (Greek: οἰκίαν; English: *oikian*) likely to indicate Joseph, Mary, and the baby were no longer temporarily living in a caravanserai, staying with Bethlehem relatives, or living in a cave, but had moved into a more permanent dwelling, supported by Joseph's skills as a carpenter/mason.

(3) To ensure that he eliminated this "King of the Jews," Herod killed all the male boys "who were two years old or under" in Bethlehem and the surrounding area. This implies Jesus could have been as old as two years when the Magi visited him. He could also have been younger, but not older.

Hoehner's concerns would not address reasons two and three, and thus it is safe to assume that Jesus was just less than two years of age when visited by these strange astrologists.

The Revelation of the Magi

Brent Landau is a lecturer in the Department of Religious Studies at the University of Texas, Austin. He translated into English the apocryphal *Revelation of the Magi*, preserved in an eighth-century AD Syriac manuscript housed in the Vatican Library. The *Revelation* is a lengthy narrative that claims to be the personal testimony of the Magi about what happened when Jesus came to Earth as a Bethlehem baby. Landau believes the earliest versions of the text may have been written by the mid-second century, less than a hundred years after Matthew's Gospel was composed.[199]

The *Revelation of the Magi* answers many questions about the Magi that he Gospel of Matthew does not, e.g., who they were, where they came from, how many there were, etc. It expresses the Magi were mystics from the far-off, mythical land of Shir, which Landau believes could possibly refer to China. Moreover, there are not just three Magi as tradition holds, but they were a group, no less than twelve, and likely many more.

These enigmatic mystics, according to *The Revelation of the Magi*, are descendants of Seth, Adam's righteous third son, and are, "The guardians of an age-old prophecy that a star of indescribable brightness would someday appear 'heralding the birth of God in human form.'"[200]

Apocryphal accounts of Jesus' birth attempt to fill in the details everyone wishes to know, but they may not get us any closer to the truth. So, what is the truth about Jesus' birth?

WHAT DO WE KNOW FOR SURE ABOUT JESUS' BIRTH?

It is not out of pure curiosity that we are interested in the year Jesus was born. As mentioned, the date of his birth impacts our understanding of the date of his death. In our study of the date of Jesus' crucifixion, that is an important issue. So, what do we know about the year of Jesus' birth?

- We know that according to Matthew 2:1 and Luke 1:5, Herod the Great was king in Judea when Jesus was born. His reign began in 37 BC and ended somewhere between 6 and 1 BC. See below.
- We know that Luke 2:1–2 placed Christ's birth within the reign of the Roman Emperor Augustus Caesar (27 BC-14 AD). Augustus established a system of census-taking during his reign. Luke refers to it in Luke 2:1.

- We know Luke informs us that Jesus was born when Quirinius (also spelled Cyrenius) took a census of Judea's inhabitants at the order of Augustus Caesar. Quirinius made the census when Archelaus was deposed from his kingdom, and Judea became a province of Rome (*Ant.*17.13.5; 18.2.1; *Wars* 2.8.1; see Acts 5:37).

- We know Roman historical evidence indicates a census was taken every fourteen years. By counting backward from a similar census taken in neighboring Egypt (also a Roman province), we can estimate a census in Judea must have been scheduled about 8 BC. Turbulent conditions in Palestine and Syria at the time may have delayed the census for a couple of years.

- We know that Quirinius was governor of Syria in 6 AD at the time of a census, but this census is too late to be related to Jesus' birth. Inscriptions have shown the probability that Quirinius was involved in the Syrian government as a joint ruler or in another office at an earlier time, about 8 BC.

- We know Jesus was born before Herod the Great died. Matthew 2:1 notes that "Jesus was born in Bethlehem of Judea in the days of Herod the king," and Luke 1:5 mentions the "days of Herod, king of Judea" as shortly before the birth of Christ.

- We know wise men from the East came to worship God's Messiah. But when they did not report back to him, Herod ordered his soldiers to kill all babies in Bethlehem, two years and under (Matt 2:16). This suggests Jesus theoretically may have been born in 5 or even 6 BC and was between one and two years old when Herod died.

- We know Tertullian wrote a treatise entitled, *An Answer to the Jews*. In it, he said, "Let us see, moreover, how in the forty-first year of the empire of Augustus, when he had been reigning twenty and eight years after the death of Cleopatra, Christ is born" (*Adversus Judaeos* 8)

- We know the first-century Roman historian Livy reported Cleopatra died on the first day of the seventh month (renamed Augustus) in 30 BC.[201] Twenty-eight years after Cleopatra's death was 2 BC.

- In his treatise *The Stromata*, Clement of Alexandria (died 217 AD) wrote, "From the birth of the Lord to the death of Commodus are, in all, 100 and 94 years, one month thirteen days." Emperor Commodus was slain on December 31, 192 AD, (*Cassius Dio* 73), which would place the date of Jesus' birth in November 2 BC.

- We know that even though Irenaeus did not speak specifically of the date of Jesus' birth, we can reckon from his treatise *Against Heresies* that he placed it a few years before the year 1 BC.
- We know that Matthew implied Jesus might have been as much as two years old when the Magi visited him in a house, and thus perhaps even older at the time of Herod's death.

The issues that bear on the year Jesus was crucified are like the pieces of a complicated puzzle. There are several good options with more than adequate proof for each. Besides the Star of Bethlehem, the slaughter of Bethlehem's innocent infants, and the date of Herod's death—all relating to the year of Jesus' birth—there is also the question of the year Jesus began his ministry. That, too, impacts our identification of the year the Savior died.

CALCULATING THE BEGINNING OF JESUS' MINISTRY

That the Gospels are not pure biographies, but rather eyewitness accounts of Jesus' life, and specifically his crucifixion and resurrection, is evident from the scarcity of references in the Gospels to Jesus' early years. See Table 1.

Table 1: The Traditional Dating of Jesus' Early Life

Jesus' Age	Approximate Year	Scripture	Gospel Event
	6 BC	Matt 1:28-13	Announcement to Joseph
	6 BC	Luke 1:26-35	Announcement to Mary
	5 BC	Luke 2:1-20	The Birth of Jesus
Eight Days	5 BC	Luke 2:22-24	Jesus' Presentation at the Temple
1-2 years	4-3 BC	Matt 2:1-6	Visit of the Magi to Bethlehem
1-2 years	4-3 BC	Matt 2:13-15	The Flight to Egypt
2+ years	3 BC	Matt 2:19-23	Return to Nazareth
12 years	11 AD	Luke 2:41-51	Boy Jesus in the Temple

Take special note of this. The Gospels tell us nothing concerning our Lord from his twelfth year to his appearance at the Jordan about his thirtieth year. That is a gap of eighteen years.

The physician/historian Luke informs us that, "Jesus, when he began his ministry, was about thirty years of age" (Luke 3:23). Logically, the adverb "about" (Greek: ὡσεὶ: English: *hōsei*) provides enough latitude for two or three years on either side of age thirty. Here are estimates for Jesus' birth year and the first year of his ministry by some notable historians.

Table 2: Jesus Begins His Ministry

Estimates for the Year Jesus Began His Ministry		
Birth Year	Proponents	Year Ministry Began
1 BC	Dionysius Exiguus	29 AD
2 BC	Tertullian; Clement of Alexandria; Epiphanius; Orosius	28 AD
3 BC	Irenaeus, Cassadorius, Origen	27 AD
4 BC	James Ussher, Emile Schürer, et al.	26 AD
5 BC	John Ratzinger (Pope Benedict XVI)	25 AD
6 BC	Grant Matthews	24 AD
7 BC	Konradin Ferrari-D'Occhieppo	23 AD
11 BC	George Ogg	19 AD
12 BC	Jerry Vardaman	18 AD
20 BC	A. T. Olmstead	10 AD

As you can see, there is a great deal of difference between these estimates. Some may be correct, but many are wide of the mark. From Luke 3:1–2, we learn two indisputable facts. (1) the word of God came to John the son of Zechariah in the wilderness, and (2) this occurred within the time frame of the lives and activities of the eight men named in those two verses:

> In the fifteenth year of the reign of Tiberius Caesar, Pontius Pilate being governor of Judea, and Herod being tetrarch of Galilee, and his brother Philip tetrarch of the region of Ituraea and Trachonitis, and Lysanias tetrarch of Abilene, during the High Priesthood of Annas and Caiaphas, the word of God came to John the son of Zechariah in the wilderness.

In the initial stages of John the Baptist's ministry, the crowds at the Jordan River thought he might be the Messiah. John slammed that door shut immediately, affirming, "I baptize you with water, but he who is mightier than I is coming, the strap of whose sandals I am not worthy to untie" (Luke 3:16).

John 1:29 picks up the account at this point and reports, "The next day he [John the Baptist] saw Jesus coming toward him, and said, 'Behold, the Lamb of God, who takes away the sin of the world!'" Just six verses later begins the account of Jesus calling his twelve disciples.

I think it is safe to deduce that John had not long been baptizing in the Jordan River when he baptized Jesus. If so, we are on relatively safe ground to believe the historical anchors used to establish the beginning of John the Baptist's ministry may also be used to establish the beginning of Jesus' ministry. These eight historical figures provide bedrock evidence for dating the commencement of Jesus' helping, healing, and saving ministry.

THE TERMINUS AD QUO AND TERMINUS AD QUEM FOR HEROD'S DEATH

In recent years, historians from East Asia have attempted to establish Jesus' birth date by linking it with special events in their Asian history. By checking their oldest records of Halley's Comet during the Han Dynasty in China (206 BC–220 AD), they discovered a reference that, "The comet heads east with its tail pointing west at night, and was appearing in the sky for more than seventy days" in 6 BC. These historians believe this comet is an independent identification of the "Star of Bethlehem" described in Matthew 2. If this were the case, and I am quite sure it is not, it would mean the birth of Jesus occurred in the summer rather than the springtime.

With what we do know, we can determine the *Terminus ad Quo* and *Terminus ad Quem* for the birth of Jesus Christ. The *Terminus ad quo* is a Latin term referring to the earliest possible date for something. The term is derived from the Latin "*terminus*" meaning "end" and "*ad quo*" meaning "to which." The opposite of *terminus ad quo* is *terminus ad quem*, which refers to the latest possible date or ending point for something. Such historical markers enable us to determine the earliest beginning point and the final limiting point for Jesus' birth and ministry.

The Birth of Jesus Christ: Terminus ad Quo

According to Luke 2:1–5, Augustus Caesar ordered Quirinius, the governor of Syria, to take a census of all the Jews living in Judea. This census was taken at the time of Christ's birth. Thus, Christ could not have been born before the census. The census referred to by Luke cannot be the 6 AD census because, if Jesus were born anywhere from 6 BC to 1 BC, he would be too old for Herod's concern when the census began. The census that interests us must be an earlier one.

> "Under no circumstance is it safe to date Jesus' birth after 5 B.C."
> —Jerry Vardaman

If Jesus were born in April 5 BC, he would have been 33 years old when he began to call his disciples (remembering there is no year zero in the calendar). A birth in 2 or 1 BC is also consistent with Luke 3:23, that he was 'about thirty' at this time his ministry commenced.

It is reasonable that Jesus could not have been born before the census, and if the census was sometime between 9 BC and 6 BC, with 6 BC being the better option, Jesus could not have been born before 6 BC. This is the *terminus ad quo* or earliest point in time for Jesus' birth.

The Death of Herod the Great: Terminus ad Quem

The *terminus ad quem* or the latest possible date for the birth of Jesus was before the death of Herod the Great. "According to Josephus, an eclipse of the moon occurred shortly before Herod's death (*Ant.*17.6.4). It is the only eclipse ever mentioned by Josephus. It happened on March 12/13, 4 BC.[202] After Herod's death, there was the celebration of the Passover,[203] the first day of which would have been April 11, 4 BC.[204] Hence, many believe Herod's death occurred sometime between March 12th and April 11th in 4 BC. Since the thirty-fourth year of his reign would have begun on Nisan 1, 4 BC (March 29, 4 BC), Herod's death may have occurred sometime between March 29 and April 11, 4 BC.[205]

Herod died in his winter palace at Jericho, after an excruciatingly painful and putrefying illness of uncertain cause, known to posterity as "Herod's Evil." A brief portion of Josephus' graphic description of Herod's death will suffice for our understanding.

> But now Herod's distemper greatly increased upon him after a severe manner . . . his entrails were also exulcerated, and the chief violence of his pain lay on his colon . . . his privy member was putrefied, and produced worms; and when he sat upright he had a difficulty of breathing, which was very loathsome, on account of the stench of his breath" (*Ant.*17.6.5).

It has been suggested that Herod died from arteriosclerosis, commonly known as the hardening of the arteries.[206] Whatever the cause of his death, Josephus states that the pain of his illness led Herod to attempt suicide by stabbing himself, an attempt that was thwarted by his cousin (*Ant.*17.7.1).

CONCLUSIONS

Modern liberal scholars make elaborate claims arguing for the impossibility of Luke's accuracy. However, modern conservative scholars offer equally plausible explanations for each liberal objection.[207]

The basis for conclusions by the entire academic community is often not matters of fact as much as they are matters of plausibility. With no tangible evidence or conflicting evidence, we must ascertain which of multiple theories is more plausible. Is it more likely that Luke erred in what he recorded historically or that modern scholars err in their present-day suppositions? Could there have been a census earlier than 6 AD? Could that census be what Luke was referring to in Luke 2:2? We do not know, but not knowing is far different from concluding that Luke's record must be inaccurate and fatally flawed.[208] This is where scholastic predisposition is most ingloriously on display.

Those who have attempted to establish the actual date of Jesus' birth in Bethlehem have not only used a variety of methods but have come to significant diversity in their conclusions. Table 3 summarizes some notable scholars who have tried to nail down the date of the birth of Jesus Christ.

Table 3: The Year of Jesus' Birth

Date	Proponent	Proponent's Profession
20 BC	A. T. Olmstead	American Assyriologist
12 BC	Jerry Vardaman	Biblical Scholar/Archaeologist
5–4 BC	Joseph Ratzinger	Pope Benedict XVI
4 BC	James Ussher	Chancellor, St. Patrick's Cathedral
4 BC	Emil Schürer	German Protestant Theologian
3 BC	Origen	Alexandrian Christian Theologian
2 BC	Clement	Alexandrian Church Father
2/1 BC	Tertullian	Christian Apologist from Carthage
1 BC	Dionysius Exiguus	A monk from Scythia Minor
1 AD	Bieke Mahieu	Herod died on March 9, 1 AD

I believe it is most likely, perhaps in another office between the years of 9 and 4 BC, that Quirinius officiated over what Luke describes as a census ordered by Augustus Caesar. I understand it is also quite plausible that Luke was reporting that Jesus' birth occurred in conjunction with a Quirinius' tax census. I suspect there is truth to I. Howard Marshall's suggestion that "Luke's full vindication lies buried somewhere, waiting to be unearthed."[209]

Moreover, if you have a high view of Scripture, you understand that in his statement, "We have the prophetic word more fully confirmed," Peter was stating reality, not bragging. And when he said, "No prophecy was ever produced by the will of man, but men spoke from God as they were carried along by the Holy Spirit," Peter included Luke 2:2 in this Spirit-supervised writing. Ultimately, your view of Scripture profoundly influences your interpretations and conclusions about Scripture.

THE BEST OPTIONS FOR JESUS' BIRTH YEAR

As strong as the temptation is, I will resist digging deeply into the details of King Herod's accession to the throne, his life, and ultimately his ghastly death. Others have prominently done this. Instead, here the focus is on the most likely options for Jesus' birth year and how that impacts the year of his crucifixion.

The option of 6 BC

Talbot Theological Seminary's Robert L. Thomas and Stanley N. Gundry, currently Senior Vice President and Publisher at Zondervan Publishing, place the date of Jesus' birth in late 6 BC or early 5 BC.[210] Grant Mathews, Director of the Center for Astrophysics at Notre Dame University, also places Jesus' birth in 6 BC. Tertullian (c. 155–245 AD) recorded a census in Judea that took place under Roman senator and imperial legate to Syria Sentius Saturninus sometime between 9 BC and 6 BC.

In his work *Adversus Marcionem*, Tertullian wrote, "But there is historical proof that at this very time there were censuses that had been taken in Judea by Sentius Saturninus, which might have satisfied their inquiry respecting the family and descent of Christ" (*Adversus Marcionem* 4:19). If born in 6 BC, Jesus was "about" thirty years old (with a 2/3± factor) between 22 and 27 AD, with 24 being the median date. If Jesus had a ministry of two and one-half to three years, encompassing three Passovers, his crucifixion would have been about 27 AD.

The option of 5 BC

The 5 BC date is preferable to 6 BC for Jesus' birth because his crucifixion cannot be earlier than 30 AD. Herod's order to kill all male babies in Bethlehem two years and under (Matt 2:16) suggests Jesus may have been born in 6 or 5 BC and was between one and two years old when Herod died. A 5 BC birth places Jesus "about" thirty years old between 23 and 28 AD, with 25 being the median date. If Jesus had a ministry of two and one-half to three years, over three Passovers, his crucifixion would have been about 28 AD.[211]

> "If Jesus was born in 6 BCE or 5 BCE, then some texts in the New Testament are difficult to reconcile with Jewish and Roman history."
> —Dennis Templeman

Pertinent to any discussion of Herod's death is what Josephus recorded about the king changing his last will. Josephus wrote, "And now Herod altered his testament upon the alteration of his mind . . . when he had done these things, he died, the fifth day after he had caused Antipater to be slain; having reigned, since he had procured Antigonus to be slain, thirty-four years; but since he had been declared king by the Romans, thirty-seven" (*Ant*.17.8.1). This information aids in pinpointing a proper year for the death of Herod and the birth of Jesus.

The option of 4 BC

The 4 BC date for Herod's death has been the accepted option for over one hundred years. This is primarily due to Emil Schürer's book, *A History of the Jewish People in the Time of Jesus Christ*.[212] Schürer concluded that "Herod died at Jericho in BC 4, unwept by those of his own house, and hated by all the people." He based his conclusion on three principal factors.

First, Josephus informs us that Herod died shortly before a Passover (*Ant*.17.8.1, *Wars* 1.33.8). As a result, Schürer claimed this made the lunar eclipse in March of 4 BC much more likely as a marker of Jesus' birth than the one in December of 1 BC.

Second, Josephus recorded that Herod reigned thirty-seven years from the time of his appointment in 40 BC, and thirty-four years from his conquest of Jerusalem in 37 BC (*Ant*. 17.8.1, *Wars* 1.33.8). Using inclusive calculation this, too, places Herod's death in 4 BC.

The Impact of Jesus' Birth Date on His Death Date

Third, Josephus recorded that Archelaus reigned over Judea and Samaria for ten years. In his tenth year, due to complaints against him from both Jews and Samaritans, he was deposed by Caesar Augustus and banished to Vienna (*Wars* 2.7.3). This means he was deposed by Caesar in AUC 759 (*Anno Urbis Conditae*) [literally "in the year the city (Rome) was founded"] or 6 AD. Counting backward places the tenth year of his reign in 4 BC (Cassius Dio, *Roman History* 55.27.6; Josephus, *Ant.*17.13.2).

In addition to Schürer's three factors, we now have coins that refer to the 43rd year of Herod Antipas' rule, placing its beginning in 4 BC at the latest. Antipas ruled over Galilee until 39 BC. He ordered the execution of John the Baptist (Mark 6:14–29) and played an ancillary role in Jesus' trial (Luke 23:7–12).[213]

In the seventeenth century, Irish Bishop James Ussher proposed the world was created precisely on October 22, 4004 BC. Bishop Ussher said Jesus was born in the year 4,000 AM,[214] which corresponds to 4 BC.[215]

In the middle of the fourth century AD, Epiphanius (Epiphanius, *Panarion*) cited 4 BC as Jesus' year of birth. On the other hand, he also noted the opinion of the "Alogi," a group of heretics who opposed the Gospel of John. ["A-logi" means "no *logos*," which is a critical concept countered in the opening lines of John's Gospel]. On the one hand, they held that the birth of Jesus occurred in 4 BC. On the other hand, they believed it happened during the consulships of Quintus Sulpicius Camerinus and Poppaeus Sabinus (B. Pompeianus). However, these men were not consuls together until 9 AD.

This glitch in dating aside, those who claim Jesus was born in 4 BC often do so because Josephus recorded there was an eclipse of the moon just before the death of Herod (*Ant.*17.13.2). Furthermore, he stated Herod died just before Passover (17.6.4), which occurred on April 11th in 4 BC. Jack Finegan, who was Professor of New Testament History and Archaeology at the Pacific School of Religion, Berkeley, believed Herod died between March 12 and April 11, 4 BC.[216] Harold Hoehner narrows the date even further to between March 29 and April 11, 4 BC.[217] This would mean when Jesus was "about" thirty years old and began his ministry, it would have been between 24 and 29 AD, with 26 AD being precisely thirty years.

The chronology derived from these historical facts provides a compelling case for the traditional date of Herod's death, the spring of 4 BC, shortly after the lunar eclipse on March 13th of that year.

The option of 3 BC

We know for certain Christ died somewhere between 26 AD and 36 AD. If we assume he died on a Friday, by astronomical calculation, we discover that only in 30 AD and 33 AD did Friday fall on *Nisan* 14. There are good arguments for both dates, which are discussed in Chapter 10. Many scholars have maintained the 30 AD date because it would make Jesus about thirty when he began his ministry. If Jesus was born on September 11, 3 BC, on the Jewish Feast of the Trumpets, he was about thirty-three years old at his death. A 3 BC birth makes Jesus "about" thirty years old between 25 and 30 AD, with 27 being the median date. If Jesus had a ministry of two and one-half to three years encompassing three Passovers, his crucifixion would have been about 30 AD. Historian Ormand Edwards holds that, given Josephus' notations in his *Antiquities* 17.8.1 and elsewhere, Herod must have died in 3 BC.[218]

The option of 2 BC

The Roman priest, historian, theologian, and student of Augustine, Paulus Orosius precisely dates Augustus's census to the year 752 on the Roman calendar or 2 BC.[219] If a general census was conducted every five years (1 *lustre*) in the Roman Empire, which Orosius deduced from those reported by Cassius Dio 55:13, the census before the one in 4 AD, which was confined to Italy, must have been taken in 2 BC.

Dating the birth of Jesus, Clement of Alexandria (*The Stromata* 1:21:145) placed the Savior's birth 194 years before Commodus's death (31 December 192 AD). Tertullian (*Against the Jews* 8:11:75) put it in the forty-first year of Augustus›s reign. He dated Jesus' birthdate from the second triumvirate of October 43 BC, and twenty-eight years after the death of Cleopatra (August 29, 30 BC). If you combine these historical accounts, the birth of Jesus would be fixed in 2 BC, between September 1 and October 30. A 2 BC birth makes Jesus "about" thirty years old between 26 and 31 AD, with 28 being the median date. If Jesus had a ministry of two and one-half to three years encompassing three Passovers, his crucifixion would have been about 31 AD.

The option of 1 BC

Dionysius Exiguus, (Dionysius Exiguus, *Liber de Paschate*) the sixth-century AD Scythian monk, said Jesus was born explicitly on December 25,

1 BC, which of course was one week before the era of BC yielded to AD.[220] However, upon what Dionysius based his conclusions is not entirely clear.

Many past and present scholars argue for the birth of Jesus in the final year of the old era—1 BC. These include George W. Rawlinson, Theodor Mommsen, Kitty Chisholm, John Ferguson, A. N. Sherwin-White, Barbara Levick, James E. C. Zetel, Paul Keresztes, Jerry Vardaman, Edwin Yamauchi, Jack Finegan, and a host of others.[221] W. E. Filmer and Andrew Steinmann believe Herod died in 1 BC, but his male heirs backdated their rule to 4 BC. This would have given greater credence to their reigns since they would then have overlapped with Herod's reign.[222]

Mentioned above as support for a 4 BC date was the eclipse of the moon that year. However, John A. Cramer, Professor of Physics at Atlanta's Oglethorpe University, points out there were other eclipses visible in Judea during the last five years of the old era. The first occurred on the night of September 15, 5 BC. The second was a partial eclipse on the night of March 12/13, 4 BC. There were two eclipses during 1 BC. The first occurred on January 9, 1 BC, and the other on December 29th, just before the new era. Either of these last two eclipses would place Herod's death and Jesus' birth in 1 BC, three years later than generally thought.[223]

Cramer asserts the eclipse of 4 BC was visible only very late that night in Judea and was a minor eclipse, as well as only a partial one. He further claims there were no lunar eclipses visible in Judea after this one until two occurred in the year 1 BC. Hence, the physicist concludes that 1 BC is the most likely year of Jesus' birth.[224]

Author Dennis M. Templeman points out, "The witness of nearly [all] writers, Church Fathers, and historians, writing before the seventh century CE are (sic) almost unanimous in speaking of the birth of Jesus in the period 4/3 BCE or (regnal dating) to 2/1 BCE."[225] Perhaps a more precise dating is impossible.

The two possible timeframes

From all the evidence available to us, two timeframes appear to be the best options for the year of Jesus' birth. The traditional date of 2/1 BC was widely accepted until Schürer wrote his *magnum opus*. Schürer's dating in *A History of the Jewish People in the Time of Jesus Christ* was frequently adopted throughout most of the twentieth century. However, there has been a resurgence of scholarly opinion for the 2/1 BC in the last several decades.

So was Jesus born in 4 BC, the traditional date, or 1 BC the date rising in popularity? It depends on the evidence that strikes you as the most weighty. None of the options fits perfectly. None fully meets all the requirements. Either date is possible. Either is plausible. Either is acceptable. A date of 4 BC for Jesus' birth tends to support a 30 AD crucifixion. On the other hand, a 1 BC birthdate lends credence to a 33 AD crucifixion.

The acceptable range for the death of Herod the Great, as well as the birth of the Savior, is in the 6–1 BC range, knowing that Jesus was "about thirty" when he began his ministry but was not yet fifty, the linkage between Jesus birth and the year of his death is another avenue of investigation for dating Jesus' death.

I have presented the thinking of much of the academic community. You cannot go wrong in choosing any of these dates for Joseph and Mary's arduous journey to Bethlehem and the subsequent birth of God in the flesh. Remember, however, that your choice of birth date impacts your choice of Jesus' death date. No one knows the date for certain, but I have made 1 BC my choice. Make yours.

Chapter 9

Calculating the Year of Jesus' Crucifixion

Jews living under Roman occupation had to keep an eye on coordinating their Jewish calendar with the Roman Julian calendar. This is true today as well. Religious Jews of the twenty-first century use their Jewish dating system in religious ceremonies but must live by the Gregorian calendar in everyday life.

IN ATTEMPTING TO ESTABLISH the date of Jesus' crucifixion, we must consider much more than whether Jesus died on Wednesday, Thursday, or Friday. It's not as simple as that. If historians, scientists, and biblical scholars have not agreed on the day, date, or year of the crucifixion, it's not likely someone who has done an Internet search or blogged about the date will arrive at an appropriate conclusion. So, let's systematically approach establishing the year of Jesus' crucifixion. We must begin by admitting there is a problem.

PROBLEMS WITH DATING THE CRUCIFIXION

The terms BC meaning "before Christ" and AD meaning "*anno Domini*" ("the year of the Lord") have historically been used to mark years in the Gregorian and Julian calendars with the birth of Jesus as the event that divides history. Often this Medieval Latin expression is understood as "the year of our Lord" because the original phrase *"anno Domini"* was translated to, "in the year of our Lord Jesus Christ." All the years before Jesus' birth received the label BC; all those years after his birth were designated as AD.[226] If Jesus had been born in 1 AD, these designations would be completely accurate, but he was not.[227] How then did the current division between BC and AD come to be? Let's begin our search for the year of Jesus' crucifixion at the most logical place—the calendar.

For the citizens of Earth in the twenty-first century, at least for those living in the Western world, using an appropriate calendar is not a problem. Most of us have only one to choose from. But did you know that Ethiopia has its own calendar? On Ethiopia's calendar, the first day of the year falls on September 11th or 12th. And even more interesting, the Ethiopian calendar is seven to eight years behind the Gregorian calendar. For example, January 1, 2025, equates to April 23, 2017, on the Ethiopian calendar.

Presented in Table 1 below are some of the many calendar systems used by people over the centuries in various locations. You may be surprised they are so numerous; however, there are many more not included in this Table.

Four different types of calendars are listed: 365 days, lunisolar, solar, and lunar. The 365-day calendar is divided into 365 days each year. The solar calendar is based on the position of Earth in its revolution around the Sun. Likewise, the lunar calendar is based on the cycles of the moon's phases. The date on the lunisolar calendar represents both the moon's phase and the time of the solar year.[228] Confused? I'd be surprised if you weren't. Perhaps Table 1 will help.

Table 1: Calendars From Various Periods and Locations

Name	Type	Period	Location
Egyptian	365	Bronze Age	Egyptian Kingdom
Roman	Solar	713 BC	Roman Empire
Old Persian	Lunisolar	Fourth Century BC	Roman Empire
Julian	Solar	45 BC	Roman World
Coptic Church	Solar	First Century AD	Coptic Orthodox World
Ethiopian	Solar	First Century AD	Christians
Qumran	364 Days	First Century AD	Qumran, Dead Sea
Islamic	Lunar	622 AD	Islamic World
Hebrew	Lunisolar	Eleventh Century AD	Jewish World

For our purposes, we need to examine only the Julian and the Gregorian calendars to investigate the date of Jesus' crucifixion. But first, we must define each and see how they differ from each other.

The Julian Calendar

The Roman calendar was the calendar used during both the Roman Kingdom (753–509 BC) and the Roman Republic (509–27 BC).

As noted in the last chapter, AUC in Latin is *Anno Urbis Conditae* meaning, "from the founding of the City (Rome)." The traditional date for Rome's founding is 753 BC. Julius Caesar proposed the Julian calendar in 46 BC (708 AUC) to reform the Roman calendar and bring it into closer alignment with the solar year.[229] The Julian calendar took effect on January 1, 45 BC (AUC 709). It was the predominant calendar in the Roman world, the most substantial portions of Europe, and European settlements in the Americas and elsewhere. The Gregorian calendar gradually replaced it. Although Caesar's reform only applied to the Roman calendar, in the following decades, many of the local and provincial calendars of the empire, as well as client states, aligned their calendars with the Julian calendar as well.[230]

Beyond this, archaeologist Jack Finegan provides valuable insight.

> In AD 525, Pope John I asked Dionysius, a Scythian monk, to prepare a standard calendar for the Western Church. Dionysius modified the Alexandrian system of dating, which used as its base the reign of Diocletian, for he did not want the years of history to be reckoned from the life of a persecutor of the church, but from the incarnation of Christ. The commencement of the Christian era was January 1, 754 AUC and Christ's birth was thought to have been on December 25 immediately preceding.[231]

Hence, today it is generally recognized that the birth of Jesus of Nazareth did not occur in 1 AD but in 4 BC or some time just before that.[232]

The Julian calendar has two types of years: "normal years" which consist of 365 days and "leap years" of 366 days. This calendar features a simple cycle of three "normal years" followed by a "leap year." This cycle repeats forever. This means the Julian year is, on average, 365.25 days long. As a result, the Julian year drifts over time with the tropical (solar) year (365.24217 days).

The Gregorian Calendar

The Gregorian calendar is the most widely used in the world, finding its most extensive use in countries of the West. It is often referred to as the Western calendar or the Christian calendar because of the momentous influence of Christianity on the West, at least in earlier years. This calendar was named after Pope Gregory XIII, who introduced it by papal bull *Inter gravissimas* ["among the most serious"], on February 24, 1582 AD. Gregory's motivation for adjusting the Julian calendar was to bring the date for the celebration of Easter into the time of year introduced by the early church.

The Gregorian year comprises twelve months of 365 days, with an extra day added every fourth year at the end of February as a leap year with 366 days. This means the average year in the Gregorian calendar is 365.2425 days long, approximating the 365.2422-day tropical year. The Gregorian calendar is solar; the dates indicate the seasons or the Sun's position relative to the stars.

LUNAR VERSUS A SOLAR CALENDAR

Suppose you belonged to a Jewish family living in Jerusalem in the first century AD. You could go outdoors any evening and observe what day of the month it was. The Jewish calendar was an observational one. In your calendar, each month began with the evening the new crescent moon was first visible. That would occur shortly after sunset.

For your family in Jerusalem, the moon was your Jewish calendar in the sky. It was to you then what a smartphone is to you now—a datebook for monthly scheduling. So important was it to discern the beginning of a new month and the ending of a current one, the priests of the Temple in Jerusalem employed a team of men who walked out to the hills west of Jerusalem to look for the new crescent moon at sunset. When at least two of the team concurred they had seen it, they would hurriedly return to the Temple. There the priests would question them, and if the priests decided the sighting was legitimate, they would blow trumpets to announce to everyone in Jerusalem it was a new moon and a new month. If you lived outside the wall of Jerusalem and could not hear the trumpets, fires were lit on the hills, and messengers were sent to spread the news throughout the land.

If you were an official observer, you would first see the new crescent moon just after sunset. It would remain visible for about thirty minutes. After half an hour, it would disappear from the sky for the rest of the night.

Why does the new moon behave in such an intriguing way? The University of Cambridge's Sir Colin J. Humphreys explains:

> At new moon time, just before sunset, the moon is slightly above the sun in the western sky. The moon is then invisible because it is too close to the sun. The sun then sets; because it moves below the horizon, the sky darkens and the thin crescent of the new moon becomes visible (typically about fifteen minutes after sunset) because the moon is no longer lost in the glare from the sun. However, the moon moves around the earth in the same direction as the sun, and thus it also sets in the western sky ... It is an astronomical impossibility for the first crescent of the new moon to be seen towards morning because the new moon is below the horizon at this time.[233]

Each lunation (the average time from one new moon to the next) is approximately twenty-nine and a half days (twenty-nine days, twelve hours, forty-four minutes, three seconds, or 29.530588 days, to be exact). As a result, it is common for the months of a lunar calendar to alternate between twenty-nine and thirty days. Since the duration of twelve such lunations (a lunar year) is only 354 days, 8 hours, 48 minutes, and 34 seconds (354.367056 days), lunar calendars lose approximately eleven days per year compared to the Gregorian calendar. This lack of intercalation causes the lunar months to cycle through all the Gregorian year's seasons in a 33 lunar-year cycle. Thus, in calculating the date of Jesus' crucifixion, we must ask if the Gospel writers were using a lunar or a solar calendar. It would make a significant difference.

MIGRATING FROM THE JULIAN TO THE GREGORIAN CALENDARS

Since the Gregorian calendar we use today was not adopted until the year 1582 AD, and Julius Caesar employed the Julian calendar, it's apparent that the Julian calendar was used in first-century AD dating. For all who use the solar Gregorian calendar, that presents some difficulty. Biblical scholars, archaeologists, and historians use the Julian calendar when addressing people and events during the days of Jesus. All dates related to Jesus' birth, his life, and crucifixion reflect the Julian calendar. So when we think about events in the New Testament, we must always be mindful that they are not dated in the calendar we use today.

The Jewish day is calculated from sunset to sunset, but the Julian day is computed from midnight to midnight. So, how do New Testament scholars or Roman historians deal with this disparity? They treat the midnight-to-midnight day in the Julian calendar as equating to the sunset-to-sunset day in the Jewish calendar. What does this mean? As we've discussed before, every day in the Roman Julian calendar was understood by the Jews of the first century AD to have begun six hours earlier than the Romans understood it.

Perhaps an example will help. Take the date of June 26th. There is nothing unique or special about that date (except it's my wife's and my wedding anniversary).[234] In the year 500 AD, June 26 fell on a Monday. This same date on the Julian calendar would have been Nisan 19 on the Jewish calendar, from 6:00 pm through midnight, plus most of Nisan 20, from midnight to 6:00 pm. Any day on the Julian calendar was split between two days on the Jewish calendar.

Jews living under Roman occupation had to keep an eye on coordinating their Jewish calendar with the Roman Julian calendar. This is true today as well. Religious Jews in the twenty-first century use their Jewish dating system in religious ceremonies but must live by the Gregorian calendar in everyday life.

Here is the bottom line. Are the first-century Gospel narratives using the lunar calendar or the solar calendar? The answer is neither. The Synoptic Gospel authors use the standard Jewish method of time reckoning, as their forefathers had been computing time for hundreds of years. While Luke 3:1–2 dates the beginning of John the Baptist's ministry explicitly in Roman time, he consistently refers to other events as they relate to the Jewish calendar. This is true both in his Gospel and in Acts, even when he was writing to Gentiles.

Luke accompanied Paul on his second and third missionary journeys. Luke was a Gentile; Paul was the apostle to the Gentiles. Still, when Luke mentions celebrating the day of Pentecost, he does not bother to identify when it occurs in Roman (Julian) time. Luke knew his readers would be well aware of when Pentecost was celebrated (Acts 2:1; 20:16). In Acts 27:9, Luke refers to the day of Atonement by merely calling it "the Fast." The doctor saw no need even to define what he meant by "the Fast." His readers knew what fast it was.

Thus, in dating the crucifixion of Jesus of Nazareth, we must be cautious not to think in terms of our calendar. While we use the Gregorian solar calendar today, the Jewish writers of the New Testament were using a Jewish lunisolar calendar that uses both the moon's phases and the sun's position to determine the date.

THE BEGINNING AND LENGTH OF JESUS' MINISTRY

We know Jesus' ministry began when he was "about thirty years of age" (Luke 3:23). Since the adverb "about" is non-specific, we have to give a little latitude in deciphering the date that Jesus began his public ministry. There are, however, a curious ensemble of hints that may seem insignificant by themselves, but when taken together give us a much clearer picture of Jesus' age when his ministry began on the Earth and when it ended with his crucifixion. Like pieces of a puzzle, let's begin collecting those hints.

The beginning of Jesus' ministry is most helpful in determining the date of his crucifixion. Most scholars accept the Gospels' uniform testimony that Jesus died during the Judean prefecture of Pontius Pilate, dating from 26 AD to 36 AD. It is possible, however, to narrow that period.

Luke 3:1-2 places John the Baptist's ministry of preaching repentance beginning in the fifteenth year of the reign of Tiberius Caesar. This date is both precise and fraught with difficulty. Joseph A. Fitzmyer lists five problematic factors in calculating the date.[235] Was this the fifteenth year of Tiberias' governance and the thirteenth year of his monarchy? Tiberias was the joint emperor for two years before Caesar Augustus died.

Many would opt for a date of August/September 28-29 AD as the beginning date of Jesus' public ministry. We do not know how much time elapsed between John the Baptist's call to ministry and the commencement of Jesus' ministry. It appears to be just a few weeks or months, but the Bible does not explicitly say. The fact that Luke turns from John's to Jesus' ministry after only twenty verses may indicate the time was short.

In John 2:20, after Jesus both cleansed the Temple and predicted its destruction, his Jewish antagonists protested that the Temple sanctuary had taken forty-six years to rebuild. Josephus (*Ant.*15.11.1; *Wars* 1.21.2) gives two different dates for rebuilding Herod's Temple, namely 23/22 BC and 20/19 BC. A forty-six-year endeavor would yield 24/25 AD and 27/28 AD, respectively for the rebuilding of the Temple. The Temple was destroyed by the Romans in 70 AD.

The length of Jesus' ministry

Many regular events of Jewish life appear in Jesus' ministry. The most prominent was the Feast of the Passover. The Gospel of John mentions three Passovers during Jesus' ministry, including the Passover at his crucifixion (John 2:13; 6:4; 13:1). Since Jesus began ministering to people before the first of the three Passovers, the length of his ministry had to be a minimum of more than two years.

In recounting the story of the feeding of the five thousand, Mark 6:39 remarks, "Then he commanded them all to sit down in groups on the green grass." Green grass would indicate springtime for the grass in Israel is parched brown all summer and fall until the winter rains return. Mark does not mention springtime again until Jesus' final Passover (Mark 14:1).

Irenaeus, in his *Adversus Haeresis*, argued that the Jew's objection to Jesus' age in John 8:57 ("You are not yet fifty years old, and have you seen Abraham?") means Jesus had to be in his forties because there would be too much of an age gap to say that to someone in their early thirties. But for Irenaeus, Jesus' ministry lasted over ten years.[236] Few others have adopted this view.

The situation is the same in the Gospel of John. There is too much historical material presented in the fourth Gospel to pack into a ministry of a year or slightly more. It appears what follows is a better solution.

The events surrounding the three Passovers

John 2:13 records that Jesus traveled to Jerusalem for the first Passover of his public ministry. Seeing the corruption that was associated with the Jerusalem Temple, Jesus made a whip of cords and drove out all the oxen and sheep salesmen. He poured out the money changers' coins and overturned their tables. When the Jews asked him for a sign that would give him authority for such unorthodox activity, Jesus made his first declaration: "Destroy this temple, and in three days I will raise it up" (John 2:19). This was at Passover number one.

When Jesus was in Galilee and fed the five thousand as they sat on the green grass, John mentioned that a second Passover was near (John 6:1–4). We cannot equate this Passover with the previous one. The geography is different. At his first Passover during his public ministry, Jesus was already in Jerusalem. At his second Passover, Jesus was in Galilee, on the north shore of the Kinneret.

Jesus' third Passover was the most significant of them all for it coincided with his crucifixion (John 11:55; 12:1; 13:1; 18:28). Jesus traveled from Galilee to Jerusalem out of duty to the Law, but he knew this journey was undertaken more out of duty to his Heavenly Father than it was to Moses the lawgiver. The Savior ascended the hills of Judea in preparation for Passover, but it appears that he did not live long enough to celebrate it.

A fourth Passover?

Jack Finegan saw a fourth Passover in John's Gospel. He argued that Jesus' words in John 4:35, "Do you not say, 'There are yet four months, then comes the harvest'?" mean that since harvest comes in April or May each year, these words must have been spoken in January or February. This, Finegan reasoned, must mean another Passover is coming, which is not explicitly referenced in the Synoptics or John. He places this unnamed Passover in between the year of Jesus' first Passover (John 2) and the one mentioned in John 6.[237]

In my possession, I have a private letter dated December 5, 1989, in which Jack Finegan explains how he understands that a fourth Passover is justified. He writes:

> Essentially, one has to understand that in the early Gk. Mss. (such as the Bodmer and Chester Beatty Manuscripts) numbers are quite often written in Greek letters . . . I believe that's what happened in Luke 3:1ff, with the source Luke used, or when Luke himself wrote, that the reading of "Year 2" was the original writing (Ei = Year 2 or "B" = 2 was the way "B" was often written in early first C. MSS); it could be confused with "E" (=5) + I (=10) = "15" as I believe was the case and that this was so close in appearance to "year 15" (EI) that the two were confused.
>
> [Author's Note: in using Greek letters as numbers, Epsilon (E) equals the number 5, Iota (I) equals the number 10, and Beta (B) equals 2].

As one with the utmost respect for Jack Finegan, I believe his contention of a fourth Passover during Jesus' ministry is mere speculation. Not many students of the Scriptures agree there was a fourth Passover in any of the Gospels.

Are we able to date the beginning of Jesus' ministry from the hints we have found? Perhaps not, but can we date it from biblical sources that are also historical sources? Yes, we can. Consider these human date indicators from Luke 3:1-2.

HUMAN DATE INDICATORS

To anchor the death of Jesus in history, we must narrow the broad Roman occupation period in Judea. We do that by human date indicators. The author of the Gospel of Luke provides no less than eight individuals that provide the best historical/biblical clues to dating the ministry of Jesus of Nazareth. Luke 3:1–2 reads:

> In the fifteenth year of the reign of Tiberius Caesar, Pontius Pilate being governor of Judea, and Herod being tetrarch of Galilee, and his brother Philip tetrarch of the region of Ituraea and Trachonitis, and Lysanias tetrarch of Abilene, during the High Priesthood of Annas and Caiaphas, the word of God came to John the son of Zechariah in the wilderness.

The physician lists eight people who have been historically confirmed and dated apart from the Bible and who help us to date the crucifixion of Jesus of Nazareth. I refer to them as human date indicators. Take note of their eminence and reputation in the Roman or Jewish communities. These are people to be reckoned with.

Emperor Tiberius: The first human date indicator

From official Roman documents, we know that Julius Caesar died on March 15, 44 BC ("the Ides of March"). If we can find a link between his death and the lives of other prominent officials whose dates are known, it may be possible to paint a broad picture of when the crucifixion of Jesus of Nazareth took place.

Caesar was followed by Gaius Octavius Thurinus, who took the name Augustus and ruled the empire from Caesar's death until his own death, August 19, 14 AD. Caesar Augustus was the Roman emperor when Jesus was born. He was followed by Emperor Tiberius, Rome's ruler when Jesus was crucified. According to Suetonius and Cassius Dio, Emperor Tiberius died on March 16, 37 AD.

From the specific dates of these Roman emperors, we have a fixed calendar from before Jesus' birth, throughout his life, and after his death. Tacitus wrote in his *Annals*: "Christus [Christ] had been executed during the rule of Tiberius by the procurator Pontius Pilatus" (*Annals* 15.44).

The Roman author Suetonius wrote a biography of Tiberius as well as other Roman emperors. In that biography, he listed and dated some of the significant events that occurred during the emperor's life. The Roman historian Cassius Dio in his *Roman History* assigned the same dates to Tiberius as did Suetonius. "These historians dated events in the standard Roman way, which was either to write that an event happened 'in the twentieth year of Tiberius' reign,' or to name the Roman consul who was in office at the time.

Since the consul changed every year, this gave the precise year in which the event occurred."[238]

With the corroboration of these ancient witnesses, we can have a high degree of confidence in the years provided by Luke and narrow significantly the years Jesus may have begun his ministry and was crucified because of it. The Roman Emperor Tiberius is himself the first human date indicator.

Pontius Pilate: The second human date indicator

Besides Jesus himself, Pilate is the central figure in the crucifixion story. Pontius Pilate was the prefect of Judea when John the Baptist began his ministry (Luke 3:1–2). Josephus' *Antiquities* 18.3 starts by relating how Pilate moved the Roman army from Caesarea to Jerusalem and made the colossal mistake of bringing the Roman ensigns into the Holy City, which permitted no idols. That is Josephus' section #1 of *Antiquities* 18.3. Section #2 follows with the account of Pilate building an aqueduct with Temple funds, another colossal blunder (*Ant.*18.3.2).

But the very next division, section #3, begins with these words, "Now, there was about this time Jesus, a wise man" (*Ant.*18.3.3). Josephus clearly placed Jesus' crucifixion within the regime of Pontius Pilate. Luke records what exactly Josephus did. As Pilate first arrived in Judea, he ordered his troops to Jerusalem for their "winter quarters." This would mean Pilate came to Judea by the fall of 27 AD. The first Passover during Jesus' ministry would be in 28 AD.[239] These dates play directly into a confirmation of the 30 AD crucifixion of Jesus of Nazareth.

We know that Jesus died, not only when Tiberius was emperor, but also when Pontius Pilate was the Roman governor of Judea. Tacitus, as well as all four Gospels, affirm these facts. From what Josephus said in his *Antiquities,* Pilate governed Judea from 26 to late 36 AD or early 37 AD.[240] The second human date indicator is well documented both in the historical sources and in the Scriptures. Now we may take a closer look at more indicators provided by Doctor Luke.

Herod, Tetrarch of Galilee: The third human date indicator

Herod Antipater was born before 20 BC. He was known by his nickname Antipas or by his regional title, Herod Tetrarch of Galilee and Perea. When Herod the Great died, his kingdom was divided among his sons. Archelaus became the "ethnarch" over Judaea or leader of an ethnic group, the Jews. Antipas received Galilee and Perea and was called a "tetrarch" or ruler over a fourth of the kingdom. Herod Philip, the half-brother of Archelaus and Antipas, was also named a tetrarch and ruled the small regions of Gaulonitis and Trachonitis in the northeast.

After much intrigue, family infighting, and assassinations, the elderly human "king of the Jews" revised his will to make Antipas his heir. Herod Antipas (Herod the Tetrarch) would rule for the next forty-two years.[241] He is notorious for having married his half-brother, Herod Philip's, wife (see next), which earned him the ire of John the Baptist and procured the Baptist's head on a platter (Matt 14).

The Passion Week episode of Pilate sending Jesus to Herod Antipas for judgment is described only in Luke 23:7–15.[242] Some scholars have questioned the authenticity of this account because it is found only in Luke's Gospel. However, I see this type of questioning as beneath the dignity of genuine scholarship. The *International Standard Bible Encyclopedia* argues that it fits well with the rest of Luke and should not be seriously questioned.[243] Although this episode affords a broader range of dates for Jesus' death, nevertheless, it still indicates that the crucifixion must have occurred before 39 AD. This is in concert with other estimates that suggest Jesus' death occurred before 39 AD.[244]

Because of espionage and intrigue, Herod Antipas lost his tetrarchy during the second year of the reign of Emperor Gaius Caesar (March 38 to March 39 AD) (*Ant*.18. 7.2; cf. 19.8.2). Coins have been found that were minted in Antipas' 43rd year as tetrarch. Alas, Herod Antipas, our third human date indicator, was deposed in 39 AD.[245]

Philip, Tetrarch of Ituraea and Trachonitis: The fourth human date indicator

Philip the Tetrarch, who is sometimes referred to as Herod Philip II, was born about 26 BC, the half-brother of Herod Antipas and Herod Archelaus. When his father Herod the Great died, Philip inherited Iturea, and Trachonitis, the mountainous regions northeast of the Sea of Galilee.

Philip was the odd man out in a love triangle that saw his half-brother, Antipas, steal his wife, Herodias, from him. Josephus tells the story.

> But Herodias, their sister, was married to Herod [Philip], the son of Herod the Great, who was born of Mariamne, the daughter of Simon the High Priest, who had a daughter, Salome; after whose birth Herodias took upon her to confound the laws of our country, and divorced herself from her husband while he was alive,

and was married to Herod [Antipas], her husband's brother by the father's side, he was tetrarch of Galilee (*Ant.* 18 5.4).

Philip ruled these northern regions of Palestine from 4 BC until he died in 34 AD. Josephus notes Philip died "in the twentieth year of the reign of Tiberius" having ruled Trachonitis and Gaulonitis for thirty-seven years (*Ant.* 17.4.6).

Lysanias, Tetrarch of Abilene: The fifth human date indicator

Luke's reference to Abilene, the territory governed by Lysanias, identifies a small realm on Mount Hermon's western slopes in the extreme northern sector of Israel. Unfortunately, this Lysanias is often confused with an earlier Lysanias, Tetrarch of Abilene, who died in 40 BC. The Lysanias mentioned in Luke 3:1-2 is also mentioned by Josephus, and his name is found on coins from that year.

In *Antiquities* 19.5.1, Josephus records Emperor Claudius was parceling out responsibility for overseeing various districts of Roman Palestine. "But for Abila of Lysanias, and all that lay at Mount Libanus, he bestowed them upon him, as out of his own territories." Here Josephus provides external confirmation of Luke's account in Luke 3:1, that Lysanias was the tetrarch of Abilene, whose capital was Abila.

Luke's account is further confirmed by Ptolemy, the great geographer when he called this city "Abila of Lysanias." In Josephus' *Wars* 2.11.5, this Lysanias is associated with "that kingdom which was called the kingdom of Lysanias." Again, in *Wars* 2.12.8, the historian mentioned "the kingdom of Lysanias, and that province (Abilene) which Varus had governed."

While our knowledge of Lysanias is limited, what we do know supports the description of Luke 3, affirming that Lysanias was the tetrarch of Abilene.

High Priest Annas: The sixth human date indicator

Annas was born into a wealthy and influential family and became head of the most prominent High Priestly family in Israel's history. In 6 AD, the Roman legate Quirinius appointed him as the first High Priest in the newly created Roman province of Judea. Annas served as High Priest, and although he was officially removed from office, he remained one of Israel's most influential political and social titans. This was due mainly to controlling his five sons and his son-in-law, Caiaphas, as something akin to puppet

High Priests. Although Annas had not been the High Priest for many years, Josephus still called him High Priest at the end of Caiaphas' tenure. In *Wars* 2.12.6, Josephus referred to Jonathan and Ananias as "the High Priests," fifteen years after Jonathan had been deposed.

The Gospels confirm Annas' behind-the-scenes power. John 18:12–14 indicates, "So the band of soldiers and their captain and the officers of the Jews arrested Jesus and bound him. First, they led him to Annas, for he was the father-in-law of Caiaphas, who was High Priest that year" (see also Matt 26:57; Acts 4:6). Jesus was sent to the current High Priest Caiaphas to stand trial for the charges made against him by Annas, to whom he was first sent.

Annas was a Sadducee, the religious/political party of the wealthy Jews in Jerusalem. He held tight control of every financial transaction that took place in the Temple. He became the Godfather of Israel, controlling a monopoly on the entire Temple enterprise. It made him fabulously wealthy.

High Priest Caiaphas: The seventh human date indicator

According to Josephus, Caiaphas was appointed High Priest in 18 AD by Valerius Gratus, the Roman prefect who preceded Pontius Pilate. In his *Jewish Antiquities,* Josephus refers to Caiaphas many times, and from the details he gives, nearly all scholars agree that Caiaphas was the High Priest from about 18 AD to 36 AD, within plus or minus a year or so.[246] Josephus confirms that, after Simon was High Priest for only a year, "Joseph Caiaphas was made his successor. When Gratus had done those things, he went back to Rome after he had tarried in Judea eleven years when Pontius Pilate came as his successor" (*Ant.* 18.2.2).

In Matthew's Gospel (Matt 26:56–67), Caiaphas and a quorum of the Sanhedrin are portrayed as interrogating Jesus. They were looking for false witnesses to frame Jesus for crimes he did not commit. Caiaphas and his cronies had already determined to kill Jesus long before this prejudicial trial. Unfortunately for them, these Jewish leaders were unable to find any credible witnesses against Jesus.

Throughout the trial, Jesus remained silent until Caiaphas demanded he say whether or not he was the Messiah. Jesus replied, "I am, and you will see the Son of Man seated at the right hand of Power, and coming with the clouds of heaven" (Mark 14:62). That enraged Caiaphas. He charged Jesus with blasphemy, called for an affirming vote from the Sanhedrin, and sentenced Jesus to death.

From historical evidence external to the Bible, Jesus died during the reign of Tiberius (14–37 AD), when Caiaphas was High Priest (about 18–36

AD), and Pontius Pilate was governor of Judea (26–36 AD). It's hard not to be impressed with Luke's precision in identifying the time of John the Baptist's ministry and, consequently, the beginning of Jesus' ministry.

John the Baptist: The eighth human date indicator

The Gospel of Luke provides another clue to the date of Jesus' crucifixion by specifying when John the Baptist began his ministry. This is relevant in determining the year of the crucifixion because after John the Baptist started preaching, Jesus came to him to be baptized. Both the beginning of Jesus' ministry and the date of his crucifixion had to be after John the Baptist commenced his ministry.

Table 2: Luke 3:1,2 Human Date Indicators

Person	Dates	Identification
Tiberius Caesar	14–37 AD	The third emperor of Rome, he ruled during the ministry of Jesus.
Pontius Pilate	26–36 AD	The governor of Roman Judea, allowed Jesus to be crucified.
Herod the Tetrarch	6–29 AD	The son of Herod the Great, Antipas was tetrarch of Galilee who wanted Jesus to entertain him.
Philip the Tetrarch	4 BC–34 AD	The half-brother of Herod Antipas, he is often called Herod Philip II.
Lysanias the Tetrarch	14–39 AD?	He ruled the territory of Abilene which is located on the slopes of Mount Hermon.
Annas the High Priest	6–15 AD	Still head of Judaism even after he was deposed; Annas interrogated Jesus.
Caiaphas the High Priest	18–36 AD	Annas' son-in-law, Caiaphas, tried Jesus and sentenced him to die.
John the Baptist	5–4 BC?	The son of Zachariah and Elizabeth, John was the "forerunner" of Jesus the Messiah.

There can be no doubt that Luke intended to pinpoint the year in which John started preaching and anchoring this in history. Luke not only specified the exact year when John the Baptist began his ministry—the fifteenth year of the Roman emperor Tiberius—he also set the scene politically by telling us who was ruling some of the Roman provinces at the time

(Luke 3:1-2). Even more importantly, Luke tells us that Annas and Caiaphas occupied the High Priest's position when John began his preaching. As a result, most scholars estimate the ministry of Jesus began around 27–29 AD and lasted between two and three and one-half years.[247]

What was the fifteenth year of Tiberius?

Of the eight human date indicators found in Luke 3:1-2, only one is dated. That is, only one indicator enables us to put our finger on a date on the calendar. That would be the first one—"In the fifteenth year of the reign of Tiberius Caesar." What year was the fifteenth year of the reign of Tiberius? "From the evidence of Suetonius and other Roman writers, most believe that Tiberius began to govern jointly with the existing emperor Augustus (his stepfather) in AD 12 and that the Roman Senate appointed him the sole emperor when Augustus died in AD 14."[248]

So, the question becomes, when Tacitus tells us Jesus died in fifteenth year of Tiberius' reign, is the historian counting the start of the emperor's reign from 12 AD, when he ruled jointly with his stepfather Augustus, or from 14 AD when Augustus died and Tiberius was appointed the sole emperor?

John Meier answers the question. "All the major Roman historians who calculate the years of Tiberius' rule—namely, Tacitus, Suetonius, and Cassius Dio—count from 14 AD, the year of Augustus' death."[249] Professional numismatists, those who study and authenticate ancient coins, also provide an answer. From the coins issued during Tiberius' reign, it is evident that Tiberius himself counted the first year of his reign from the death of Augustus in 14 AD. Numismatic experts say, "The coinage of Tiberius can be dated very closely. The first issue is dated by year 1 of Tiberius and year 45 of Actium (August-November 14 AD)."[250] Augustus died on August 19, 14 AD, and the Roman Senate appointed Tiberius as the new emperor less than a month later, on September 17, 14 AD.

If we were calculating Tiberius' reign today, the first year would appear on our calendar as September 17, 14 AD to September 16, 15 AD. This would make the fifteenth year of Tiberius' reign from September 17, 28 AD to September 16, 29 AD. However, since The Roman year used the Julian calendar, which started on January 1, Roman historians would have counted the first year of Tiberius' reign as January 1 to December 31, 15 AD. This would make the last year of Augustus' rule January 1 to December 31, 14 AD.

Colin Humphreys clarifies:

> Luke probably meant by the "fifteenth year of the reign of Tiberius" the period January 1 to December 31, AD 29 . . . Thus,

the earliest possible date for John the Baptist to have begun his ministry is autumn AD 28, and so the crucifixion of Jesus could not have occurred as early as AD 27 [as some have contended]. This is consistent with what we know about the life of Pilate. Pilate became the governor of Judea in AD 26. Most scholars believe that Pilate had been governor for some time before the crucifixion (see Luke 13:1 and 23:12). Thus, on these grounds alone, an AD 27 crucifixion is highly unlikely.[251]

Many variables in dating Jesus' crucifixion are often overlooked by those who attempt to establish one date or another. For example, if Luke used the Syro-Macedonian calendar, which he could have since he was writing to a fellow Greek living in Antioch, Syria, he would have counted the interval between August 19 and the beginning of the new year (October 1) as the first regnal year. In that case, the fifteenth year extended from October 1, 27 until September 30, 28 AD. This would mean Jesus was baptized toward the end of the year 27 AD. It also would tend to support a 30 AD crucifixion date.

In the New Testament language, the word for "fifteen" is *dekapent* (Greek: δεκαπέντε; English: *dekapente;* see Acts 27:28; Gal 2:18). When Luke spoke of the "fifteenth" (Greek: πεντεκαιδεκάτῳ; English: *pentekaidekatō*) year of Tiberius (Luke 3:1), he used a compound word composed of "deka" (Greek: δεκα), related to ten, and "pente" (Greek: πεντε), related to five, ten plus five.

It is also possible that Luke's record used dynastic calculation, meaning he was recording from Tiberius' accession on August 19, 14 AD. The fifteenth year would have been from August 19, 28 AD to August 18, 29 AD. Thus, the first Passover of Jesus' ministry might have been in 29 or 30 AD. This later calculation and a three-and-a-half-year ministry places Jesus' crucifixion in 33 AD.[252]

The controversial testimony from Josephus

All four canonical Gospels reference the fact that Jesus was crucified at Golgotha during the Roman prefecture of Pontius Pilate, governor of Judea.[253] Josephus also chronicled in his *Antiquities of the Jews*, written about 93 AD, that Pilate crucified Jesus.[254] Here is what Josephus said.

> Now, there was about this time Jesus, a wise man, if it be lawful to call him a man, for he was a doer of wonderful works—a teacher of such men as receive the truth with pleasure. He drew over to him both many of the Jews, and many of the Gentiles. He was [the] Christ; and when Pilate, at the suggestion of the

principal men amongst us, had condemned him to the cross, those that loved him at the first did not forsake him, for he appeared to them alive again the third day, as the divine prophets had foretold these and ten thousand other wonderful things, concerning him; and the tribe of Christians, so named from him, are not extinct at this day.

Most modern scholars agree that the *Testimonium Flavianum* (the passage just quoted from *Antiquities* 18.3.3) has been subjected to some interpolation. Still, they also admit that it originally consisted of an authentic core containing the execution of Jesus by Pilate.[255] James Dunn, Emeritus Lightfoot Professor at the University of Durham, weighs in saying there is "broad consensus" among scholars that the reference to the crucifixion of Jesus in the *Testimonium* is authentic.[256]

Thus, while there are likely later additions to Josephus' history of Jesus and the cross, the core of what was written is to be trusted. Joseph confirms that Jesus was crucified under Pontius Pilate.

Trusted testimony from Tacitus

According to Gerd Theissen, professor of New Testament at the University of Heidelberg, Germany, Tacitus is one of the greatest Roman historians.[257] Writing in *The Annals* about 116 AD, Tacitus both described the persecution of Christians by Nero and referred to the crucifixion of Jesus, stating that Pilate ordered his execution.[258]

It is important to recognize that Tacitus was not a Christian sympathizer; he was a patriotic Roman senator.[259] His writing does not display any sympathy towards Christians at all.[260] As a result, Tacitus' reference to the execution of Jesus Christ by Pontius Pilate appears to be genuine and of historical value as an independent Roman source.[261] Since Pontius Pilate was governor of Judea from 26 AD until 36 AD, being replaced by Marcellus, either in 36 or 37 AD, we can establish definitively that the date of Jesus' death had to be before 37 AD.[262]

The result of wading through all this Roman history is that in Luke 3:1-2 the Gospel author knew what he was talking about when he dated the beginning of John the Baptist's ministry. The dating of Luke's Gospel is anchored in the dating of Roman history, and no reasonable person doubts it. By understanding when John began his ministry of repentance, and consequently, when Jesus began his ministry of redemption, we have one more clue to help us determine the year Jesus of Nazareth was crucified.

EVENTS IN THE LIFE OF PAUL THAT HELP DATE JESUS' CRUCIFIXION

Luke 3:1–2 contains the most pinpointed, most poignant, and most precise 50 words (in Greek) demonstrating how secular history corroborates biblical history. But Luke's testimony is not the only New Testament witness to the date of Jesus' death. There are many other events recorded in the New Testament that act as historical markers as well. Among these additional biblical and historical markers are the following.

The conversion of Paul

A different approach to estimating a *terminus ad quem* for the year of Jesus' crucifixion is by dating Saul's conversion on the road to Damascus and his transformation from Saul the persecutor to Paul the apostle. The date of Paul's conversion is critical. Both the Pauline epistles and the Acts of the Apostles affirm Paul's conversion took place after Jesus' death.[263] Here are some essential keys to dating Paul's conversion after Jesus' crucifixion and resurrection.

- Paul says in 1 Corinthians 15:3–8 that Jesus "appeared to Cephas, then to the twelve. Then he appeared to more than five hundred brothers at one time, most of whom are still alive, though some have fallen asleep. Then he appeared to James, then to all the apostles. Last of all, as to one untimely born, he appeared also to me." Don't miss the historical order of Jesus' post-resurrection appearances: Peter, the Twelve, 500 fellow believers, James, other apostles, and lastly Paul. The apostle certainly presents Jesus' death, burial, and resurrection appearances as preceding his conversion.

- The Acts of the Apostles incorporates three separate references to the conversion of Saul of Tarsus.[264] Acts 9:1–5 records the incident on the road to Damascus saying, "Now as he went on his way, he approached Damascus, and suddenly a light from heaven shone around him. And falling to the ground, he heard a voice saying to him, 'Saul, Saul, why are you persecuting me?' And he said, 'Who are you, Lord?' And he said, 'I am Jesus, whom you are persecuting.'" The light and the voice came "from heaven" indicating Paul's conversion event occurred after Jesus' ascension back to heaven (Acts 1:1–11).

- Standing on the Roman army barracks' steps after being arrested for preaching to the mob that wanted his head, Paul repeated the touching story of his conversion on the Damascus Road (Acts 22:1–11).

Obviously the Saul to Paul experience on the road to Damascus occurred after Jesus' death, burial, resurrection, and even his ascension into heaven from which he called out to Saul.

- While defending himself in the court of King Agrippa, Paul again rehearsed the story of his conversion, placing it after Jesus Christ's crucifixion and resurrection (Acts 26:12-18). Also obvious is that the events of Acts 26 transpired after those of Acts 22.

Thus, the book of Acts places the conversion of Rabbi Saul to the Apostle Paul later than the crucifixion of Jesus of Nazareth. If we can confidently date the conversion of Paul, we have another clue for dating Jesus' crucifixion.

Paul's trial before Gallio in Corinth

We may calculate the date of Paul's conversion by working backward from a well-established date—Paul's trial before Junius Gallio in Corinth, Greece (Acts 18:12-17). This took place around 51-52 AD, a date proven credible because of the discovery of four stone fragments that were part of the Delphi Inscriptions. These inscriptions constitute a collection of nine fragments of a letter written by the Roman emperor Claudius in 52 AD. They were discovered early in the twentieth century at the Temple of Apollo in Delphi, Greece.[265]

Gallio was the proconsul [prefect] of Achaia (Acts 18:12) and the brother of the famous Roman Stoic philosopher, Seneca. He became the prefect between the spring of 51 AD and the summer of 52 AD. His term as prefect ended no later than 53 AD.[266] Thus, Paul's conversion must have taken place before 51-52 AD and Jesus' crucifixion and resurrection of Jesus Christ had to have occurred before that.

Here are some additional facts that relate to Paul's conversion and Jesus' crucifixion.

- Paul's trial is thought to have occurred in the earlier part of Gallio's tenure as prefect, based on the reference (Acts 18:2) to his meeting in Corinth with Priscilla and Aquila who had been expelled from Rome by the order of Emperor Claudius, along with all the other Jews living in Rome. This expulsion dates to 49-50 AD.[267]

- The book of Acts indicates Paul spent eighteen months in Corinth, approximately seventeen years after his conversion.[268] Galatians 2:1-10 informs us that fourteen years after his conversion, he went back to Jerusalem. "There are strong early traditions, dating back to the second century AD, that Paul's conversion occurred eighteen months after the crucifixion."[269]

- This time interval is consistent with many events known to have occurred between the crucifixion of Jesus and Paul's conversion.[270] "Hence the crucifixion cannot have been as late as spring 34 AD. There is no positive evidence in favor of 34 AD, and therefore it can be ruled out."[271]

Armed with this biblical information, the best factual estimate for the date of Paul's conversion is sometime between 34 and 36 AD, likely in 34. This means that the death and resurrection of Jesus had to occur before 34 AD.[272] Hence, the conversion and life of the Apostle Paul are important date indicators that help us narrow the terminal date when the crucifixion of Jesus could have occurred.

THE DECREE OF ARTAXERXES HELPS DATE JESUS' CRUCIFIXION

Is the decree of Persian king Artaxerxes in Ezra 7:11–26 a marker for Jesus' crucifixion? Or is the decree of Nehemiah 2:1–8 the marker? Does Ezra or Nehemiah contain a commandment to rebuild Jerusalem, a commandment that was prophesied by Daniel? Does this impact the death of Jesus Christ? These are the questions now to be addressed.

Most readers will be familiar with the Seventy-Weeks Prophecy of Daniel 9:25–26. Many Christians believe the decree of Artaxerxes in Ezra 7:11–26 is the beginning of those Seventy Weeks. Writing in *The Expositor's Bible Commentary*, Edwin Yamauchi explains:

> Many scholars regard the Letter of Artaxerxes I permitting Ezra's return in 458 (or 457) as the *terminus a quo*, the beginning point, of Daniel's first 69 weeks (Dan 9:24–27). If each week represented a solar year, then 69 times 7 years equals 483 years, added to 457 BC equals AD 26, i.e., the traditional date for the beginning of Christ's ministry. Others, however, regard the commission of the same king to Nehemiah in 445 BC as the starting point (Neh 1:1, 11; 2:1–8). From this date by computing, according to a lunar year of 369 days, the same date of AD 26 is reached.[273]

First, a little background. The Jews began to lay the foundations for the Second Temple in 536 BC. However, construction came to a halt not long after and did not begin again until the second year of Darius I (520 BC). The resumption of building the Temple came as a direct result of the preaching of Haggai and Zechariah (Ezra 4:24; 5:1-2; Hag 1:1-15; 2:1-9). It was completed in Darius's sixth year (Ezra 6:15), which would be approximately 516 BC.

This is another way to mark the seventy-year interval of exile, from the destruction of Solomon's Temple in 586 BC to the completion of the Zerubbabel's Temple in 516 BC. Here are some keys to understanding this prophecy and how it relates to Jesus' crucifixion.

- The Old Testament's final historical events occurred during the reign of Artaxerxes I (464-23 BC). Ezra was permitted to take a delegation of Jews to Jerusalem in the seventh year of Artaxerxes (Ezra 7:7-9), about 458 BC.

- To assist Ezra and the Jewish community, Nehemiah received an appointment as governor of the land that permitted him to return in the twentieth year of Artaxerxes (Neh 1:1). That would be about 444 BC. There appears to be an interval between this first journey to Jerusalem (Neh 2:1-11) and a second journey in the forty-third year of Artaxerxes (Neh 13:6). This would be 432 BC.

- Daniel predicted the Messiah would redeem his people after seventy sets of seven years (which Daniel metaphorically calls "weeks"), beginning with Nehemiah's return to Jerusalem in 444 BC (Dan 9:24). The Messiah would be "cut off" at the end of sixty-nine sets of "sevens" (Dan 9:25-26), or 483 years starting with the proclamation of Artaxerxes in 444 BC. As the Sovereign God orchestrated it, this is the Passion Week at the end of which Jesus was crucified. Don't let this slip by you too quickly. This cannot be a coincidence. Put this on the sticky side of your mind.

- As you read books that deal with this prophecy, you discover a healthy variety of interpretations to identify the year of Jesus' crucifixion. Those who advocate a 30 AD crucifixion often combine 26 AD and a three-and-one-half-year ministry for Jesus or 27 AD and a two and one-half-year ministry to reach 30 AD.

- Some scholars combine 27 AD and Jesus' ministry of three and one-half-years to reach 31 AD. These usually argue for a Tuesday night or Wednesday crucifixion on April 25. The Reformed Jewish Calendar of Hillel II, which established the Jewish calendar, placed the Passover Sabbath on Wednesday in both years (see also the Reformed Jewish Calendar for 1-39 AD).

- Harold Hoehner claimed 29 AD as the year in which Jesus began his ministry.[274] If Jesus' ministry began in the fall of 29 AD and continued for three and one-half years, that would produce a Friday, 33 AD crucifixion. In 33 AD, on the Reformed Jewish Calendar, Friday, April 3, was Nisan 14. This means the Passover Sabbath would have been Saturday, April 4, but as the Jews reckon time by a lunar calendar, it would have begun Friday night at sunset.

Many Christian scholars hold that the crucifixion occurred in 30 AD and that Jesus' ministry began in 26 AD. Others identify 31 AD as the crucifixion year and opt for 27 AD as the first year of Jesus' ministry. The established range of dates, then, seems to be 29–34 AD. More will be said later, defining the year with greater clarity.

THE REMODELING OF THE TEMPLE HELPS DATE JESUS' CRUCIFIXION

John 2:13—3:21 documents Jesus' first recorded visit to Jerusalem after his ministry began. On this occasion, he cleansed the Temple. Immediately the Jews demanded Jesus give them a sign to verify his authority to do such a thing. His answer, "Destroy this temple, and in three days I will raise it up," made the hair rise on the back of the Jewish religious leaders' necks. They responded, "It has taken forty-six years to build this temple, and will you raise it up in three days?"[275]

According to secular history, Herod initiated the Temple renovation sometime in 20 or 19 BC. This exchange between Jesus and his antagonists occurred at the first Passover of his public ministry. The "forty-six years" therefore furnishes another means of identifying the year his earthly ministry began.[276] Here are some things to keep in mind.

- This extensive project still had not been completed when Herod died in 4 BC. It was still in progress when the Jews uttered those words of John 2:20. Completion did not come until 64 AD, many years after Jesus' crucifixion, resurrection, and ascension.
- By counting forty-six years from 20 or 19 BC, you arrive at 26 or 27 AD. Hence the first Passover of Jesus' ministry would have been in the spring of 27 AD, a date that supports the 30 AD crucifixion.
- There are two Greek words for "Temple" that Josephus carefully distinguished. The first (Greek: ἱερόν; English: *hieron*) refers to a sacred

- place. For the Jews, this was the entire sacred area of the Temple that encompasses all three courts.

- The second term (Greek: ναὸς; English: *naos*) is far more restrictive and denotes the central sanctuary, the sacred building itself. Josephus located it within the Priests' Court (*Ant*.15.11.5). Both terms are translated as "Temple" in English with no distinction.

- However, the Gospels make a distinction just as Josephus did. When the Synoptics referred to the whole sacred area, ἱερόν was used (Matt 21:12; Mark 11:15; Luke 23:45). John's Gospel is consistent with this individualism. Notice in 2:14–15 Jesus encountered the money changers in the Temple court, that is, τo ἱερὸν (cf. John 5:14; 7:14, 28; 8:2, 20, 59; 10:53; 11:56; 18:20) while in 2:19–20 John uses ὁ ναὸς when describing the Jews' chatter about the destruction of the Temple edifice.

- It is reasonable to assume the Jews were speaking of the Temple edifice, and not the whole of the sacred precincts when they challenged Jesus' claim to rebuild in three days.

- Josephus indicated the initial task in rebuilding Zerubbabel's Temple was the Temple edifice. The priests accomplished this in just a year and a half (*Ant*.15.11.6). This reconstruction was started in 20 or 19 BC, and the sanctuary was completed in 18 or 17 BC. Remembering there is no year 0, the years 18 or 17 BC with forty-six years of rebuilding brings us to 29 or 30 AD. What the Jews meant was that the edifice portion of their Temple had stood for forty-six years. This squares with the fact that Jesus was baptized in the summer or autumn of 29 AD. That means between Christ's baptism and his first Passover, somewhere between four and nine months expired.[277] This calculation points to a 33 AD crucifixion.

REFERENCES TO JESUS' AGE HELP DATE JESUS' CRUCIFIXION

There are two references in the Gospels to Jesus' age in the Gospels that help us refine the date of his crucifixion. One is the *terminus ad quo* and the other is the *terminus ad quem* for Jesus' age during his ministry on Earth.

"About Thirty Years Old"

In my opinion, this phrase is the key that unlocks the question of the year Jesus was crucified. The physician/historian Luke informs us that, "Jesus, when he began his ministry, was about thirty years of age" (Luke 3:23). The Greek word for "thirty" (Greek: τριάκοντα; English: *triakonta*) can mean in his "third decade." This may be why Luke is imprecise, indicating Jesus was "about" thirty years old. He may have been suggesting that Jesus was in his third decade, not that he was precisely thirty years old.

The adverb "about" (Greek: ὡσεί; English: *hōsei*) provides enough leeway for two or three years on either side of age thirty. This is the word used in Matthew 14:21 and Luke 9:14 to estimate the number Jesus fed: "There were about five thousand men." It was not designed to be precise. The expression "about thirty years of age" may signify any age between twenty-five/twenty-six and thirty/thirty-three. Luke is well known for his precision in recording details, especially in precise chronological information (cf. Luke 1:5; 2:1–2; 3:1–2). But in this case, he provided an approximate age. Consider, therefore, these calculations.

- If Jesus' birth occurred in 4 BC, Jesus' thirtieth birthday was sometime in 25 AD. If the Savior was born in 5 BC, he reached thirty years in 24 AD.

- The traditional day of Jesus' baptism is January 6, 28 AD. At that time Jesus would have been 33 or 34 years old, depending on the calendar, or as Luke recorded, "about thirty years old."

Table 4 shows the importance of flexibility in the phrase "about thirty years." Bearing in mind that Luke may have been saying Jesus was in his third decade instead of thirty years, and also keeping in mind the flexibility of the word "about," the following scenarios present themselves. If Jesus was born in 5 BC, he would have turned thirty in 24 AD. But if the "about" allowed flexibility of two-three years, he may have reached thirty in 26 or 27 AD. And if the same flexibility would allow for three-five years, Jesus could have turned thirty in 27, 28, or 29 AD. This would place his crucifixion anywhere from 29 to 33 AD, depending on flexibility.

The more information we consider, the more difficult it becomes to pinpoint the date of that dark day at Golgotha. But there is another age reference on which we must reflect, the *terminus ad quem* of Jesus' age.

Table 3: Jesus' Birth, Ministry, and Flexible Crucifixion Dates

Birth Date	Year Turned Thirty	Flexible 2–3 Years	Crucifixion Date
6 BC	23 AD	25–26 AD	28 AD
5 BC	24 AD	26–27 AD	29 AD
4 BC	25 AD	27–28 AD	30 AD
3 BC	26 AD	28–29 AD	31 AD
2 BC	27 AD	29–30 AD	32 AD
1 BC	28 AD	30–31 AD	33 AD

"Not yet fifty years old."

Another biblical marker that helps us date Jesus' ministry and the Passion Week is found in John 8:56–58. Involved in yet another skirmish with the scribes and Pharisees, Jesus said to them, "Your father Abraham rejoiced that he would see my day. He saw it and was glad." To this, the Jews rapidly responded, "You are not yet fifty years old, and have you seen Abraham?" Equal in his rapid response, Jesus said to them, "Truly, truly, I say to you, before Abraham was, I am" (John 8:56–58). This so frustrated the Jews they picked up stones to kill Jesus right there, but somehow he mingled with the crowd and slipped out of the Temple.

Why did the scribes and Pharisees say Jesus was not yet fifty years of age? Why not sixty or forty years? Consider these facts.

- *Pirke Abot* is a compilation of the ethical teachings and maxims allegedly passed down to the rabbis from Moses. According to *Pirke Abot* 5.21a, a man is only fit to give counsel once he reaches the age of fifty. Hence the Levites were dismissed from any physical service at age fifty because it was thought more proper for them to advise than to bear burdens or do manual labor.

- As the Hebrew language was not generally in use by Jews for centuries after their Babylonian captivity, a methurgeman, or interpreter, stood by the side of the reader (cp. 1 Cor 14:27–28) and translated verse by verse into Aramaic what the reader in the synagogue read in Hebrew. Aramaic is a sister language to Hebrew; it was spoken in daily conversation by the Jews. Even the methurgeman was not chosen until he reached the age of fifty (Talmud Babylonian, *Chagiga*, 14.1; *Juchasin*, 44.2).

- In the Jewish community, if a man died before he was fifty, the Jews referred to this as the death of cutting off; it was a death thought to be inflicted by God as punishment (Jerusalem Talmud, *Biccurim,* 64. 3. Babylonian Talmud, *Moed Katon,* 28. 1; *Macsecheth Semachot,* c. 3. sect. 9. See Rabbi Kimchi on Isa 38:1). Thus, if you lived past fifty, you were thought to be righteous enough both to give advice and assume a leadership role in the Jewish community.

Christ had not lived to age fifty. He was well short of it. In the initial days of his ministry, Jesus entered the synagogue in Capernaum and began to teach. Mark 1:22 records the reaction of those in attendance. "And they were astonished at his teaching, for he taught them as one who had authority, and not as the scribes."

When the Jews remarked that Jesus was not yet fifty years of age, the scribes and Pharisees wondered how a man of such a young age could possess such wisdom and speak so confidently (John 8:57). The scribes' and Pharisees' statement adds weight to the argument that Jesus was somewhere in his early thirties when he was executed at Golgotha.

These historical markers from the Bible enable us to establish the broad framework of the birth, life, and death of Jesus of Nazareth. Some of these markers are more pointed and more important than others, but each confirms and contributes to our understanding of the historical life of Jesus Christ. Dating Jesus' death would be pure conjecture without these historical and biblical time markers.

ASTRONOMY HELPS DATE JESUS' CRUCIFIXION

Astronomy has played a principal role in narrowing the possible date of Jesus' crucifixion, just as it did his birth. If Jesus died on the 14th of Nisan, we must ask in which years during Pilate's prefecture did that date fall on Thursday/Friday? Two independent, astronomical methods have been used to determine this, and, remarkably, both suggest the same date.

One method goes back to Sir Isaac Newton's calculation of the relative visibility of the new moon's crescent between the Hebrew and Julian calendars.[278] The other way uses a lunar eclipse model and independently arrives at the same date, i.e., April 3, 33 AD.[279] Scholars generally assume Jesus died between 30 and 36 AD.[280]

The ability to see the new moon in Palestine was indispensable for determining the Jewish calendar months. Since their calendar was lunar, leap months had to be added to synchronize with the solar calendar year.

Joachim Jeremias comments there are no historical records related to adding leap months in 27–30 AD.[281] To further complicate calculating the year of Jesus' death, we must employ the Julian calendar, which was in use by the Romans during the New Testament days. Also, the authors of the Gospels used the lunisolar calendar which was the basis for the Jewish calendar. This is partially the reason that astronomers have come up with different results.

Joachim Jeremias gave an admirable accounting of how much scholarly opinions have changed and changed again during the 1920s, 1930s, and 1940s.[282] Jeremias[283] and Oxford scholars Colin Humphreys and W. Graeme Waddington,[284] claim the 14th of Nisan in 30 AD fell on Thursday/Friday and in 33 AD the 14th of Nisan also fell on Thursday/Friday.

THE TERMINUS AD QUEM AND TERMINUS AD QUO FOR JESUS' CRUCIFIXION

Given the historical and biblical information we have at hand, it is possible to determine the earliest possible date for Jesus' crucifixion and the latest possible date for that dark day. Here is what we know about the earliest possible date. First, the facts in evidence for the beginning of Jesus' ministry.

- Jesus' ministry began after John the Baptist's ministry commenced. John was the forerunner of the Messiah. Matthew 3:11, "He who is coming after me is mightier than I, whose sandals I am not worthy to carry."
- John the Baptist began his ministry in the fifteenth year of the reign of Tiberius Caesar (Luke 3:1–2).
- Tiberius' reign began on August 19, 14 AD. It is not certain whether Luke used the accession or non-accession year in defining the fifteenth year of the reign of Tiberius Caesar.[285]
- According to Suetonius, Tiberius was declared "co-Princeps" by the Roman Senate in 12 AD after returning from Germania.[286] Augustus died in 14 AD, a month before his seventy-sixth birthday (Velleieus Paterculus, *Roman History* 2.123). At that time, Tiberius was confirmed as Augustus's sole heir (Tacitus, *Annals* 1.8) and Rome's emperor.
- If Luke used the non-accession year, we must reckon Tiberius' reign from the year of the decree that made him co-regent with Augustus (12 AD). This would make John's ministry commence around 27 AD and Jesus' ministry shortly after that.

- If Luke was referring to the Julian calendar used by the Romans, Tiberius' first year would have been January 1 to December 31, 15 AD, making his fifteenth year 30 AD.
- The mention of Pontius Pilate places the beginning of John the Baptist's ministry in the decade between 26 AD and 36 AD.
- Jesus' ministry could not have begun at the very beginning of Pilate's tenure. John P. Meier comments:

> Tiberius' entrance upon his fifteenth year (at the earliest, 26 AD), the Baptist's commencement of his public activity, and then Jesus' beginning of a ministry that lasted at least one year—make it impossible that Jesus could have been executed as early as 26 AD. Hence, just as one cannot place Jesus' execution at the very end of Pilate's tenure (36 AD), so one cannot place it at its very beginning (26 AD).[287]

- John the Baptist's ministry, therefore, began no earlier than the autumn of 27 AD. John baptized Jesus sometime after that (Luke 3:21-22).

This discussion is quite confusing to many, but that is largely because determining the day and year of Jesus' crucifixion is confusing. It is not as easy as it appears on the face of it. Multiple issues may sometimes be contradictory and must be addressed from multiple historical sources. We must all be careful not to jump to a conclusion too quickly.

Having explored the *terminus ad quem* and *terminus ad quo* for the beginning of Jesus' ministry as it relates to the beginning of John the Baptist's ministry, in the next chapter, we must focus on establishing the year in which Jesus of Nazareth was crucified.

Chapter 10

Candidates for the Year of Jesus' Crucifixion

Pilate was rapidly running out of friends and just as rapidly gaining enemies. After the death of Sejanus, both Pilate and Antipas did whatever they could to distance themselves from Sejanus and gain the favor of Emperor Tiberius. Each one was willing to do whatever it took to implicate the other in any disturbance or dust-up.

IN THE LAST CHAPTER, we did the hard work of uncovering all the historical facts and dates that bear on the ministry of Jesus and, ultimately, his crucifixion. In this chapter, the equally hard work of choosing a year for the crucifixion of the Messiah will be explored.

German Roman Catholic theologian and priest Josef Blinzler (1824–1890) investigated the published statements on the year of Jesus' death by approximately a hundred biblical scholars in his day. He found the years 26, 27, 28, 29, 30, 31, 32, 33, 34, and 36 AD had all been suggested. The most popular dates were 29 AD [thirteen scholars], 30 AD [fifty-three scholars], and 33 AD [twenty-four scholars].[288] Other dates were also given and some of them deserve a cursory examination.

THE MOST VIABLE YEARS FOR JESUS' CRUCIFIXION

Since not all of these proposed dates are of equal weight or plausibility, we will explore only those that seem to be the more likely year of Jesus' death. Here are the facts for each year. You decide.

27 AD

Although Friday, April 11, 27 AD could have fallen on either Nisan 14 or 15, Luke 3:1-2 indicates that John the Baptist's ministry started in Tiberius' fifteenth year, 27 or 29 AD. Jesus' ministry followed this, and therefore the 27 AD date is not only questionable astronomically but impossible biblically. This is confirmed in John 2:20, when, at the first Passover of Christ's ministry, the Jews spoke of the Temple edifice having been in construction for forty-six years. Since the Temple sanctuary was completed in 18/17 BC, forty-six years later would be the year 29/30 AD. Therefore, the 27 AD date is not a viable option for Christ's crucifixion. It is almost certainly too early.

30 AD

The 30 AD crucifixion can boast of the most advocates. This date is much preferred to the earlier date of 27 AD or the later date of 36 AD. Herod's reconstruction of the Temple is a major event supporting the 30 AD date. Josephus records that the Jews began to refurbish the Second Temple in the eighteenth year of Herod's rule; that would be about 19 BC (37 BC minus eighteen years; *Ant.*15.11.1). When he visited Jerusalem for Passover, Jesus was told the reconstruction was already a forty-six-year project (John 2:13-14, 20). This would mean Jesus' first visit was in 27 AD. We assume that Jesus had already begun his ministry when he visited Jerusalem so he would have begun his work sometime in the fall of 26 AD or early in 27 AD. This would support a crucifixion date of 30 AD.

33 AD

The 33 AD date is also very reasonable for Jesus' crucifixion. First, it is sound astronomically.[289] Second, it is not limited to one dating system (the accession system), as is 30 AD, for reckoning the beginning of the Baptist's ministry in Tiberius' fifteenth year (Luke 3:1-2). Third, the 33 AD date allows more time for Jesus' public ministry. It permits a ministry of three-plus years, beginning in the summer or autumn of 29 AD and ending at the Passover of 33 AD. Fourth, it explains John 2:20 as the Temple edifice, which had stood for forty-six years since it was completed, making the Passover of 30 AD the first Passover of Jesus Christ's ministry.

34 AD

Sir Isaac Newton favored 34 AD as the date of Jesus' crucifixion. His reason appears to be that April 23rd is St. George's Day. This 34 AD date is also almost certainly not the correct year because it conflicts with the likely date of Paul's conversion. By confidently establishing the dates in Paul's life, which are much less problematic than dating the years in our Lord's life, we can use the time spans given by Paul himself to infer that his conversion was in 34 AD.[290] There is no definite evidence for 34 AD as the year of the crucifixion since it does not coordinate well with the date of Paul's conversion.

36 AD

Considering the *terminus ad quem*, Luke 3:1 makes a shipwreck of this late date. There is no indication in the Gospels or anywhere that Jesus' ministry lasted six years. Those who hold to this late date do so on the supposition that John the Baptist was not beheaded until shortly before 36 AD. The basis for this belief is an inference from Josephus that John the Baptist's death occurred just before the victory of King Aretas IV of Nabatea over Herod Antipas in retaliation for Antipas divorcing Phasaelis, the king's daughter. Unfortunately, this theory abandons the Gospels' chronology completely. It is far more logical to date Jesus' crucifixion based on the four Gospel eyewitnesses than on a single interpretive inference from Josephus. As a result, the 36 AD date for the crucifixion must be rejected.

The conclusion of Colin J. Humphreys is helpful:

> There are only two possible crucifixion dates: Friday, April 7, 30 AD, and Friday, April 3, 33 AD. Both these dates are on Nisan 14 in the official Jewish calendar. Thus the Last Supper cannot have been a Passover meal held on the appointed day, Nisan 15, in the official Jewish calendar. John is, therefore, correct in placing the crucifixion on Nisan 14. The belief of many scholars that John locates the crucifixion on Nisan 14 for the sake of theological symbolism at the expense of historical fact is hence incorrect.[291]

Are there any references in early extra-biblical literature that date Jesus' death? The apocryphal *Gospel According to Peter* (verse 3) states unambiguously that Jesus' death was on the eve of Passover, or Nisan 14. A Jewish source, the Babylonian Talmud (*Sanhedrin* 43a), reports that on the eve of Passover, they hanged Yeshu'(or "Jesus," the Greek equivalent of the Hebrew *Yeshu'*), earlier referred to as "Yeshu' the Nazarene." There is astonishing agreement from all historical sources that the crucifixion was on Nisan 14. Consequently, the only two plausible dates for Jesus' death are Friday, April 7, 30 AD, or Friday, April 3, 33 AD.

We have already seen the science of astronomy helps establish the year of Christ's crucifixion. Since the Jewish calendar was based on lunar months, by observing the dates of the new moons' appearances during the reign of Pontius Pilate (26 to 36 AD), it is possible to establish the years in which Nisan 14 fell between Thursday at sundown and Friday at sundown.

So the question remains: which date is the correct one? This requires further investigation.

THE CASE FOR A *30* AD CRUCIFIXION

The arguments for a 30 AD crucifixion of Jesus of Nazareth are both robust and convincing. Here are some of those arguments.

Four Passovers

Many regular events in Jewish life appear in Jesus' ministry. The most prominent was the Feast of the Passover. The Gospel of John mentions three Passovers during Jesus' ministry (John 2:13; 6:4; 12:1). In his *Harmony of the Gospels,* however, A. T. Robertson believes that John 5:1 also refers to a Passover feast, which, if so, would indicate a fourth Passover. If as the Gospels seem to indicate Jesus began his ministry before the first of these Passovers, the length of his ministry was three-and-one-half years, beginning sometime in the fall of 26 AD it would conclude at the spring Passover of 30 AD. This argues for a 30 AD crucifixion.

The death of Tiberius

According to Luke's Gospel, Tiberius Caesar had been in office for fifteen years at the beginning of John's ministry. His fifteenth year would have been 27 AD or 29 AD, depending on whether Josephus used the accession or a non-accession year dating. Jesus began his ministry shortly after that. If Jesus had a ministry of two and a half years and was about thirty years old when he began (Luke 3:23), a problem surfaces immediately. Josephus' date for Tiberius's death compels Jesus' death to have occurred in 32/33 AD. However, advocates of the 30 AD implore us to remember that Tiberius ruled as co-regent with Augustus Caesar for two years before Augustus died. This means we could date the beginning of his rule to about 12 AD. If we use the accession system of dating, the fifteenth year of Tiberius' reign was actually in 26 or 27 AD, with 26 as the better choice for the beginning of John's and Jesus' ministries because 26 AD better squares with the 5–4 BC date of Jesus' birth. This argues for a 30 AD crucifixion.

30 AD better fits a birth-to-death calendar

The date of Jesus' birth impacts the date of his death in several ways. Since Jesus was "about thirty," plus or minus two years given some flexibility in the meaning of "about," if the birth of the Savior took place in 4± BC, he would have turned thirty in 26 AD, ± two years. Thus, Jesus would have begun his ministry anywhere from 24 to 28 AD, enduring his crucifixion in 30 AD. You can see how the flexibility of the word "about" plays a vital role in dating Jesus' crucifixion.

> "The fourteenth of Nisan (7 April) of the year A.D. 30 is, apparently in the opinion of the majority of contemporary scholars as well, far and away the most likely date of the crucifixion of Jesus."
> —Rainer Riesner

Unfortunately for any student of the Bible, there is just no neat package of dates that all contribute perfectly to the identity of the year Jesus died. The arguments for a 30 AD crucifixion are quite strong. Still, some scholars have found valid reasons to question this date.

ARGUMENTS AGAINST A *30* AD CRUCIFIXION

The two British physicists, Colin J. Humphreys and W. G. Waddington, who have shown that only 30 and 33 AD are suitable years for Jesus' crucifixion, contend further that 30 AD is impossible for several reasons. These are also reasons proposed by biblical scholars.

Luke used a Roman calendar

First, Luke indicates that John the Baptist's ministry began in Tiberius' fifteenth year (Luke 3:1-3). By the Roman method of reckoning the calendar (see, for example, in the histories written by Tacitus, Suetonius, and Cassius Dio), the fifteenth year of Tiberius' reign began on January 1, 29 AD. It continued until the beginning of the following year, January 1, 30 AD. Luke positioned the commencement of the Baptist's ministry no earlier than Nisan 28 AD, and the first Passover of Jesus' ministry no earlier than Nisan 29 AD. Humphreys and Waddington contend Luke likely used the official Roman method of dating when identifying the reign of Tiberius.

We know from the third verse of Luke's Gospel that he addressed his narrative to a man named Theophilus. Luke also addressed the book of Acts to the same man, even referencing his Gospel in his greeting of Acts 1:1. According to tradition, Luke and Theophilus were friends, and both natives of Antioch in Syria. Since this man's name means "lover of God," it is likely Theophilus adopted the name upon his conversion to Christianity.

The fact that Luke addressed him as "most excellent Theophilus" indicates he was highly esteemed, perhaps a Roman official. Thus, it is likely Luke used ordinary Roman calendar reckoning in dating Roman authorities in Luke 3:1-2. This means John the Baptist's ministry began in 29 AD. We should assume if Luke wanted his Gospel to be understood in every part of the Roman Empire, he would not use a method of dating recognized only in Judea and perhaps the adjacent provinces. There seem to be too many events in Jesus' ministry to squeeze into one short year, beginning in 29 AD and ending with a crucifixion in 30 AD. This seems logical.

No evidence of a co-regency

About a century ago many scholars and Bible teachers began to prefer 30 AD as Jesus' crucifixion year. They did so assuming the non-accession year system of dating a king's reign, believing that when Luke calculated Tiberius's regnal years, he included his co-regency years with Augustus before Caesar's death. Discoveries of the twentieth century, however, have somewhat moderated this view. No trace of a co-regency appears in any papyri, coins, or inscriptions that have come to light in recent decades of excavation.[292]

Pilate became prefect over Judea in 26 AD. He succeeded Valerius Gratus after Gratus had served eleven years (*Ant.*18.2.2). It is historically well established that Emperor Tiberius relied heavily on his trusted ally Sejanus to rule the empire on a day-to-day basis.[293] It is well established that Sejanus was quite influential in the emperor awarding Pilate the post of prefect in Judea. And there was one other more troubling note about Sejanus that is well established, according to the Jewish writer Philo. Sejanus was rabidly anti-Semitic.[294]

It is quite likely that, at least in his early years, Pontius Pilate shared Sejanus' hatred for the Jews, and that figured heavily in lobbying the emperor to award Pilate the governorship of Judea. This anti-Jewish feeling was not always well hidden during Pilate's tenure as prefect. On several occasions, Pilate offended the Jewish religious conscience, and on at least one occasion, he severely punished those who dissented.[295]

While a high number of scholars hold to the 30 AD crucifixion date, if John's ministry began in Tiberius' fifteenth year, 28/29 AD (Luke 3:1-2), Jesus Christ would have had a ministry of only a year or perhaps a bit more. That doesn't seem logical.

A flawed timeline

This timeline for a 30 AD crucifixion is flawed for two reasons. First, as noted, there is no evidence from historical documents, coins, etc. that Tiberius' reign was ever reckoned from his co-regency.[296] On the contrary, his reign is always recognized from when he became the sole ruler after Augustus' death on August 19, 14 AD. Josephus stated that Tiberius reigned twenty-two years and five or six months (*Ant.*18.6.10; *Wars* 3.9.6). Reckoning backward from his death on March 16, 37 AD brings us to 14 AD as the first year of his solo reign.

Second, those who hold this theory are not all in agreement about the beginning of the co-regency. Scholars such as Josef Blinzler avow we must account for Tiberius' reign using the Syrian accession year chronology.[297] Blinzler believed this because Luke was born in Syria, where Tiberius' first year reigning would be Elul 19 to Tishri 1, 14 AD (August/September), making the fifteenth year Tishri 1, 27 AD to Tishri 1, 28 AD. Blinzler then claimed Jesus Christ's ministry would have been only two years and a few months.

However, Blinzler's view does not take into account John 4:35: "Do you not say, 'There are yet four months, then comes the harvest'? Look, I tell you, lift up your eyes, and see that the fields are white for harvest." This would be March/April, not September/October. While Jesus was speaking of a harvest of men's and women's souls, he used the present grain harvest as his point of reference. He told his disciples to look around the well of

Samaria at the many barley fields, ready to be cut. Blinzler's view fails the season test.

It also does not adequately address what John meant in John 5:1, "After this there was a feast of the Jews, and Jesus went up to Jerusalem." Of the Jewish feasts in September/October, only Sukkot (Tabernacles) is a pilgrimage feast where the Jews were required to go "up to Jerusalem." The other two pilgrim feasts were Passover (Unleavened Bread) and the Shavuot (Feast of Weeks) in early and late Spring.

The 30 AD crucifixion view limits Christ's ministry to less than two years, which requires the reversal of events recorded in John chapters 5 and 6. The argument here is that the contents of chapter 6 fit perfectly at the end of chapter 4. However, a three-year± ministry for Jesus doesn't face this problem. It fits much better with the meaning, context, and setting of these verses.

The close relationship of Passover to Jesus' crucifixion

Finally, an abbreviated ministry does not explain the time note of John 4:35 or the unnamed feast of John 5:1. The word (Greek: ἑορτὴ; English: *heortē*) used for "feast" in the New Testament is found two dozen times in the Gospels in Greek. While it can mean any of several festivals of the Jews, of those twenty-four times, only in Luke 22 and John 7 is it used for *Sukkot* (the Feast of Tabernacles or Booths). In John 10:22, another word (Greek: ἐγκαίνια; English: *enkaínia*) is used for the Feast of Dedication which was instituted by Judas Maccabeus (*1 Macc* 4:59). All the other times the word *heortē* occurs in the Gospels it refers to Passover, the most revered feast of the Jewish year.

After discussing the scholarly preference for dating Jesus' crucifixion to April 7, 30 AD, Helen K. Bond from the School of Divinity at the University of Edinburgh, Scotland, writes, "The precise date can no longer be recovered. All we can claim with any degree of historical certainty is that Jesus died sometime around Passover (perhaps a week or so before the feast) between 29 and 34 CE."[298]

Many scholars find Professor Bond's pronouncement both unacceptable and somewhat silly. Frankly, dismissing the possibility of an April 7, 30 AD crucifixion, or placing the date of the crucifixion "perhaps a week or so before the feast [Passover]," is ridiculous. Here are just some of those scholars who strongly disagree with Bond's assertion. Interestingly, they represent the gamut of theological persuasions.

- "There is a relatively widespread consensus that Jesus was crucified on April 7, 30."—J. D. G. Dunn[299]
- "Jesus was dead by the evening of Friday, April 7, 30."—John P. Meier[300]
- "As regards Jesus, it is certain that he was crucified in Jerusalem on April 7, 30."—J. Murphy O'Connor[301]
- "The fourteenth of Nisan (April 7 of the year 30 AD) is, apparently in the opinion of the majority of contemporary scholars as well, far and away the most likely date of the crucifixion of Jesus."—Ranier Riesner and Douglas W. Stott[302]
- "I conclude that Jesus died on Nisan 14 (April 7) in 30 AD."—Ben Witherington[303]

As these scholars illustrate, April 7, 30 AD is widely regarded by many New Testament scholars as the day on which Jesus died.[304] Some historians favor the year 30 AD without specifying the particular day or month.[305] E. P. Sanders accepts 30 AD as a useful approximation but, like Bond, strictly holds that specific dates are impossible. Others propose more idiosyncratic dates. For example, Jerry Vardaman argues for Friday, Nisan 15, 21 AD.[306] Leo Depuydt argues for 29 AD,[307] as does Daniel J. Lasker.[308]

While the case for the 30 AD crucifixion of Jesus of Nazareth is strong and accepted by a wide variety of well-qualified historians and theologians, that is equally true for a 33 AD crucifixion. We now must explore the case for and against dating Jesus' death in 33 AD.

THE CASE FOR A *33* AD CRUCIFIXION OF JESUS

Oxford scholars Humphreys and Waddington have researched and written extensively about the date of Jesus' crucifixion. Their paper, "The Date of the Crucifixion," published in the 1985 edition of the *Journal of Scientific Affiliation*[309] a standard among both biblical and scientific scholars. In summary, Humphreys and Waddington's paper concluded:

(1) astronomical calculations permit only two dates for Jesus' crucifixion, April 7, 30 AD, and April 3, 33 AD. Other textual evidence strongly favors Friday, April 3, 33 AD as the date of the crucifixion; and

(2) there was a lunar eclipse visible from Jerusalem at moonrise on the evening of Friday, April 3, 33 AD. There are three textual references confirming this: the Acts of the Apostles, the writings of Cyril of Alexandria, and the "Report of Pilate" [found in Greek in the *Acts of Peter and Paul* and as an appendix to the *Gospel of Nicodemus* in Latin]. There are, therefore,

compelling convergent arguments pointing to April 3, 33 AD as being the date of the crucifixion.[310]

Table 5 provides a potential timeline for the events of Jesus' life assuming either a 4 BC birth or a 1 BC birth and a 30 AD crucifixion or a 33 AD crucifixion. Both Luke 3:1 with its specific reference to the "fifteenth year of the reign of Tiberius" and Luke 3:23 with the note that Jesus was "about thirty years of age" provided the strongest evidence for 29 AD as the year Christ began his public ministry. Consequently, many scholars have concluded Christ's ministry began sometime in the summer or autumn of 29 AD[311]

Table 1: 30 AD and 33 AD Crucifixion Timelines

4 BC Birth	Important Dates	1 BC Birth
4 BC	Jesus' Birth	1 BC
8 AD	Jesus' Visit to the Temple at Age 12	11 AD
Fall, 26 AD	Jesus Begins His Ministry; It is the Fifteenth Year of Emperor Tiberius	Fall 29 AD
Spring 27 AD	First Passover of Jesus' Ministry (John 2:13)	Spring 30 AD
Spring 28 AD	Second Passover of Jesus' Ministry (John 5:1)	Spring 31 AD
Thursday, Nisan 14 April 2, 29 AD	Third Passover of Jesus' Ministry (John 12:1)	Thursday, Nisan 14 April 2, 32 AD
Friday, Nisan 14 April 7, 30 AD	Jesus' Passover Trial and Crucifixion	Friday Nisan 14 April 3, 33 AD
Sunday Nisan 16 April 9, 30 AD	Jesus has risen from the dead. Hallelujah!	Sunday, Nisan 16 April 5, 33 AD

Jesus was "about thirty" when he began his ministry

As often noted, Luke says Jesus was about thirty years old when he began his ministry (Luke 3:1–2, 21–23). But why is age thirty significant? We know priests began their service at age thirty, but Jesus was not a Levitical priest. This age stipulation did not bind him. So why is the mention that Jesus was "about thirty" important to us?

From a Jewish perspective, a man of thirty was of sufficient age to be respected. A man of thirty was not too young to hold a position of spiritual authority or prominence. Simultaneously, a man of thirty was not too old to robustly engage in a public ministry that would take him south of Jerusalem and northwest of Galilee to the regions of Tyre and Sidon (Matt 15:21).

If Jesus was about thirty when his ministry began, and he had a three-and-one-half-year ministry, that makes him about age 33 at his crucifixion. If his birth year was 1 BC, this fits well with a 33 AD crucifixion.

The most important historical event bearing on the date

While the 30 AD date provides explanations for many issues related to Christ's death, the 33 AD date best explains the change in Pilate's attitude toward the Jews. Amidst suspicions of a conspiracy against Tiberius, his right-hand man Sejanus was arrested on October 18, 31 AD. He was found guilty of treason, strangled, and his body cast down the Gemonian Stairs. With the influence of Sejanus in Rome gone, Pilate was now on shaky ground, and the Jews knew it. The Gospels indicate they also took advantage of it.

S. G. F. Brandon thinks that the characterization of Pilate in the Gospels as being a weak, abject figure as opposed to that given in Josephus and Philo is ludicrous.[312] Given his bias, Brandon sides with the secular historians. He says Mark was writing an apology to explain away Pilate's responsibility for Christ's death and to place that responsibility on the Jews. He also argued that the Gospels' picture of Pilate's attempt to save Jesus and his yielding to the pressures of the Jews is inaccurate in light of the remarks in Josephus and Philo indicating how inflexible and disrespectful he was toward the Jews.[313] Along similar lines of argumentation, William Riley Wilson contends that in the light of Josephus and Philo, the Gospels give a distorted portrait of Pilate.[314]

You must have a very low view of Scripture to side with Josephus and Philo against Matthew, Mark, Luke, and John. Brandon and Wilson's weak view of the Bible causes them to brush aside those who are said to have been led by the Spirit of God in what they wrote (2 Pet 1:21; 2 Tim 3:16). They can be pardoned for their lack of faith, but not for their lack of understanding. Their characterization of Pilate as strong as opposed to waffling may have been true at the beginning of his prefectureship, but not toward the end, not after the fall of Sejanus.

Accepting the 30 AD date for the crucifixion, as Brandon and Wilson do, impedes their understanding of the historical metamorphosis Pontius Pilate underwent making him accurately depicted in the Gospels. The evangelists' portrayals of Pilate do not contradict Josephus' and Philo's description of a ruthless ruler at all. They simply describe the man in two different situations in life, during two different timeframes.

Pilate's earlier versus later administration

In John 19:12, the Jews very aggressively shout that if Pilate does not release Jesus to them, the Roman prefect will prove he is not a friend of the Roman Emperor. The term "friend of Caesar" (Latin: *amicus Caesaris*) was a technical term reserved for meritorious senators, knights, and administrators favored by the emperor.[315] To lose this title was the equivalent of being surreptitiously removed from the U.S. President's cabinet and disparaged by every major media outlet in the country. Losing the *amicus Caesaris* was to lose not only your imperial post but to be completely ostracized from Roman life, as was the case for Gallus in 26 BC under Augustus.[316]

A little background is necessary here. For a complete discussion of Sejanus's influence over Pontius Pilate, see Chapter 7 of Book Two in this crucifixion series.

Clearly, Lucius Aelius Sejanus was a force to be reckoned with during the reign of Emperor Tiberius. Sejanus rose to power as prefect of the Praetorian Guard, the elite unit of the Roman army formed by Augustus in 27 BC, to serve as a bodyguard to the emperor and the imperial family. Sejanus commanded the Praetorian Guard from 14 AD until he died in 31 AD. Throughout those years he gradually grabbed more and more power by consolidating his influence over Tiberius and eliminating all potential political opponents, including the emperor's son.

When the mentally unstable Tiberius withdrew to Capri in 26 AD, Sejanus was left in complete control of the administration of the empire. Suetonius records that in 31 AD, Sejanus shared the consulship with Tiberius *in absentia* (*Life of Tiberius*, 65). Equestrians came to Sejanus for favors as if he was the emperor. The masses publicly celebrated his birthday. The ancient historian Cassius Dio wrote in his *Roman History*, "Sejanus was so great a person by reason both of his excessive haughtiness and of his vast power, that, to put it briefly, he himself seemed to be the emperor and Tiberius a kind of island potentate, inasmuch as the latter spent his time on the island of Capreae" (58.5.1–2). Sejanus began nominating those loyal to him for positions in the service of Rome. Pontius Pilate was one of them. He was made prefect of Judea about the time Tiberius abandoned Rome for Capri.

However, Tiberius heard how Sejanus usurped his authority in Rome and immediately took steps to remove him from power. Tiberius deceptively set up Sejanus for a fall. The Roman historian Cassius Dio noted that Tiberius, "Wrote the Senate many contradictory letters, some of which praised Sejanus and his friends, and others denounced them. Tiberius sometimes announced that he would arrive in Rome the next day and, at other times, reported that he was at the point of death (*Roman History*,

58.6.3–5). Eventually, Tiberius stepped down as consul, forcing Sejanus to do the same. The Senate issued a *damnatio memoriae* on Sejanus. [*Damnatio memoriae* is the Latin phrase "condemnation of memory," meaning that a person is to be expunged from official accounts]. His name was eradicated from all public records.

Philo records that Tiberius executed Sejanus for sedition on October 18, 31 AD. At that time, the emperor began to root out Sejanus's appointees and allies. Since Pilate was one of those appointees, he was now skating on thin ice and Caiaphas knew it. It is inconceivable the Jewish religious leaders would threaten Pilate with the "no friend of Caesar" ploy as long as Sejanus was still in power. Such a threat makes sense only if Emperor Tiberius was back in control of the empire and if Pilate was running scared because of his former association with Sejanus.

Pilate's concern becomes intelligible only after the events of 31 AD when Sejanus was deposed. If the crucifixion of Jesus of Nazareth occurred in 30 AD, the Jewish religious leaders' threat against Pilate would have been meaningless. However, in 33 AD, the threat to take an accusation against Pilate to the emperor had real consequences. The Jews knew Pilate was wounded and they were not afraid to use the "nuclear option" to get him to comply with their demands. The *Sitz im Leben* for Pilate in 33 AD was much different from that of 30 AD and provides an honest and plausible explanation for the two sides of Pilate's character presented in historical documents[317]

A. D. Doyle posits a possible thesis that, after Sejanus' fall, Herod's four sons complained about the golden shields at the Passover of 32 AD, when they would naturally be together in Jerusalem with Jesus' crucifixion taking place a year later.[318]

The shields affair was a dart to the heart of Pilate. Herod Antipas reported the episode to Tiberius for his own benefit and Pilate's harm. Because Pilate saw Jesus' trial as an even more threatening case, when he learned that Jesus was from Galilee, he quickly referred the case to Herod Antipas, the tetrarch of Galilee (Luke 23:6–12). Pilate was not about to do anything that would get the attention of Tiberius. Thus, a 33 AD crucifixion date justifies Luke's statement as being accurate.[319] It also fits more reasonably with the events of history at that time.

One final item in favor of a 33 AD crucifixion is direct patristic evidence from Eusebius. In his *Chronicon*, 2, the renowned Church Father stated that Christ suffered "in the nineteenth year of the reign of Tiberius," i.e., 33 AD, and cited Phlegon's reference to the abnormal solar eclipse that took place in the "fourth year of the 202nd Olympiad." This period extended from July 1, 32 AD to June 30, 33 AD. Since Christ was crucified at Passover, spring 33 AD would be the year.[320]

The claim of Romanian astronomers

Shortly after the turn of this millennium, two Romanian astronomers, Liviu Mircea and Tiberiu Oproiu from the Astronomic Observatory Institute in Cluj, Romania, maintained they had pinpointed the exact time and date of Christ's crucifixion and resurrection. They cited their research that showed Christ died at 3:00 pm on a Friday and rose again at 4:00 am on a Sunday.

Mircea and Oproiu used a computer program to check biblical references against historical astronomical data. From data collected on the stars between 26 and 35 AD, they established that the first full moon in those nine years after the vernal equinox was registered only twice—on Friday, April 7, 30 AD, and again on Friday, April 3, 33 AD. But it was only in the latter year that records show a solar eclipse as having occurred in Jerusalem (Mark 15:33).

The Romanian astronomers are convinced the date of the crucifixion was 33 AD because of the solar eclipse that occurred in Jerusalem that year, as depicted in the Bible at the time of Jesus' crucifixion[321]

Possible evidence from an earthquake study

In 2012, NBC News published a story from Discovery News with the headline, "Quake reveals the day of Jesus' crucifixion, researchers believe." *The International Geology Review* investigated an earthquake that was said to have occurred on the same date as Jesus' crucifixion.

Geologist Jefferson Williams of Supersonic Geophysical, and his colleagues Markus Schwab and Achim Brauer of the German Research Center for Geosciences, analyzed earthquake activity in the Dead Sea area by studying three core samples from the En Gedi Spa Beach.

Varves (annual layers of deposition in sediments, somewhat akin to the rings of a tree) reveal that at least two major earthquakes affected the core. One was a widespread earthquake in 31 BC, and the second was a seismic event that happened sometime between the years 26 and 36 AD. Geologist Williams noted, "The latter period occurred during the years when Pontius Pilate was procurator of Judea and when the earthquake of the Gospel of Matthew is historically constrained"[322] The evidence for Jesus' crucifixion on Friday, April 3, 33 AD, from 9:00 am to 3:00 pm is exceptionally strong.

Nonetheless, some reputable scholars have argued against it. Those arguments are worthy of our investigation to gain a fair and balanced view of the date of the crucifixion.

ARGUMENTS AGAINST A 33 AD CRUCIFIXION OF JESUS

The arguments against this later date for Jesus' crucifixion are as rational as those against the earlier date. It is this balance of pros and cons that makes deciding between a 30 AD or a 33 AD crucifixion so difficult.

The argument of age: Jesus would be too old in 33 AD

Those who oppose the 33 AD date advance a dual-threat argument. First, they say that Jesus would have been too old by that date. The argument is that Jesus would have been almost forty when he died and that doesn't seem to square with the Luke 3:23 reference that Jesus was "about thirty years of age" when he began his ministry. This argument, however, is dependent on Jesus' birth being in 5 or 4 BC. If it was in 1 BC, the argument does not stand.

Second, critics of the 33 AD crucifixion believe this makes the public ministry of Jesus too long. If Jesus was near forty instead of "about thirty," his earthly ministry would have been some four years. Thus, many scholars prefer the 30 AD date for Jesus' death and resurrection. But this second argument is based on the first. If the first is false, the second is as well.

The argument for a Passover Crucifixion

As you know, the Synoptics do not agree with John on the date of the month Jesus was crucified. According to the Gospel of John, Jesus died on the 14th of Nisan, corresponding with the sacrifice of the paschal lambs. But it would be highly unusual for an execution to occur on the eve of a Jewish holiday. According to the Gospels of Matthew, Mark, and Luke, Jesus died on the 15th of Nisan (the first day of Passover). Again, it was highly unusual to execute someone on Passover (*Sanhedrin* 4.1). Many scholars have offered clarifications for this apparent discrepancy, but few have succeeded. Perhaps the most ingenious explanation comes from nineteenth-century Russian-Jewish orientalist Daniel Chwolson.

Chwolson assumed Jesus died on Nisan 14th and accounted for the discrepancy in Matthew 26:17 by a mistranslation of the original.[323] Chwolson's artificial construction of the law regarding Passover (when Nisan 15 was on Saturday), however, would not remove the impediment of a Friday execution, the eve of a Sabbath, as well as the eve of a high Jewish holiday.

This objection is lessened if the Jews could try Jesus, condemn him, and then hand him over to the Romans to carry out judgment, which is what they did.

The argument of execution just before the Sabbath

It is also argued that the most significant difficulty for a 33 AD crucifixion date, from the viewpoint of the Jewish penal procedure, is presented by the day and time of Jesus' execution. According to the Gospels, Jesus died on Friday, the eve of the Sabbath. Yet on that day, because of the rapidly approaching Sabbath, executions lasting until late in the afternoon were not likely (*Sifre*, ii. 221; *Sanhedrin* 35b; *Mekilta* to *Wayakhel*). Some see this as negating the possibility of a mid-Friday afternoon crucifixion and a late Friday burial.

But this argument fails to take into account that it was not the Jews who were conducting executions but the Romans. The Jews had shoved responsibility for the cruelty and death of their Messiah onto the Romans because the Jews could not conduct the execution themselves.

"Forty years before the fall of the Temple," the Jews of the Sanhedrin lost the right to inflict penal justice in capital cases. This meant the crucifixion of Jesus was the physical act of the Roman government. In Roman eyes, this Messiah, this "king of the Jews," was a rebel, and dissidents in the empire were crucified (Suetonius, *Vespas*, 4; *Claudius*, 25.; Josephus, *Ant.* 20. 5.1; 8.6; Acts 5:36–37).

The inscription on the cross of Jesus reveals the Roman law he had broken for which he was crucified. In Rome's eyes, Jesus was a rebel, a pseudo-leader, and a would-be king of the Jews. He was an insurrectionist and a potential threat to the stability of Roman rule, all in a province that was well-known to be unruly.

Perhaps some of the concerns we have in the twenty-first century in determining the correct year of Jesus' crucifixion were not concerns of the first century. We are often guilty of determining first-century realities through twenty-first-century possibilities.

CHOOSING A YEAR

Faced with the difference between John's record and that of the Synoptics, most scholars accept that we are left with simply having to choose between the two options. But which one—John or the Synoptics? Recent scholars have tended to give preference to John.[324] Others hold confidently to the Synoptics.

This choice impacts choosing between a 30 AD or a 33 AD crucifixion, and that is the real task here. Making matters even more complicated, there is no consensus among biblical scholars about which date is the correct one. Table 6 indicates a sampling of scholars and the year of Jesus' crucifixion they hold to be the actual date.

Table 2: Scholars Date Jesus' Crucifixion

Scholars	Date of Jesus' Death
Jerry Vardaman, Robert Eisler	April 15, 21 AD
Paul Winter	28 AD
C. H. Turner	29 AD
Josef Blinzler, Helen K. Bond	30 AD
Jack Finegan, Joachim Jeremias, Ben Witherington John P. Meier, Gerd Theissen, Andreas J. Kostenberger, et al.	April 7, 30 AD
Ethelbert Stauffer, Ernst Bammel	32 AD
J. K. Fotheringham, Harold Hoehner, Colin J. Humphries, Paul L. Maier, W. G. Waddington, Darrell L. Bock, et al.	April 3, 33 AD

At first sight, John's outline has two significant advantages over the Synoptics. First, John's account is internally consistent, while Mark's account has some difficulties. Second, John's low-key version of Jesus' informal Jewish hearing on the day of Preparation aligns more precisely with Jewish jurisprudence in the first century than does the Synoptic record.[325]

Solving the dilemma with the help of a computer

There are two ways to solve this puzzle. While an earlier generation of scholars relied on ancient calendrical tables,[326] modern scholars have benefited from the computer. Whichever method is employed, today astronomers can pinpoint the beginning of months in the first century by locating the lunar conjunction (when the moon is between the Earth and the Sun), and then, by adding two weeks, they can identify the date for the Passover full moon.

Nisan was the first month of the Jewish year, which roughly corresponds to our March/April. In the first century, the Passover always took place after the vernal equinox, i.e. usually March 21st. This changed after the fall of the Temple in 70 AD. The beginning of months in antiquity was then calculated by observing the new crescent moon in the evening sky. Still, without knowing specific atmospheric or climatic conditions, it is impossible to know precisely what would have been visible in Palestine in antiquity.[327]

The more recent calculations by British physicists Colin Humphreys and D. G. Waddington, published in the science journal *Nature,* claim to have surmounted all these difficulties. Still, their dates are almost entirely in line with earlier proposals.[328] Nisan 14 fell on only two possible dates within our broader period—Friday, April 7th, 30 AD, or Friday, April 3, 33 AD. By way of comparison, using the Synoptic dating, Nisan 15 fell on a Friday only in 27 AD and 34 AD, both of which are only marginally possible dates. This information from astronomy appears to have reinforced the Johannine tradition.

Hence we are left with the two most popular dates for Jesus' death, with those who favor a shorter ministry (or who date Luke 3:1–2 reasonably early) supporting April 7, 30 AD, and those who prefer a more extended ministry opting for April 3, 33 AD. Neither date fulfills every detail in the Gospel account of Jesus' birth and ministry. I am inclined to believe the observation of Roman Catholic theologian Raymond E Brown, "I see no possibility of coming to a decision choosing one of the two years."

I quite agree. When you line up the facts for the AD 30 date and the AD 33 date, you come to a draw. If you ask my opinion, and I must be cautious here, it appears to me that the stronger case belongs to AD 33. Here's why.

My reasoning is not biblical but historical. I believe the New Testament accounts are not specific enough to favor one date over the other. However, I do believe an account in Roman history favors AD 33.

Sejanus had a choke hold on the empire while Emperor Tiberius dallied in Capri, but when Tiberius turned on Sejanus and had him killed, both the political and historical environment changed. Suddenly those favored by Sejanus were not favored by Tiberius. Those whom Sejanus engineered to be in places of authority, now were running scared and afraid they may lose their appointments in the Roman Empire, and maybe their life as Sejanus did. One of those was a man named Pontius Pilate. Pilate was rapidly running out of friends and just as rapidly gaining enemies. After the death of Sejanus, both Pilate and Antipas did whatever they could to distance themselves from Sejanus and gain the favor of Emperor Tiberius. Each one was willing to do whatever it took to implicate the other in any disturbance or dust-up.

Pilate was certainly anti-Semitic and had a consistent record of hostility toward the Jews. On three occasions—the Roman standards (*Ant.* 18.3.1), the construction of an aqueduct with Temple funds (*Ant.* 18.3.2), and producing coins engraved with a symbol of Emperor-worship[329]—Pilate showed that he knew how to push Caiaphas's buttons. But Caiaphas and the Jewish leaders also knew how to push Pilate's buttons and the most notable occasion of their button-pushing was when they accused Pilate of not being a friend of Caesar Tiberius. "From then on Pilate sought to release him, but the Jews cried out, 'If you release this man, you are not Caesar's friend. Everyone who makes himself a king opposes Caesar'" (John 19:12).

While the Gospel authors were clearly cognizant of Pilate's past behavior and his reputation as a tyrant, their narratives of Jesus' crucifixion indicate a much different man. Rather than reject the Gospel narratives of Pilate as inaccurate and unhistorical, we should embrace them as an authoritative account of Pilate after Sejanus. There is brilliant historical evidence for what would cause such a drastic change in Pilate's behavior. That evidence stems from the accounts of the deposition of Sejanus and the concern of his cronies that they might face the same fate. That was the trump card that the Jews used to get Pilate's authorization to have Jesus crucified. That was the knife that Caiaphas stuck in Pilate's back and twisted with glee.

Sejanus's fall came in AD 31. Since that event appears to have emboldened the Jews to throw the loss of *Amicus Caesaris*[330] into Pilate's face, Jesus' crucifixion could not have occurred in AD 30. Because of this historical evidence, I lean toward the AD 33 date.

Conclusion

Which date is correct? Never in my academic life have I seen so many competent scholars use the same historical information and come to such different conclusions. Many bloggers who are cocksure they have cracked the case of dating Jesus' death and resurrection are perhaps unschooled in the depth of discussion about Jesus' crucifixion. Perhaps some are unwilling to accept the validity of the arguments in favor of a position they do not hold. Again, we are faced with another issue in which we must practice charity toward those with whom we disagree. Who knows? Perhaps we are all wrong.

A growing number of scholars and others are voicing their opinion that we are becoming too focused on precision dating. They say our modern methods of time precision should not be read back into the Gospel narratives. The first century was a period when no standardization of timepieces, no specification of time, or no exact recording of hours and minutes were available. To mark time, Matthew, Mark, Luke, and John used methods that were available to them and a part of their culture. Our only guarantee of pinpoint accuracy is the supervision of the Holy Spirit as the evangelists wrote their accounts.[331]

Nevertheless, here is what is important to remember. "Christ Jesus came into the world to save sinners" (1 Tim 1:15). He accomplished this by dying on Calvary's Cross to pay the penalty for my sin, your sin, and the sin that infests the whole world.

Determining unquestionably the year of Jesus' crucifixion is not nearly as important as the fact of it. If you trust the fact, the year will take care of itself.

Conclusion

It was Passover weekend. Jesus had journeyed from Galilee to Jerusalem for the annual feast. We can place the date because it was fixed by God and will never change.

WHAT TIME IS IT? Did you look at your watch? Your response was instinctive, wasn't it? It could be a Rolex or a Timex, the price is insignificant. We all depend on our watches or cellphones to tell us the time, day or night.

One of my favorite books is Yogi Berra's *"What Time Is It? You Mean Now?*[332] It's filled with "Yogisms" from, as the book's subtitle says, "the Zennest Master of Them All." The title is worth the price of the book. When someone asks you the time, of course, they mean now! They want to know the time at that very moment. Otherwise, what's the point? The question would be superfluous, unwarranted, redundant, unnecessary (like these words).

In summary, what do we know from exploring the Gospel narratives of Jesus' Passion Week? Specifically, what do we know about the year he was crucified? Do we know the exact date of that year? Can we settle on which day of the week Jesus was executed? And quite importantly, can we determine the time of day he hung on the cross and the moment he died? I think there are strong clues that help us answer each of these questions.

THE YEAR OF JESUS' CRUCIFIXION

Here's what we know about the year Jesus was crucified. There is a significant amount of evidence that helps us determine the year of the Savior's death. We even have that cadre of human date indicators in Luke 3:1–2 that help.

Unfortunately, all that evidence doesn't lead us to just one year, but two. Jesus was crucified either in the year 30 AD or in 33 AD. The evidence is strong for either year, and scholarship, both liberal and conservative, is almost evenly divided between them. For me, the strongest evidence for 30 AD is that it better fits a birth-to-death calendar. Since Jesus was "about thirty" (three ± years for "about") and if he was born around the traditional 4 BC date, he would have turned thirty in 26 AD ± three years. These dates are a better fit for a 30 AD crucifixion than a 33 AD one. The year 33 is difficult to square with a 4 BC birth.

If Jesus was born in 1 BC, however, he would have turned thirty in 29 AD, and again, given the flexibility of "about" with two years ±, he would have begun his ministry anywhere from 27 to 31 AD. This squares with a 33 AD crucifixion date.

To my thinking, however, the greatest indicator in favor of the 33 AD date for Jesus' crucifixion is that pesky threat to take an accusation to the emperor against Pilate if he did not crucify Jesus. Such a threat would have little teeth in 30 AD, but gigantic canines by 33 AD. When Sejanus lost his power with Emperor Tiberius in 31 AD, Pilate too lost most of his power and he feared a recall to Rome. He was on thin ice already because of the incident with the Roman shields. The Jews had Pilate right where they wanted him, and that better fits a 33 AD crucifixion.

Perhaps we cannot pinpoint the year of Jesus' death conclusively, but we can narrow it down to a very concise period of three years. We must live charitably and gird our discussions with kindness.

THE DATE OF JESUS' CRUCIFIXION

When dating the year of Jesus' death we have lots of helpful indicators, both within and without the Bible. Events in the life of Paul help us. Artaxerxes' decree aids us. The rebuilding of the Temple gives us a time indicator. Jesus' age helps date the year of his crucifixion. Even astronomy gives us valuable information about that momentous year.

> "God has arranged all of the preceding centuries, all of the intervolutions of time, all of the events from Genesis 1:1 up to this moment—has arranged and molded them, has had them converge in such a way that there would be a place for this hour, the hour in which His Son will be bound . . . He allowed neither the forces above nor the forces below to tamper with the clock of history."
> —Klass Schilder

But when it comes to the actual date of Jesus' death at Calvary, we don't need all those indicators. The Bible provides sufficient information to unquestionably set the date. It was Passover weekend. Jesus had journeyed from Galilee to Jerusalem for the annual feast. We can place the date because it was fixed by God and will never change.

Exodus 12 reports both the first Passover that dark night in Egypt and God's command to make the Passover an everlasting commandment. Here are some selected verses:

> And the Lord said to Moses and Aaron, "This is the statute of the Passover . . .
>
> It shall be eaten in one house; you shall not take any of the flesh outside the house, and you shall not break any of its bones. All the congregation of Israel shall keep it . . . All the people of Israel did just as the Lord commanded Moses and Aaron. And on that very day the Lord brought the people of Israel out of the land of Egypt by their hosts.

Leviticus 23:4-6 establishes the order for Passover and gives us the date.

> These are the appointed feasts of the Lord, the holy convocations, which you shall proclaim at the time appointed for them. In the first month, on the fourteenth day of the month at twilight, is the Lord's Passover. And on the fifteenth day of the same month is the Feast of Unleavened Bread to the Lord; for seven days you shall eat unleavened bread.

The date of Jesus' crucifixion is inextricably tied to Passover. This was no coincidence; this was intentionality by God. More about this is below.

Passover was in the first Hebrew month of Nisan, corresponding to March/April on our Western calendar. It was also the fourteenth day of the month. On the very next day, the fifteenth of the month began the weeklong Feast of Unleavened Bread symbolizing the hardship of the Jewish Exodus from Egypt.

The Babylonian Talmud (*Sanhedrin* 43a) claims Jesus "was hanged [crucified] on the eve of Passover." The eve of Passover would be near the end of the day of Preparation.

Since the Savior was crucified on the day of Preparation for the Passover, and since the Passover was always the fourteenth day of the month, Jesus must have been crucified in the hours just before the beginning of the annual Passover festival.

In the year that Jesus was executed, the "high day" Sabbath or Passover Sabbath coincided with the regular Saturday Sabbath, making that day even more special.

THE DAY OF JESUS' CRUCIFIXION

We spent considerable time exploring the way time was determined in antiquity. The method of inclusionary calculation was standard in the ancient Middle East. Inclusive calculation counted any portion of a day as a day itself. This was true in Jonah's day, Esther's day, and Jesus' day. It was always the same.

Inclusive calculation allows only Friday of the Passion Week as the day upon which Jesus was crucified. A few hold to a Wednesday crucifixion and a few more to a Thursday crucifixion, but Friday has both the weight of tradition and the enormous weight of the facts behind it. I am confident Jesus was crucified on the day we call Good Friday.

Given our two probable choices for the year of Jesus' crucifixion, the day and date of Jesus' death would either be Friday, April 6, 30 AD, or Friday, April 3, 33 AD. Science and history are laser-focused on these two Fridays. I believe the second choice is the correct one.

THE HOUR OF JESUS' CRUCIFIXION

From all we have explored in the chapters of this book, one issue of time strikes me as the most significant display of God's sovereignty. It does not have to do with the year of Jesus' crucifixion. It does not even have to do with the day Christ died. It has everything to do with the time of day he died.

Jesus was crucified in the month of Nisan when Passover occurs. By the Law of Moses, the Passover lambs were sacrificed on 14 Nisan, just about the middle of the month. This occurred on the day of Preparation, the day before the Passover celebration. Jesus' crucifixion occurred on exactly the same day. That was not by chance nor by accident. That was God's eternal plan and displayed his sovereignty over people, places, events, and time.

Here is what the Gospel authors report about the time of Jesus' crucifixion and death. Although Mark is the shortest of the Gospel narratives, it fills in quite a bit of detail related to the timing of Jesus' death. Here are the words of Mark 15:25, 33, 34, 37, and 42.

> And it was the third hour when they crucified him... And when the sixth hour had come, there was darkness over the whole land until the ninth hour. And at the ninth hour Jesus cried with a loud voice, "Eloi, Eloi, lema sabachthani?" which means, "My God, my God, why have you forsaken me?"... And Jesus uttered a loud cry and breathed his last... And when evening had come, since it was the day of Preparation, that is, the day before the Sabbath, Joseph of Arimathea, a respected member of the council, who was also himself looking for the kingdom of God, took courage and went to Pilate and asked for the body of Jesus.

The Jews divided the daylight hours of their days into four quarters. The first began at sunrise. The second three hours after. The third was at midday. The fourth after 3:00 pm during the hours that continued until sunset. While Mark was using Jewish time calling this third quarter "the third hour," clearly John used Roman time. John is somewhat stingy with time references in his account, but John 19:14–16 does indicate, "Now it was the day of Preparation of the Passover. It was about the sixth hour. He said to the Jews, 'Behold your King!' They cried out, 'Away with him, away with him, crucify him!' Pilate said to them, 'Shall I crucify your King?' The chief priests answered, 'We have no king but Caesar.' So he delivered him over to them to be crucified."

According to Roman time, the sixth hour was noon. Modern translations like the NIV or The Message have abandoned the terminology of "the sixth hour" for the simple word "noon" (cp. John 4:6 in the Geneva Bible, KJV, RSV, etc., although the HCSB oddly translates this as "it was about six in the morning").

Regardless of whether an author used Jewish time or Roman time, Jesus was dead at 3:00 pm on that Good Friday. He had been hanging from the cross since 9:00 am and would only be taken down after his death.

> "Jesus dies at the moment when the Passover lambs are being slaughtered in the Temple. Jesus dies as the real lamb, merely prefigured by those slain in the Temple."—Pope Benedict XVI

Nevertheless, there is something more remarkable in the timing of God. Since Jesus died at 3:00 pm on the day he was tried, harassed, beaten, spat upon, and worse (Mark 15:1–37), there was great significance to the timing of his death. Three o'clock on the day of Preparation for the Sabbath is precisely the time when the hoard of Jewish priests began the ritual of slaughtering the lambs for sacrifice. This continued for approximately two hours, the deadline for every Jewish family to have a lamb to roast.

The sacrificed animal was given back to Sah-bah (Grandpa), the head of the household, who rushed home from the Temple to find Sav-tah (Grandma) with a waiting fire. The Passover meal itself would have been eaten after sunset as the day of the 14th (Preparation) ended, and the day of the 15th (Passover) began.

When Jesus died at the very hour the sacrificial lambs were being killed, it was not a coincidence. It was the eternal coordination of time by Almighty God. What may be even more difficult for the human mind to grasp is that this time was coordinated, not on the day of Jesus' crucifixion, but in the ageless expanses of eternity past (Acts 2:23). Only God could do that! Thank him that he can, and did!

What Does It Mean to Me?
A final observation

When Jesus died at the very hour the sacrificial lambs were being killed, it was not a coincidence. It was the eternal coordination of time by Almighty God. What might be even more difficult for the human mind to grasp is this time was coordinated, not on the day of Jesus' crucifixion, but in the ageless expanses of eternity.

AT THE END OF any presentation, whether the scholar in a seminar or the Sunday school teacher in the Junior High boys' classroom, the audience has the right to say, "So what?" "What did that presentation tell me that I didn't already know?" And even more importantly, "What does it mean to me?" "How does it impact my life?"

Of course, pinpointing the year, day, date, etc. of the most famous crucifixion in history benefits each of us. It demonstrates that when the biblical scholar and scientist work together without preconceived notions, amazing discoveries can be made. Second, pinpointing these events in Jesus' life, most specifically his death, reaffirms our faith in the accuracy of the Gospel authors. While the Synoptics and John differ on some of the dating details, the general timeline of Passion Week fits with the understanding of all four of the evangelists. Additionally, knowing the day Jesus died and the day he arose from the dead gives us concrete dates on the calendar to celebrate these events. Unlike the date of Jesus' birth, the date of his death is fixed and available for our worship of him around the world.[333]

Yet answering some of these great questions about dating Jesus' death does not bring us eternal peace and happiness. That's because knowing the exact year or date of Jesus' death is not the central issue for humankind. It's not the "So what?" issue.

The answer to the "So what?" question relates, not to all the arguments made by scholars, but to the absolute control the sovereign God has over his world, and specifically over the events at Calvary. The Romans viewed Jesus' crucifixion as a victory. But look around you. The Roman Empire has vanished and the cross of Christ has vanquished all the crucifiers. The Roman Eagle is gone; the cross of Jesus is here and held high.

The Bible always connects Jesus' death on Calvary's Cross with our salvation. Furthermore, it always says ours is an eternal salvation (Heb 5:9), by which Jesus' sacrifice provides for us eternal life (John 3:15-16, 36; 4:14; 5:24; 6:40, 47, 54, 68; 10:28; 17:2-3; Acts 13:48; Rom 2:7; 5:21; 6:22-23; Gal 6:8; 1 Tim 1:16; 6:12; Titus 1:2; 3:7; 1 John 1:2; 2:25; 5:11-13, 20; Jude 1:21).

When Jesus died at the very hour the sacrificial lambs were being killed, it was not a coincidence but an eternal coordination of time by Almighty God. Central to Peter's message on the day of Pentecost was the sovereignty of God demonstrated in Jesus' crucifixion as the Passover Lamb at the very hour the Passover lambs were being sacrificed. Peter boldly said to his Jewish audience, "This Jesus, delivered up according to the definite plan and foreknowledge of God, you crucified and killed by the hands of lawless men" (Acts 2:22-24).

Paul confirmed what Peter said in his Epistle to the Ephesians. "Of this gospel I was made a minister . . . to bring to light for everyone what is the plan of the mystery hidden for ages in God . . . This was according to the eternal purpose that he has realized in Christ Jesus our Lord" (Eph 3:8-11).

Because of the events at Calvary, the Apostle Paul was able to see clearly what God had hidden through the centuries of the Old Testament. God's eternal plan was always to save his own by the sacrificial blood of the Lamb of God who takes away the sin of the world.

Because of what took place outside Jerusalem on that Friday afternoon, the day of Preparation for the Passover, at 3:00 pm, we can now clearly see the hidden mystery of God's eternal plan to save us from the penalty of our sin.

The year of Jesus' crucifixion. The date, the day, and the hour. That's not God's message at Golgotha. Certainly, the crucifixion was about Jesus, but it was about you too. Jesus hung there for you and for me. He died there for you and for me. That's what Jesus' crucifixion is all about. It was all about God's gift to you and me.

"As Moses lifted up the serpent in the wilderness, so must the Son of Man be lifted up, that whoever believes in him may have eternal life. For

God so loved the world, that he gave his only Son, that whoever believes in him should not perish but have eternal life" (John 3:14–16).

Dating Jesus' death is of little consequence if we do not embrace what his death was about. It was God's expression of love for you and me and his way of freeing us from the penalty of our sin. Remember these words:

> For while we were still weak, at the right time Christ died for the ungodly. For one will scarcely die for a righteous person—though perhaps for a good person one would dare even to die—but God shows his love for us in that while we were still sinners, Christ died for us (Rom 5:6–8).

That's what the cross was about. It was about God's love for you and me, such love that he sent his only Son to die a bloody, painful, shameful death on a Roman cross. Yet it brought glory to the Father and good to us. The slaughter of the Lamb of God was not a pretty sight, but what Jesus accomplished on Calvary's Cross was a beautiful thing. Embrace it. Enjoy it. Share it. Thank God for it.

> The love of God is greater far
> Than tongue or pen can ever tell;
> It goes beyond the highest star,
> And reaches to the lowest hell;
> The guilty pair bowed down with care,
> God gave His Son to win;
> His erring child He reconciled,
> And pardoned from his sin.
>
> Could we with ink the ocean fill,
> And were the skies of parchment made,
> Were every stalk on earth a quill,
> And every man a scribe by trade;
> To write the love of God above
> Would drain the ocean dry;
> Nor could the scroll contain the whole,
> Though stretched from sky to sky.
>
> Oh, love of God, how rich and pure!
> How measureless and strong;
> It shall forevermore endure,
> The saints' and angel's song.
> —Frederick M. Lehman

Endnotes

1. Macrobius, I.12.3; *Macrobius*, Robert A Kaster, editor *Saturnalia*, vol. I, Loeb Classical Library, No. 510.
2. Adler, et al., *The Jewish Encyclopedia*, vol. 4, 475.
3. ———, *The Jewish Encyclopaedia* vol. 4, New York: Funk and Wagnall's, 1906, 475.
4. The Jerusalem Talmud, *Shabbath* 9.3; see also the Babylonian Talmud, *Pesahim* 4a.
5. In the Roman army, a legion was composed of 6,000 soldiers; each legion was divided into ten cohorts, with each cohort containing six *centuria*. A centurion, such as Cornelius, commanded approximately 80–100 men. The designation "Italian Cohort" likely defines this group of 600 men as being Italians as opposed to conscripted soldiers from conquered countries.
6. Bruce, *Acts*, 218.
7. Luke's Gospel and Acts are both addressed to the same Roman official, Theophilus. In addressing this man, Luke uses the formal term "most excellent" in his Gospel (Luke 1:3). This was common etiquette in addressing Roman officials. Both Felix and Festus were addressed this way by the Apostle Paul (Acts 24:2; 26:25). But, at the beginning of Acts, Luke no longer calls Theophilus "most excellent Theophilus." Instead, he addresses him as, "O Theophilus" (Luke 1:3; Acts 1:1). Since many minor Roman officials were appointed to an office for only a year, this may indicate Theophilus was no longer in office by the time Luke penned the book of Acts. However, Luke must still have been residing in a region where Theophilus continued to command some respect. Theophilus could have been proconsul of Achaia, the region in which Jerome indicates Luke was living when he wrote the Gospel. We simply do not know for certain.
8. Humphreys, *Mystery*, 23–24.
9. See Finegan, *Handbook*, 1988.
10. Bruce, "Calendar," *Illustrated Bible Dictionary* vol. 1.
11. Borg, *The Last Week*, ix-x.
12. Humphreys, *Mystery*, 26–27.
13. Bacher, *JQR*, July 1893, vol. 5, 684, 687.
14. *De Doctrina Temporum Commentarius in Victorium Aquitanum nunc Primum post M.C.LXXVII Annos in Lucem Editum aliosque Antiquos Canorum Paschalium Scriptores*, [Gilles Bouchier] Antwerp, 1634.
15. Schürer, *History*, 5.3.242.
16. Philo, *Special Laws 2*, sec. 148, 149.
17. *Tractatus Primus de Raerificio Paschall*, 12.
18. Benoit, *Passion*, 150.

19. Zodhiates, *Dictionary*, 1113.
20. *Palestine Exploration Fund, Quarterly Statement*, January 1902, 82.
21. Barnett, *Early Christianity*, 21.
22. Philo, *"De Specialibus Legibus 2.145;* Josephus, *Wars* 6.9.3; Mishnah, *Pesahim* 5.1.
23. Brown, *Death*, 959–60.
24. Cox, *Harmony*, 323; see also Niswonger, *History*, 173–74.
25. Kostenberger, *Cradle*, 538.
26. See J. V. Miller, "The Time of the Crucifixion" JETS 26 (1983)
27. Westcott, *John*, 2:325–25. See also Lenski, *Interpretation*, 150–51.
28. ———, *John*, 2.325–26.
29. Plummer, *John*, 328–29.
30. ———, *John*, 342.
31. Franke, *Saturday* People's Christian Bulletin,1.
32. Lançon, *Rome*, 132.
33. Bruce, *John*, 374.
34. Brown, *Death*, 1352.
35. Humphreys, *Mystery*, 26–27.
36. Jeremias, *Eucharistic Words*, 1966.
37. For brief explanations of these 14 parallels, see Theissen, *Historical Jesus*, 423–27.
38. I Howard Marshall, "The Last Supper," in *Key Events in the Life of the Historical Jesus*, Darrell L. Bock and Robert L. Webb, eds. Grand Rapids, MI: Eerdmans, 2010, 543–47.
39. Marcus, "Passover," NTS, 303–24
40. Jeremias, *Eucharistic Words*, 41–56; Higgins, *Lord's Supper*, 20–23; Dalman, *Jesus-Jeshua*, 106–32; Robinson, "Alleged Discrepancy," *BibSac*, II (August 1845), 406–36.
41. ———, *Eucharistic Words*, 55.
42. R. T. Beckwith, "The Day, Its Divisions, and Its Limits, in Biblical Thought," *EQ* 43 (1971), 219.
43. Jeremias, *Eucharistic Words*, 44–46.
44. Hoehner, *Chronological Aspects*, 76–77.
45. ———, *Eucharistic Words*, 62–84; Higgins, *Lord's Supper in the New Testament*, 16–20; Ogg, "Chronology," 76–77; Frederick, "Eat the Passover?" *BibSac*, 68 (July 1911), 503–9; Stauffer, *His Story*, 94–95; Zeitlin, "The Last Supper," *JQR* 42, No. 3, (January 1952), 251–60.
46. Torrey, "Paschal Meal?" *JQR* 42, No. 3, (January 1952), 237–50.
47. Robinson, "Alleged Discrepancy," *BibSac*, 2 (August 1845), 426–27.
48. See Glatzer, *The Passover Haggadah*, 24, 64.
49. Barrett, "Luke XXII.15," *JTS*, 9 (October 1958), 305–7.
50. Excerpts of Mishnah, Seder Moed, *Pesachim* 10.
51. See Dalman, *Jesus-Jeshua*, 93–106; Strack, *Kommentar*,2, 815–34.
52. To learn more about the parallels between the *Didache* and the Jewish *Birkat ha-Mazon*, see Mazza, *The Celebration*, 19–26. Here Mazza discusses these parallels; on pages 307–9, he provides translations of the texts.
53. Box, "Jewish Antecedents," *JTS*, 3 (April 1902), 357–69.
54. Jeremias, *Eucharistic Words*, 26–29.
55. Lietzmann, *Mass*, 170–71.
56. Jeremias, *Eucharistic Words*, 30.
57. D. A. Carson, "Matthew," in The Expositor's Bible Commentary, edited by Frank E. Gaebelein, Grand Rapids: Zondervan, 1984, 8:528–32; Craig L. Blomberg, The Historical Reliability of John's Gospel. Downers Grove, IL: InterVarsity, 2001, 187–88, 237–39, 246–47, 254).

58. John Nolland, "The Gospel of Matthew," in *The New International Greek Testament Commentary*. Grand Rapids, MI: Eerdmans 2005, 1044–46.

59. See Markus Bockmuehl, *This Jesus*. Downers Grove, IL: InterVarsity, 1996, 92–94; N. T. Wright, *Jesus and the Victory of God*, vol 2. Minneapolis, MN: Fortress Press, 1997, 555–56; Scott McKnight, *Jesus and His Death*. Waco, TX: Baylor University, 2006, 264–73].

60. Bockmuehl, *This Jesus*. Downers Grove, IL: InterVarsity, 1996, 92–94.

61. Joseph Tabory, *The JPS Commentary on the Haggadah: Historical Introduction, Translation, and Commentary*. Philadelphia, PA: Jewish Publication Society, 2008, 51–70.

62. Jeremias, *Eucharistic Words*, 23.

63. Bacchiocchi, *The Time*, 16.

64. Scroggie, *Gospels*, 569–77.

65. This idea began with the noted Bible scholar and seminary professor A. T. Robertson. He advanced the concept of 'silent days' during Passion Week in his monumental work *A Harmony of the Gospels*.

66. This day-by-day description of Passion Week is from the website of the United Church of God, https://www.ucg.org/the-good-news/the-chronology-of-the--and-Resurrection-of-jesus-christ and faithfully represents the reasoning of those who advocate a Wednesday.

67. Barnes, *Notes*, 1983.

68. Note that in the John 2 passage, the expression is "in three days" with no reference to three days and three nights.

69. Small terracotta lamps used to light the dark passageways of these Christian underground cemeteries also feature the Jonah story. A typical Jonah cycle of three scenes is carved on the front of a late third-century sarcophagus, which is now in the Vatican Museum.

70. Bacchiocchi, *The Time*, 18–19.

71. R. A. Torrey, *Difficulties in the Bible*. New York: Fleming H. Revell, 1907, 107–8.

72. Bruce Gore, "Good Friday - Easter Sunday: It Didn't Happen That Way! | United Church of God (ucg.org). Mar 31, 2004

73. Armstrong, *Not on Sunday*, 13, note 1.

74. Leviticus 23:11; Josephus and Philo both attest that Pentecost was celebrated 50 days after the first day of the Passover.

75. Bruce, *John*, 374.

76. Humphreys, *Mystery*, 127.

77. ———, *Mystery*, 126–27.

78. For similar twenty-first-century calls for a solemn assembly of repentance and forgiveness, see Richard Owen Roberts, *Sanctify the Congregation: A Call to the Solemn Assembly and to Corporate Repentance*. Solemn assemblies were a crucial part of the Christian's life in America's early years. It is well documented that many American revivals of years gone by began with a solemn assembly. Within the Sprague Collection of Early American Pamphlets in the Widener Library at Harvard University, there are many sermons preached at Fast Days and Solemn Assemblies. These convocations were frequently summoned in attempts to revive the temperature of a constantly dying spirituality in America. The Founders of America believed God was offended by sin, and many of them were deeply troubled by the unconfessed sin of America. Although there is little evidence of it, America's leaders should be similarly troubled today, along with the leaders of every nation. We need a solemn assembly again!

79. According to the Naval Meteorology and Oceanography Command, the United States Naval Observatory (USNO) has as its primary mission to produce Positioning,

Navigation, and Timing (PNT) for the United States Navy and the United States Department of Defense. Former USNO director Gernot M. R. Winkler initiated the "Master Clock" that provides precise time to the GPS satellite constellation run by the United States Air Force.

80. The director's letter was published in the *American Sentinel* of September 1934, 3.
81. Navy Department Letter File, EN23/H5(1)(652).
82. Bradshaw, *Christian Worship*, 78–80.
83. Johnson, *Worship*, vol 1, 224.
84. Woolfenden, *Daily Liturgical Prayer*, 26.
85. Novatianism was an early Christian sect devoted to Novatian (c. 200–258 AD). Novatian refused to accept back into the church's fellowship those baptized Christians who had denied their faith but now denounced their denial. The church of Rome declared the Novatianists a heretical sect.
86. Zenos, "Life of Socrates," x–xi.
87. Woodrow, *Three Days*, 18–19.
88. Vass, *Microbiology Today*, vol. 28. Nov. 2001, 190.
89. Franke, *Not on Sunday*, 19.
90. Babylonian Talmud, *Sanhedrin* 43a; see Cohn, *The Trial*, 298).
91. Humphreys, *Mystery*, 50.
92. Although a rather imprecise measurement depending on the size of the person, a cubit was the distance between the elbow and the tip of the tallest finger. This standard was differently interpreted in various periods of history. Still, it is generally reliable to say that one cubit is equal to approximately 18± inches.
93. The end of a day, when the sun started to set, and the start of a new day for the Jews, with the first three stars' appearance, was a gradual event, lasting in Jerusalem usually around eighty minutes. Modern astronomers define this period as "twilight," the same period in the New Testament was between sunset and the first three stars' appearance.
94. See Humphreys, *Mystery*, 2011.
95. Farmer, "Ignatius of Antioch," 220.
96. Hanegraaff, *Esotericism*, 20.ft.
97. *First apology of Justin, Weekly Worship of the Christians*, Chapter 68.
98. See *Pliny: A Self-Portrait in Letters*, 9–11.
99. Lee, *The Covenantal Sabbath*, 242.
100. See Rokeah, "Ben Stara," *Tarbiz*, 39, 1969, 9–18 [in Hebrew]; Schafer, *Jesus in the Talmud*, 9, 17, 141.
101. Robert Travers Herford also identifies this Ben Stada with Jesus of Nazareth. As to the meaning of the name, he relates it to "seditious" and suggests [page 345, note 1] that it originally designated "the Egyptian" mentioned in Acts 21:38 and Josephus, *Ant.* 20.8.6. Herford, *Christianity*, 37.
102. Tertullian, *The Writings of Tertullian*, vol. 3, 309.
103. Gill, *An Exposition*, 1980.
104. Geva, "Jerusalem's Population in Antiquity," *Tel Aviv 41* (2), (2013):131–60.
105. Magen Broshi, "Estimating the Population of Ancient Jerusalem" *Biblical Archaeological Review* 4:02, June 1978.
106. If 256,000 lambs needed to be slain at Passover and the priests had but 2 hours in which to accomplish the task, 128,000 lambs an hour must be slain. Hypothetically, at an unrelenting pace of one lamb every two minutes, this would still require 4,267 priests. While this sounds like an impossible amount, it really isn't. There were likely 7,200 priests in Jesus' time, but unlike the chief priests, most of them lived outside Jerusalem in Judean and Galilean towns and villages.

107. The principle of God first, then ourselves is entirely biblical. "All the firstborn males that are born of your herd and flock you shall dedicate to the Lord your God" (Deut 15:19). In speaking of the Macedonian churches that gave money for the relief of the poor saints in Jerusalem, the Apostle Paul noted, "but they gave themselves first to the Lord and then by the will of God to us" (2 Cor 8:5). Jesus himself advised, "But seek first the kingdom of God and his righteousness, and all these things will be added to you" (Matt 6:33). God first, then us.

108. See Zohary, *Domestication*, 59–69.

109. See Katz, *Meaning in Midrash*,162.

110. The word *týpos* occurs sixteen times in the New Testament, mostly by the Apostle Paul (John 20:25; Acts 7:43–44; 23:25; Rom 5:14; 6:17; 1 Cor 10:6,11; Phil 3:17; 1 Thess 1:7; 2 Thess 3:9; 1 Tim 4:12; Titus 2:7; Heb 8:5; 1 Pet 5:3), but it is variously translated depending on the context.

111. John P. Meier, *Jesus: A Marginal Jew*. New York/London: Doubleday, 1991, 402.

112. These aromatic, often pungent spices had a diversity of benefits. Spices were used in the worship service of the Temple. Some of the spices, used as sacred oils for anointings (Exod 30:23–25), include the following:

- Balsam (*Pistacia lentiscus*) was a product of Gilead exported to Egypt, as well as Tyre. Jeremiah 46:11 apprises us this desert plant's resin was used for medicinal and cosmetic purposes.
- Myrrh (*Commiphora abessinica*) is the resinous gum of a plant, primarily used to prepare the holy anointing oil (Exod 30:23). It has sweet-smelling aromatic properties (Ps 45:8) and was one of the precious gifts given to Jesus at his birth by the Magi (Matt 2:11). It was offered as a drink when he was dying on the cross (Mark 15:23).
- Cinnamon was used as a condiment, in the preparation of perfumes (Prov 7:17), and in the holy oil for anointing (Exod 30:23). Revelation 18:13 indicates that Babylon was the origin country where cinnamon was grown.
- Cassia (*Flores cassia*) was a dried bark used in the preparation of the anointing oil. Cassia pods and leaves were also useful as medicine.
- Calamus, Hebrew *Kaneh*, is listed in Exodus 30:23–25 as one of the holy anointing oil ingredients. Calamus is an Oriental plant called "sweet cane" (Isa 43:24; Jer 6:20) because of its aromatic smell. It is one of the sweet scents in the Song of Solomon 4:14. And it was a trade item sold in the markets of Tyre (Ezek 27:19).

113. Hoehner, "Chronology," 1992.

114. The Greek *engýs* meaning "near" can be used either as a time or a distance reference. For example, when John noted, "Jesus therefore no longer walked openly among the Jews, but went from there to the region *near* the wilderness, to a town called Ephraim, and there he stayed with the disciples" (John 11:54), he was using the term as a distance reference (see also: Luke 19:11; John 3:23; 6:19, 23; 11:18; 19:20, 42, even Rom 10:8 and Eph 1:13, 17). But, in the next verse when John recorded, "And the Passover of the Jews was near, and many went from the country up to Jerusalem *before* the Passover, to purify themselves," (John 11:55 NKJV) he was using it as a time reference (see also Matt 2432–33 26:18; Mark 13:28–29; Luke 21:30–31; John 2:13; 6:4; 7:2; Phil 4:5; Rev 1:3; 22:10).

115. Carl Johnson, http://mb-soft.com/public/crucif.html).

116. Fred Espenak, "Year Dating Conventions" NASA Eclipse Web Site, NASA.

117. See Cassini, Tables Astronomiques (1740), Explication et Usage, 5 (PA5), 7 (PA7), Tables page 10 (RA1-PA10); Newcomb, "Tables of the Motion," vol vi:, 27, 34–35.

118. Humphreys, *Mystery*, 169–90.

119. Girod, *Words and Wonders*, 59.

120. Benoit, *Passion*, 175.
121. ———, *Passion*, 150.
122. ———, *Passion*, 213.
123. Maier, "The Date of the Nativity," 113–29.
124. Borg, *Two Visions*, 236.
125. Ramm, "Evangelical Christology," 19.
126. Sherwin-White, *Roman Society*, 162.
127. Edwards, *Luke*, 68–69; Gruen, "The Expansion," 157.
128. Conzelmann, *Primitive Christianity*, 30.
129. Schürer, *History*, 1891.
130. Meier, *A Marginal Jew*, 1:213.
131. Dio, *Roman History*, 55. 25:3–4, 9 vols.
132. ———, *Roman History* 55.25:3–4.
133. ———, *Roman History*, LV 25:5–6.
134. Schürer, *History*, vol. 1, 411–13.
135. Finegan, *Handbook*, 234–38.
136. Bruce, *Christian Origins*, 193.
137. The word "stadia" means a level staff or leveling rod used by surveyors to measure differences in level or to measure horizontal distances by sighting the stadia hairs. In Roman times, one stadium equaled 0.11495 miles. Thus, 35 stadia were about four miles.
138. Sir William Mitchell Ramsay was a Scottish archaeologist and New Testament scholar. By his death in 1939, he had become the foremost authority of his day on the history of Asia Minor and a leading New Testament scholar. Initially, however, Ramsay was at best ambivalent toward Christianity. Like other Tübingen scholars of his day, he assumed the New Testament writings, including Luke and Acts, emerged well after the events they claimed to report, and were largely the stuff of legend and mythology.

In an initial chapter of his highly acclaimed book *St. Paul the Traveller and Roman Citizen,* Ramsay admits a bias against the trustworthiness of the book of Acts that many other scholars have but are not willing to admit. Ramsay wrote:

I may fairly claim to have entered on this investigation without any prejudice in favour of the conclusion which I shall now attempt to justify to the reader. On the contrary, I began with a mind unfavourable to it, for the ingenuity and apparent completeness of the Tübingen theory had at one time quite convinced me. It did not lie then in my line of life to investigate the subject minutely; but more recently I found myself often brought in contact with the book of Acts as an authority for the topography, antiquities, and society of Asia Minor. It was gradually borne in upon me that in various details the narrative showed marvellous truth" (Ramsay, *St. Paul*, 19).

In his research, Ramsay was surprised at all the archaeological finds he made that verified the veracity of Luke's writings. Despite his early dismissal of Christianity and New Testament historicity, he became convinced of the impeccable accuracy of Luke-Acts, and by extension the other biblical gospels. Ramsay's archaeological research led him to conclude that the early history of Christianity was not legendary at all but was entirely rooted in historical fact.

139. Schürer, *History*, 1891.
140. ———, *History*, 399–427. This is also the position of Brown, *Birth*, 552–53.
141. Hoehner, *Chronological Aspects*, 14–23. See also Pearson, "The Lucan Censuses, Revisited," in *CBQ*, 61, 1999, 269–70.
142. Johnson, *Luke*, 49.
143. Meier, *A Marginal Jew*, 412, note 9.
144. Brown, *Birth*, 547–56.

145. Hayles, "The Roman Census," *Buried History* 9/4 (December 1973) 113–32; 10 (March 1974), 16–31.
146. Ogg, "The Quirinius Question Today," *ExpTim* 79/7 (April 1968) 231–32.
147. Tertullian, *Adversus Marcionem*, 4.19.
148. See Finegan, *Handbook*, 235.
149. Bruce, *Christian Origins*, 193–94; Habermas, *Ancient Evidence*, 152–53; Boyd, *Lord or Legend?*, 142–43. See also a complete treatment of dating the two censuses by Gerard Gertoux at https://www.academia.edu/3184175/Dating_the_two_Censuses_of_Quirinius.
150. Witherington, *Beyond Strange Theories*, 101–2.
151. Vardaman, *Chronos*, 61.
152. Boyd, *Tells*, 175.
153. Bock, Luke 1:1—9:50, 903–10. See Maier, The Date, 115.
154. Stauffer, *His Story*, 31.
155. Bock, Luke 1:1—9:50, 905. Barnett alternatively suggested that this apographē (a.pografh) was the "machinery" established to facilitate, not taxation, but a "nationwide oath taking" to Caesar. Barnett, "Apographē," *ExpTim* 85 [September 1973], 378–79.
156. Dio, *Roman History*, 53.253.
157. ———, *Roman History*, 54.28.4.
158. Livy, *T Livii Patavini Historiarum Libri Qui Supersunt Cum Deperditorum Fragmentis et Epitomis Omnium: Ad Optimarum Editionum Fidem Scholarum in Usum*, v. 3 (Latin Edition) 2009, 138–39.
159. *Corpus inscriptioum latinarum*, vol. 13: no. 1668. See Lewis, *Roman Civilization*, 2:131–34). The Lyon Tablet is an ancient bronze tablet bearing the transcript of Claudius's speech while he was emperor of Rome. Only the bottom portion of the tablet survives. It was discovered by a dealer in cloth and dry goods in 1528 in his vineyard on Croix-Rousse Hill, which is today the site of the Sanctuary of the Three Gauls in Lyon, France. The Lyon Tablet can be seen in the Gallo-Roman Museum of Lyon.
160. Bruce, *Christian Origins*, 193–94.
161. *Duumviri* is Latin for "two men." Originally *duoviri* (the English term is *duumvirs*) were joint magistrates in ancient Rome.
162. Vardaman, "Jesus' Life," 62–63.
163. See Bruce, Christian Origins, 193–94; and Boyd, *Tells*, 175.
164. Finegan, *Handbook*, 304; cf. Justin, *Apology* 1.34.
165. Stauffer, *His Story*, 29.
166. Schürer, *History*,1:424–25; Bock, Luke 1:1—9:50, 908.
167. Ramsay, *Bethlehem?* 232–33.
168. Schürer, *History*, 1:423; cf. Luke 3:1, 23.
169. Alternatively, his *nomen* could be spelled Quintilius. See Rist, "Luke 2:2," *JTS*, vol 56, Issue 2, 1 October 2005, 489–91, especially 489, note 3.
170. Josephus recorded Herod's death in *Ant.* 17.8.1. He then portrayed Varus's role in settling Herod's affairs in *Ant.* 17.9.3; 10.1, 9; 11.1 cf. also Tacitus, *History* 5.9 and 1:257–58. C. Sentius Saturninus preceded Varus, a Roman general and politician in Syria (*Ant.*16.9.1; Schürer, *History*,1:257; Sherwin-White, *Roman Society*, 169.
171. ———, *Roman Society*, 169.
172. Wallace, *Greek Grammar*, 304.
173. Bruce, *Christian Origins*, 192.
174. See Wallace, *Greek Grammar*, 304.
175. Hoehner, *Chronological Aspects*, 21.

176. For other New Testament locations where πρῶτος occurs, and just as correctly could be translated "before," consider these: Matthew 7:5; Mark 3:27; Luke 11:26; 2 Timothy 1:5; and 1 John 4:19. In each case, the word πρῶτος was translated "before" and made perfect sense. Thus, many conservative scholars argue that the Luke 2:2 passage could be translated: "This was before (πρῶτος) the registration when Quirinius was governor of Syria."

177. Turner, *A Grammar*, vol 3, 29–32.
178. ———, Turner, *Grammatical Insights*, 23–24.
179. Hoehner, *Chronological Aspects*, 22.
180. Higgins, "Sidelights," *EQ*, XLI (October 1969), 300–301.
181. Fitzmyer, *Luke I-IX*, vol. 6, 393, 399–407.
182. Templeman, "The Death of Herod," 97. Academia.edu. (99+) Discussion: The Death of Herod the Great in early 1 BCE Updated 14 09 2020 Google Docs - Academia.edu.
183. For an excellent account of the Magi's origin and their relation to astrology and magic, see Yamauchi, "The Episode of the Magi,"1989.
184. For anyone interested in non-biblical, apocryphal but fascinating tales of Jesus' birth, the Christian Apocrypha is replete with such tails. Read the *Protoevangelium of James*, the *Arabic Infancy Gospel*, the *Armenian Infancy Gospel*, or these apocryphal works dedicated to the Magi—the *Legend of Aphroditianus*. On the star or *The Revelation of the Magi* see Tony Burke, "Christmas Stories in Christian Apocrypha," in *BAR*, 12/13/2017.
185. The Armenian Infancy Gospel was an apocryphal book that drew from *the Protoevangelium of James*, the *Infancy Gospel of Thomas*, and *Pseudo-Matthew*.
186. "Magi," *Encyclopædia Britannica*, April 1910; see also Freed, *The Stories*, 93.
187. Bond, "Black King," *Hyperallergic* Jan. 6, 2020.
188. See MacGregor, *Seeing Salvation*, 2000; and Leclercq, "Mages," 980–1070.
189. Vermes, The Nativity, 22.
190. Metzger, *New Testament Studies*, 1980.
191. There are different interpretations about the gifts the Magi brought—gold, frankincense, and myrrh. The traditional belief is that these valuable items were standard gifts to honor a king or deity in the ancient world: gold as a precious metal, frankincense as perfume or incense, and myrrh as anointing oil. Some interpret the gifts as symbolic, chosen for their special spiritual symbolism about Jesus—gold representing his kingship, frankincense a symbol of his priestly role, and myrrh a prefiguring of his death and perfuming. And thirdly, a few scholars interpret the gifts not as regal but as medicinal. Researchers at Cardiff University have demonstrated that frankincense has an active ingredient that can help relieve arthritis by inhibiting the inflammation that breaks down cartilage tissue and causes arthritis pain. Of course, the gifts were presented to a very young Jesus who, presumably, had no difficulty with arthritis (see: Strata: The Magi's Gifts—Tribute or Treatment? *BAR* 38:1, January/February 2012).
192. See Metzger, "Names for the Nameless," vol 1:79–99, 1970, 23–29.
193. "Magi," *Encyclopaedia Britannica*.
194. See Jensen, "Witnessing the Divine" *BAR*, November 17, 2016.
195. See Tabor, "His Star," *BAR*, December 30, 2021.
196. Parpola, "The Magi" in *BR* 17:6, December 2001.
197. This is not to suggest that only the teachers in Catholic schools, Hebrew schools, or Sunday schools are steeped in incorrect traditions. Almost anyone you ask believes three wise men followed a star to Bethlehem.
198. An example of a common misconception is that Paul spent three years in the Arabian desert while God revealed divine truth to him. But that's not what the Bible

says. Galatians 1:16–18 clearly says, "I did not immediately consult with anyone; nor did I go up to Jerusalem to those who were apostles before me, but I went away into Arabia, and returned again to Damascus. Then after three years, I went up to Jerusalem to visit Cephas." Read this in any version you want; they all say Paul went to Arabia, returned to Damascus, and then after three years, he went to Jerusalem Another misconception is the Bible nowhere claims the lion will lie down with the lamb. It does say: "The wolf shall dwell with the lamb, and the leopard shall lie down with the young goat" (Isa 11:6), and "The wolf and the lamb shall graze together; the lion shall eat straw like the ox (Isa 65:25). But the Bible is completely void of claiming a lion lies peacefully with a lamb. It is a widely believed falsehood.

199. Biblical Archaeology Society staff, "Brent Landau," November 29, 2011.
200. ———, "Brent Landau," November 29, 2011.
201. Rahner, *Encyclopedia of Theology*, 731; Novak, *Christianity*, 302–3; Hoehner, *Chronological Aspects*, 29–37; Scarola, "Nativity Era." 61–68; Kostenberger, *The Cradle*, 114.
202. Schürer, *History*, 325–28 n. 165.
203. *Wars* 2.1.3 §10, *Ant.*17.9.3.
204. Parker, *Babylonian Chronology*, 45.
205. ———, *Babylonian Chronology*, 45.
206. "Loathsome Disease," *The Straight Dope*, November 23, 1979.
207. See a similar conclusion in Porter, "Lukan Census," 187–88.
208. For excellent online research into Luke's accuracy concerning Quirinius, see Brindle, "The Census And Quirinius: Luke 2:2," *JETS* (March 1984) 43–52.
209. Marshall, Luke, 102.
210. Thomas, "The Day," 320–324.
211. Barnes, "The Date," *JTS* 19 (1968); Lynn, "The Eclipse, 253."
212. Schürer, *History*, vol. 1, 2000.
213. See Jensen, "Antipas," *BAR*, September/October 2012.
214. Anno Mundi, abbreviated as AM, or Year After Creation, is a calendar era based on the biblical accounts of the world's creation.
215. Elrington, ed, *Whole Works*. Ussher's date for Creation in October generally corresponds with the estimation of Judaism, which holds that Rosh Hashanah, celebrated in mid-to-late September, marks the anniversary of Creation.
216. Finegan, *Handbook*, 231.
217. Hoehner, *Chronological Aspects*, 13.
218. Edwards, "Herodian Chronology" *PEQ*, 114:1, 29–42 (1982).
219. Orosius, *Seven Books*, 6: 22:1; 7:3:4.
220. There is a date suggestion even later than this one. Bieke Mahieu understands the moon eclipse of December 29, 1 BC as the one that specifies the time of Herod's death. She proposes that Herod died on the 9th of March, 1 AD. See Mahieu, *Between Rome and Jerusalem*, 310–317.
221. Rawlinson, *Egypt and Babylon*, 214, 218; Mommsen, *History of Rome*, 39; Chisholm, *The Augustan Age*, 100; Sherwin-White, *Roman Foreign*, 325; Levick, *Augustus*, 183; Zetzel, *New Light*, 1970; Keresztes, *Imperial Rome*, 1–43. Vardaman, "The Nativity and Herod's Death," 85–92; Finegan, 300, §516.
222. Filmer, "Chronology," *JTS* ns 17 (1966), 283–98; see also Beyer, "Josephus Reexamined," 85–96; Steinmann, "Herod the Great Reign?" *NT*, vol 51, no 1, 2009,1–29. Also, Steinmann's book, *From Abraham to Paul*, 219–56
223. See Cramer's response at the Queries and Comments page of the *BAR* 39:4, July/August 2013 article by Suzanne Singer entitled "Strata: Herod the Great." For those who are interested, NASA publishes a website that includes a "Five Millennium Catalog of Lunar Eclipses" at https://eclipse.gsfc.nasa.gov/LEcat5/LE-0099-000.html.

224. Cramer, *BAR* 39:4, July/August 2013, Queries and Comments.

225. Templeman, "The Death" Academia.edu. (99+) Discussion: The Death of Herod the Great in early 1 BCE Updated 14 09 2020 Google Docs - Academia.edu.

226. In academic circles, the designations BC and AD have been exchanged for BCE ("before the common era") and CE ("the common era"). Many academics today shun the older BC and AD for a variety of reasons. American lawyer and founder of *Kol HaNeshamah*, The Center for Jewish Life and Enrichment, Adena K. Berkowitz' has explained the primary reason for the change. "Given the multicultural society that we live in, the traditional Jewish designations—BCE and CE—cast a wider net of inclusion, if I may be so politically correct." William Safire, "B.C./A.D. or B.C.E./C.E.?" *The New York Times*, August 17, 1997.

227. The traditional 4 BC date for Herod's death has been challenged by W. E. Filmer, "The Chronology of the Reign of Herod the Great," *JTS*, n. 17 (1966), 283ff., as well as many others.

228. With the lunisolar calendar, if the solar year is defined as a tropical year [the time the Sun takes to return to the same position in the cycle of seasons], then a lunisolar calendar will indicate the season. If it is considered a sidereal year [the time taken by Earth to orbit the Sun one time regarding the fixed stars], the calendar will predict the constellation nearest which the full moon may occur. As is the case with all calendars that divide the year into months, there is the need to add a thirteenth intercalary or leap month. The Hebrew, Jainist, Buddhist, Hindu, Kurdish, Burmese, Chinese, Japanese, Tibetan, Vietnamese, Mongolian, and Korean calendars—virtually all cultures in the East Asian sphere—use the lunisolar calendar.

229. Richards, *Explanatory Supplement*, 595.

230. Stern, *Calendars in Antiquity*, 259–297.

231. Finegan, *Handbook*, 132–34.

232. See Ben Witherington's piece entitled "The Turn of the Christian Era" in the November/December 2017 issue of *BAR*.

233. Humphreys, *Mystery*, 40–43.

234. Actually, several important events took place on this day: 363 AD--Roman Emperor Julian was killed during the retreat from the Sassanid Empire; 1870—Richard Wagner's opera "Valkyrie" premiered featuring "Ride of the Valkyries"; 1940—the end of the USSR's experimental calendar with the readoption of the Gregorian calendar; 1945--United Nations Charter signed by fifty nations; 1963—US President John F. Kennedy gave his "Ich bin ein Berliner" speech; 1997—J. K. Rowling published the first book in the Harry Potter series, etc.

235. Fitzmyer, *Luke*, 1.455.

236. Irenaeus, *Adversus Haereses*.

237. Finegan, *Handbook*, 283.

238. See Humphreys, *Mystery*, 15–16.

239. *Ant.* 18.4.2; see also Schürer, *History*, 388 n. 145.

240. ———, *History*, 388. n. 145; Hoehner, *Chronological Aspects*, 30; and Finegan, *Handbook*, 362.

241. Bruce, *Acts*, 8.

242. Majerník, *The Synoptics*, 181; Patella, *Luke*, 16; Card, *Luke*, 251.

243. It is unreasonable to doubt the existence of Jesus if you do not doubt a spiritual reformer will come from a foreign land (outside Bharat) with his disciples (companions). His name will be Mahamad (Muhammad). He will dwell in a desert. (*Bhavisyath Purana* 3:5–8) Bromiley, *ISBE*, vol E-J, 694–95.

244. Harding, *The Content*, 88–89; White, *The Emergence*, 11.

245. *Ant.* 17. 7.1–2; Hoehner, *Herod Antipas*, 262; Losch, *All the People*, 159.

246. Finegan, *Handbook*, 352.

247. Anderson, *The Riddles*, 200; Knoblet, *Herod the Great*, 183–84; Evans, "John the Baptist," 55–58; Maier, "The Date of the Nativity," 113–29.

248. Finegan, *Handbook*, 329–44.

249. Meier, *A Marginal Jew*, 384.

250. Burnett, *Roman Provincial Coinage*, vol. 1, 621.

251. Humphreys, *Mystery*, 63–66.

252. Evans, *Matthew-Luke*, vol. 1, 67–69; *Eerdmans Dictionary*, 249.

253. Jensen, *Herod Antipas*, 42–43.

254. *Ant.* 18.3.3; See White, *The Emergence of Christianity*, 48.

255. Hoehner, *Herod Antipas*, 28, 125–27; Dapaah, *The Relationship*, 48.

256. Bromiley, *ISBE*, A-D 686–87 and K-P 929.

257. Theissen, *Historical Jesus*, 81–83; Kostenberger, *The Cradle*, 104–8.

258. *Annals* 15.44; White, *The Emergence of Christianity*, 48; Evans, *Jesus and His Contemporaries*, 316.

259. Wansbrough, *Oral Gospel Tradition*, 185.

260. Voorst Van, *Jesus Outside*, 39–42; Ferguson, *Backgrounds*, 116.

261. Flavius Josephus, *Ant.* 18.4.2; Green, *Luke*, 168.

262. Carter, *Pontius Pilate*, 44–45; Schäfer, *History*, 108; Ferguson, *Backgrounds*, 416.

263. Meyer, *The Word*, 112; Barnett, *Early Christianity*, 19–21; Kostenberger, *The Cradle*, 77–79.

264. Polhill, *Paul and His Letters*, 49–50; Craig, *The Blackwell Companion*, 616.

265. Marrow, *Paul*, 45–49; Novak, *Christianity*, 18–22.

266. Dunn, *The Cambridge Companion*, 20; Morrow, *Paul*, 45–49; Novak, *Christianity*, 18–22.

267. ———, *Christianity*, 18–22; Jeffers, *The Greco-Roman World*, 164–65.

268. Evans, *Acts–Philemon*, 248.

269. Riesner, *Paul's Early Period*, 64–71.

270. ———, *Paul's Early Period*, 64–71; Jewett, *Dating Paul's Life*, 29–30.

271. Humphreys, *Mystery*, 66.

272. Meyer, *The Word*, 112; Barnett, *Early Christianity*, 19–21; Köstenberger, *The Cradle*, 77–79.

273. Yamauchi, "Ezra-Nehemiah," 651.

274. Hoehner, Chronological Aspects, *BibSac*, 132 [1975]; 47–65; Yamauchi, Ezra-Nehemiah, 651.

275. The Jews were referring to the remodeling project initiated by Herod the Great forty-six years earlier that involved the renovation of Zerubbabel's broken-down Temple.

276. Maier, "The Date of the Nativity," 113–29.

277. See Hoehner, *Chronological Aspects*, 40–43.

278. Riesner, *Paul's Early Period*, 19–27; Blomberg, *Jesus and the Gospels*, 431–36.

279. Köstenberger, *The Cradle*, 114; Sanders, *The Historical Figure*, 249.

280. Meyer, *The Word*, 112; Maier, "The Date of the Nativity," 113–29.

281. Jeremias, *Eucharistic Words*, 37.

282. ———, *Eucharistic Words*, 39–41.

283. ———, *Eucharistic*, 37.

284. Humphreys, "Dating the Crucifixion," *Nature* 306 (1983) 743–46.

285. In the eastern prefectures of the Roman Empire, years were calculated from the reigning emperor's accession. The second year of his reign began the first New Year's Day after his accession. Luke may have counted Tiberius' accession year [the

time between Tiberius' August accession and the following New Year's Day] as his first regnal year. The earliest possible New Year's Day may have been in Tishri's Jewish lunar month (September/ October). In the Talmud, Rabbi Hisda commented, "The rule [that New Year for kings is in Nisan] was only meant to apply to the kings of Israel, but the years of non-Israelitish kings were reckoned from Tishri" (Talmud, *Rosh HaShanah*, 3a). See Brown, *The Jerome Bible Commentary*.

286. Speidel, *Riding for Caesar*, 19.
287. Meier, A *Marginal Jew*, 375.
288. Blinzler, *The Trial*, 101–26. For further information about the range of the possible dates for Jesus' crucifixion and death, see Sanders, *The Historical Figure of Jesus*, 282–90.
289. Goldstine, *New and Full Moons*, 1973.
290. Jewett, *A Chronology*, 30; Edwards, *The Time of Christ*, 174.
291. Humphreys, *Mystery*, 66ff.
292. See Ogg, *The Chronology*, 178, 270–271; Maier, "Sejanus," *Church History* 37 (1968): 6; Kindler, "More Date," *IEJ* 6 (1956): 54–57.
293. Maier, "Sejanus," *Church History* 37 (1968), 8–9.
294. Philo, *De Legatione ad Gaium* 24, *In Flaccum* 1.
295. Blaiklock, *Archaeology*, 52–55; Maier, "Sejanus," *Church History* 37 (1968), 9–12.
296. See Hoehner, *Chronological Aspects*, 31–32, or Marshall, *Luke*, 133 for evidence that dating by co-regency was not used in Roman calculation.
297. Blinzler, *The Trial*, 73.
298. Bond,
299. Dunn, *Jesus Remembered*, 312.
300. Meier, *Marginal*, 402.
301. Murphy-O'Connor, *Jesus and Paul*, 53.
302. Riesner and Stott, *Early Period*, 58.
303. Witherington III, *Narrative Account*, 134.
304. For a survey of older authors who favored April 7, 30 AD, see Blinzler, *The Trial*, 72–80.
305. Theissen, *The Historical Jesus*, 160.
306. "Jesus' Life" in *Chronos*, 55–82.
307. "The Date," *Journal of the American Oriental Society.* 122 (2002), 466–80.
308. "The Date," *Journal of the American Oriental Society* 124 (2004), 95–99.
309. Humphreys and Waddington, *JASA* 37, March 1985, 2–10.
310. A useful discussion that supports the 33 AD date and involves astronomical calculation is offered by Husband, *The Prosecution*, 34–69.
311. Harold W. Hoehner, "Chronological Aspects of the Life of Christ Part II: The Commencement of Christ's Ministry," *BibSac*, 131:521 (Jan 1974) 53–54).
312. Brandon, *The Trial*, 99, 190, n 100.
313. ———, *The Trial*, 146–50.
314. Wilson, *The Execution of Jesus*, 17–23, 131–34.
315. Sherwin-White, *Roman Society*, 47n.
316. Stauffer, *His Story*, 133.
317. See an interesting post by Gary DeLashmutt entitled *Sejanus and the Chronology of Christ's Death* (xenos.org).
318. See Doyle, "Pilate's Career," *JTS* 42 (1941), 190–93. *Cambridge Ancient History* also favors the 33 AD dating, 10, 649; Fotheringham, "The Evidence," *JTS*, 35 (1934), 146–62.
319. Hoehner, *Chronological Aspects*, 106–13.

320. For further discussion, see Maier, "Sejanus," *Church History*, 37 (March 1968), 3–13.

321. *The Orlando Sentinel*, "Scientists Date Crucifixion," May 17, 2003.

322. Jerusalem Quake Seasonality, Jefferson Williams,12 publications, Research Project (researchgate.net).

323. See Khvol'son [Chwolson], *Das Letzte Passamahl*, 13.

324. Blinzler, *Trial of Jesus*. 101–8; Brown, *Death*, 1351–73; Meier, *A Marginal Jew*, 1:395–401; Theissen, *Historical Jesus*, 37; Crossan, *Who Killed Jesus?* 100; and Fredriksen, *Jesus of Nazareth*, 221.

325. For a detailed discussion, see Sanders, *Judaism*.

326. Ancient calendrical tables: Langdon, *The Venus Tablets*, 1928; Parker, *Babylonian Chronology*, 1956. Applications of these ancient calendrical tables to the date of Jesus' death include articles by Fotheringham, "The Date of the Crucifixion," *Journal of Philology* 29, (1903), 100–118; "Astronomical Evidence for the Date of the Crucifixion," *JTS* 12 (1910), 120–27; and "The Evidence of Astronomy and Technical Chronology for the Date of the Crucifixion," *JTS* 35 (1934), 146–62; also Karl Schoch, "Christi Kreuzigung am 14. Nisan," *Biblica* 9 (1928), 48–56; and Olmstead, "The Chronology of Jesus' Life," *Anglican Theological Review*. (1942), 1–26.

327. Stern, *Calendar and Community*. 100; Jeremias, *Eucharistic Words*, 36–41. See also the earlier article by Kraeling, "Olmstead's Chronology of the Life of Jesus," *Anglican Theological Review* 24 (1942), 334–54, esp. 336–37; and more recently, Beckwith, "Cautionary Notes," in *Chronos*, 183–205.

328. Humphreys, "Dating the Crucifixion," *Nature*. (1983), 743–46.

329. Ethelbert Stauffer, Jerusalem und Rom (Bern and Munchen, 1957), pp. 17,134 n. 7, cited in Harold W. Hoehner, Chronological Aspects of the Life of Christ, Part V: The Year of Christ's Crucifixion, p. 343.

330. A. N. Sherwin-White, Roman Society and Roman Law in the New Testament (Oxford: Clarendon Press, 1963), p. 47n.

331. Köstenberger, *The Cradle*, 538; Niswonger, *New Testament History*, 173–74; Cox, *Harmony of the Gospels*, 323–23.

332. Berra, "What Time Is It?

333. Lancon, *Rome in Late Antiquity*, 132.

Bibliography

Adler, Cyrus, et al. *The Jewish Encyclopedia,* 12 vols., "Day," vol. 4. New York: Funk and Wagnall's, 1906.
Anderson, Paul N. *The Riddles of the Fourth Gospel: An Introduction to John.* Minneapolis, MN: Fortress, 2011.
Armstrong, Herbert W. *The Resurrection Was Not on Sunday.* Pasadena, CA: Ambassador College, 1972.
Bacchiocchi, Samuele. *The Time of the Crucifixion and the Resurrection.* Berrien Springs, MI: Biblical Perspectives, 1985.
Bacher, Wilhelm. *JQR,* July 1893, vol. 5, 684, 687.
Barnes, Albert. Barnes' *Notes on the Old and New Testaments,* 14 vols. Grand Rapids, MI: Baker, 1983.
Barnes, Timothy D. "The Date of Herod's Death," *JTS* 19 (1968).
Barnett, Paul. "Apographē and *apographesthai* in Luke 2:1–5," *ET 85* [September 1973], 378–79.
———. *Jesus & the Rise of Early Christianity: A History of New Testament Times.* Downers Grove, IL: InterVarsity, 1999.
Barrett, C. K. *The Gospel According to John: An Introduction with Commentary and Notes on the Greek Text,* second edition. Philadelphia: Westminster, 1978.
———. "Luke XXII. 15: To Eat the Passover," *JTS* 9 (October 1958).
Benoit, Pierre. *The Passion and Resurrection of Jesus Christ.* New York: Herder and Herder, 1970.
Berra, Yogi with Dave Kaplan. *"What Time Is It? You Mean Now?"* New York: Simon & Schuster, 2003.
Beyer, David W. 'Josephus Reexamined: Unraveling the Twenty-Second Year of Tiberius', in Jerry Vardaman (ed.), *Chronos, Kairos, Christos II: Chronological, Nativity, and Religious Studies in Memory of Ray Summers.* Macon, GA: Mercer University Press, 1998.
Biblical Archaeology Society staff. "Bible Scholar Brent Landau Asks 'Who Were the Magi'?" in *The Bible History Daily,* November 29, 2011.
Blomberg, Craig. *The Historical Reliability of John's Gospel.* Leicester, England: InterVarsity, 2001.
Bock, Darrell L. Luke 1:1—9:50 in *Baker Exegetical Commentary on the New Testament.* Grand Rapids, MI: Baker, 1994.
Bokser, Baruch M. "Was the Last Supper a Passover Seder?" *Bible Review* 3 (1987).

Bond, Sarah E. and Nyasha Junior. "The Story of the Black King Among the Magi," *Hyperallergic* Jan. 6, 2020.

Borg, Marcus J. and John Dominic Crossan. *The Last Week*. San Francisco: HarperSanFrancisco, 2007.

Borg, Marcus. *The Meaning of Jesus: Two Visions, A Vision of the Christian Life*. HarperCollins: 1999.

Box, G.H. "The Jewish Antecedents of the Eucharist," *JTS*, 3 (April 1902).

Boyd, Gregory A. and Paul Rhodes Eddy. *Lord or Legend? Wrestling with the Jesus Dilemma*. Grand Rapids, MI: Baker, 2007.

Boyd, Robert. *Tells, Tombs, and Treasure*. Grand Rapids, MI: Baker, 1969.

Bradshaw, Paul F. *The Search for the Origins of Christian Worship*. Oxford: Oxford University Press, 2002.

Brindle, Wayne. "The Census And Quirinius: Luke 2:2." *JETS* (March 1984) 43–52.

Brown, Raymond E. *The Birth of the Messiah: A Commentary on the Infancy Narratives in the Gospels of Matthew and Luke*. New York: Doubleday, 1993.

———. *Death of the Messiah*, Volumes 1 & 2. New York: Doubleday, 1999.

———. *New Testament Essays*. London: Image, 1965.

Bruce, F. F. *The Acts of the Apostles*. Grand Rapids, MI: Eerdmans, 1990.

———. "Calendar," *The Illustrated Bible Dictionary* vol. 1, D. Douglas Hillyer, ed. Wheaton, IL: InterVarsity, 1980.

———. *Jesus and Christian Origins Outside the New Testament*. Grand Rapids, MI: Eerdmans, 1974.

Burke, Tony. "Christmas Stories in Christian Apocrypha" *BAR*, 12/13/2017.

Carroll, Sean M. *From Eternity to Here: The Quest for the Ultimate Theory of Time*. Boston, MA: Dutton, 2009.

Carson, D. A. *The Gospel According to John*. Grand Rapids: Eerdmans, 1991.

Carter, Warren. *Pontius Pilate: Portraits of a Roman Governor*. Collegeville, MN: Liturgical Press, 2003.

Cassini, Jacques. *Tables Astronomiques* (1740), *Explication et Usage*, 5 (PA5), 7 (PA7), Tables page 10 (RA1-PA10), et al.

Chisholm, Kitty and John Ferguson, eds. Rome: *The Augustan Age*. Oxford: Oxford University Press, 1981.

Chwolson, Daniel. *Das letzte Passmahl Christi und der Tag seines Todes* (2nd edition). Leipzig: Haessel, 1980.

Cohn, Haim. *The Trial and Death of Jesus*. New York: Harper & Row, 1967.

Conzelmann, Hans. *History of Primitive Christianity*. Nashville, TN: Abingdon, 1973.

Cox, Steven L. and Kendell H. Easley. *Harmony of the Gospels*. Nashville, TN: Holman Bible Publishers, 2007.

Cramer, John A. Queries and Comments, *BAR* 39:4, July/August 2013.

Dalman, Gustaf. *Jesus-Jeshua*, translated by Paul P. Levertoff. Eugene, OR: Wipf and Stock, 2004.

Davies, William David. *Setting of the Sermon on the Mount*. Cambridge: Cambridge University Press, 1964.

Dio, Cassius. *Roman History*, 55. 25:3–4, 9 vols. Translated by Earnest Cary and Herbert Baldwin Foster. Cambridge, MA: Harvard University Press, 1914–1927.

Driver, G. R. "Two Problems in the New Testament," *JTS*, 16 (October 1965).

Dunn, James D. G. *The Cambridge Companion to St Paul*. Cambridge: Cambridge University Press, 2003.

———. *Jesus Remembered*. Grand Rapids: Eerdmans, 2003.
Edwards, James R. *The Gospel of Luke*. Grand Rapids, MI: Eerdmans, 2015.
Edwards, Ormand. "Herodian Chronology." *PEQ*, 114:1, 29–42 (1982).
Elrington, Charles Richard, ed. *Whole Works; with Life, and an Account of His Writings*. Dublin, Ireland: Hodges and Smith, 1847.
Evans, Craig A. *The Bible Knowledge Background Commentary: Matthew-Luke*, vol. 1. Colorado Springs, CO: Cook, 2003.
———. "Josephus on John the Baptist," *The Historical Jesus in Context*, Amy-Jill Levine et al., editors. Princeton: Princeton University Press. 2006.
Farmer, David Hugh. "Ignatius of Antioch," *The Oxford Dictionary of the Saints*. New York: Oxford University Press, 1987.
Ferguson, Everett. *Backgrounds of Early Christianity*. Grand Rapids, MI: Eerdmans, 2003.
Filmer, W. E. "Chronology of the Reign of Herod the Great." *JTS* ns 17 (1966), 283–98.
Finegan, Jack. *Handbook of Biblical Chronology: Principles of Time Reckoning in the Ancient World and Problems of Chronology in the Bible*. Peabody, MA: Hendrickson, 1988.
Fitzmyer, Joseph A. *Anchor Bible: The Gospel According to Luke I-IX*, vol. 6. Garden City, NY: Doubleday, 1981.
Franke, Elmer Ellsworth. *The Resurrection of Christ on Saturday Not on Sunday* (5th edition). People's Christian Bulletin,1963.
Frederick, William. "Did Jesus Eat the Passover?" *BibSac* 68 (July 1911).
Freed, Edwin D. *The Stories of Jesus' Birth: A Critical Introduction*. London: Continuum International, 2001.
Fuller, Reginald H. *The Mission and Achievement of Jesus*. London, SCM, 1956.
Geldenhuys, J. Norval. *Commentary on the Gospel of Luke*. Grand Rapids, MI: Eerdmans, 1951.
Geva, Hillel. "Jerusalem's Population in Antiquity: A Minimalist View." *Tel Aviv 41* (2), (2013):131–60.
Gill, John. *An Exposition of the Old and New Testaments*, vol. 5. Grand Rapids, MI: Baker, 1980.
Girod, Gordon H. *Words and Wonders of the Cross*. Grand Rapids, MI: Baker, 1962.
Glatzer, Nahum N. *The Passover Haggadah* New York: Schocken, 1981.
Green, Joel B. *The Gospel of Luke: New International Commentary on the New Testament*. Grand Rapids, MI: Eerdmans, 1997.
Gruen, Erich S. "The Expansion of the Empire Under Augustus" in *The Cambridge Ancient History* 10, Alan K. Bowman; Edward Champlin; Andrew Lintott, eds. Cambridge: Cambridge University Press, 1996.
Habermas, Gary R. *Ancient Evidence for the Life of Jesus*. Nashville, TN: Thomas Nelson,1984.
Hanegraaff, Wouter. *Esotericism and the Academy: Rejected Knowledge in Western Culture*. Cambridge: Cambridge University Press, 2012.
Harding, Mark and Alana Nobbs, eds. *The Content and the Setting of the Gospel Tradition*. Grand Rapids, MI: Eerdmans, 2010.
Hayles, David J. "The Roman Census and Jesus' Birth," *Buried History* 9/4 (December 1973) 113–32; 10 (March 1974), 16–31.
Herford, Travers. *Christianity in the Talmud*. London: Forgotten Books, 2015.
Higgins, A. J. B. *The Lord's Supper in the New Testament*. London: SCM, 1956.

Hoehner, Harold W. "Chronological Aspects of the Life of Christ Part II: The Commencement of Christ's Ministry." BibSac, 131:521 (Jan 1974) 53–54.
———. *Chronological Aspects of the Life of Christ*. Grand Rapids: Zondervan, 1977.
———. "Chronology," *Dictionary of Jesus and the Gospels*, Joel B. Green, General Editor. Downers Grove, IL: Intervarsity, 1992.
———. *Herod Antipas*. Grand Rapids, MI: Zondervan, 1999, 28.
Humphreys, Colin J. *The Mystery of the Last Supper*. Cambridge: Cambridge University Press, 2011.
Jaubert, Annie. *La date de la cène* (EBib, Paris: Gabalda, 1957; the English translation is by Isaac Rafferty, *The Date of the Last Supper*. Staten Island, NY: Alba House, 1965.
Jensen, Morten Hørning. "Antipas—The Herod Jesus Knew." *BAR*, September/October 2012.
———, *Herod Antipas in Galilee: The Literary and Archaeological Sources*. Tübingen, Germany: Mohr Siebeck, 2010.
Jensen, Robin M. "Witnessing the Divine: The Magi in Art and Literature." *BAR*, November 17, 2016.
Jeremias, Joachim. *The Eucharistic Words of Jesus*. Translated by Norman Perrin. New York: Scribner's, 1966.
Johnson, Lawrence J. *Worship in the Early Church: An Anthology of Historical Sources*, vol 1. Collegeville, MN: Liturgical. 2009.
Johnson, Luke T. *The Gospel of Luke*. Collegeville, MN: Liturgical, 1991.
Katz, Michael and Gershon Schwartz. *Searching for Meaning in Midrash: Lessons for Everyday Living*. Philadelphia, PA: The Jewish Publication Society, 2002.
Keresztes, Paul. *Imperial Rome and the Christians: From Herod the Great to About 200 AD*. Lanham, MD: University Press of America, 1989.
Klausner, Joseph. *Jesus of Nazareth*, translated by Herbert Danby. London: Macmillan, 1925.
Kostenberger, Andreas J. et al., *The Cradle, the Cross, and the Crown: An Introduction to the New Testament*. Nashville, TN: B&H Academic, 2009.
Lagrange, Marie-Joseph. *The Gospel of Jesus Christ*, 2 vols. Translated by Members of the English Dominican Province. Westminster, MD: Newman, 1951.
Lançon, Bertrand. Translated by Antonia Nevill. *Rome in Late Antiquity*. New York: Routledge, 2000.
Leclercq, Henri. "Mages," in the *Dictionnaire d'archéologie chrétienne et de liturgie* 10.1, 1920.
Lee, Francis Nigel. *The Covenantal Sabbath*. Leominster, UK: Lord's Day Observance Society, 1972.
Lenski, R. C. H. *The Interpretation of St. John's Gospel*. Minneapolis, MN: Augsburg, 1943.
Levick, Barbara. *Augustus: Image and Substance*. Abingdon-on-Thames, England: Routledge, 2010.
Lewis, Naphtali and Meyer Reinhold. *Roman Civilization*. New York: Columbia University Press, 1955.
Lichtenstein, Yechiel Tzvi. *Commentary on the New Testament*. Leipzig, Gustav Fock, 1885.
Lietzmann, Hans. *Mass and Lord's Supper*. Leiden, Netherlands: Brill, 1979.
Livy. *T Livii Patavini Historiarum Libri Qui Supersunt Cum Deperditorum Fragmentis et Epitomis Omnium: Ad Optimarum Editionum Fidem Scholarum in Usum*, v. 3 (Latin Edition) 2009.

Lynn, W. T. "The Eclipse of Josephus" (letter) *The Observatory,* June (1900), 253.
MacArthur, John. *The Murder of Jesus.* Nashville: Word, 2000.
MacGregor, Neil. *Seeing Salvation: Images of Christ in Art.* New Haven, CT: Yale University Press, 2000.
Macrobius, I.12.3; *Macrobius,* Robert A Kaster, ed. *Saturnalia,* vol. I, Loeb Classical Library, No. 510. Cambridge, MA: Harvard University Press, 2011.
Mahieu, Bieke. *Between Rome and Jerusalem: Herod the Great and His Sons in Their Struggle for Recognition. A Chronological Investigation of the Period 40 BC-39 AD.* Leuven, Belgium, Peeters, 2012.
Maier, Paul L. "The Date of the Nativity and Chronology of Jesus" in Jerry Vardaman and Edwin M. Yamauchi, editors, *Chronos, Kairos, Christos: Nativity and Chronological Studies.* Winona Lake, IN: Eisenbrauns, 1989.
Marcus, Joel. "Passover and Last Supper Revisited," *NTS* 59.3 (2013), 303–24.
Marshall, I. Howard. *The Gospel of* Luke. Grand Rapids, MI: Eerdmans, 1978.
———. *Last Supper and Lord's Supper.* Exeter: England, Paternoster, 1980.
Mazza, Enrico. *The Celebration of the Eucharist: The Origin of the Rite and the Development of Its Interpretation.* Collegeville, MN: Liturgical, 1999.
Meier, John P. *A Marginal Jew: Rethinking the Historical Jesus,* vol.1: *The Roots of the Problem and the Person.* New York: Doubleday, 1991.
Metzger, Bruce. "Names for the Nameless in the New Testament: A Study in the Growth of Christian Tradition," in *Kyriakon: Festschrift Johannes Quasten,* 2 vols. Edited by Patrick Granfield & Josef A. Jungmann. Münster, Germany: Verlag Aschendorff, vol. 1:79–99, 1970, 23–29.
———. *New Testament Studies: Philological, Versional, and Patristic,* vol. 10, Leiden, Netherlands: Brill, 1980.
Meyer, Paul William and John T. Carroll. *The Word in This World: Essays in New Testament Exegesis and Theology.* Louisville, KY: WJK, 2004.
Mommsen, Theodor. *The History of Rome.* Cambridge University Press, 2010.
Morgenstern, Julian. "The Calendar of the Book of Jubilees, its Origin and its Character," *VT,* V (January 1955).
Morris, Leon. *The Gospel According to John.* Grand Rapids, MI: Eerdmans, 1971.
Murphy O'Connor, Jerome. *Jesus and Paul: Parallel Lives.* Minnesota: Liturgical Press, 2007.
Newcomb, Simon. "Tables of the Motion of the Earth on its Axis and Around the Sun" in Astronomical Papers Prepared for the Use of the American Ephemeris and Nautical Almanac, Volume VI: Tables of the Four Inner Planets. United States Naval Observatory, 1898.
Niswonger, Richard L. *New Testament History* Grand Rapids, MI: Zondervan, 1992.
Novak, Ralph Martin. *Christianity and the Roman Empire: Background Texts.* Harrisburg, PA: Trinity, 2001.
Ogg, George. "The Chronology of the Last Supper" in *Historicity and Chronology in the New Testament,* edited by D. E. Nineham. London: SPCK, 1965.
———. "The Quirinius Question Today," *ExpTim* 79/7 (April 1968) 231–32.
Orosius, Paul. *Orosius: Seven Books of History Against the Pagans* 6: 22:1; 7:3:4. Liverpool, England: Liverpool University Press, 2010.
Parker, Richard A. and Waldo H. Dubberstein. *Babylonian Chronology 626 BC-AD 75,* 2nd edition. Providence, RI: Brown University Press, 1956.
Parpola, Simo. "The Magi and the Star: Babylonian Astronomy Dates Jesus' Birth" in the *BR* 17:6, December 2001.

Pearson, Brooke W. R. "The Lucan Censuses, Revisited," in *CBQ*, 61, 1999, 269–70.
Philo. *Special Laws 2*, sec. 148, 149. Translated by F. H. Colson. Loeb Classical Library, vol. 7, Cambridge: Harvard University Press, 1935.
Pliny. *A Self-Portrait in Letters*. London: The Folio Society, 1978.
Plummer, Alfred. *The Gospel According To St John, With Maps, Notes And Introduction*. Charleston, SC: Nabu, 2011.
Polhill, John B. *Paul and His Letters*. Nashville, TN: B&H Academic, 1999.
Porter, Stanley. "The Reasons for the Lukan Census." In *Paul, Luke and the Graeco-Roman World: Essays in Honour of Alexander J. M. Wedderburn*, A. J. M. Wedderburn and Alf Christophersen, eds. London: Sheffield Academic, 2002.
Rahner, Karl. *Encyclopedia of theology: a concise Sacramentum mundi*. London: Burns & Oates 2004.
Ramm, Bernard L. *An Evangelical Christology: Ecumenic and Historic*. Vancouver, BC: Regent, 1993.
Ramsay, Sir William. *St. Paul the Traveler and Roman Citizen*, edited by Mark Wilson Grand Rapids, MI: Kregel, 2001.
———. *Was Christ Born at Bethlehem? A Study in the Credibility of Luke*. Eugene, OR: Wipf and Stock, 1999.
Rawlinson, George W. *Egypt and Babylon from Sacred and Profane Sources*. London, Forgotten Books, 2012.
Riesner, Rainer and Douglas W. Stott. *Paul's Early Period: Chronology, Mission Strategy, Theology*. Grand Rapids, MI: Eerdmans, 1998.
Rist, John M. "Luke 2:2: Making Sense of the Date of Jesus' Birth," *JTS*, vol. 56, Issue 2, October 2005, 489–91.
Roberts, Richard Owen. *Sanctify the Congregation: A call to the Solemn Assembly and to Corporate Repentance*. Wheaton, IL: International Awakening, 1994.
Robinson, Edward. "The Alleged Discrepancy Between John and the Other Evangelists respecting Our Lord's Last Passover," *BibSac*, II (August 1845).
Rokeah, David. "Ben Sṭara is Ben Pantira. To the clarification of a philological problem and historic." *Tarbiz*, 39, 1969.
Rudgley, Richard. *The Lost Civilizations of the Stone Age*. New York: Simon & Schuster, 1999.
Scarola, Jack V. "A Chronology of the Nativity Era" in *Chronos, Kairos, Christos 2*. Edited by Ray Summers and Jerry Vardaman. Macon, GA: Mercer University Press, 1998.
Schäfer, Peter. *The History of the Jews in the Greco-Roman World*. London: Routledge, 2003.
———. *Jesus in the Talmud*. Princeton, NJ: Princeton University Press, 2009.
Schnabel, Eckhard J. *Jesus in Jerusalem. The Last Days*. Grand Rapids, MI: Eerdmans, 2018.
Schürer, Emil. *A History of the Jewish People in the Time of Jesus Christ*, 5 vols. Edited by Geza Vermes, et al., Edinburgh, Scotland: T & T Clark, 2014.
Scroggie, W. Graham. *A Guide to the Gospels*. London: Pickering and Inglis, 1948.
Sherwin-White, A. N. *Roman Foreign Policy in the East, 168 B.C. to A.D. 1*. Norman, OK: University of Oklahoma Press, 1984.
———. *Roman Society and Roman Law in the New Testament*. Oxford: Clarendon Press, 1953.
Singer, Suzanne. "Strata: Herod the Great—The King's Final Journey." *BAR*, February 13, 2013.

Stauffer, J. Ethelbert. *Jesus and His Story*. Translated by Dorothea M. Burton. New York: Knopf, 1960.
Steinmann, Andrew. *From Abraham to Paul: A Biblical Chronology*. St. Louis, MO: Concordia, 2011.
———. "When Did Herod the Great Reign?" *NT*, vol. 51, no 1, 2009,1-29.
Stern, Sacha. *Calendars in Antiquity: Empires, States and Societies*. Oxford: Oxford University Press. 2012.
Strack, Hermann L. and Paul Billerbeck. *Kommentar zum Neuen Testament*. Munchen: Verlag C. H. Beck, 1996.
Tabor, James D. "We Have Seen His Star in the East: What Was the Christmas Star?" *BAR*, December 30, 2021.
Tabory, Joseph. *JPS Commentary*. Philadelphia, PA: Jewish Publication Society, 2008.
Taylor, Vincent. *The Cross of Christ* London: Macmillan, 1956.
Templeman, Dennis M. "The Death of Herod the Great in Early 1 BCE" *Academia.edu*. (99+) Discussion: "The Death of Herod the Great in early 1 BCE." Updated 14 09 2020 Google Docs—Academia.edu.
Tertullian. *Adversus Marcionem (Against Marcion)*, Books 1-5. Translated by Ernest Evans. Oxford: Oxford University Press, 1972.
———. *The Writings of Tertullian, Ante-Nicene Christian Library*, vol. 3. Peabody, MA: Hendrickson Publishing, 1995.
Theissen, Gerd and Annette Merz. *Historical Jesus: A Comprehensive Guide*. Minneapolis, MN: Fortress, 1998.
Thomas, Robert L. and Stanley N. Gundry. "The Day and Year of Christ's Birth and Crucifixion" in *A Harmony of the Gospels*. San Francisco, CA: HarperOne, 1986.
Torrey, Charles C. "In the Fourth Gospel the Last Supper Was the Paschal Meal?" *JQR* 42, No. 3, (January 1952).
Torrey, R. A. *Difficulties in the Bible*. New York: Fleming H. Revell, 1907.
Turner, Nigel. *Grammatical Insights into the New Testament*. Edinburgh: T. & T. Clark. 1966.
VanderKam, James C. *Calendars in the Dead Sea Scrolls: Measuring Time*. London: Routledge, 1998.
Vardaman, Jerry and Edwin M. Yamauchi, eds. *Chronos, Kairos, Christos: Nativity and Chronological Studies Presented to Jack Finegan*. Warsaw, IN: Eisenbrauns, 1989.
Vardaman, Jerry. "Jesus' Life: A New Chronology," Jerry Vardaman and Edwin M. Yamauchi, eds. *Chronos, Kairos, Christos: Nativity and Chronological Studies Presented to Jack Finegan*. Warsaw, IN: Eisenbrauns, 1989.
Vass, Arpad A. *Microbiology Today*, vol. 28. Nov. 2001, 190.
Vermes, Geza. *The Nativity: History and Legend*. London: Penguin, 2006.
Voorst Van, Robert. *Jesus Outside the New Testament: Introduction to the Ancient Evidence*. Grand Rapids, MI: Eerdmans, 2000.
Wallace, Daniel B. *Greek Grammar Beyond the Basics: An Exegetical Syntax of the New Testament*. Grand Rapids, MI: Zondervan, 1996.
Wansbrough, Henry. *Jesus and the Oral Gospel Tradition*. Sheffield, England: Sheffield Academic, 1991, 185.
Westcott, Brooke Foss. *The Gospel According to St. John: the Authorized Version with Introduction and Notes*. Grand Rapids, MI: Eerdmans, 2000.
White, Cynthia. *The Emergence of Christianity: Classical Traditions in Contemporary Perspective*. Minneapolis, MN: Fortress, 2010.

Witherington, Ben III. "Biblical Views: The Turn of the Christian Era: The Tale of Dionysius Exiguus," *BAR* 43.6 (2017).

———. *New Testament History: A Narrative Account*. Grand Rapids, MI: Baker Academic, 2001.

———. *What Have They Done with Jesus? Beyond Strange Theories and Bad History—Why We Can Trust the Bible*. New York: HarperSanFrancisco, 2006.

Woodrow, Ralph. *Three Days and Three Nights—Reconsidered in Light of Scripture*. Palm Springs, CA: Ralph Woodrow Evangelistic Association, 1993.

Woolfenden, Gregory W. *Daily liturgical prayer: origins and theology*. Farnham, England: Ashgate, 2004.

Wright, N. T. *Jesus and the Victory of God*. Minneapolis, MN: Fortress, 1996, 438.

Yamauchi, Edwin M. "The Episode of the Magi" in Jerry Vardaman and Edwin M. Yamauchi, editors, *Chronos, Kairos, Christos: Nativity and Chronological Studies*. Winona Lake, IN: Eisenbrauns, 1989.

———. "Ezra-Nehemiah," *The Expositor's Bible Commentary*, vol. 4. Edited by Frank E. Gaebelein. Grand Rapids, MI: Zondervan, 1988.

Zeitlin, Solomon. "The Last Supper as an Ordinary Meal in the Fourth Gospel," *JQR* 42, No. 3, (January 1952)

Zenos, A. C. "Life of Socrates," in *A Selected Library of the Nicene and Post-Nicene Fathers*, series 2, vol. 2, Henry Wace and Philip Schaff, editors. New York: Christian Publishers, 1887–1900.

Zetzel, James E. C. *New Light on Gaius Caesar's Eastern Campaign*. Harvard University presentation, 1970.

Zodhiates, Spiros. *The Complete Word Study Dictionary*: New Testament. Chattanooga, TN: AMG Publishers, 1992.

Zohary, Daniel and Maria Hopf. *Domestication of Plants in the Old World: The Origin and Spread of Cultivated Plants in West Asia, Europe, and the Nile Valley*, 3rd edition. Oxford: Oxford University Press, 2000.

Subject Index

14th of Nisan, 39, 42, 131, 162, 163, 255, 256, 272
Abilene, 219, 238, 241, 243
Abomination of Desolation, the, 110
"About thirty years old," 253, 262, 267
Abraham, 4, 82, 161, 236, 254
Achaia, 22, 167, 248, 287
Actium, 202, 244
Adam (person), 172, 216
Adam (town), 168, 169
Advent, xiv, 127
Advent Calendar, 127
"After the Sabbath," 45, 53, 54, 55, 96, 97, 100, 101, 103, 108, 109, 112, 114, 119, 120, 136, 143, 144, 149, 166, 168, 170, 171, 177
"After three days," 18, 24, 25, 26, 27, 28, 47, 91, 117, 137, 138, 139, 147
Against Heresies, 218
Ahasuerus (see Xerxes)
Aloes, 125, 137, 177
Amalek/Amalekites, 12, 16
America/American(s), 32, 44, 46, 64, 86, 95, 98, 174, 197, 209, 212, 222, 231, 289, 296, 305
American Sentinel, 105, 290
"*Amicus Caesaris*" (see no friend of Caesar), 269, 270, 276
An Essay on Criticism, 187, 193
Ananias, 242
Ancient Near East, 10, 91
Angel, 19, 38, 77, 79, 114, 118
Anglo-Saxon, 211
Annals, 198, 204, 238, 246, 256

Aanno Domini, 229, 230
Anno Urbis Conditae, 225, 231
Ante-Nicene Fathers, 153
Antiquities of the Jews, 156, 169, 245
Anti-Semitic, 15, 264, 276
Anti-type (see Type)
Annas, 163, 188, 189, 190, 193, 219, 238, 240, 241, 242, 243, 244
Apocalypse, the, 102
Apocrypha(l), 178, 212, 216, 261, 294
Apostles' Creed, The, 195
April 3, 33 AD, 260, 261, 266, 267, 271, 274, 275, 298
April 7, 30 AD, 260, 261, 265, 266, 267, 271, 274, 275, 298
Aqueduct, 21, 239, 276
Aramaic, 47, 62, 160, 254
Archaeology/archaeological, xviii, xxv, 29, 206, 225, 292
Aretas IV, King, 260
Aristobulus, 38, 40, 42
Armenia, 198, 210, 213
Armenian Infancy Gospel, 210, 213, 294
Asia/Asian, 10, 166, 167, 207, 211, 220, 292, 296
Assyria(n), 14, 156
Astrology, 210, 294
Astronomy, 105, 210, 213, 255, 261, 275, 279, 299

Babylon/Babylonian, 16, 35, 210, 213, 254, 291
Balthazar, 213
Baraith, 120

Ben Stada, 157, 158, 290
Bethany, 65, 129, 130, 131, 132, 133, 134, 135
Bethlehem, 196, 197, 199, 200, 201, 203, 206, 210, 213, 214, 215, 216, 217, 218, 220, 222, 224, 228, 294
Bible, xiii, xiv, 2, 10, 11, 14, 15, 23, 24, 25, 26, 29, 38, 42, 56, 86, 90, 92, 95, 98, 106, 110, 113, 119, 123, 125, 145, 153, 165, 166, 173, 181, 183, 187, 214, 235, 238, 242, 255, 262, 263, 268, 271, 279, 280, 282, 285, 289, 294
Biblical Archaeology Review (BAR), 29, 163
Birth, 2, 8, 9, 10, 31, 197, 198, 200, 202, 207, 209, 210, 212, 213, 216, 217, 218, 219, 220, 221, 222, 223, 224, 225, 226, 227, 228, 229, 230, 231, 233, 238, 240, 253, 254, 255, 262, 267, 268, 272, 275, 279, 284, 291, 294
Bishop of Durham, 51, 123, 174
Blood, 38, 41, 47, 64, 68, 74, 78, 79, 80, 81, 82, 109, 164, 165, 285
Boise, ID, xxv
Books, extra-biblical,
  Enoch, 40
  Epistle to the Trallians, 153
  Esdras, I, 38, 39
  Jubilees, 40
Boston, MA, xxv

Caesar Augustus, 200, 201
Caesarea Maritima, 8, 19, 239
Caiaphas, 66, 107, 163, 188, 189, 190, 191, 193, 219, 238, 241, 242, 243, 244, 270, 276
Calendars, xiv, xv, 2, 3, 4, 5, 6, 7, 8, 9, 11, 31, 32, 33, 40, 42, 43, 59, 72, 85, 88, 96, 98, 105, 106, 111, 120, 127, 128, 141, 148, 149, 151, 154, 161, 165, 170, 173, 189, 190, 221, 226, 229, 230, 231, 232, 233, 234, 238, 244, 245, 250, 251, 253, 255, 256, 257, 260, 261, 262, 263, 279, 280, 284, 295, 296
  Advent, 127
  Gregorian, 4,5,6,7,32, 85, 190, 229, 230, 231, 232, 233, 234, 296
  Julian, 4, 85, 105, 106, 190, 229, 230, 231, 232, 233, 234, 244, 255, 256, 257, 296
  Lunar, 5, 7, 11, 41, 42, 49, 190, 224, 225, 227, 230, 232, 233, 234, 249, 251, 255, 261, 266, 274, 298
  Luni-solar, 230, 234, 256, 296
  Solar, 5, 7, 72, 190, 230, 231, 232, 233, 234, 249, 255
  Syro-Macedonian, 245
Calvary, xviii, 81, 87, 190, 280, 285
Calvary's Cross, 57, 82, 175, 277, 285, 286
Capernaum, 51, 52, 90, 172, 255,
Capri/Capreae, 269, 275
Caspar, 213
Catacombs, 91, 92, 93, 211,
  Peter and Marcellinus, 212
  Priscilla, 211
  Saint Callixtus, 92, 93
  Saint Domitilla, 92, 212
  Saint Sebastiano, 92
  Via Latina, 93
Catechism, 3, 65, 70
Catholic(s), 10, 50, 85, 174, 209, 214, 258, 275, 294
Chester Beatty manuscripts, 237
Chief priests, 2, 18, 26, 27, 28, 35, 47, 48, 49, 84, 89, 117, 120, 137, 138, 139, 143, 144, 147, 159, 191, 194, 282, 290
Christ, xiii, xv, 2, 20, 45, 48, 57, 69, 71, 76, 82, 86, 87, 88, 92, 93, 94, 95, 106, 108, 118, 121, 137, 142, 144, 145, 149, 154, 160, 162, 167, 172, 174, 179, 181, 184, 185, 190, 196, 198, 200, 209, 213, 217, 220, 226, 227, 246, 248, 255, 264, 267, 270, 271, 277, 281, 285, 286, 289
Christ-follower(s), xiii, 27, 42, 63, 70, 71, 72, 75, 85, 107, 111, 118, 127, 249, 153

Subject Index   311

Christ Jesus, 20, 57, 92, 93, 172, 277, 285
Christian Church, 33, 42, 70, 86, 153
Christian Orthodox Church, (see
    Eastern Orthodox Church)
Christianity, xiv, 35, 212, 232, 263, 292,
    294
Christians, xiii, xvii, 10, 20, 26, 27, 33,
    42, 45, 47, 56, 57, 62, 64, 65,
    174, 175, 181, 184, 200, 211,
    212, 214, 222, 230, 231, 232,
    246, 249, 251, 289, 290
Christmas, 36, 43, 58, 82, 128, 196, 197,
    212
Church Fathers, 155, 160, 175, 185, 202,
    212, 222, 227, 270
Church of the Holy Sepulchre, 181
Circumcision, 9, 10, 71, 110
Cleopas, 26, 118, 119, 127, 171, 188
Cleopatra, 217, 226
Coptic Church, 230
Constantinople, 107, 210
Corinth(ian), 20, 22, 56, 70, 166, 248
Cornelius, 19, 20, 287
Council, the (see Sanhedrin)
Council of Nice[a], 106
Creation, xv, 3, 4, 35, 73, 75, 160 161,
    164, 295
Cross, xi, xii, xiii, 17, 36, 42, 43, 46, 49,
    74, 76, 77, 83, 84, 88, 100,
    111, 118, 120, 138, 144, 145,
    146, 148, 157, 162, 163, 168,
    169, 182, 183, 185, 188, 189,
    190, 194, 246, 273, 278, 282,
    285, 286, 291
Crucifixion, xi, xiii, xvii, xxv, 2, 17, 22,
    24, 26, 27, 32, 33, 36, 41, 44,
    45, 46, 48, 49, 52, 54, 55, 56,
    58, 70, 79, 86, 87, 88, 90, 92,
    93, 94, 95, 96, 97, 103, 104,
    106, 107, 108, 109, 111, 112,
    113, 114, 115, 117, 118, 120,
    121, 123, 125, 126, 135, 136,
    137, 140, 141, 142, 143, 144,
    147, 148, 150, 152, 153, 154,
    155, 156, 157, 158, 159, 160,
    161, 162, 165, 166, 169, 170,
    174, 177, 178, 179, 180, 182,
    183, 184, 187, 188, 189, 190,
    192, 193, 196, 212, 217, 222,
    223, 225, 229,232, 233, 234,
    235, 237, 238, 239, 242, 244,
    245, 246, 247, 248, 249, 240,
    242, 243, 255, 256, 258, 259,
    260, 261, 262, 264, 265, 266,
    268, 269, 270, 272, 272, 273,
    275, 276, 278, 280, 281, 283,
    284, 285, 297
Cyrenius (see Quirinius)

Damascus, 246, 247, 294
Daniel, 183, 248, 249
Darius I, 37, 248
David, 12, 15, 22, 87, 92, 187, 299
Dawn, 20, 52, 53, 54, 55, 83, 95, 96, 103,
    108, 112, 113, 114, 118, 119,
    135, 140, 142, 143, 153, 169,
    170, 174, 177, 180, 187, 190,
    191, 209
Day of Atonement, 6, 98, 101, 233
Day of Preparation, 18, 32, 35, 45, 46,
    47, 48, 49, 50, 54, 64, 65, 70,
    82, 87, 94, 102, 107, 110, 116,
    119, 137, 138, 142, 143, 144,
    145, 153, 155, 156, 158, 159,
    160, 166, 175, 176, 178, 183,
    187, 191, 279, 280, 282, 284
Days of the week
    Sunday, xv, xxv, 7, 9, 26, 27, 32,
        38, 44, 52, 53, 54, 55, 56, 87,
        88, 92, 93, 94, 95, 97, 102,
        103, 106, 107, 108, 111, 112,
        113,114, 115, 117, 118, 119,
        123, 124, 125, 128, 130, 135,
        136, 137, 138, 139, 141, 142,
        143, 147, 148, 149, 150, 152,
        153, 154, 155, 160, 165, 166,
        169, 170, 172, 174, 176, 177,
        178, 179, 180, 183, 184, 185,
        188, 194, 215, 268, 272, 284,
        295
    Monday, xv, 7, 8, 9, 15, 32, 35, 87,
        88, 93, 94, 111, 128, 130, 131,
        132, 133, 134, 149,180, 235
    Tuesday, 7, 9, 15, 31, 87, 88, 93, 94,
        104, 105, 106, 111, 115, 128,
        130, 131, 132, 133, 134, 149

Subject Index

Days of the week (*cont.*)
  Wednesday, 8, 15, 26, 53, 86, 87, 88, 90, 92, 93, 94, 95, 96, 97, 99, 101, 102, 103, 104, 105, 106, 107 108, 110, 111, 112, 113, 114, 115, 116, 117, 118,120, 121, 122, 123, 125, 126, 130, 135, 136, 140, 141, 142, 143, 150, 152, 165, 167, 170, 173, 175, 178, 179, 180, 181, 184, 185, 188, 189, 190, 191, 229, 251, 281, 290
  Thursday, xxv, 2, 26, 32, 33, 53, 59, 65, 86, 88, 89, 91, 94, 95, 97, 100, 103, 104, 108, 111, 115, 116, 117, 119, 123, 124, 125, 126, 127, 128, 130, 131, 136, 137, 138, 141, 142, 143, 144, 146, 147, 148, 149, 151, 152, 163, 165, 167, 170 173, 175, 178, 179, 180, 181, 184, 185, 188, 189, 190, 193, 229, 255, 256, 261, 267, 281
  Friday, 2, 7, 27, 33, 34, 35, 36, 37, 46, 47, 54, 59, 65, 66, 72, 86, 87, 88, 89, 94, 95, 96, 98, 103, 104, 105, 107, 110, 112, 115, 116, 117, 118, 120, 121, 123, 124, 125, 126, 127, 130, 131, 136, 137, 138, 141, 142, 143, 144, 145, 148, 151, 152, 153, 154, 158, 159, 160, 161, 163, 164, 165, 166, 167, 170, 173, 174, 175, 176, 177, 178, 179, 180, 181, 184, 185, 188, 189,190, 193, 194, 226, 229, 251, 255, 256, 259, 260, 261, 266, 267, 271, 273, 275, 281, 282, 285
  Saturday, 7, 33, 34, 37, 55, 56, 57, 87, 88, 89, 94, 95, 96, 97, 98, 103, 104, 107, 108, 110, 112, 113, 115, 116, 117, 118, 119, 120, 124, 125, 126, 129, 130, 132, 133, 134, 135,136, 137, 138, 140, 141, 142, 143, 144, 148, 150, 151, 154, 156, 161, 166, 167, 169, 170, 175, 177, 178, 179, 180, 181, 184, 188, 251, 273, 281

Dead Sea, 46, 230, 271
Death, xi, xiii, xvii, xxv, 4, 6, 10, 13, 14, 18, 22, 23, 26, 27, 28, 29, 35, 38, 42, 43, 45, 48, 58, 59, 65, 66, 72, 78, 79,80, 82, 91, 92, 95, 101, 109, 119, 122, 124, 125,127, 130, 138, 153, 156, 157, 162, 164, 167, 172, 179, 183, 184, 185, 186, 188, 191, 194, 196, 197, 199, 201, 207, 209, 216, 217, 218, 220, 221, 223, 224, 225, 226, 227, 228, 237, 238, 240, 242, 244, 246, 247, 248, 249, 255, 256, 258, 259, 260, 261, 262, 263, 264, 266, 268, 269, 272, 273, 274, 275, 276, 278, 279, 280, 281, 282, 284, 285, 286, 292, 293, 294, 295, 296, 299
Didache, 46, 70, 106, 160, 288
Didascalia Apostolorum, 106, 107
Dio, Cassius, 199, 204, 217, 226, 238, 269
Dionysius Exiguus, 219, 222, 226, 229

Early morning, 50, 56, 66, 148, 191
Earthquake, 26, 194, 271
Easter, 43, 53, 85, 86, 107, 161, 185, 232
Eastern Christianity, 35, 63, 212
Eastern Orthodox Church, 85, 230
"Ecce Homo," 52
Eclipse, 230, 280, 290, 291
Egypt/Egyptians, 10, 11, 12, 13, 23, 35, 38, 39, 41, 42, 44, 49, 60, 63, 68,74, 75, 82, 83, 111, 130, 164, 165, 176
Elders, 2, 27, 90, 137, 156, 174, 191
Elizabeth, 200, 243
"Eloi, Eloi, lema sabachthani," 192, 282
Emmaus/Emmaus Road, 26, 118, 171, 188
Encyclopaedia Britannica, The, 106, 213
"End of the Sabbath(s)," 53, 54, 87, 94, 131, 136
Ephraim, 180, 291
Epistles, 185, 247
Erev Shabbat, 46, 192
Ethnarch, 239
Eucharist(ic), 61, 70, 73, 80
Europe/European, 10, 221, 231

Subject Index   313

Evening, xxv, 8, 22, 33, 34, 37, 38, 39,
    40, 44, 47, 48, 49, 51, 52, 53,
    56, 59, 63, 65, 66, 70, 88, 89,
    90, 102, 103, 106, 107, 114,
    117, 119, 120, 130, 131, 141,
    142, 143, 151, 160, 161, 163,
    165, 167, 169, 177, 179, 192,
    193, 194, 232, 266, 275, 282
Exodus, the, 4, 61, 74
Eyewitness(es), 218, 260
Ezra, 16, 249, 250

Feasts/festivals, 3, 5, 10, 14, 32, 36, 37,
    38, 39, 40, 41, 44, 45, 46, 47,
    56, 57, 60, 66, 69, 70, 71, 97,
    98, 99, 100, 102, 103, 107,
    127, 145, 146, 148, 160, 163,
    164, 166, 169, 173, 265, 280
  Atonement, Day of, 6, 36, 99, 102
  Firstfruits, 32, 43, 45, 49, 57, 97, 99,
    100, 101, 112, 113, 148, 149,
    160, 166, 167, 168, 169, 170,
    172, 173
  Passover (see Passover)
  Pentecost, 32, 33, 38, 41, 42, 57, 97,
    99, 102, 120, 160, 161, 166,
    234, 265, 285, 289
  Pilgrimage, 38, 60, 265
  Tabernacles/Booths, 38, 98, 99, 100,
    102, 265
  Trumpets, 36, 99, 101, 102, 226, 232
  Unleavened Bread, 36, 37, 38, 41,
    42, 43, 44, 49, 57, 59, 60, 61,
    63, 66, 67, 71, 73, 88, 90, 96,
    97, 98, 99, 100, 101, 112, 120,
    121, 136, 137, 141, 144, 146,
    160, 161, 163, 164, 165, 166,
    167, 169, 265, 280
  Weeks (see Pentecost)
Fig tree, 53, 88, 135, 188
Fortress of Antonia, 22
"Forty-six years," 137, 235, 251, 252,
    259, 260, 297
French, 9, 39, 55, 107
Friday crucifixion, 27, 54, 72, 87, 98,
    105, 115, 124, 141, 142, 151,
    152, 153, 158, 161, 163, 170,
    173, 174, 175, 176, 178, 179,
    180, 181, 184, 185

Gabbatha, 47, 65
Galilee, 27, 90, 91, 103, 108, 139, 147,
    159, 176, 219, 225, 236, 238,
    239, 240, 241, 243, 267, 270,
    278, 280
Gaul, 203, 204, 293
Gaulonitis, 240, 241
Gemonian Stairs, 268
Gentile, 19, 22, 28, 73, 82, 102, 165, 166,
    194, 234, 245
Gethsemane, xxv, 63, 69, 130, 163, 189,
    193
Gilgal, 167, 169
God, xiii, xiv, xv, 2, 4, 6, 8, 11, 12, 15,
    16, 19, 20, 22, 23, 26, 31, 32,
    34, 35, 36, 37, 38, 39, 40, 41,
    42, 43, 44, 45, 47, 48, 49, 57,
    60, 63, 64, 65, 68, 69, 70, 74,
    75, 76, 77, 78, 79, 80, 81, 82,
    84, 87, 90, 93, 96, 98, 100, 102,
    105, 111, 112, 117, 118, 119,
    120, 127, 138, 139, 141, 145,
    146, 148, 149, 154, 155, 156,
    161, 162, 164, 165, 168, 169
    172, 174, 180, 183, 192, 193,
    194, 195, 209, 210, 215, 216,
    217, 219, 223, 228, 238, 250,
    255, 263, 268, 278, 279, 280,
    281, 282, 283, 284, 285, 286,
    289, 291, 294
Golgotha, 43, 47, 52, 181, 182, 183, 188,
    189, 191, 193, 194, 245, 253,
    255, 285
Good Friday, 86, 131, 132, 152, 177,
    184, 185, 281, 282
Gospels, xiii, 1, 25, 27, 30, 33, 43, 46, 58,
    59, 66, 67, 80, 83, 84, 87, 93,
    105, 118, 126, 136, 137, 138,
    139, 144, 145, 151, 152, 153,
    155, 156, 158, 159, 178, 181,
    183, 185, 189, 190, 191, 193,
    197, 218, 235, 237, 239, 242,
    245, 252, 256, 260, 261, 265,
    268, 272, 273, 292
Gratus, Valerius, 242, 263

Subject Index

Greek, xiv, 2, 17, 19, 20, 24, 31, 36, 40, 46, 53, 54, 55, 56, 65, 66, 67, 68, 69, 97, 110, 113, 119, 123, 136, 137, 138, 145, 147,156, 159, 160, 167, 171, 172, 173, 180, 182, 184, 191, 192, 203, 206, 207, 208, 209, 210, 214, 215, 218, 237, 245, 247, 251, 252, 253, 261, 265, 266, 291
Greeks 10, 31, 88

Haburah meal, 71
Hadassah (see Queen Esther)
Haggadah, 58, 65
Halakha(ic), 39, 121
Halley's Comet, 220
Haman, 6, 15
Hanukkah, 6, 72
Heaven, 1, 8, 32, 72, 80, 130, 172, 195, 242, 247, 248
Heavenly Father, 148, 236
Hebrew, xiv, 2, 4, 6, 7, 12, 32, 34, 36, 41, 61, 67, 97, 98, 99, 100, 101, 102, 121, 130, 136, 146, 148, 158, 161, 165, 173, 181, 214, 230, 254, 255, 261, 280, 291, 294, 296
Hebrew people, 10, 11, 13, 38, 40, 44, 60, 164, 64, 179, 201, 208, 215, 225, 251, 274, 291
Hell, 194, 286
Hellenistic, 40, 47, 160, 203, 208
Helper, the, 139
Herod, 209, 214, 215, 216, 217, 218, 220, 221, 222, 223, 224, 225, 226, 227, 228, 235, 243, 251, 259, 272, 293, 294, 295, 296, 297
   the Great, 2, 181, 197, 198, 200, 202, 207
      Antipas, 2, 17, 52, 189, 193, 219, 225, 238, 239, 240, 241, 243, 260, 272
      Archelaus, 202, 217, 225, 239, 240
      Lysanias, 219, 238, 241, 243
      Philip II, 240, 243
Herod's Evil, 221
High Day, 36, 37, 46, 47, 48, 49, 96, 99, 103, 111, 120, 121, 137, 140, 141, 144, 146, 160, 161, 177, 180, 281
High Priest, 43, 88, 102, 107, 157, 163, 219, 238, 240, 241, 242, 243, 244
High Sabbath, 36, 37, 57, 58, 59, 89, 97, 98, 103, 104, 111, 136, 160
Historian(s), xi, xxv, 23, 31, 33, 43, 46, 55, 71, 107, 154, 155, 156, 163, 164, 196, 197, 198, 199, 200, 206, 212, 217, 218, 219, 220, 226, 226, 228, 229, 233, 238, 241, 244, 246, 253, 266, 268, 269
Historical writings,
   Acts of Peter and Paul, 266
   Didache, 46, 70, 106, 160, 288
   Gospel of Nicodemus, 266
   Gospel of Peter, 178
   Martyrdom of Polycarp, 46, 160
   Teaching of the Twelve Apostles (see Didache)
Holy City, 184, 239
Holy Spirit, xiii, 17, 33, 42, 76, 209, 223, 277
House, 19, 20, 22, 34, 38, 40, 41, 53, 60, 64, 66, 68, 79, 98, 107, 112, 120, 127, 128, 130, 131, 145, 146, 151, 163, 164, 165, 167, 177, 179, 187, 191, 192, 214, 215, 216, 218, 224, 280, 283

India, 176, 210, 213
Internet, 3, 108, 181, 184, 185, 228
Invasion of time, xiv
Israel/Israelites, 6, 7, 8, 11, 13, 14, 16, 26, 31, 32, 34, 35, 36, 38, 39, 44, 45, 48, 57, 60, 61, 63, 68, 73, 74, 75, 76, 77, 81, 82, 83, 98, 99, 100, 101, 102, 111, 118, 128, 145, 148, 149, 157, 162, 163, 165, 166, 167, 168, 177, 210, 236, 241, 242, 280, 298
Italian Cohort, 19, 287
Ituraea, 219, 238, 239

James (person), 68, 108, 114, 139, 147, 159, 167, 176, 247

Subject Index   315

Jericho, 130, 131, 151, 167, 168, 169, 180, 221, 224, 132, 135, 150
Jerusalem, 2, 5, 14, 17, 26, 32, 34, 38, 39, 42, 43, 45, 46, 56, 57, 60, 61, 62, 63, 64, 68, 69, 80, 82, 84, 88, 89, 105, 111, 118, 127, 128, 129, 130, 132, 132, 141, 151, 163, 164, 171, 174, 177, 180, 181, 183, 188, 191, 192, 194, 197, 200, 208, 210, 211, 214, 215, 224, 232, 236, 239, 242, 248, 249, 250, 251, 255, 259, 265, 266, 267, 270, 271, 278, 280, 285, 290, 291, 295
Jesus, xi, xiii, xv, xvii, xxv, 1, 2, 16, 17, 18, 22, 23, 24, 26, 27, 28, 29, 30, 33, 34, 35, 37, 42, 43, 44, 46, 47, 50, 51, 52, 53, 55, 56, 57, 60, 62, 63, 64, 66, 67, 68, 69, 70, 71, 72, 73, 74, 75, 76, 77, 78, 80, 81, 82, 84, 85, 87, 88, 89, 90, 91, 92, 93, 94, 95, 96, 97, 101, 103, 104, 106, 107, 109, 111, 112, 113, 115, 116, 117, 118, 119, 121, 124, 125, 126, 127, 128, 130, 131, 136, 137, 138, 139, 141, 142, 143, 145, 147, 148, 149, 151, 152, 153, 154, 155, 156, 157, 158, 159, 160, 161, 162, 163, 164, 167, 170, 171, 172, 173, 174, 175, 176, 177, 178, 179, 180, 181, 182, 183, 184, 185, 186, 188, 190, 191, 192, 194, 197, 198, 200, 212, 215, 216, 217, 218, 219, 220, 221, 223, 224, 225, 226, 227, 228, 229, 230, 235, 236, 237, 238, 239, 240, 242, 243, 244, 245, 246, 247, 248, 249, 250, 251, 252, 253, 254, 255, 256, 258, 259, 261, 262, 264, 265, 266, 267, 268, 269, 270, 272, 273, 276, 278, 279, 280, 281, 282, 283, 284, 285, 286, 290, 291, 294, 296, 304
Jesus Christ, xiii, 2, 48, 57, 87, 88, 93, 95, 142, 145, 149, 154, 160, 172, 185, 198, 201, 220, 222, 224, 227, 246, 248, 249, 255, 260, 264
Jesus of Nazareth, xi, xiii, xvii, xxv, 1, 26, 42, 113, 151, 152, 158, 173, 231, 234, 238, 239, 246, 258, 255, 257, 261, 266, 270, 290
Jew(s), xi, 1, 2, 3, 4, 5,6, 7, 8, 9, 11, 12, 15, 16, 17, 18, 19, 22, 31, 32, 34, 35, 36, 38, 41, 42, 43, 44, 47, 49, 54, 57, 61, 65, 66, 70, 72, 73, 80, 82, 90, 91, 92, 100, 111, 112, 120, 121, 125, 126, 128, 130, 137, 144, 146, 157, 158, 160, 163, 169, 177, 179, 180, 199, 206, 215, 220, 225, 226, 229, 234, 236, 242, 248, 249, 250, 251, 252, 254, 255, 259, 265, 268, 270, 273, 276, 279, 282, 291, 297
Jewish, xi, 1, 3, 4, 5, 6, 7, 8, 9, 10, 11, 12, 13, 14, 15, 16, 17, 18, 19, 20, 21, 22, 24, 26, 27, 31, 32, 33, 34, 35, 37, 38, 39, 40, 42, 43, 44, 45, 46, 47, 49, 50, 51, 52, 55, 56, 57, 58, 59, 60, 62, 64, 65, 67, 70, 82, 84, 92, 96, 98, 105, 106, 113, 115, 116, 117, 118, 119, 120, 121, 124, 126, 131, 141, 145, 146, 148, 149, 151, 156, 157, 161, 162, 163, 164, 166, 169, 178, 180, 181, 188, 191, 200, 211, 213, 224, 226, 227, 229, 230, 232, 233, 234, 235, 238, 242, 250, 251, 255, 256, 260, 261, 264, 265, 267, 270 272, 273, 274, 275, 276, 280, 282, 283, 285, 298
Jewish Encyclopedia, The, 9, 10, 181
Jewish historian(s), xi, 33, 43, 156, 163, 164, 206, 241
John (person), 37, 42, 46, 50, 51, 52, 53, 59, 60, 64, 65, 66, 68, 71, 84, 95, 96, 98, 114, 115, 118, 120, 130, 138, 139, 145, 147, 154, 160, 167, 177, 189, 191, 194, 219, 225, 236, 237, 238, 252, 260 265, 272, 274, 277, 282, 284, 291

Subject Index

John the Baptist, 50, 200, 219, 220, 225, 234, 235, 239, 240, 243, 244, 245, 246, 256, 257, 259, 260, 261, 262, 263
Jonah (person), 22, 23, 29, 87, 88, 89, 90, 91, 92, 93, 116, 121, 124, 153, 154, 281, 289
Jordan (river), 17, 168, 169, 218, 219
Joseph, father of Jesus, 197, 199, 200, 201, 214, 215, 218, 228
Joseph of Arimathea, 47, 48, 55, 69, 88, 115, 124, 125, 139, 142, 143, 144, 146, 154, 177, 181, 182, 183, 188, 192, 193, 194, 282
Joseph's tomb, xxv, 18, 29, 55, 88, 89, 115, 117, 120, 121, 126, 175, 182, 192
Josephus, xi, 33, 38, 39, 40, 41, 42, 43, 45, 46, 49, 60, 156, 157, 163, 164, 166, 169, 180, 198, 201, 202, 204, 206, 207, 221, 224, 225, 226, 235, 239, 240, 241, 242, 245, 246, 251, 252, 259, 260, 261, 262, 264, 268, 273, 293
Joshua, 42, 167, 168, 170
Judah, 13, 38, 61, 162, 201
Judah kings, 13, 14, 16
    Amaziah, 13, 14
    David, 12, 13, 16, 23, 88, 93, 188, 200
    Hezekiah, 14, 60
    Jehoahaz, 13
    Jehoash, 13
    Joash, (see Joash)
    Josiah, 38, 60, 61
    Rehoboam, 13, 16
    Solomon, 13, 60, 176, 250
Judaism, 1, 3, 4, 5, 6, 7, 16, 31, 33, 46, 69, 70, 145, 158, 160, 192, 243, 295
Judea(n), 138, 198, 200, 202, 204, 206, 216, 217, 219, 220, 223, 225, 227, 235, 236, 237, 238, 239, 241, 242, 243, 245, 246, 263, 264, 269, 271, 290
Julian calendar, 4, 85, 105, 106, 190, 229, 231, 232, 233, 234, 244, 255, 256, 257
Julius Caesar, 4, 231, 233, 238

King of Kings, 80, 215
Kingdom,
    Egyptian, 230
    God, of, 47, 48, 69, 192, 282, 291
    Heaven, 80
    Lysanias, 241
    Millennial, 192
    Roman, 4, 217, 231, 239, 240
    Solomon, 13
Koiné Greek, 54

Lamb of God, 76, 100, 164, 219, 285, 286
Last Supper, 37, 46, 50, 58, 59, 60, 61, 62, 63, 64, 65, 66, 67, 68, 70, 71, 72, 73, 75, 77, 81, 82, 83, 84, 85, 89, 188, 189, 190, 260
"Late on the Sabbath," 54, 113, 114, 119
Latin, 10, 85, 204, 205, 220, 230, 231, 270
Lazarus, 93, 109, 111, 127, 128, 130, 131, 151, 177, 179, 180
Leaven, 44, 98, 164, 165
Levites, 39, 61, 74, 81, 254
Lincoln, NE, xxv
Lord, LORD, the, 11, 12, 23, 33, 35, 36, 37, 41, 42, 44, 48, 49, 57, 60, 63, 67, 68, 70, 75, 81, 98, 99, 100, 101, 102, 107, 120, 139, 145, 149, 162, 172, 178, 180, 184, 192, 196, 217, 280, 291
Lord Jesus, 57, 67, 81, 106, 149, 172, 192
Lord Jesus Christ, 20, 102, 184, 230
Luke (person), 10, 17, 19, 20, 22, 26, 28, 52, 56, 59, 64, 69, 92, 108, 109, 114, 118, 124, 154, 159, 171, 176, 189, 192, 196, 197, 198, 199, 200, 201, 202, 203, 204, 206, 207, 208, 209, 215, 216, 217, 218, 220, 222, 223, 234, 235, 237, 239, 240, 241, 243, 244, 245, 246, 247, 253, 256, 257, 261, 263, 264, 267, 268, 270, 272, 277, 287, 293, 295, 298

Lunar,
  Calendar, 11, 230, 232, 233, 234,
    251, 255
  Conjunction, 274
  Eclipse, 190, 224, 225, 227, 230,
    255, 266
  Month, 5, 41, 42, 49, 233, 261, 298
  Year, 7, 230, 233, 249

Magdala, 158, 172
Magi, 209, 210, 211, 212, 213, 214, 215,
  216, 218, 291, 294
Manuscript(s), xvii 24, 39, 97, 157, 216,
  237
Mark (person), 17, 19, 24, 27, 28, 33, 46,
  50, 53, 55, 56, 66, 72, 109, 114,
  136, 159, 176, 177, 182, 191,
  192, 236, 268, 277, 281, 282
Mary Magdalene, 53, 56, 97, 108, 114,
  118, 119, 120, 125, 126, 136,
  143, 159, 170, 171, 176, 178,
  181
Mary, the other, 53, 97, 114, 119, 120,
  136, 143, 170
Mary, mother of James, 108, 159, 176
Mary, mother of Jesus, 194, 197, 199, 201
Mary, sister of Martha and Lazarus, 151
Martha, 109, 127, 128, 151, 177
Matthew (person), 2, 17, 19, 27, 28, 34,
  49, 52, 53, 54, 59, 88, 90, 96,
  114, 117, 119, 136, 138, 143,
  144, 154, 177, 191, 192, 197,
  200, 209, 210, 211, 212, 213,
  214, 215, 216, 218, 242, 268,
  271, 272, 277
Matzah, 61, 67, 82
Melchior, 213
Messiah, xiv, 28, 76, 83, 90, 92, 118, 187,
  201, 211, 213, 214, 215, 217,
  219, 242, 243, 250, 256, 258,
  273
Middle Ages, 40, 42, 146
Middle East, 9, 14, 29, 166, 212, 281
Mishnah, 21, 45, 55, 67, 71, 77, 84, 120,
  157, 158, 169, 170
Month/months, 4, 5, 6, 7, 10, 36, 37, 38,
  39, 40, 41, 42, 44, 49, 60, 63,
  75, 100, 101, 102, 105, 130,
  131, 167, 169, 217, 232, 244,
  256, 272, 275, 280, 281, 298
Moon, xv, 5, 8, 11, 35, 40, 105, 106, 221,
  225, 227, 232, 233, 255, 271,
  274, 275, 295
Morning, xxv, 9, 10, 12, 21, 44, 53, 59,
  63, 89, 108, 114, 124, 136, 143,
  148, 151, 153, 163, 167, 177,
  178, 190, 191, 192, 210, 233
Mosaic Law, 82, 88, 128
Moses, 4, 11, 16, 36, 38, 39, 40, 42, 44,
  48, 73, 74, 75, 76, 79, 90, 101,
  102, 111, 128, 145, 162, 168,
  172, 236, 254, 280, 281, 285
Mount(s),
  Hermon, 242, 243
  Libanus, 241
  Moriah, 82
  Olives, 8, 84, 88, 106, 127, 130
  Sinai, 11, 162
Muslim(s), 5, 35
Myrrh, 125, 137, 177, 212, 291, 294

Nazarene, 17, 120, 158, 261
Nazareth, xi, xiii, xvi, xxv, 1, 26, 42, 113,
  151, 152, 158, 173, 197, 199,
  218, 231, 234, 238, 239, 246,
  248, 255, 257, 261, 266, 270,
  290
Nebraska, 32
Nehemiah, 249, 250
New covenant, 68, 88
New creation, 73, 75, 164
New Testament, xiv, 2, 10, 16, 17, 19, 24,
  25, 27, 29, 33, 36, 38, 46, 47,
  48, 53, 56, 62, 64, 68, 70, 84,
  91, 109, 117, 119, 145, 167,
  170, 172, 173, 174, 175, 184,
  185, 197, 198, 199, 203, 209,
  213, 215, 225, 233, 234, 245,
  246, 247, 256, 265, 266, 275,
  290, 291, 292, 294
Nicodemus, 55, 115, 124, 125, 137, 177,
  181, 182, 183, 193, 194, 266
Nineveh, 23, 92

Nisan/Nissan, 37, 41, 42, 49, 60, 263, 275, 280, 281, 298
  1st, 121
  7th, 132, 150
  8th, 111, 128, 129, 132, 135, 150, 151
  9th, 128, 129, 132, 133, 134, 135, 150, 151
  10th, 112, 129, 130, 132, 133, 134, 135, 150, 151, 169
  11th, 112, 129, 132, 133, 134, 135, 151
  12th, 129, 132, 134, 135, 151
  13th, 66, 129, 132, 133, 134, 135, 151
  14th, 37, 39, 41, 42, 45, 50, 60, 66, 71, 98, 105, 111, 121, 129, 130, 131, 133, 134, 135,140, 141, 148, 150, 151, 161, 162, 163, 164, 165, 166, 167, 168, 169, 226, 251, 255, 256, 259, 260, 261, 262, 266, 267, 272, 273, 275, 281
  15th, 37, 42, 50, 58, 59, 66, 97, 112, 129, 130, 133, 134, 135, 136, 140, 141, 148, 150, 160, 161, 163, 164, 165, 166, 167, 169, 260, 266, 272, 273, 275
  16th, 32, 33, 42, 45, 112, 136, 137, 140, 141, 148, 161, 167, 169, 170, 173, 267
"No friend of Caesar," 270
"Not yet fifty years old," 236, 254, 255
Novatianism, 107, 290
Numbers,
  cardinal, 15, 16, 18, 91, 93, 152
  ordinal, 15, 16, 18, 91, 118, 152, 170

Old Testament, 2, 11, 12, 16, 34, 36, 38, 41, 63, 66, 75, 83, 84, 102, 161, 162, 167, 170, 172, 173, 249, 285
Olivet Discourse, the, 88, 188
Olympic Games, 10, 31
Omer, 6, 48, 166
Onah, 16, 17

Palestine, 62, 156, 176, 201, 217, 241, 255, 275

Passion Week, 37, 42, 50, 53, 72, 73, 87, 88, 95, 96, 97, 100, 102, 105, 106, 108, 109, 111, 117, 120, 121, 123, 128, 131, 138, 143, 144, 146, 149, 160, 161,166, 173, 179, 180, 187, 188, 189, 190, 192, 193, 194, 240, 250, 253, 278, 281, 284, 289
Passover, 5, 6, 33, 34, 36, 37, 38, 39, 40, 41, 42, 43, 44, 45, 46, 49, 50, 57, 59, 60, 61, 63, 64, 65, 66, 67, 68, 69, 71, 72, 74, 75, 78, 79, 81, 82, 83, 84, 93, 94, 95, 96, 97, 99, 100, 101, 102, 103, 105, 106, 107, 117, 120, 121, 127, 128, 131, 139 , 144, 145, 146, 149, 151, 157, 158, 159, 161, 163, 165, 165, 166, 167 168, 169, 179, 180, 187, 188, 189, 191, 221, 223, 224, 225, 226, 235, 236, 237, 239, 245, 251, 252, 259, 260, 261, 263, 265, 267, 270, 271, 272, 273, 275, 280, 281, 283, 285, 291
  Calendar, 127, 128
  Cups, 68
  Eve, 120
  Meal (see Passover Seder)
  Moon, 105, 274
  Offering, 42
  Pardon, 84
  Preparation, 47, 49, 50, 282
  Sacrifice, 49, 58, 128, 131
  Week, 32, 66, 96, 97, 102, 112, 122, 136, 142, 170, 278
Passover Lamb, 40, 42, 43, 44, 49, 59, 63, 64, 66, 74, 75, 77, 79, 100, 111, 149, 162, 163, 164, 165, 166, 169, 172, 281, 282, 285, 290
Passover Sabbath, 37, 59, 95, 97, 103, 104, 108, 110, 111, 120, 121, 131, 137, 143, 160, 168, 177, 179, 180, 184, 249, 250, 281
Passover Seder, xi, 37, 46, 50, 58, 59, 60, 61, 62, 63, 64, 65, 67, 68, 69, 71, 72, 73, 74, 75, 77, 82, 83, 84, 88, 89, 97, 141, 260, 283

Paul, the Apostle, xvii, 2, 20, 38, 39, 44, 45, 46, 56, 67, 70, 90, 93, 112, 123, 127, 149, 164, 166, 167, 185, 234, 247, 248, 249, 260, 266, 279, 284, 287, 291, 292, 294, 295
Pentecost, 32, 33, 38, 41, 42, 57, 97, 120, 160, 161
Periods,
  Coptic, 230
  Egyptian, 230
  Ethiopian, 230
  Hebrew, 230
  Intertestamental, 16
  Islamic, 230
  Julian, 230
  Mishnaic, 120
  Old Persian, 230
  202nd Olympiad, 270
  Paleolithic, xv
  Roman, 206, 230, 237
  Second Temple, 38 42, 130, 160
Persia(ns), 14, 16, 38, 176, 210, 213, 230
Persian Kings, 213, 249
  Artaxerxes, 38, 249, 250, 279
  Cyrus, 38
  Darius, 38, 249
  Xerxes, 14, 15, 162
Peter (person), 19, 20, 64, 68, 84, 90, 114, 118, 123, 127, 139, 147, 171, 188, 189, 223, 247, 285
Pharisee(s), 17, 18, 35, 47, 48, 49, 88, 90, 117, 120, 128, 138, 143, 147, 159, 253, 254
Pilate, xi, 18, 36, 46, 47, 48, 49, 50, 51, 52, 59, 65, 84, 111, 117, 119, 120, 123, 124, 125, 138, 142, 143, 144, 145, 146, 147, 153, 155, 159, 163, 181, 182, 183, 188, 189, 190, 191, 192, 193, 194, 195, 219, 235, 238, 239, 240, 242, 243, 244, 245, 246, 255, 256, 258, 261, 263, 264, 266, 268, 269, 270, 271, 275, 276, 279, 282
Pilate's Palace, 65, 182, 183
Place of the Skull, 191

Planets, 213, 261
  Earth, xxv, 2, 3, 4, 18, 23, 35, 41, 73, 90, 92, 116, 124, 127, 154, 184, 190, 192, 197, 211, 216, 230, 233, 235, 252, 274, 286, 296
  Jupiter, 213
  Regulus, 213
  Venus, 213
Pontius Pilate (see Pilate),
Possible/probable, 23, 27, 197
Portland, ME, xxv
Portland, OR, xxv
Preparation Day (see Day of Preparation),
Promised Land, 60, 74, 75, 168, 169
Prophets, 23, 26, 43, 57, 61, 73, 81, 90, 91, 92, 93, 156, 223, 245
Protoevangelium of James, 212
Psalms, 62, 73, 74, 81

Quaestor, 155, 202
Queen Esther, 14, 15, 16, 162, 281
Queen of Sheba, 176
Queen Vashti, 14, 15
Quirinius, Publius Sulpicius, 197, 198, 199, 200, 201, 202, 203, 204, 205, 206, 207, 208, 209, 217, 220, 222, 241, 294
Qumran, 72, 230

Rabbinic, 3, 61, 174
Rabbi(s),
  Bacher, Wilhelm, 39
  Eleazar ben Azariah, 16
  Eliezer, 157
  Hisda, 298
  Hillel II, 7
  Kimchi, 254
  Lamm, Maurice, 4
  Saul of Tarsus, 247
  Simon bar Yochai, 6
  Zeitlin, Solomon, 174

Resurrection, xxv, 18, 19, 22, 23, 24, 25, 26, 27, 29, 45, 53 54, 55, 56, 57, 81, 87, 91, 92, 94, 96, 101, 104, 107, 108, 112, 113, 115, 117, 118, 124, 125, 127, 130, 136, 139, 140, 142, 144, 149, 152, 155, 161, 162, 166, 167, 171, 173, 178, 179, 181, 184, 185, 218, 247, 248, 251, 271, 272, 276

Resurrection Day/Sunday, 26, 56, 98, 112, 115, 116, 118, 125, 154, 156, 166, 167, 170, 171, 178, 184, 187

Revelation, 167, 216

Roman Emperors,
    Augustus, Gaius Octavius Thurinus, 157, 197, 198, 199, 201, 203, 204, 207, 216, 217, 220, 222, 225, 226, 235, 238, 244, 256, 262, 263, 264, 269
    Claudius, 201, 241, 248, 293
    Commodus, 217, 226
    Constantine, 155
    Diocletian, 231
    Nero, 43, 246
    Tiberius, 198, 219, 235, 238, 239, 241, 242, 243, 244, 245, 256, 258, 259, 261, 262, 263, 264, 267, 268, 269, 270, 275, 276, 279, 297, 298
    Vespasian, 180

Roman,
    Army, 19, 239, 247, 269, 287
    Census, 43, 197, 198, 199, 200, 201, 202, 203, 204, 206, 207, 208, 209, 216, 217, 220, 221, 222, 223, 226
    Governors,
    Piso, 205
    Quirinius, Publius Sulpicius, 197, 198, 199, 200, 201, 202, 203, 204, 205, 206, 207, 208, 209, 217, 220, 222, 241, 294
    Saturninus, 202, 205, 223, 294
    Varus, 205, 207, 241, 293

Historians, 31, 155, 163, 198, 199, 217, 226, 233, 238, 244, 246, 269

Prefect/procurators, xi, 206, 235, 239, 242, 245, 248, 255, 263, 264, 268, 269, 297

Shields, 270, 279

Soldier(s), 21, 46, 117, 125, 178, 188, 189, 193, 217, 242, 287

Rome, xi, 31, 155, 199, 203, 204, 206, 211, 217, 231, 238, 242, 243, 248, 256, 268, 269, 273, 279, 290, 293

Rooster, 22, 53, 84, 188, 189

Rosh Hashanah, 6, 295, 298

Sabbath/Shabbat, 1, 7, 31, 33, 34, 35, 36, 37, 44, 45, 46, 47, 48, 49, 53, 54, 55, 56, 57, 58, 59, 69, 71, 83, 87, 88, 89, 94, 95, 96, 97, 98, 99, 100, 101, 102, 103, 104, 107, 108, 109, 110, 111, 112, 113, 114, 117, 119, 120, 121, 124, 125, 127, 128, 130, 131, 136, 137,1 41, 143, 144, 145, 146, 149, 151, 154, 155, 156, 157, 158, 159, 160, 161, 166, 168, 169, 170, 171, 172, 173, 175, 176, 177, 179, 180, 181, 182, 183, 184, 192, 193, 250, 273, 281, 282
    Double, 96, 98, 108, 109, 111, 136, 144
    High, 36, 37, 57, 58, 59, 89, 97, 98, 103, 104, 111, 120, 121, 136, 137, 137, 140, 144, 146, 136, 160, 161, 177, 180, 281
    Passover, 37, 58, 59, 95, 97, 103, 108, 110, 111, 120, 121, 131, 137, 143, 160, 168, 177, 179, 180, 184, 250, 281
    Saturday, 37, 59, 89, 95, 98, 103, 104, 108, 112, 136, 137, 144, 154, 169, 281

Sacrifice, xv, xvii, 21, 39, 40, 41, 42, 43, 44, 49, 50, 57, 59, 60 74, 77, 80, 82, 87, 111, 130, 131, 161, 163, 164, 166, 272, 281, 283, 285

Subject Index   321

Salome (faithful woman), 53, 108, 114, 159, 176
Salome (daughter of Herodias), 240
Salt Sea (see Dead Sea)
Salvation, 3, 32, 76, 285
Samaria, 13, 14, 52, 154
San Francisco, xxv
Sanhedrin, 5, 69, 157, 181, 188, 191, 193, 242, 273
Sanhedrin (Talmud), 157, 158, 181, 261, 272, 273, 280
Satan, 17, 28, 138
Saturninus, Sentius, 201, 204, 222, 293
Saul of Tarsus (see Paul, the Apostle)
Savior, xiv, 2, 22, 23, 29, 52, 56, 58, 68, 71, 75, 82, 101, 108, 117, 156, 158, 163, 166, 172, 174, 181, 190, 196, 214, 217, 225, 227, 235, 252, 261, 277, 279
Scholar(s)/scholarship, xi, xii, xiv, 16, 27, 39, 42, 46, 50, 51, 58, 61, 63, 64, 65, 68, 69, 70, 84, 85, 97, 109, 122, 123, 146, 152, 158,160, 173, 174, 175, 181, 189, 189, 190, 197, 198, 200, 202, 203, 205, 207, 209, 213, 222, 226, 229, 233, 235, 240, 242, 244, 245, 246, 249, 250, 251, 255, 256, 258, 260, 262, 263, 264, 265, 266, 267, 272, 274, 276, 284, 285, 289, 292, 294
Scribes, 2, 27, 35, 88, 90, 137, 156, 181, 194, 202, 254, 255, 286
Scripture(s), xiv, xvii, xviii, 10, 11, 13, 22, 26, 29, 40, 55, 56, 93, 99, 108, 114, 116, 119, 125, 138, 139, 144, 145, 147, 152, 167, 171, 173, 218, 223, 237, 239, 268
Sejanus, Lucius Aelius, 258, 263, 264, 268, 269, 270, 275, 276, 279
Seneca, 248
September, 4, 6, 226, 227, 230, 235, 244, 245, 264, 290, 295, 298
Seleucus I, 31
Seminaries,
    Asbury Theological Seminary, 203
    BIOLA, 95

Candler School of Theology, 201
Dallas Theological Seminary, xii, 64, 174
Duke Divinity School, 62
Newton Theological Seminary, 51
Pacific School of Religion, Berkeley, 225
Spurgeon's College in London, 87
Talbot Theological Seminary, 223
Sephardic Judaism, 42, 146
Seventh-Day Adventist, 35, 87, 94
"Seventy-two-hours," 12, 15, 19, 20, 23, 24, 55, 87, 89, 91, 96, 103, 104, 109, 112, 113, 115, 121, 123, 139, 142, 143, 144, 161, 170, 178, 179
Shanghai, xv, 210
Silent Day Wednesday, 87, 188
Simon of Cyrene, 69
Sin, 43, 44, 74, 75, 77, 167, 219, 277, 285, 286, 289
Sinai, 11, 162
Sivan, 5, 6, 161
Solar eclipse, 270, 271
Solemn assembly, 98, 102, 289
Son of David, 88, 188
Son of God, xiii, 79, 93, 118, 138
Son of Man, 23, 27, 28, 79, 90, 91, 92, 116, 124, 137, 154, 194, 242, 285
Sovereignty, xiii, 4, 43, 63, 250, 281, 285
Star of Bethlehem, The, 213, 218, 220
Suetonius, 238, 244, 256, 263, 269, 273
Sulpician Fathers, 50, 174
Sun, the, 5, 8, 9, 31, 40, 41, 49, 52, 55, 60, 104, 108, 113, 114, 115, 130, 136, 154, 159, 165, 170, 171, 172, 176, 190, 192, 210, 230, 233, 274, 290, 296
Sunset(s), 5, 8, 20, 31, 34, 39, 41, 46, 49, 55, 56, 59, 60, 63, 88, 89, 94, 95, 96, 97, 98, 103, 104, 113, 114, 115, 116, 117, 119, 120, 125, 126, 130, 136, 140, 141, 142, 143, 146, 151, 154, 162, 171, 178, 179, 181, 183, 192, 193, 232, 233, 234, 251, 282, 283, 290

Synoptic Gospels, 46, 50, 52, 58, 59, 63, 64, 65, 67, 83, 84, 85, 189, 234, 237, 252, 272, 274, 275
Syria, 31, 43, 106, 107, 198, 199, 200, 202, 203, 204, 205, 206, 207, 208, 209, 210, 212, 217, 220, 223, 245, 263, 264, 294

Talmud, 5, 121, 148, 157, 158, 298
    Babylonian, 120, 157, 158, 181, 254, 255, 261, 280
    Jerusalem, 84, 157, 255
Taxation, 199, 200, 206, 207, 293
Temple, 4, 21, 33, 37, 38, 40, 42, 43, 45, 53, 56, 60, 61, 70, 74, 81, 88, 92, 111, 115, 125, 128, 130, 137, 138, 139, 141, 148, 149, 160, 166, 188, 218, 232, 235, 236, 239, 242, 248, 249, 250, 251, 252, 254, 259, 260, 267, 273, 275, 276, 279, 282, 283, 291, 297
Terminus ad quem, 220, 221, 247, 252, 253, 256, 257, 260
Terminus ad quo, 57, 220, 221, 252, 256, 257
Tetelestai, 17
Tetrarch, 2, 219, 238, 239, 240, 241, 243, 270
"The fifteenth year," 13, 14, 219, 235, 238, 243, 244, 245, 256, 262, 263, 264, 267
"The Ides of March," 238
Theophilus, 19, 20, 203, 263, 287
"Third day," 26, 38, 45, 47, 89, 91, 106, 107, 116, 117, 118, 119, 126, 127, 143, 144, 147, 148, 149, 154, 155, 161, 162, 170, 171, 173, 178, 185, 192, 194, 195, 246
"Three days," 12, 13, 15, 16, 18, 20, 23, 24, 25, 26, 27, 28, 47, 92, 115, 117, 125, 137, 138, 139, 147, 171, 236, 251, 252, 289
"Three days and three nights," 12, 13, 15, 16, 18, 22, 23, 24, 25, 26, 27, 29, 44, 55, 86, 87, 88, 89, 90, 91, 92, 93, 94, 96, 112, 115, 116, 121, 123, 124, 125, 126, 127, 136, 141, 142, 152, 153, 154, 179, 289
Three stars, 8, 12, 90, 113, 130, 151, 193
Time, xiv, xv, xvii, xxv, xxvi, 1, 2, 3, 4, 6, 7, 8, 9, 10, 11, 12, 13, 14, 15, 16, 17, 19, 20, 21, 22, 23, 24, 25, 26, 27, 28, 29, 30, 31, 32, 33, 34, 35, 38, 39, 40, 44, 49, 50, 51, 52, 54, 55, 56, 57, 61, 62, 64, 69, 71, 72, 74, 81, 83, 86, 90, 93, 94, 98, 100, 102, 103, 105, 106, 109, 110, 116, 118, 119, 121, 124, 126, 130, 131, 138, 142, 143, 147, 152, 153, 159, 160, 163, 164, 168, 169, 171, 175, 177, 181, 183, 184, 185, 189, 190, 191, 192, 193, 197, 199, 201, 202, 203, 204, 206, 207, 209, 214, 215, 217, 218, 219, 220, 221, 223, 224, 227, 230, 231, 232, 233, 234, 235, 239, 243, 245, 247, 249, 251, 253, 255, 256, 260, 265, 269, 270, 271, 273, 276, 277, 278, 279, 280, 281, 282, 283, 284, 285, 286, 287, 290, 291, 292, 295, 296, 298
Torah, 4, 6, 38, 42, 45, 50, 146
Tosefta, 157, 158
Trachonitis, 219, 238, 240, 241
Trial(s), xi, xxv, 37, 50, 51, 59, 84, 135, 157, 188, 189, 190, 193, 225, 242, 248, 267, 270
Triumphal Entry, 89, 93, 111, 112, 129, 131, 132, 133, 134, 135, 150, 151, 188
Trumpets, 36, 99, 101, 102, 226, 232
Twelve, the, 55, 56, 63, 69, 70, 91, 116, 194, 247
Twilight, 8, 37, 44, 60, 74, 77, 100, 130, 142, 165, 280, 290
Type/Anti-type, 58, 82, 172, 173, 211, 230, 240
Tyre, 176, 267, 291

United States (see America)

Universities,
  Bar Ilan, 81
  Berlin, 71
  Cambridge, 189
  Catholic University of America, 209
  Dropsie College, 46
  Durham, 67, 246
  Edinburgh, 265
  Erlangen, 95
  Heidelberg, 246
  Helsinki, 213
  Leeds, 209
  Leipzig, 95
  Manchester, 19
  Notre Dame, 223
  Oglethorpe, 227
  Oxford, xiv, 71, 72, 121, 174, 203, 256, 266
  Queen Mary University of London, 59
  Tennessee, 109
  Texas, Austin, 216
  Yale, 95
  Zimbabwe (Rhodesia), 208
Upper Room, 60, 63, 188
U.S. Naval Observatory (USNO), 104, 105, 289, 290

Varus, P. Quinctilius, 207, 241, 293
Varus Saturninus, 205
Varves, 271
Vatican Library, 216
Vatican Museum, 211, 289
Vernal equinox, 5, 40, 105, 106, 271, 275
Via Dolorosa, 52, 188

Western,
  Asia, 166
  Calendar, 232, 280
  Catholic Church, 35, 85, 213, 231
  Christianity, 212
  Civilization, 5
  Greece, 167

Pennsylvania, 32
Sky, 233
World, xiv, 230
Wine, 61, 62, 67, 73, 75, 81, 82, 88, 139, 149, 163
Winter season, 55, 221, 236, 239
"Without blemish," 74, 76, 77, 78, 149, 165, 168
Worldwide Church of God, 87, 174

Xanthicus, 41, 42, 49
Xerxes, 14, 15, 16

Year/years, xi, xv, xvi, xxvi, 1, 3, 4, 5, 6, 7, 10, 13, 14, 16, 19, 22, 31, 32, 33, 35, 36, 37, 38, 39, 41, 42, 43, 44, 45, 49, 54, 55, 59, 60, 61, 74, 77, 82, 87, 95, 96, 99, 106, 107, 111, 120, 121, 126, 157, 160, 164, 165, 168, 169, 170, 174, 175, 181, 183, 185, 187, 189, 190, 191, 192, 196, 197, 198, 200, 202, 203, 204, 206, 207, 209, 213, 215, 216, 217, 218, 219, 220, 221, 222, 223, 224, 225, 226, 227, 228, 229, 230, 231, 232, 233, 234, 235, 236, 237, 238, 239, 240, 241, 242, 243, 244, 245, 246, 247, 248, 250, 251, 252, 253, 254, 255, 256, 257, 258, 259, 260, 261, 262, 263, 264, 265, 266, 267, 268, 269, 270, 271, 272, 273, 274, 275, 277, 278, 279, 281, 284, 285, 287, 289, 294, 295, 296, 297, 298
Yeshu', 157, 261
YHWH, 60, 130

Zarethan, 168, 169
Zechariah (father of John the Baptist), 200, 219, 258
Zerubbabel, 250, 252, 297

Author/Person Index

Augustine, Saint, 226

Bacchiocchi, Samuele, 94
Bacher, Wilhelm, 39
Bammel, Ernst, 274
Barnes, Albert, 92, 111
Barrett, C. K., 67
Beatty, Chester, 237
Bede, Venerable, 211
Berra, Yogi, 278
Billerbeck, Paul, 69
Bisagno, John, 174
Blinzler, Josef, 258, 265, 265, 274
Bock, Darrell L., 62, 203, 204
Bockmuehl, Markus, 72
Bond, Helen K., 265
Borg, Marcus, 197
Box, George Herbert, 71
Brandon, S.G.F., 174, 268
Brooks, Phillips, 196
Broshi, Magen, 163, 164
Brown, Raymond E., 50, 59, 174, 178, 201, 214, 275
Bruce, F.F., 19, 97, 98, 174, 200, 206, 207
Bucherius, Aegidius, 39

Chisholm, Kitty, 227, 295
Chwolson, Daniel, 272, 273
Clarke, Adam, 111
Clement of Alexandria, 217, 219, 226
Cohn, Haim, 174
Cox, Steven L. 50
Cramer, John A., 227, 295
Cyril of Alexandria, 265

Dalman, Gustaf, 68
Depuydt, Leo, 266
Doyle, A.D., 270
Dunn, James, 246, 266

Easley, Kendell H., 50
Ehrman, Bart D., 174
Eichelberger, W. S., 105, 106
Eisler, Robert, 274
Epiphanius, 107, 219, 225
Eusebius, 270
Evans, Craig A., 174

Ferguson, John, 227
Ferrari-D'Occhieppo, Konradin, 219
Filmer, W.E., 227
Finnegan, Jack, 174
Fitzmyer, Joseph A., 209, 235
Fotheringham, J.K., 274, 299
Franke, Elmer E., 105

Geva, Hillel, 163
Gill, John, 111, 160
Green, Joel B., 174
Gregory of Tours, 107
Gundry, Stanley N., 223

Hayles, David J., 201
Hoehner, Harold H.,
Hengel, Martin, 174
Higgins, A.J.B., 209
Hirsch, Emil G., 181

Hoehner, Harold, 64, 179, 201, 208, 215, 225, 251, 274, 291
Hopkins, John Henry, Jr., 212
Hovey, Alvah, 51, 52
Humphreys, Colin, 27, 59, 98, 121, 131, 135, 189, 190, 233, 244, 256, 260, 262, 263, 266, 275, 297

Ignatius of Antioch, 153
Irenaeus, 218, 219, 236

Jeremias, Joachim, 61, 62, 63, 84, 256, 274
Johnson, Luke, 201
Josephus, xi, 33, 38, 39, 40, 41, 42, 43, 45, 46, 49, 60, 156, 157, 163, 164, 166, 169, 180, 198, 201, 202, 204, 206, 207, 221, 224, 225, 226, 235, 239, 240, 241, 242, 245, 246, 251, 252, 259, 260, 261, 262, 264, 268, 273, 293
Justin Martyr, 154, 200

Kepler, Johannes, 213
Keresztes, Paul, 227
King Edward VII, 203
Kohler, Kaufmann, 181
Kostenberger, Andreas J., 50, 274

Lagrange, Marie-Joseph, 208
Lançon, Bertrand, 55
Landau, Brent, 216
Langton, Stephen, 119
Lasker, Daniel J., 266
Lehman, Frederick M., 286
Levick, Barbara, 227
Lietzmann, Hans, 71
Livy, 204, 217
Lucian of Samosata, 156

MacArthur, John F., 174
Mahieu, Bieke, 222, 295
Maier, Paul L., 174, 274
Maier, Walter, 174
Marcus, Joel, 62, 63
Marshall, I Howard, 62, 223
Martin, Ernest L., 174
Matthews, Grant, 219

Meier, John P., 174, 175, 201, 244, 257, 266, 274
Miller, J.V., 50
Mircea, Liviu, 271
Mommsen, Theodor, 227
Murphy O'Connor, Jerome, 266
Maimonides, 39, 42, 146

Newton, Sir Isaac, 255, 260

Ogg, George, 202
Olmstead, A.T., 219, 222, 299
Oproiu, Tiberiu, 271
Origen, 212, 219, 222
Orosius, Paulus, 219, 226

Papola, Simo, 213
Philo, 21, 38, 40, 45, 166, 268, 270, 289
Pliny the Younger, 155, 156
Pope, Alexander, 187, 193
Pope Gregory XIII, 232

Ramm, Bernard, 197
Ramsey, Sir William, 200, 203, 292
Ratzinger, Joseph, 219, 222
Rawlinson, George W., 227
Riesner, Rainer, 262, 266
Robertson, A.T., 261, 289
Robinson, J.A.T., 174

Sanders, E.P., 266
Schürer, Emil, 201, 219, 222, 224, 227
Schwab, Markus, 271
Scott, Douglas W., 266
Scroggie, W. Graham, 87
Sherwin-White, A.N., 174, 198, 227
Sproul, R.C., 174
Spurgeon, Charles Haddon, 42
Stauffer, Ethelbert, 203, 274
Steinmann, Andrew, 227

Tabory, Joseph, 81
Tacitus, 163, 198, 199, 204, 238, 239, 244, 246, 256, 263
Templeman, Dennis M., 209, 224, 227
Tertullian, 160, 202, 217, 219, 222, 223, 226
Theissen, Gerd, 146, 274

Thomas, Robert L., 223
Torrey, Charles C., 46
Torrey, Reuben Archer, 95
Turner, C.H., 274
Turner, Nigel, 208

Ussher, James, 219, 222, 225, 295

Vardaman, Jerry, 199, 203, 206, 219, 220, 222, 227, 266, 274
Vass, Arpad A., 109

Waddington, W. Graeme, 121, 256, 262, 263, 266, 274, 275

Webb, Robert L., 62
Wesley, John, 111
Westcott, B. F., 51, 123
Williams, Jefferson, 271
Wilson, William Riley, 268
Winter, Paul, 274
Witherington, Ben, xv, 29, 30, 203, 274
Woodrow, Ralph, 109
Wright, N.T., 174

Yamauchi, Edwin, 227, 249

Zeitlin, Solomon, 46, 47, 174
Zetel, James E.C., 227

www.ingramcontent.com/pod-product-compliance
Lightning Source LLC
Chambersburg PA
CBHW071228230426
43668CB00011B/1346